Applause for My Diary Unlocked

"Authenticity is more than just the key to happiness and high self-esteem; it is the doorway to greater connectedness, empathy and peace—both within ourselves and within the world. *My Diary Unlocked* offers the heartfelt experiences of girls and women who have made this journey, along with a treasure chest of transformational insights and tools to guide readers toward their own path of self empowerment." Jack Canfield, America's #1 Success Coach, founder of the book brand *Chicken Soup for the Soul*®, and a leading authority on Peak Performance and Life Success

"A must read for every woman who has ever been a teen girl ... enlightening, entertaining and educational." Susie Walton, San Diego Parent Educator of the Year, author of *Keys to Personal Freedom*

"This book gives women of all ages the insight and tools needed to live their lives deeply and confidently. It is thoroughly researched and beautifully written. I will wholeheartedly recommend this book to my counseling clients, family, and friends. It is an inspiring, empowering, and practical guide to overcoming life's challenges and embracing one's authentic self." Amy Torn, MFT

"Regardless of our age or education, our self-concept—the way we view ourselves in relation to the world around us—filters our experience of reality and defines the boundaries of what we believe we can and cannot do, be, and accomplish. In sharing the innermost struggles and victories of teen girls and women, *My Diary Unlocked* offers a compelling, true-to-life understanding of how we create our own limitations, and—more importantly—how we can harness the power of awareness and personal responsibility to become more self-directed and emotionally free." David Sablatura, Ed.D., School District Educational Leader, Houston, Texas

"A powerful and compelling book for teen girls and their parents. The real diary entries and expert commentary bring insight, compassion, humor, and hope for the many challenges facing not only the modern teen girl, but the esteem of the human condition as a whole." Julie Anderson, MSFA, Developmental Research Psychologist, Childhood Cognitive Development

"The guiding light of diarists whose own transformation led to a more loving and peaceful state of being inspires us all to choose a better way. *My Diary Unlocked* carries within its pages a modern day compass filled with ancient wisdom to transcend personal and family dynamics from fear-based patterns to soul-driven practices." Gerald Jampolsky, MD, best-selling author of numerous books, including the perennial classic *Love is Letting Go of Fear*. Founder of The Center for Attitudinal Healing; www.ahinternational.org

"This is not a book just for teenage girls. Rather it is a mirror from which everyone can learn from their reflection. As the sacred oracle said, "Know Thyself." This book will enlighten the reader, and as such, may well trickle down to all with whom they come in contact." Emilie Winthrop, retired theatre critic and former executive editor of *Décor and Style Magazine*.

"With a modern answer to the old adage that 'it takes a village to raise a child,' Janet Larson has pulled together a wealth of wisdom, insight and practical resources to support teens and those who love them in navigating the often turbulent waters of adolescence. Written in large part by teen girls who struggled with and overcame all-too-common obstacles to developing self-esteem and self-reliance, *My Diary Unlocked* delivers information and inspiration in a voice that will resonate with adults and teenagers alike." Sally Grablick, author of *The Reason: Help and Hope for Those Who Grieve*

"Through collections of genuine diary excerpts, *My Diary Unlocked* reveals the heart and flesh experiences of young women who share their hidden stories of pain and possible paths to living healthy and well. *My Diary Unlocked* is a gift to teenaged girls and the people who love and care for them. Parents, family members, teachers and members of the healing profession will benefit from reading this remarkable book." Joanna Poppink, MFT, eating disorder recovery psychotherapist working with adult women. Author of *Healing Your Hungry Heart*. www.eatingdisorderrecovery

Notes From Contributing Diarists:

"Unlocking the words I have held in my diary since childhood feels cathartic and hopeful in its ability to possibly help someone else heal. Growing up was a very lonely place. This book gives a voice to so many as it helps them feel less alone."—Sherry Duquet

"Hopefully my entry will make an impact on someone in a way that they can see that the events of our past do not have to define our future."—Christy Dyer

"As a mother of three children who are approaching the teenage years, I plan on reading this book cover-to-cover. Contributing my own experiences made me realize how much I wish I had an adult to help guide me through those troubled years. *My Diary Unlocked* gives me the tools, guidelines and emotional fortitude to assist my children through the teen years and into well-balanced young adults."—Contributor

"If sharing my story helps just one person not take their loved ones for granted, this will be worth it. Live your life with no regrets."—Kimberlee Dale Bishop-VanHeulen

"Keeping a diary, something I've done for more than 30 years now, helps us connect more fully with ourselves. Through this book, Janet is taking the power of this great ritual to help us to connect more deeply with each other."—Melissa Braverman

"Feeling for the first time that my experience could be helpful to others is exciting and heart expanding."—Contributor

"In the age of social media, we are all diarists. *My Diary Unlocked* reveals the long and powerful history of this tradition. The timeless guidance that comes out of lives lived reflected in the passages throughout this collection provides feelings of understanding and connectedness. All diarists, whether digitally or on paper, have extended the reflections of our very human interactions with each other as painful, honest, elated and at times searing. This collection does the same but with an intention to help."—Contributor

"It is an honor to be included in a project encouraging young women to be courageous in telling their truth and their stories."—Nathalie Hardy

"If my story reaches one heart, I am happy. If you allow it to help you find your way out of darkness, I am fulfilled."—Kristen Moeller

"I am grateful for the opportunity to share my diary entries. I would be thrilled if they are helpful to others."—Linda Smith

"Sometimes it's not friends or family who teach us to be brave. Sometimes it's complete strangers. As a contributor to this book, I am grateful to be one of those strangers."—Contributor

"I wish I had someone to share their experiences with me when I was a teen ... I am incredibly honored and willing to share my experiences to help young people out—or anyone who is searching their soul. I have found my voice in this project."—Contributor

"*My Diary Unlocked* examines the issues we face during adolescence and how we carry them into adulthood. They shape us in both positive and negative ways. By understanding the common themes so many women have woven through their journals, we can further use this book as a tool towards healthier, more meaningful living. I am proud to contribute to a book dedicated to helping women everywhere live authentically and true to their inner selves."—Karina Larson Greenway

My Diary
UNLOCKED®

Linda,
I honor you for
living your life
unlocked. You are
a beacon of light
for others.
Janet Larson

My Diary
UNLOCKED®

Stories of Teen Girls Heal the
Inner Adolescent of Our Soul

Janet Larson

 My Diary Unlocked Press

SELF-HELP / Personal Growth / Self-Esteem / Parenting / Women—Psychology

My Diary Unlocked Press
3525 Del Mar Heights Rd Ste. 1000 San Diego, CA 92130
www.mydiaryunlocked.com

First Printing: July 2014
ISBN 13: 978-1940711096
Library of Congress Control Number: 2014904862

2   4   6   8   10   9   7   5   3   1

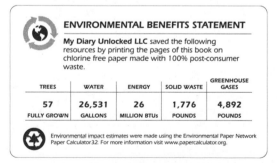

ENVIRONMENTAL BENEFITS STATEMENT

My Diary Unlocked LLC saved the following
resources by printing the pages of this book on
chlorine free paper made with 100% post-consumer
waste.

TREES	WATER	ENERGY	SOLID WASTE	GREENHOUSE GASES
57	26,531	26	1,776	4,892
FULLY GROWN	GALLONS	MILLION BTUs	POUNDS	POUNDS

Environmental impact estimates were made using the Environmental Paper Network
Paper Calculator32. For more information visit www.papercalculator.org.

Printed in Canada on 100% postconsumer-waste recycled paper
Cover and interior design by Janet Larson © 2014
Selected design elements by Paul Quarry

Ordering Information:
Special sales may be available on quantity purchases by associations, organizations, schools and others.
For U.S. trade bookstores and wholesalers, please contact the publisher at: info@mydiaryunlocked.com.
For more inspiration, sign up for eblasts at www.mydiaryunlocked.com

This book is dedicated in loving memory to my dear friend Mary Sorgdrager,
who taught me the real meaning of living;
to my parents with deep gratitude for teaching me the power of forgiveness;
and with love and devotion to my precious daughter Angela ...
May you remain forever true to every aspect of your BEING.

Contents

Other Noteworthy Entries

Acronym	Page Introduced	Acronym	Page Introduced
ABC	133	Fearself	21
Affirm	68	Gossiping	150
Awake	62	Grace	193
Aware	62	Grief	252
Awareness	62	Help	175
Bar	104	Key	19
Being	18	Listen	134
Breath	195	Me	293
Breathe	195	Numb	175
CEU	269	React	130
Choice	35	Real	294
Denial	200	Respond	130
Diary	8	Soul	6
Empathy	293	Soulself	6
Fear	21	Us	293

(SEE DETAILED GLOSSARY OF ACRONYMS ON PAGE 305)

Foreword by Jack Canfield

I have spent the better part of the last forty years teaching that high self-esteem is fundamental to building successful relationships and careers, fulfilling our soul's purpose, and experiencing true happiness as an internal state of being. Although two generations have passed since I began developing and leading self-esteem programs, the majority of those who participate in them are—and always have been—women. Most are drawn to this work by a desire to break free from perceptions and beliefs they formed in childhood, often in their teenage years, which are still limiting the expression of their full potential.

At the time of this writing, a staggering three out of four women and girls exhibit patterns of disordered eating. Forty-one percent of our country's teenage girls report that they have been bullied. Between the years 2000 and 2010, rates of depression among women and girls have doubled. Yet despite the fact that the life scripts of so many women and girls share similar and recurring themes, very few feel safe enough to tell their stories openly.

The "delusion of uniqueness" is a psychological phenomenon that occurs with greatest frequency during our teenage years. It is very common for a young woman to believe that she alone is plagued with self-doubt and insecurities around body image, social status or sexuality; that she is the only one who feels picked on or excluded at school, or who comes home at the end of each school day to dysfunctional family dynamics. Of course, every one of us is unique; the delusion lies in believing that we are also alone.

Convinced that our past, our pain, or our present circumstances are different and therefore unacceptable, we mask our vulnerability—and in so doing, we lose access to the parts of ourselves that are real and alive and authentic. The diarists whose stories you will read on these pages dispel the delusions of separation that plague us at every age by demonstrating what research professor Dr. Brené Brown has called "the courage to be imperfect." Paradoxically, the act of sharing that which we believe makes us different reveals the common thread that connects us all.

When Mark Victor Hansen and I began compiling the very first *Chicken Soup for the Soul*® book, we agreed to include only those stories that awaken the spirit and inspire readers to express more of who they truly are—in other words, they had to evoke either tears or goose bumps. The stories you'll read here do both. After sifting through thousands of diary entries written by teenage girls, author Janet Larson selected those that reflect what is most raw, real and pure within each one of us. The uncensored words of these girls and women, along with Janet's powerful account of her own transformation, beautifully underscore an observation made by psychologist Carl Rogers: The most personal is, in fact, the most universal. There is much we can learn from the private sorrows, internal struggles and ultimate victories of another, for in retracing their choices we have an opportunity to review and revise our own.

My Diary Unlocked creates a safe space that makes more authentic exchange possible between mothers and daughters; sisters and friends; teachers and students. By choosing to share this book with the important women in your life, you extend this safe space to them, forging a common bond that allows you to more deeply connect with one another, learn from one another and empower one another. I believe our ultimate goal should be to expand this connection so that women and girls feel safe to speak their minds and hearts, not only in the presence of their peers but also in the presence of partners, parents or mentors. Today's teenage girls are tomorrow's mothers, and today's mothers are the guardians of our shared future. We have allowed too much of our collective wisdom to fall through the generation gap. The time has come to reclaim it and move forward in high esteem.

The 21st century has witnessed a resurgence of conflict and war. All over the world, violence, discrimination and exploitation are inflicting unspeakable harm upon our children. Mother Earth herself is suffocating. The very real problems facing us today are born of hatred and intolerance. *My Diary Unlocked* imparts a message we urgently need to hear and become inspired by: The willingness to truly connect with one another is the path to a healthier way of being.

One thing is true about this period in human history, and that is that none of us can afford to be silenced by self-doubt or shame, or to keep secrets that stop us from speaking out. We need everybody—young and old, male and female—to step up, to bring forth that which brings us alive, and to summon the courage to be ourselves. In our vulnerability, we are connected as a powerful force that defuses conflict and generates peace. As Janet wrote in *My Diary Unlocked*: Vulnerability is the new power.

Jack Canfield
Fall 2012
Santa Barbara, California

Jack Canfield, America's #1 Success Coach, is the co-creator of the best-selling series *Chicken Soup for the Soul®,* the co-author of *Chicken Soup for the Teenage Soul* and *Chicken Soup for the Mother's Soul.* Author of *The Success Principles,* Jack is a leading authority on Peak Performance and Life Success. www.jackcanfield.com

Author's Note

The diary entries and later reflections you are about to read are real and they are raw. For the past decade, I have collected diary entries submitted by hundreds of women and teens for potential inclusion in the My Diary Unlocked self-esteem project and/or this book. I have pored through thousands of entries received from friends, friends of friends, and through word of mouth and media query sites. I have personally communicated with each diarist whose entries appear on these pages. Outside of minor edits and occasional composite entries written to maintain readability and protect the privacy of diarists who wished to remain anonymous, the entries and reflections are authentic and presented in the form in which they were first written—when there was no intention for them to ever be read.

Upon learning about the goal of the My Diary Unlocked movement, these brave diarists changed their minds about the secret nature of their diaries, opening the pages along with their hearts to share with others the truths revealed within. As one diarist put it when she first contacted me, "I heard about this project after just finding my journals from high school and college last weekend. I cringed at how obsessed I was with guys back then, and wondered what to do with the journals. Burning them was an option, but reading them helped me realize how much I have grown as a person, and now I'm so glad I kept them. Helping someone else keep a proper perspective as she learns to come into her own truth is more than I could hope for in contributing my entries."

As the author of this work, my goal is to touch people so deeply that they are inspired to go out and change the world; not only for our teen girls—our mothers of tomorrow—but for the inner adolescent within each of us who yearns for a deeper understanding of ourselves. Its purpose is to educate and inspire, and is in no way intended to treat psychological or mental disorders. The exercises, processes and other healing modalities shared throughout the book are those from which I personally derived value. I offer them here in the same spirit that has long inspired women to share their wisdom with other women; not as an expert dispensing professional advice. I want people to walk away determined to love and cherish both their children and themselves and to take a stand for the equal rights of all the girls of the world. My hope is that readers become passionate in their understanding of how sacred are our children and teenagers, and how much they look to adults for guidance. For teen readers, I wish for you to learn through the examples and insights provided between these covers that no matter what anyone says, no matter what circumstances you find yourself in, no matter what mistakes you've made in the past or what fears you hold about the future, you are lovable and capable of achieving your dreams.

My Diary Unlocked features the issues teen girls and many grown women encounter day after day and year after year—some personal and some universal. The reason I titled the book *My Diary Unlocked* is because of this merging of selves—we are individual, and yet we are one. In essence, my diary is your diary. At the end of the day, we share the same joys and fears whether we are young or old, female or male. The fact is that teenage boys endure countless pressures of stereotypes and assumptions of their character. They have long suffered the indoctrination to stuff their emotions in the face of suffering and to appear fearless in the midst of that which scares them. While I do not overlook this sad truth, my focus in this volume is on the diaries and experiences of teenage girls. Of course, nobody functions in isolation, and we all know that the tangled web of the experiences of teen girls certainly does not exclude boys—in fact, in many cases, they are the central figures.

The quotations from experts and others shared throughout this book are independent of other contributors, and do not necessarily endorse the opinions or modes of healing outside of their own contributions. Likewise, the diarists contributing to this book have done so independently of other contributors, and do not necessarily take a position on the written narrative or tools of healing outside of their own contributions. The primary intent of every contributor is to open their hearts to others who may have walked or will walk a similar path.

A note about the format of the book: The diary entries, diarist reflections and commentary by subject matter experts are indented and slightly italicized to separate them from my narrative.

To whom ever is about to
Read this Journal:

Enclosed are very private and
personal words that came from
deep within my life.
If you feel you must read this
then I warn you - I am very open,
blunt and honest. Some of the
things you read could possibly
hurt or offend.
This journal is a place I vent
my fears and emotions. Everyone
who I write about is someone I
love very much and would never
want to hurt.
SO - if you are someone please
reconsider what you are doing. It
could be to your own benifit.

Opening page of a
contributor's diary ...
telling it like it is.

"We read to know we are not alone, we write to find ourselves," wrote psychologist and author Judith Ruskay Rabinor, PhD, quoting her college English Professor O'Hara. Rabinor added, "there is something about writing it down which is different from talking it out. Writing builds trust in one's ideas and beliefs. Writing reveals the self. Writing connects one to ones' insides. Perhaps writing offers another kind of reparative experience: where one can eventually build a bridge to the inner world, to "the frozen seas within."

he won't. What will I do
if he goes to.
and bes with her? All
I'st hate him if he does
that to me again. I
don't know if I'm all
worried for nothing or
if I need to be. I wish I
had a mom I could talk
to. Mine can't even sit at the
table.

If you intend to read
this, please understand you
will be going against my
wishes and violating my
privacy. I can only ask you
to respect my decision and
keep your eyes to yourself.
However, if you do read
these words contained in this
book, I ask you keep them
private. Thank you.

Please someone hear my cry &
reach out and grab my hand
guide me along the way
show me the short cuts and the
right roads to take but most
of all stand there and be
my friend. I need it.

Keep Out

Maybe I'll be an artist
or preferably an actress.
I think I'll major in
communications. I want 3

Help this has been an
emotional week for me. I
had a Blood Test & Chest X-ray
on Wed. The X-Ray showed something
in one of my lungs later. It's
centeresting or insisting how I
didn't want to tell anyone until
I get the results back. What
short support for me. I was
thinking the other person &
how they would feel

Well I am really excited
to start a new journal.
It's as if each completed
one marks an accomplishment
and more I understand
about myself.
Anywho, this week has
been hell. Being grounded
sucks, but either/or this
week has been hell.

I could   Dear Diary,
then he
broken.
bis
ice.
at another
a girl
e Thold

Help! I need to go on a diet and
lose 20-25 pounds except I never have any
will power. Please help me get through it and
lose all that weight. I also got a last put on
my foot. All that junk food does is put
the herbs on rolls. So mmm more fun
However long until I lose it all!!!!

FAT FAT FAT FAT! I don't care

Introduction

I want to write, but more than that,
I want to bring out all kinds of things that lie buried deep in my heart.
—Anne Frank

I never had a Mrs. Duncan. You know, Oprah's beloved fourth grade teacher who recognized her potential, shone a light in the midst of a dark and troubled childhood, and forever changed the trajectory of her life.

Growing up, I saw no such light guiding me towards my authentic self or urging me to live my highest truth. I do, however, remember the junior high school teacher who came up behind me in class with a snow shovel and a metal wastebasket. He banged them together as loud as he could to wake me from the nap I was taking after I'd been awake all night listening to my parents fight. My classmates were hysterical with laughter as the sound of clamoring metal jolted through my body and nearly shot me through the roof. I almost saw stars, but in no way was I seeing the light. Little did I know back then there *was* a light; not one coming from an external source, but a source of illumination centered deep within my own heart.

On the outside, my teen years were filled with the activities that defined a "normal" life: birthday parties, boyfriends, pom-pom practice, piano recitals and student council meetings. But on the inside I was a bundle of nerves, filled with self-doubt and plagued with near constant feelings of unworthiness. It wasn't until I was in my 30s and read Mary Pipher's *Reviving Ophelia* that I came across a description of the teenage years that resonated with my own experience. Adolescence, Pipher explained, is a time when girls are under enormous social pressure to abandon their authentic selves, and—in a desperate search for acceptance—express only a small portion of their full potential. Lacking the sturdy foundation only a strong sense of oneself can provide, I was the proverbial "sapling in a hurricane" she wrote about, rooted to nothing in particular and being blown in every direction.

By the time I hit my late teens, I'd been pregnant, had an abortion, and nearly committed suicide—and yet amazingly, I kept all of this from even my closest of friends. I thought no one would understand me. I thought no one could relate to the way I felt. I thought I was alone. I know now I

And the day came when the risk to remain tight in a bud was more painful than the risk it took to blossom.
—Anais Nin

was wrong. After devoting decades of my life to personal growth and self-discovery, I now understand that even though I couldn't see it at the time, a broader, deeper, more natural expression of myself was available all along. This is the message I wish to impart to teen girls, their mothers and everyone whose inner adolescent is either under-expressed or wildly running the show; whose relationships with themselves or others are still mired in teenage dramas: Now is the time to let ourselves bloom. There is no denying the fact that teenagers today face challenges—physical, emotional, psychological and spiritual—that are radically different from those faced by any previous generation. On the whole, statistics concerning today's teenager paint an undeniably grim picture: Nearly every two hours, a person under the age of 25 commits suicide in America. Since the December 2012 Sandy Hook Elementary shooting that left 26 people dead to the first printing of this book 54 weeks later, there has been a shooting in one of America's schools almost every four school days. Close to 1,800 teen girls in the U.S. become pregnant every day. Almost half of our nation's teens have been bullied, while over 43 percent have been cyberbullied, repeatedly, via their cell phones or the Internet. One in 12 young people, the vast majority of whom are girls, engage in self-mutilation—cutting, burning, or deliberately taking life-threatening risks. Obesity rates among teens are skyrocketing, even as they are coming to age in a culture that condemns anything less than a perfect airbrushed body. For far too many young girls today, the road to womanhood is paved not only with hormone swings and broken hearts, but also with anxiety, depression, loss of personal power, 24/7 cyberbullying and—most tragically—a disconnection from their true selves. Unfortunately, the emotional baggage accumulated along the way often becomes lodged in the heart until a conscious choice is made to unlock its grip and release its toxic drama.

My Diary Unlocked presents a rarely seen, deeply intimate glimpse into the inner world of teenage girls, shedding light on concerns haunting parents and children alike. However, unlike most books aimed at helping teens and parents survive and ultimately thrive during this tumultuous time, *My Diary Unlocked* provides a direct window into the hearts and souls of teenage girls who never considered they would someday share their privately written words. Their thoughts and feelings strike a chord in anyone searching for meaning and identity, for they resonate with an inner vibration of truth. In a one-of-a-kind anthology of actual diary entries written by teenage girls themselves, this book brings to life the gut-wrenching, serious, funny, heartbreaking, heartwarming and liberating experiences that are par for the course during the adolescent years. This range of emotions is also felt by boys, and although they do not journal as much, they and their parents can learn, grow and reap the benefits of this book as well as anyone else. These entries may be separated by time and generation, but the hopes, dreams, trials and triumphs expressed through each one forge a universal bond between parents and teens, sisters and friends.

Each chapter explores one of the many issues that have occupied the minds and hearts of teenage girls for decades, if not centuries: body image, family, relationships, romance, sexuality, pregnancy, self-esteem, bullying, addictions, coping with loss, change and even death. No body of text captures these struggles more purely than the words written in a private diary, for with every stroke of the pen or computer key, the writer plunges to the depths of her soul, sharing her heart on the page and drawing the reader into her innermost thoughts and feelings. This in and of itself is a tremendous source of comfort to teens and parents alike, for it imparts the message that they are not alone. Then, in an effort to light a path through the struggles, these diary entries are followed with insights, inspiration and practical action steps contributed by some of today's leading authorities on human potential, parenting and teen issues. Reflections later shared by the diarists themselves reveal the resilience of the human spirit as they offer inspiration and encouragement to those walking a similar path.

The seed that eventually blossomed into *My Diary Unlocked* was first planted in 1979, when I spent weekends away from college visiting my grandmother, born in 1895, as she was slowly losing her battle against colon cancer. Hearing story after story about the lessons she learned from being raised on the prairies of Minnesota, the realization hit me that this woman possessed a depth of wisdom and experience that—unless captured in print—would be lost forever. As she talked, I found myself taking copious notes, until one day she gently stopped me, and with a smile assured me she had already written it all down. Sure enough, in her desk drawer buried under stacks of papers was an inconspicuous notebook containing an accounting of her life's history, dating all the way back to a blizzard she recalled in 1904:

"One Christmas nite coming home from a party, we got lost in a raging blizzard but as luck would have it we had thotfull [sic] neighbors and they hung out lanterns just in case someone was lost on the prairie, and we drove in circles for hours but finally saw a light and headed for it, and when we got there we were just a 1/4 of a mile from home. That was the good old days, when we drove horses and sleighs and put quilts over our heads to keep warm. That storm must have been about 1904."

As citizens, we are guardians of all living things; as parents, we are the trailblazers for our young; and as mothers, we have a responsibility to do all we can to help our daughters emerge victorious from the struggles they will inevitably face as teenage girls on the road to adulthood. After all, these young women are the mothers of tomorrow. It is time to keep the pain and drama that is right now filling the hearts and diaries of millions of girls from defining their perception of who they are, and from allowing their limiting beliefs to determine who they will become. Today, as I write these words, there exists a very real threat to humanity and to the planet. Only the feminine spirit of compassion, empathy and understanding, whether expressed through females or males, will prevail in lighting the path in the stormiest and darkest of nights. We have spent ages going around in circles and have borne a rut of deep suffering to the point we must realize there is a better way. A wiser way. The diarists and teachers on the pages of this book open the door for a course correction as they share the fears that keep us weathering storms created by self-rejection. In so doing, they hand us the keys to the age of wisdom.

Whether you are a parent, a teen or a grown adult whose inner adolescent is still struggling to find the courage to listen to your heart, follow your dreams and live your fullest life, the diary entries captured on these pages are lanterns set out just for you. When you choose to follow the light, you will realize—just as my Grandma Tillie did—that indeed, you were never really far from home.   Janet Larson, Winter 2013

Chapter 1

My Journey:
An Introduction to the SOULSELF

The journey is my home.
—*Muriel Rukeyser*

It's true what they say. When we ignore the quiet whispers of the soul, its voice becomes louder and its lessons more painful until finally we have no choice but to turn our attention within and listen. One of my first experiences of this occurred in seventh grade. Despite her fear I would become a hippie, my mother finally relented and allowed me to get John Lennon wire-rimmed glasses. Wearing them with pride, I sat at my desk in English class, looking down to admire the swirling colors of my psychedelic bell-bottom jeans. My private daydream was cut short by an announcement from the teacher: each student would take turns reading one page from a book, out loud. As the snake of readers slithered its way closer to my row and to my desk, my heart began pounding so hard I became lightheaded. By the time it was my turn to read, beads of sweat had formed on my upper lip and my mind was blank. Feeling physically ill, I bolted out of the room, barely making it to the girls' bathroom before getting sick to my stomach. What on earth was going on? I had no idea. I do know from that moment on, the thought of speaking in front of a group terrified me—even if I was just reading someone else's words off a page, never mind expressing my own opinions. I'd stopped that long before, after every attempt of doing so at home left me feeling shamed. This event in English class marked the onset of anxiety and panic attacks that plagued me for years, often without warning and for no reason in particular. Ultimately, these episodes of "stage fright," while a source of embarrassment at the time, became a powerful source of

Me in my "John Lennon" wire-rims. Age 12

inspiration that urged me to listen to my feelings, search patiently for the words to express them, and do so by reconnecting with a more authentic part of myself.

From the trenches of anxiety and depression through which I've travelled, I learned that by honoring my authentic self and expressing my inner truth with confidence, I realign with my soul—the very essence of who I am. Over many years of teaching self-esteem workshops to Girl Scouts, pregnant teens, girls in gangs and women in weight-loss programs and domestic abuse shelters, I have seen this same transformation take place. There comes a moment when something clicks within them and the light returns to their eyes.

When we merge with the soul and reconnect to our truth, we operate from a sacred space I call the SOULSELF. After writing this word in my own diary years ago, I realized the letters help to clarify its meaning:

SOULSELF ... SOURCE OF UNIVERSAL LIFE SERVING TO EXTEND LOVE FOREVER

The SOULSELF is the voice that speaks through the silent whispers of our hearts. It is the state of being we enter when we've expanded our breath, silenced our minds and once again have access to inner peace. When we are at one with the SOULSELF, our self-esteem is high enough to listen to our intuition and allow it to guide us gently through the river of wisdom. We embrace the message of "Peace, be still," as we express our uniqueness in service to humanity. We are *authentic*. The SOULSELF is not something we need to create or improve, for it is always with us—always at hand.

authentic:
au·then·tic [aw-then-tik] of undisputed origin; genuine; real

The SOULSELF is present in parents who recognize their teen daughters' backtalk and rolling eyes not as a prompt for punishment, but as a call for love. It is present in teens when they deflect rather than absorb hurtful words directed toward them, their confidence unshaken by insults as they stand strong in the truth of their being. It is present in women like Stephanie, whose diary entry you will read in Chapter 2, who, instead of reaching for a quart of ice cream to numb her pain, learned to feel compassion when emotional scars surfaced from her past. When we relate to one another from this higher ground, meaningful connections become possible. We understand that within *each of us* lives an inner adolescent struggling to refine and reclaim her identity. Relationships are no longer experienced as battlefields where old dramas are reenacted in endless loops. They become opportunities to heal and to grow, because we are now dwelling in a place where it is safe to express our true feelings. As we model for others what it is to live from the SOULSELF, we instill it more deeply within our own hearts. Speaking from my own experience and from the perspective I've gained as a result of reading thousands of diary entries of hundreds of teenage girls—from all walks of life, raised in different households and in different decades—I know one thing for sure. Most of us grow up in families that not only discourage the blooming of the SOULSELF, but actually encourage us, whether consciously or not, to conceal our authentic selves behind one of any number of masks. Our daughters, our mothers and our own wounded inner teens need us to engage with them at a soul level, not on an inauthentic level that creates further pain and separation.

Teach peace
Live Peace
Learn Peace
Have Peace
—Angela Melugin

My Journey to the SOULSELF

In most alcoholic, workaholic, shopaholic, or "fill in the blank"-aholic homes, children often assume whatever role they believe will help to keep the peace. Alcoholism was the card my family was dealt, and anxiety was my initial reaction. It wasn't easy for anyone. My dad wasn't Mr. Congeniality when he wasn't drinking, but he became ultra-critical when he was drunk. Growing up, I felt nothing I did was good enough to secure his love, and making a mistake was a risk I could not afford to take. One night, I sat on my bed, aching in frustration over the gap between how perfect I was expected to be and how imperfect I felt. I went to my nightstand, grabbed a notebook and wrote the following poem—not realizing that this marked the very first entry in what would become a lifelong practice of keeping a diary.

No Mistakes

If I make sure I get straight As
And keep my room clean too,
Would you love me all the time?
The way that I love you?
The coach is always telling me
"You're good; try out for the team!"
But you'd be so mad if I missed a shot,
So I watch from the stands, and dream.

My friends all ask, "Why don't you play?"
You're tall and quick and strong.
I tell them you'd be so embarrassed
If I ever did something wrong.
I wish that I could make mistakes
I'd try so many new things
And you would love me just the same
With all the acceptance that real love brings.

Over time, my dad's criticism engulfed me like a cloak; my shoulders slumped and my head hung low beneath its weight. I was too young to understand then that he, too, was in pain. Yet somewhere deep within me, I felt the presence of an inner light that yearned to grow brighter. In search of inspiration and hope, I turned to words written by others, and soon books became my constant companions. There wasn't a bookstore in my hometown, so I'd go the local Hallmark store and read uplifting greeting cards, collections of poems and inspirational books to keep my airway above the emotional waters of despair. My inner compass had led me to seek the truth in the midst of chaos, and the words written by sages and poets—recently or long, long ago—fed my soul and nourished my heart. One quote that served as a lifeline I returned to time and again was Eleanor Roosevelt's famous observation that "No one can make you feel inferior without your consent." Potent messages like these are sprinkled throughout this book, by the way, as my experience has revealed that words can re-ignite the spark of the SOULSELF, however dimmed it may have become by negativity or circumstance.

Around the same time I began collecting a treasure chest of personal favorite quotes, I started using my diary for something other than fashion critiquing and reporting my emotional weather forecast. It became an outlet to express my thoughts and insights—which is why I now consider a DIARY a representation of the:

DIARY ...   **DEVOTED INSIGHTS ABOUT THE REAL YOU**

It started one Sunday when I was seventeen, when a special guest speaker wandered off the path of the fire-and-brimstone–themed sermon typical at the church I attended and instead delivered a talk that was alive and spoke directly to my heart. The message moved me to the point that words and ideas hidden deep within me sprang to the surface, bursting to be expressed. Arriving at home, I jumped on the bed, crossed my legs and opened to a blank page in my diary and wrote:

> **Janet, Age, 17**
> **September. 28.** *Best sermon I have ever heard. I started crying. The guest talked about loneliness, and how people sit and cry because they are lonely, and tension builds up and they get chronic head-aches and things like that. Sure sounds like me. He said, "What you need is solitude. You have to find yourself." I don't really understand what I'm supposed to do, but I will go hear him tomorrow night, and pray to get John out of my mind once and for all. Bad headache today.*
> **September 29.** *I went back to hear that guy talk about your sub-conscious mind and how you can control your own destiny. He said that thoughts and words have power. For example, if every day I tell myself, "I don't like John," and imagine myself releasing my attachment to him, then pretty soon I'll begin to believe it, and I won't feel so desperate! The talk really cheered me up and helped me have a better attitude.*

Make time for
SOULITUDE:
Solitude for the soul.
—Janet Larson

This was my introduction to the power of the mind and the now widely accepted concept—confirmed not just by mystics and philosophers but also by scientists and scholars—that "where your attention goes, energy flows." On that early autumn night, sitting in the third pew from the front of the altar, the seeds that would one day sprout into my life's purpose were planted.

You get what you focus on, so focus on what you want.
—Unknown

Where I once was running on empty, encouraging quotes now fueled me with emotional and spiritual inspiration, and they appeared in the most unexpected of places. One day in the spring of my senior year in high school, while I was working as a bank teller, my boss saw me reading inspirational quotes from note cards I had made. The next day, she walked over to my desk and right on top of my paperwork of reconciling bank accounts, she plopped down a nearly 2,000-page book she had cherished for years, a 1939 edition of *Familiar Quotations* by John Bartlett. Any time business was slow at the bank, I'd read that book and take notes. Shakespeare, Whitman, Emerson, Robert Frost, Mark Twain ... all became my dearest and most trusted friends. The book sits next to me to this day as a dependable resource guide.

Not long after, I was off to college, my newfound love of inspiration and my diaries in tow. And although these had given me a powerful glimpse of my true passion and an inkling of my ultimate destiny, I was still out of touch with my true purpose and how to honor it, and lacked the courage to take the road less travelled. I thrived on my daily serving of quotes, but I had yet to integrate one of the most famous of them all: "This above all, to thine own self be true," by Shakespeare. I was good at math and had been told I would be guaranteed a job if I majored in accounting, which is what I did. So, in a twist of irony, I started my career specializing in journal entries, but these were journal entries of an entirely different purpose!

The Dark Night of the Soul

In my sophomore year of college, while mourning the ordeal of my pregnancy and abortion and still keeping the secret, I became critically ill and was hospitalized while doctors tried to figure out what was wrong. Besides my having a severe rash, my white blood count was through the roof, my fever was so high my skin blistered and peeled down to the tissue, and I was nearly comatose. A couple of friends came to see me in between classes when they could. My then-boyfriend visited once, but left after a few minutes because he didn't like hospitals. My parents didn't come. I had never felt so alone in all my life. Every morning as I woke up, tears of sadness rolled down my face in recognition I was still alive. My joints were too stiff and my muscles too weak to wipe away my own tears, so they flooded my ears and soaked my pillow.

Sometimes when we think we are keeping a secret, that secret is actually keeping us.
—Frank Warren

Discharged from the hospital a week later after a battery of tests, I had no diagnosis from the doctors other than being identified as a "strange case." My body began to heal, but emotionally I fell into a deep depression. I went through the motions of college life and flew to Daytona Beach, Florida for spring break with friends. At a party on a high floor of a beachfront hotel, I stood on the edge of the balcony as laughter from the party echoed in the back of my mind. In the forefront, however, I was telling myself I didn't matter. I was worthless. Just as I was working on getting up the courage to hurdle the railing and end my misery, a guy appeared through the glass sliding door and whispered in my ear, "don't do it," then disappeared back into the room. This startled me enough that I lost my concentration and went back to the party. When I got back from break, I was touched by a stroke of serendipity as I saw a flyer for the Big Sister program and became a big sister to a sweet 9-year-old girl. Suddenly, I mattered to someone. Reaching out in service to others has always helped me at least as much as it helped them, and it is one of the cornerstones toward living in the presence of the SOULSELF discussed throughout this book. A footnote to this story is that several months later, my illness was identified. More females around the country developed the same symptoms, and many died. It was toxic shock syndrome, a rare bacterial disease caused by the use of tampons. As it became a headline news topic, I called the TV station to say I'd had that, but declined a TV interview to share my story because I was too insecure to think about being on TV, even though it may have helped others.

Out of college and in my 20s, I was working full time and had a number of friends. Emotionally, however, I was once again hanging out at the lower levels of Maslow's Hierarchy of Needs I'd learned about in my psychology classes—the level of survival. I was far from the top level of thriving or reaching my peak potential. Soon, my outer world began reflecting my inner disconnection with myself: I became involved in an emotionally abusive relationship that was insidious and poisonous, feeding on and perpetuating my low self-esteem. My spirit was so low and my thoughts so dark I began having recurring nightmares of standing inside the front door of my house, trying desperately to get out, but the door to the outside was locked, and prison bars lined the windows. As I plunged deeper into despair—my own version of the proverbial dark night of the soul—I clung to the poems I'd collected in my diaries with the tenacity that a baby clings to its blanket. The following is one I kept in my purse 24/7 during this time:

Don't Quit

When things go wrong as they sometimes will,
When the road you're trudging seems all uphill,
When funds are low and the debts are high,
And you want to smile, but you have to sigh.
When care is pressing you down a bit,
Rest, if you must, but don't you quit.
Life is queer with its twists and turns
As every one of us sometimes learns.
And many a failure turns about
When she might have won had she stuck it out.
Don't give up though the pace seems slow—
You may succeed with another blow.
Success is failure turned inside out—

The silver tint of the clouds of doubt.
And you never can tell how close you are.
It may be near when it seems so far:
So stick to the fight when you're hardest hit
It's when things seem worst that you must not quit.
—Author Unknown

I cherished the message contained within those last few lines, for just when it seems things cannot get any darker, a silver lining can reveal itself from the most unforeseen places. The faintest flicker of desire is all it takes to awaken the SOULSELF from its slumber. Here, I realized that words—when fused with intention and followed by action—have the ability to lift us out of our own mental gutter, free us of self-doubt, and re-establish us once again in a place of true power.

With the help of a friend, I left the abusive relationship. In fact, I left the state, my mind set on moving to California. I got only as far as Arizona before I realized—in the words of Jon Kabat-Zinn—"wherever you go, there you are." It turns out, I had taken myself with me. Sobbing in a phone booth on the side of a desert road, I called my parents. My dad—now many years sober yet terrified of flying—took a bus from North Dakota to Utah, where we had decided I would drive from Arizona to meet up. Although I was emotionally numb driving to Utah, I'll never forget the journey across the Hoover Dam that day. My mind raced in response to a voice telling me to step on the gas as hard as I could to see if I could make the car barrel off the edge and end my pain right then and there. Divine intervention is not a myth, by the way. Someone in a higher place than me must have taken the wheel that day, because the next thing I knew, I was still driving along the highway, the dam in my rearview mirror.

That night in the hotel room, I had my very own "bathroom floor" experience that Elizabeth Gilbert describes in her book, *Eat, Pray, Love*. I sobbed the whole night, allowing myself to truly come apart at the seams. In the morning, I used the last square of remaining toilet paper to wipe away my final tear, walked out of the hotel bathroom, pasted a smile on my face, and said good morning to my dad. We packed the car to head back home and drove all day, stopping for dinner when our stomachs growled.

I've finally stopped running away from myself. Who else is there better to be?
—Goldie Hawn

A Full-Circle Walk Between Generations

After dinner my dad and I went for a long walk before checking into the next hotel along our journey home. He never let on that he had heard me crying through the night, but on that sunset walk, he opened up to me like he never had before. He told me of his heartbreaks growing up, about being an All-Star basketball player and a record-holding track star whose parents had never come to a single game or track event. Instead of celebrating his accomplishments, they told him he would never measure up to his brother, an academic achiever, whose success they valued over "silly games" and sports. Dad's voice cracked and his eyes filled with tears when he spoke of searching the stands amid a sea of parents cheering their kids on to victory, and of the void he felt when he realized his own parents were nowhere to be found. He was a champion lost in the judgmental shadows of his parents. I later learned my dad had suffered whippings from his stern Norwegian father, who asserted his power nearly every night with a leather strap. From his toddler years through age 11, this was the primary role model of parenting my dad received.

I've learned that simple walks with my father around the block on summer nights when I was a child did wonders for me when I was an adult.
—Andy Rooney

As he spoke, I saw for the first time that inside my dad was a wounded boy, with a story that preceded his alcoholism, his workaholism and—outside of providing financially—his lack of any meaningful presence in the lives of his own children. His vulnerability that night opened the door to a miraculous healing in our relationship. For the first time, I was able to let go of my attachment to how my dad "should have" been and opened my heart to the truth of who he was. In other words, I forgave him. I saw the irony of how patterns of judgment are passed down from one generation to the next. My dad was judged for playing sports, and I felt too judged to attempt sports, as reflected in my poem. I recognized that beyond his imperfections as a parent, he had risen above his own experience to do better, to the best of his ability. By the time he died two decades later, he and I had enjoyed many years of a mutually enriching relationship.

Hurt people hurt people.
—Unknown

Forgiveness is giving up hope that the past could have been any different.
—Gerald Jampolsky

The Road to Healing

I arrived back in North Dakota just as autumn was setting in and my parents were heading for their snowbird trek to Florida for the winter. In too fragile an emotional state to do anything else, I followed along and stayed with them for the remainder of the year, using the time to heal from what I believed to be a nervous breakdown that began when I set out for California.

I went to the library and devoured every motivational book I could find. I rested at the beach. I began cognitive-based therapy. Although I was only twenty-something, I attended yoga classes for senior citizens, in part because my anxiety-driven weight loss had withered my body away to almost nothing, (to the point I hadn't had a period in months), and—well, in part because in Florida, senior yoga classes were easy to find!

During this time, I read Leo Buscaglia's book, *Living, Loving and Learning,* multiple times, and—although I had never dealt with any prescription drug issues—I relished the book, *I'm Dancing as Fast as I Can.* Its author, Barbara Gordon, had also been to hell and back, and offered me hope that there was a way out of personal bondage and into true liberation of the soul. Following my therapy sessions, when the knots in my stomach were a little less tightly wound, I was once again able to nourish my body with healthy food. The initial phase of my post-traumatic healing was officially underway.

Remembering the words I'd heard years earlier from the guest speaker who visited at church, I decided to explore in greater depth how our thoughts create our destiny. I was drawn to a book on the shelf called *Creative Visualization*, and the moment I read the first paragraph, I knew I had been led to another important signpost along my journey toward personal growth. "Creative visualization," Shakti Gawain wrote, "is the technique of using your imagination to create what you want in your life. There is nothing at all new, strange, or unusual about creative visualization. You are already using it every day, every minute in fact. It is your natural power of imagination, the basic creative energy of the universe which you use constantly, whether or not you are aware of it." I began using the techniques in the book. Together with everything else I was doing to dig myself out of my personal hell, I went on to complete graduate school at the University of Oregon and then moved to the city of my dreams, San Diego, California.

And yet, two steps forward often meant one step back. My fear of speaking was still interfering with my ability to succeed at work and in other areas of my life, but because my eyes were now open to seek wisdom, they fell upon the perfect quote at the perfect time. (Oh, the magic of synchronicity!) I opened a book to a random page and was awestruck by

You'll see it when you believe it.
—Wayne Dyer

these words by Mark Twain: "Do the thing you fear the most, and the death of fear is certain." My determination to feel the fear and do it anyway became instilled "at the soulular level," a phrase I learned from my friend and author Azim Khamisa.

I joined a Toastmasters group. (Fortunately, the group met in a hospital conference room, so if I fainted or came close to death from speaking, the response time to spare my life would be nil, because a Code Blue could be called on the spot!) Later, I became president of the local chapter. I enrolled in the Dale Carnegie Course and went on to assist the instructor for several subsequent courses, all of which helped solidify its lessons within me. Infinitely more comfortable in my own skin, I became an instructor at three leading universities and eventually launched my own consulting business. My confidence was building, the evolution of my soul was picking up speed, and my life was moving in the right direction. Instrumental in my personal development was my recognition that I, little Janet Larson, had the power of choice. Realizing that every day and each moment presented a choice between fear and love, I meditated—and when my depression took me to a place too deep and chronic to dig out of, I medicated. Because I was big on "mind over matter," I resisted medication, until a close friend suggested it when she witnessed firsthand the depths of my despair. I had her pegged as a "Do Not Medicate" proponent, and her open mind showed me that I could be open-minded too. On Prozac, I was able to stay out of the "hole" of negativity long enough to establish a baseline level of functioning, resume a regular exercise routine and become more mindful in my everyday experiences—all the while circling back to meditation to deepen my connection with the golden light within, my SOULSELF. From that position, I was able to make moment-to-moment choices that tethered my inner truth to my outer actions—choices that enhanced my accountability to the truth of my being.

Balancing the inward exploration of meditation with the camaraderie and external emotional support I received from structured personal growth programs was the key to my continued growth. Each workshop I have attended has been a breadcrumb on the path toward my destiny. Today, I feel blessed to have had the privilege of receiving personal training from some of the most brilliant thinkers and human potential leaders of our time, including Eckhart Tolle, don Miguel Ruiz, Marianne Williamson, Deepak Chopra, Byron Katie, Wayne Dyer, John Gray, John Bradshaw

There are two ways to live your life—one is as though nothing is a miracle, the other is as though everything is a miracle.
—*Albert Einstein*

From making one choice … you reorder the entire magnetic flow of the whole of your life on this planet. You shift the dynamic of your entire life.
—*Caroline Myss*

Bradshaw and many more. In a workshop led by Stephen R. Covey in Waikiki, I learned to customize the *Seven Habits of Highly Effective People* just for me. I have basked in the warmth of the Dalai Lama's radiant smile and listened deeply to Maya Angelou's immortal voice of truth. I have played and replayed the audio teachings of both Eckhart and Deepak, and studied the works of Neville, Joel Goldsmith, Caroline Myss and Joseph Campbell. I learned the power of asking meaningful questions from watching Oprah. At a pivotal point along my journey, Jack Canfield mentored me, and he was instrumental in my decision to lead self-esteem—building seminars for girls and women from ages 5 to 85.

My Diary Unlocked

My Diary

One Saturday afternoon, some 15 years after graduating from high school, I emerged from the storage unit at my apartment in Del Mar, California and took a box cutter to the tape that sealed a dusty box bearing the word "memories" on the outside. I opened its flaps and there it was: the red diary I had written in during my senior year of high school. Blowing the dust from the lock, I opened it and—as if by instinct—drew it close and sniffed the words to smell if the strawberry scented ink, sealed for years in this box, had endured the test of time. The scent had faded, but the memories evoked by ink were all too vivid. With each page I turned, feelings of insecurity, self-loathing and self-doubt came flooding back as if the events that triggered them had happened only yesterday. I nestled in, cross-legged on the floor, and read it from cover to cover. I cried, I laughed, I cringed, I became angry; but more than anything, I wanted to stretch my arms back across time and give that girl a great big hug. Unlocking my diary gave me a greater appreciation than ever before of the contrast between the girl I used to be and the woman I had become. The realization of how far I had come empowered me to more purposefully chart a course to even greater freedom and to share my secrets with others.

By this point, I'd learned I was not alone in the experiences, emotions, losses and lessons that had defined my teenage years. I understood every teenager faces similar challenges that can manifest in different ways and through different circumstances, including emotional or physical abuse, addiction, the loss of a loved one, romantic break-ups, issues around sexuality or body image, or long-standing feelings of inadequacy or abandonment. In fact, I realized that in no other demographic are these expressed more dramatically than in teenage girls. I understood that nearly every woman deprived of the opportunity to process these emotions while she is young carries within her psyche a wounded inner child stuck in the adolescent stage of development in one or more aspects of her life. She strives to understand her authentic, inherently lovable self but looks to the outer world for validation that she is worthy. Unless it is healed, this cycle of dysfunction continues to be passed down through generations, because children live what they learn.

From the pages of my diary I saw just how drastically I'd changed over the years, how dramatically I had improved my capacity to reclaim my own personal power, to find compassion, to develop meaningful values, to love, laugh and listen to myself—even in the midst of struggle. I had become my own best friend, choosing more moments of peace and fewer moments of anxiety and chaos. Reflecting on the resources and tools that gradually transformed my life from one of quiet desperation to one built upon a foundation of peace and happiness, I realized my journey back to freedom required me to clarify my daily choices in relation to what I have now categorized into five key aspects of my being.

There is nothing more vital to your life than living an authentically empowered life.
—Oprah Winfrey

In this moment of heightened awareness, I envisioned each of these aspects as a template that represented the fullness of my being. The more responsibility I took for the choices I made in each one of these key aspects, the more I was able to access the keys to unlock the innermost core of my SOULSELF. This template—what I call the Freeing Your BEING Compass—will serve as a tool for personal direction to help you recognize the source of your own choices more objectively, while also offering a gauge to identify your own true north. In effect, it is a roadmap to high self-esteem. As you gain awareness of the diarists' stories as they unfold, you will be in a better position to seize opportunities to respond differently when faced with your own challenges or dramas—even those that may have previously shaken you to the core. When you objectively view your actions and choices through your bearing on this compass, you are able to more clearly see the destination that each choice is moving you towards. Is it fear, or is it your own inner truth—your soul? By paying attention to more subtle cues offered by our inner compass, we maintain its calibration as we bypass pain and suffering.

Calibrating Your Compass

Mark this page and refer to it often as you consider which of the five aspects are causing stress or keeping you from the happiness you deserve. (Also, mark the page entitled "Glossary of Acronyms" following the last chapter, as there are more words that spell out their meaning.) You will not be walking this path alone. We are all in this together, with the diarists as our torchbearers.

Keys to the SOULSELF
The Freeing Your BEING Compass

BEING ...   BEING: BODY, EMOTIONS, IMAGINATION, NATURAL SELF, GENIUS MIND

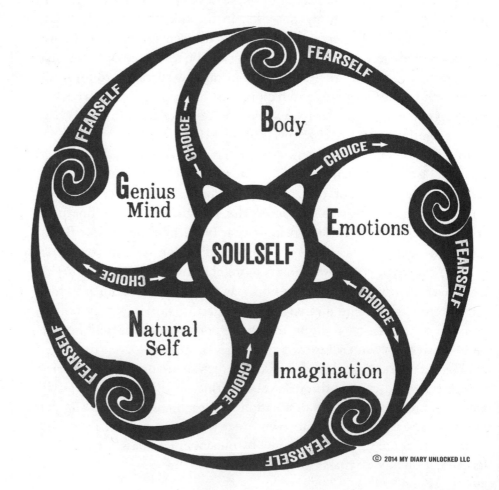

© 2014 MY DIARY UNLOCKED LLC

Body
Emotions
Imagination
Natural Self
Genius Mind

In truth, at the very core of our BEING,
in the stillness of all life, lies our essence.
Living this essence— this BEING—
is the KEY to high self-esteem.
It is about having the courage to face the fears
that pull us in every direction—away from our
true guiding compass, and choosing to come back
home to our own soul—to free our BEING.

essence:
es·sence [es-uhns]
the invariable nature
of a thing; Origin late
Middle English: via
Old French from Latin
essentia, from esse 'be.'

KEY
KNOWING THE ESSENCE OF YOU

... KEY

In the context of the Freeing Your BEING Compass, let's look at each acronym of this compass one word at a time. We have already defined the SOULSELF as the:

SOURCE OF UNIVERSAL LIFE SERVING TO EXTEND LOVE FOREVER

SOULSELF

SOURCE: The core element of the SOULSELF is its source—the symbolic womb from which truth arises. It is the hub from which all activity of our BEING springs forth, and the center toward which we ultimately return on our journey through life. It is the gateway to transformation and the elixir that sheds light on the darkness.

OF: Expresses the inherent relationship between the source and universal life.

UNIVERSAL: Universe means one song or one story. *Uni* means one. *Verse* is song or story. Within the SOULSELF, the universe is the connection we share with others, whether it is recognized or not. It is the wave as part of the ocean and the ocean as part of the wave. The acknowledgment of unity with our source invites a life of peace.

LIFE: The SOULSELF is vital energy that cannot be created nor destroyed. It is the pulse of the universe, the chills we get when we hear a song we love, the heart that feels pain when mourning and joy when we unveil the truth of love's presence.

SERVING TO: The purpose of the SOULSELF is to serve, to share and to join in the connectedness with all life.

EXTEND: The SOULSELF manifests as the divine and unique extension of the love within our hearts to others.

LOVE: The SOULSELF knows only love, for only love is real.

FOREVER: The love rooted within the SOULSELF is as eternal as it is divine. Because the SOULSELF is generated from love, its essence lives on into infinity. Only that which is manufactured or made up by humans is temporary.

The outermost edge of the Freeing Your BEING Compass represents what I have named the FEARSELF. As we did with the word SOULSELF, let's decode this next acronym—the FEARSELF—to better understand its full meaning:

FRAGILE EXPERIENCE OF ANXIETY OR REGRET SEEKING EVIDENCE OF LIMITATIONS FOREVER

FEARSELF

FRAGILE: The FEARSELF is fragile because when faced with truth, it dissolves. The FEARSELF has no foundation; it is not who we really are. Like the proverbial castle made of sand, it is all fluff and no substance - an illusion, a dream.

EXPERIENCE OF: The feelings we have and the interpretations we make, based on our beliefs and perceptions.

ANXIETY OR: Anxiety is based on the fear of the future.

REGRET: Regret is living in the past.

SEEKING: The FEARSELF keeps us on an endless cycle of seeking; it keeps us from just *being*.

EVIDENCE OF: Seeking "proof" that we are not good enough, the FEARSELF finds validation to support our limiting beliefs.

LIMITATIONS: Remaining smaller than or achieving less than our full potential.

FOREVER: Yes, forever - until we become awake enough to challenge its false authority.

The FEARSELF is what many refer to as the ego. It is the part of us that assumes the worst, takes everything personally and eclipses the truth of our inherent worthiness in its fog of misconceptions. Look at the black dot at the center of this image for 30 seconds. By remaining focused on the core of the SOULSELF—represented by the dot, you may see the surrounding gray area—representing the fog of the FEARSELF that obscures the truth— begin to change, shrink or perhaps even go away. It's an optical illusion that leads us to question what other illusions may be filtering the truth. False or sabotaging beliefs keep the FEARSELF in charge. When the FEARSELF is directing our thoughts and actions, we are not operating in present-moment awareness but are bound instead by our own limiting interpretations of past experiences we then project into the future.

If we bite the hook, the FEARSELF achieves its goal—to trigger within us negative emotions that take us out of the present. Even when we resolve not to lose ourselves in anxiety or regret, the FEARSELF has a backup plan to keep us from occupying the empowered present, where the SOULSELF resides. It does this by stirring in us a more subtle kind of fear—the FRAGILE EXPERIENCE OF ANTICIPATION OR REMEMBRANCE—in other words, by luring our attention to an anticipated unpleasant event in the future or an unpleasant memory from the past. But even if these more subtle tactics are used, the bottom line is, they also spell FEAR. Anticipation may be nice to build excitement, but its value is lost when it clouds what is currently happening. Of course, we need to make plans for the future; it is when our attachment to a specific outcome of our plans causes us to sacrifice peace in the present moment that we shift into a state of FEAR. It is a sense of trust or faith that our vision *or something better* will unfold that keeps us anchored to our soul. And while it is fine to have the gift of remembrance, when we remain stuck in our memories at the expense of being mindful of the present, we sacrifice the most precious moments of life—the only place where peace is possible—the Now. Sometimes, the effects of the FEARSELF at play are not so subtle, like when they are played out as the FRAGILE EXPERIENCE OF ANGER OR RESENTMENT. When our choices are driven by the FEARSELF, we spin around and around in the turbulence of the outermost superficial edge of the circle, like a hamster

If you are depressed, you are living in the past. If you are anxious, you are living in the future. If you are at peace, you are living in the present.
—*Lao Tzu*

on a wheel. We endure pain because we believe the stories that induced the pain.

The following chapters unveil the many faces of FEAR that show up in our lives regardless of our age. In truth, although these stories were played out in real life, they were engineered behind the scenes from our misguided beliefs. Suffering everywhere, going nowhere and exhausted, we may think we're just sleep deprived, but in truth we are spirit deprived, as Anne alludes to in her entry. In the FEARSELF, there is no peace. When the light of truth is recognized and embraced, the FEARSELF simply ceases to exist, just as darkness disappears when a single light is turned on.

Anne Frank
January 22, 1944. *Dearest Kitty, can you tell me why people go to such lengths to hide their real selves? Or why I always behave differently when I'm in the company of others? Why do people have so little trust in one another?*

In the SOULSELF, nothing can separate us from peace. Living from the SOULSELF—the brilliant inner core of this hub—we find truth is like the unchanging axle around which our experiences revolve. It is here we become teachers of integrity and truth to adolescents everywhere, including the one that lives within each of us. Robert Frost captured this beautifully in his poem, *The Secret Sits*. "We dance round in a ring and suppose," he wrote, "But the Secret sits in the center and knows."

On the Compass, the lines that move in both directions from the innermost core of the SOULSELF to the outer edge of the FEARSELF remind us that in every aspect of our lives—and in each and every moment—we have the power to choose which direction to take. Every action we take represents a choice between the FEARSELF and the SOULSELF, between doubt and faith, weakness and strength, fear and love, illusion and truth, constriction or expansion, isolation or connection. With every action, we move closer towards or farther away from truth and love. When we allow the SOULSELF to guide us back to the innermost core truth of our BEING, we discover the keys to our own kingdom, where truth really is our protector. Here, we gain access to the freedom and the confidence we need to live our lives unlocked. In this place, the five aspects of our BEING merge together in the present moment to function in harmony with each other and as a natural expression of our true essence in our relationships with others.

The Five Aspects of BEING

A key acronym in the Freeing Your BEING Compass is—BEING.

BODY
EMOTIONS
IMAGINATION
NATURAL SELF
GENIUS MIND

BODY: The *Body* aspect of our being is the vehicle or conduit that drives the outward expression of our inner state of BEING. It is the physical form we have to communicate and connect with others. When the perception of our bodies is held captive by the FEARSELF, we are plagued with insecurities and preoccupations about our looks. We have mistaken our bodies for ourselves. As a result, if we feel our bodies are not good enough, we believe the lie that we are not good enough. We think we are unlovable as we are, and too often we unconsciously seek to prove it in a variety of self-destructive ways: eating disorders, obsessions and compulsions about food, weight or appearance. On the other hand, when the Body is aligned with the SOULSELF, we radiate inner beauty, which is the source of real beauty, and treat it with the respect it deserves—as a conduit; an instrument; a temple. We nourish ourselves with healthy food; we celebrate life with movement, and energize our bodies with the breath of life provided by exercise. As we continue to evolve into the age of wisdom, I'm not surprised by the trend of physical exercise programs, such as yoga and Pilates, which focus more on unblocking stuck energy and building core strength. These disciplines place emphasis on the solar plexus area—the Body's powerhouse, located between the rib cage and navel—the center of our physical foundation and the source point for personal power. Hugging into the source of truth, we literally become grounded at the core and are more able to express the truth of our BEING from that place. When our inner compass is pointed toward the SOULSELF, we use our bodies only in ways that honor and express our higher purpose; we literally live and breathe as instruments of peace.

bel

iefs
storm

tran

Unlock your feelings peace, be still
layers of emotion... sadness, anger, fear,
hurt, forgiveness, sadness, anger, fear,
turn fear into love, happiness, joy, peace
Anxiety about love. Express yourself
Regretting the future steals the moment
becoming present sets me free —
embrace compassion emotional

EMOTIONS: The aspect of *Emotions* reflects the quality of our relationships. Caught in the headlights of the FEARSELF, we waver between numbing our Emotions and permitting anxiety or depression to torture the spirit within. Believing we are unworthy of others' love, we easily become withdrawn, angry, jealous or self-centered. We become more susceptible to addictions. Aligned with the SOULSELF, our emotional intelligence lives up to its name, and we demonstrate compassion and empathy for others and ourselves. We feel our feelings, but we don't allow them to run the show. We have feelings, but we are not our feelings. They represent only one aspect. We seek to understand and resolve conflicts with respect and dignity for all.

follow your intuition for your wishes to be fulfilled. creation
idea unlock your imagination. The key is in your heart. I am capable of achievement
insight visualize wish dream aspire picture this creativity
create imagine intuition perception inspiration inspired

IMAGINATION: *Imagination* is the aspect of our BEING that fuels our dreams. This is the part of ourselves where true vision and creativity are born; where we are able to conceive and believe in a future that has not yet been made manifest. Imagination is also at the core of our perceptions at any given time, for in order to perceive something—whether positive or negative, we must imagine it to be so. It follows that Imagination is a critical aspect to develop empathy and compassion for others. To understand their suffering, we must be able to imagine what they may be experiencing. In the realm of the FEARSELF, Imagination is extinguished before it has a chance to bloom. Feeding on a "can't, won't, don't, no, never" mentality or perception, our dreams are suffocated by a blanket of doubt as they turn into nightmares—or, worse, into resignation. Fear of failure sabotages our chances of success, or prevents us from even imagining a world in which we can get what we really want and deserve. Operating from the FEARSELF, the reality of the suffering of others remains distant, as we are unwilling to "put ourselves in their shoes." But at the core of the SOULSELF, Imagination is the engine urging us to reach the threshold of the Divine, reel in our dreams, and make manifest their reality. True Imagination is the spark of electricity occurring when the hand of the Creative Source touches our own. It triggers the goose bumps we feel when we experience or stand witness to an act of loving kindness to one in need, or how we feel when a new idea is born within us, opening the doors to the powers of intuition to lead the way to manifestation.

NATURAL SELF: The aspect of *Natural Self* reflects who we are when our behavior aligns with our authentic essence. Before they take on the pretenses of the world, children are pure, beautiful expressions of their inner truth; their essential, Natural Self. But, when co-opted by the FEARSELF, we no longer feel the freedom to be who we really are, and instead—in search of external validation—begin to mold ourselves to meet the expectations of others. Our lack of authenticity prevents us from truly connecting with others, leaving us feeling like the odd girl out, isolated and alone. When the Natural Self is united with the SOULSELF, integrity, honesty, happiness and abundance are inevitable manifestations. Speaking our truth becomes *natural.* We are empowered to "feel the FEAR and do it anyway," because we are not preoccupied with the opinion of others.

GENIUS MIND: *Genius Mind* is the aspect of our BEING that gives us the ability to evaluate and make decisions. From this aspect we gain the uniquely human ability to observe our own thoughts. In the realm of the Genius Mind, we can consciously re-establish our habits and the nature of our self-talk. When operating from the FEARSELF, the Genius Mind is corrupted by beliefs that limit our potential; beliefs that we are phonies, impostors, stupid or unworthy. They convince us to stifle our unique gifts and withhold our contributions, sabotaging the present and limiting our future. To live our lives plagued by self-doubt is to remain undeniably miserable. Choosing to embrace the potential of our Genius Mind from the perspective of the SOULSELF, we become confident, focused, goal-oriented, open-minded and disciplined. We are mindful—not mindless. We gain access to the "genie" within—the guardian spirit referenced in the root word *genius*, coined in the 14th century. From that state of genius, we direct our course of action in unity with Infinite Intelligence, for we have reached a genuine understanding of ourselves.

The diarists you will meet in the following chapters have come face to face with the FEARSELF in each and every aspect of their BEING at one point or another. At times, they felt like giving up. If we also feel that circumstances have led us down a life path that we are helpless to change, perhaps we will relate. Before getting comfortable with this attitude, however, we would do well to consider the words of Viktor Frankl, who suffered horrors as a Holocaust prisoner: "The last of one's freedoms is to choose one's attitude in any given circumstance." By choosing an attitude inspired by a SOULSELF-directed life in each of the five key areas in our lives, we blossom into our full potential—BEING the person we were meant to be, instead of just *doing* what we think we should do.

Making Choices: The Journey to Freedom

The last piece of the Freeing Your BEING Compass includes the lines or "spokes" that lead from the center to the outer edge of the Compass, between each of the five aspects of BEING. This is where the action in life takes place. Just as a rudder steers a ship in one direction or the other, our choices are dynamic forces that lead us into or out of our highest good. With every choice we make, we face the positive and negative polarities of being human.

In the same way that it is the nature of an acorn to become an oak tree and a caterpillar to become a butterfly, it is the nature of every human being to seek and express love, and to claim the full power of Divine Intelligence. Yet as humans, we are also born with a gift not given to any other living thing on earth: free choice. An acorn cannot choose whether to bloom into an oak, nor can a caterpillar decide it is unworthy of becoming a butterfly. Their growth unfolds naturally and without conscious participation. Human beings alone have the dubious ability to choose to grow or to remain the same. I use the word "dubious" here to describe this gift because to a large extent we also have the ability to determine the course our growth will take. In other words, we can allow ourselves to act unconsciously from the FEARSELF or to be guided by the SOULSELF. In every instant that we make a choice that leads to the expression of our highest potential, we carry whatever aspect of our BEING is related to that choice directly to the core of the SOULSELF. As a result, we feel more alive and free to be ourselves. In recognition of the truth that we are constantly making choices, I have coined this acronym to remind us of this ever-present power. CHOICE is:

CONSTANTLY HAVING OPTIONS IN CREATING EXPERIENCE   . . . CHOICE

At an awards ceremony in India, the Dalai Lama gave a speech on "The Power of Women," during which he made a plea to women around the world to reclaim the feminine virtues of compassion and affection, that we may unite and redirect our moral compass to the spirit within rather than to the madness without. Our teens—whether they live in our homes or in our hearts—are repressed and weary from the escalating aggression and violence happening on our planet. There is a yearning in our collective soul to stop feeling numb and start feeling understood. There is a thirst to end the insanity of our cultural identity crisis and to choose peace. We can't keep doing the same things over and over and expect different results. The time has come for our society to stop acting self-centered and start BEING soul-centered. We are living in a time when our youth need us to take up this challenge and make new CHOICES, for they are depending on us to mentor their emergence into adulthood equipped with the tools to create a morally grounded future.

Regardless of whether you are reading this book from the perspective of a mother, a daughter or a grown adult whose own wounded inner teen is in need of healing, you are both the teacher and the student; a bearer of peace and a beneficiary of it. That this book is in your hands is testament to the fact that you are ready to accelerate your journey to the SOULSELF, and to facilitate that journey for others.

The sharing of stories has long been a doorway to greater self-awareness, and those told to us by our mothers and grandmothers, our sisters and our daughters give us a deeper understanding of them, as well as ourselves. When any woman or any girl has the courage to tell the truth about her sorrows, her struggles, and her ultimate victories, she opens the door for others to become vulnerable enough to do the same. And in that space of defenselessness, we are not *powerless* but *powerful* as we begin to understand—and learn from—one another's pain. Above all, we learn that we are not alone.

These pages hold firsthand accounts of girls and women who faced and triumphed over challenges that affected their self-esteem in one direction or the other. It is my deepest hope that unlocking their diaries, as well as

You have but two emotions, love and fear.
—A Course in Miracles

my own, will unite us as change-makers and as leaders committed to sharing, caring and daring to make a difference in changing the trajectory down a path of fear to a path of love. Together, we have the power to hasten the journey toward a life of joy and a culture of peace that awaits each one of us.

Painting is just another way of keeping a diary.
—Pablo Picasso

Natalie Fry

Chapter 2

From Body as an Image to Body as an Instrument

For beautiful eyes, look for the good in others; for beautiful lips,
speak only words of kindness; and for poise,
walk with the knowledge that you are never alone.
—*Audrey Hepburn*

Three days after my best friend Mary—to whom this book is dedicated—lost her life to breast cancer, a crumpled wad of paper was found on her desk at the social services office where she worked as a child abuse investigator. No one had seen the note before, but here it was, being handed to me by her former co-worker. In Mary's own handwriting were printed these words:

IN THIS MOMENT,

MY MIND AND HEART OPEN

TO RECEIVE MY GOOD

MY GOD

I AM A CONDUIT OF ENERGY

I AM THE FLOW OF SPIRIT

I DIRECT THIS FLOW OF ENERGY TO ALL WHICH

AWAKENS ME TO MY DIVINE NATURE

WITH GRATITUDE, I FLOW AS THE FLOW OF SPIRIT

BODY

I reread this passage hundreds of times, for it expressed so eloquently the miracle that is the human body. In the months following Mary's death, every possible emotion seeped through me. Among them, eventually—and thanks in large part to this note—was an overwhelming feeling of peace. Mary's words confirmed that before her time in a human body came to an end, she had come to understand its true purpose. To this day, Mary's words remind me that our bodies *are* conduits of the Spirit that animates them.

Body Image and Eating Disorders

Science tells us only 1 percent of the body is solid matter; if we took the protons, neutrons and electrons that comprise each cell and compressed them together, all solid matter would fit on the tip of a needle. So what, then, exists in the 99 percent of "empty" space? Our bodies are instruments that connect us as individuals to the universe in which we live and make it possible to commune with everyone and everything we love. If only we could see our bodies through this broader perspective; if we would stop to appreciate all they do for us and all they enable us to do, I have no doubt we would care for them as the temples they truly are.

Tragically, however, these are not the eyes through which an overwhelming percentage of young girls and grown women alike view their bodies. Rather than standing in awe at the miracle of the human body, we stand in judgment of all we perceive they are not. The depth of despair that our distorted body image causes us as women is best revealed through the words of the diarists in this chapter:

Once you are Real you can't be ugly, except to people who don't understand.
—Margery Williams

Janet, Age 14
I put on beauty mud last night. It didn't work. I'm still ugly.

Jenny, Age 14
I have no self-esteem because I'm too ugly, too fat, my feet and hands and legs and butt and stomach are too big, and I'm too damn flat-chested. Why is everything else on my body bigger than it is on all my friends, but my chest has to be small—so it turns people away that much more? Why can't I stop crying, and why do soft warm tears keep rolling down over my cheek and onto you, my dear diary?

Toianna, Age 16
I HATE my body and how my boobs flop around. They are three times as big as the girls I go to school with. I look like a freak and no one ever chooses me to be on their teams for sports, I guess because I feel so awkward with big, flapping boobs. It scared me when Colin wanted to pay me ten dollars for me to lift up my shirt so he could see my boobs. Matt always tries to corner me at the neighbor's house to tease me. He gets too close and scares me.

Kayla, Age 19
March 15. I weighed in today at 131lbs. It seems I can't get out of the bloody 130's, but what else is new, really? Today is my ninth day without food and my wasting away goes unnoticed.
April 19. Just so we're clear, I've been starving myself for 44 days, so the two slices of apple I ate today really hurt my stomach. It probably got used to just having liquids I've been feeding it at work where I drink water—and coffee, sure—I'm a Starbucks barista. Green tea frapp and soy chai, which is far better than nothing. I know all about that nothing stuff.

Sara, Age 14
Julie pinched all my knee fat today and everyone in the whole car started laughing. I'm just worthless shit to everyone including my incredibly ugly, dirty, disgusting self. Love, Sara

Erin T., Age 16
I'm very pissed with myself; I have about 5 or 6 very evident zits! I was ugly before, but now I just feel as though I'm a nothing and ugly, which is just great!!

Beauty is the illumination of your soul.
—John O'Donohue

In the simplest of terms, our body image is the sum total of the thoughts, feelings, and images that arise within us when we contemplate our physical appearance. It is both a reflection of the way we perceive ourselves and of the way we think others perceive us. The regard (or disregard) we hold toward our bodies is intimately tied to the value we place upon on ourselves as females.

While writing this book, the "meta-research" (research of all the research) I conducted on teens with body image issues forced me to acknowledge the profound lack of self-esteem that manifests in one or more areas of their lives. I also learned that leaving the teen years does not necessarily

Definition of self esteem: Knowing that you are lovable and capable just the way you are, and that you are worthy of achieving your dreams.

mean leaving behind teen fears. Judgments and insecurities around physical appearance may be more prominent in adolescence, but they continue to plague many women well into adulthood. A few months before her death at age 85, my own mother told me she couldn't stand to look in the mirror because she thought she was "so ugly with all those wrinkles." The same wrinkles I saw as a softening of muscles held tight with bitterness in her younger years, she viewed with disdain.

In the absence of high self-esteem, body image becomes tainted by the FEARSELF and directed by the limitations it seeks to impose—including comparison, condemnation, and self-deprecation. And when in contrast we hold a healthy and positive image of our bodies, the path that returns us to the SOULSELF—to the truth of who we are—again opens wide. We feel comfortable in our own skin and accept ourselves unconditionally.

Experience of Body Image	
FEARSELF	**SOULSELF**
External appearance defines internal worth	The physical body is viewed as a vehicle to commune, express, and serve
Outer beauty is valued over connection to inner truth	Breath is used to reconnect the body back to its non-physical source
Physical boundaries are non-existent or disregarded	Physical boundaries are established and respected
Obsessive dieting, issues with weight, or eating disorders are present	Food is used for nourishment and enjoyment of flavors
Self-judgment is frequent—and in some cases, constant.	Attention and care are lovingly offered to maintain the body's health

Ideally, the body image of every man, woman and child would be something over which we alone have jurisdiction. In reality, however, the way we feel about our physical appearance is highly variable; it fluctuates day by day and in response to each new situation. Body image is also powerfully influenced by the messages we absorb from our parents, our culture and the mass media—and, unfortunately, many of these messages are negative.

In the 1980s, while researching collective group behavior and social movements, I wrote an essay about the devastating effect fad diets can have on young women's self-esteem. The marketing of these programs was, and still is, brilliant—and also deeply destructive. Most are designed to ensnare teen and pre-teen girls into a preconceived notion of what it means to be "beautiful" at precisely the time in their lives when they are the most vulnerable; when they are making the transition from childhood into womanhood. Their bodies are gaining new curves and their weight is in a constant state of flux. Growing into unfamiliar bodies while comparing themselves to the idealized images of female "perfection" they see around them, many young girls accept the premise that to be lovable they, too, must look like the models they see in music videos and fashion magazines. The average height and weight for a model is 5 feet, 10 inches and 110 lbs., while the Centers for Disease Control and Prevention (CDC) reported the height and weight for the average woman was 5 feet, 4 inches and 166 lbs. in the U.S. in 2012. The National Institute of Health (NIH) calculates ideal body weight for adult (age 20 and over) females as 100 lbs. plus 5 lbs. for every 1 inch over 5 feet tall. A female who is 5 feet, 4 inches tall has an ideal body weight of 120 lbs. A 5-foot, 10-inch-tall woman has an ideal body weight of 150 lbs.

From where did this notion that women are objects arise, and how has it managed to gain such a stranglehold? In large part, the answer is sitting no farther than the TV set, the magazines lining the checkout stands of grocery stores, the movie theater down the street or social media reaching everywhere. Family members, teachers and athletic coaches, too, may unwittingly contribute in some way—although not necessarily on purpose. After all, most of them were conditioned by a similar set of social values and are merely continuing to teach what they learned. However, of all the factors that come together to mold and shape a young woman's developing sense of self, perhaps the most significant of all is the influence of her parents—and especially her mother. Disparaging comments about looks, fashion CHOICES and weight can make a deep and lasting impact on a young girl's psyche.

Fat is an "F" word that carries a lot of emotional charge. When a young girl hears a parent using it in reference to *anyone,* that negative charge

Every time a woman passes a mirror and criticizes herself, there's a girl watching.
—Gloria Steinem

intensifies. Even praising our daughters' appearance can backfire, for it can easily be received as criticism in disguise. While there's no harm in complimenting someone who looks nice—perhaps she just did her hair for a special occasion—our daughters may interpret some "compliments" to mean that the depth of our love is tied to the way they look. Saying, "Wow, you've really slimmed down," while smiling from ear to ear and bubbling with pride can imply conditional acceptance based on weight. Backhanded compliments like these are proverbial wolves in sheep's clothing. They may be dressed in a cloak of positivity, but they deliver the powerfully negative message that skinny is good, and not skinny is not good. And while weight is certainly one of the most common self-criticisms chipping away at the healthy body image of our teens, it is by far not the only one.

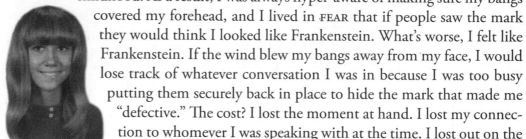

Me with my bangs perfectly in place.

When I was a teen, I didn't have a weight issue but I did have a mark on my forehead due to a rare skin disorder I was diagnosed with in early childhood. As a result, I was always hyper-aware of making sure my bangs covered my forehead, and I lived in FEAR that if people saw the mark they would think I looked like Frankenstein. What's worse, I felt like Frankenstein. If the wind blew my bangs away from my face, I would lose track of whatever conversation I was in because I was too busy putting them securely back in place to hide the mark that made me "defective." The cost? I lost the moment at hand. I lost my connection to whomever I was speaking with at the time. I lost out on the experience of real life. This same phenomenon is happening right now, in the hearts and minds of countless young girls conditioned to value outer appearance more than inner character. No wonder insecurities about body image have reached epidemic proportions.

At age 17, 78 percent of American girls are "unhappy with their bodies."
—National Institute on Media and the Family

Several years ago, I was asked to conduct a self-esteem workshop for a hospital-based weight management group consisting primarily of women. On the second day, I assigned a homework exercise: Participants were to go home and look at themselves in the mirror, *in the nude*, and find something about their bodies to compliment. Hearing this, a woman sitting in the back row called out, "Yeah, and watch the mirror break!" The room broke into laughter and the group instantly bonded as they related to this participant's issues around her body image, which obviously mirrored their own. "Jokes" such as these are common *practice*, but with regards to fostering a healthy body image and high self-esteem—at any stage of life—they do not make common *sense*.

Having spent nearly a decade reading thousands of diary entries written by women—young and old and from all walks of life—I am forced to acknowledge just how ruthlessly critical of ourselves most women are, and how adept we are at focusing with laser sharp clarity on our every so-called flaw. Jenny's entry reveals her self-judgment about being too flat chested, while Toianna resents her "big, flapping boobs." It's always something.

Whether we're judging imperfections on our skin, legs that are too short, or hips that are too wide—when we look in the mirror and see only what's wrong, we miss out entirely on everything that is wonderfully right and all that makes us uniquely ourselves. Most tragic of all, we begin to subscribe to the myth that a woman's body is a measure of her worth.

By the time our girls hit their teenage years, this self-deprecating message has been reinforced countless times by sources both near and far. And with social networking and media sources flooding our daughters' senses for up to ten hours each day, they receive a constant barrage of "pop-up" messages that distort their concept of real beauty. At some point, most "accept the prompt" and inadvertently download a belief system far more dangerous than any computer virus. According to a 2014 poll conducted by The National Campaign to Prevent Teen and Unwanted Pregnancy, a depressing 74 percent of teen girls say they often get the message that attracting boys and looking sexy is one of the most important things they can do. The diary entries that follow lay bare the private thoughts which occupy the minds of a huge percentage of the 20+ million pre-teen and teen girls in our country, confirming that the spell that was first cast upon us—by our parents, our culture, or by the media as a whole—still has us deep in a trance.

47 percent of girls in fifth through twelfth grade reported wanting to lose weight because of magazine pictures.

69 percent of girls in fifth through twelfth grade reported that magazine pictures influenced their idea of a perfect body shape.

42 percent of first grade through third grade girls want to be thinner.

81 percent of 10 year olds are afraid of becoming fat.
www.kidshealth.org et al

Diana, Age 15
I'm 5'4" and weigh 115 pounds. I always wish I weighed about 100 but lately I am more content the way I am. I have dark brown hair almost to my waist. My eyes are too small but with eye make-up I think they look better.

Tracy, Age 15
Is it my image? Is it because of the way I look, you don't take me out? Is my body or my face the reason you don't show me off to your friends? Yes I'm a little big, with brown spots on my face, and everybody talks about me. Baby, am I not perfect enough for you?

Am I too big, or too ugly for you? Because if I am, baby I want to know.

Sasha, Age 14
I'm so ugly sometimes, diary; it's like, I look at myself and all I see is failure. Whenever I am happy I'm just "copying" someone else. I look at pictures of me and all I see is UGLY, UGLY UGLY. Maybe when I get my braces off, and my hair has grown long I will be pretty and I can smile again. I feel fat—and like I don't add up; like I have some good qualities but not enough to be anyone worthwhile.

Elise, Age 16
I feel like a complete failure. Seriously, I'm not pretty enough, smart enough, sweet enough, happy enough or good enough for anyone. The image of myself has been changed from beautiful to lost and broken-hearted.

The range of feelings, from unrealistic expectations to worthlessness shared in these entries reveals the grip of the FEARSELF in each one of these girls. In reality, the "ideal" body type portrayed in advertising is naturally possessed by only 5 percent of American females, yet our desperation to measure up to this arbitrary standard of beauty causes untold pain. Like cigarette companies whose tactics are designed to get teens addicted before they understand the consequences, the diet and beauty industry sells promises of attractiveness, with their own profits (to the tune of $50 billion per year)—and not our girls' health—in mind.

Three-quarters of the word "diet" spells die.

On any given day, nearly 116 million adults—55 percent of the total adult population—are dieting, and 80 percent of our nation's children will have already been on a diet by the time they enter the fourth grade. Despite this, only Mexico has an obesity rate higher than the U.S. At the time of this writing, 17 percent of teenagers in America are obese. Often, this is no fault of the children themselves. The unhealthy eating habits of the parents and their lack of understanding about the importance of fresh, whole foods are sometimes passed on to kids before they are old enough to understand that there are, in fact, other CHOICES. The results of a long range study including 31,000 people indicated that those who consumed seven or more servings a week, an average of one per day of sugar-sweetened beverages were at a 29 percent higher risk of death from heart disease than those who consumed one serving or less. Fortunately, activists like

Chef Jamie Oliver are leading the way to create a movement to educate every child about food, inspire families to cook again and empower people everywhere to fight obesity. However, we still have a long way to go.

That Diana, at 5 feet, 4 inches and 115 pounds, thought she "should" weigh in at 100 is disturbing. That Elise, a 16-year-old girl whose self-image was changed from "beautiful" to "lost and broken-hearted" because she was not "... enough" is nothing short of a tragedy. We live in a culture that is obsessed with beauty, physical perfection, and—in particular—thinness. And we are putting our girls' souls at stake.

What's Eating America's Girls?

In 1983, when Grammy Award–winning singer Karen Carpenter died weighing a shocking 82 pounds, I had just begun my research of the effect that fad diets have on the self-esteem of teens and young women. Up until that time, very little was known about the disease that claimed her life and was silently afflicting the lives of many other young women. Carpenter's tragic death may have opened the country's eyes to the very real dangers of eating disorders (EDs), but their prevalence continues to rise at an alarming rate, especially among young people. Up to 24 million people suffer from an eating disorder in the U.S. The National Association of Anorexia Nervosa and Associated Disorders (ANAD) revealed that eating disorders are the third most common chronic condition among adolescent girls; a full 95 percent of those diagnosed with the disease are between the ages of 12 and 25.

It should be noted that those who suffer from an eating disorder rarely intend to get to the point where the disorder is controlling them. Quite the opposite. Often, they are looking for one thing in their lives over which they can exercise control. Some resolve to throw up their food just for a month to lose a little weight. Others go on what they consider a simple diet, and the dieting spirals out of control. In the entries that follow, notice how many of our diarists exhibited one or more of these common warning signs:

Common Eating Disorder Warning Signs
- Has low self-esteem
- Shows strong tendency toward perfectionism or need for control

- ✸ Denies feeling hungry and denies there is anything wrong
- ✸ Makes excuses to avoid mealtimes or situations involving food
- ✸ Seems to be preoccupied with weight, food, calories, and dieting
- ✸ Hides body with baggy clothes
- ✸ Makes frequent trips to the bathroom, especially after eating
- ✸ Engages in excessive tooth brushing
- ✸ Has a history of being sexual abused

The day I met Stephanie for an interview at a coffee shop after she'd volunteered to contribute her entries about her battle with anorexia, we discovered we were both celebrating our birthdays. Although I have never struggled with an eating disorder, it was a gift to meet a kindred spirit willing to share her heart's truth at the level of the SOULSELF.

Stephanie, Age 17

December 5. *I had a horrible Thanksgiving. Everything seems to be getting worse. I am fat and maybe it is not a distortion. I can't stop eating. I just eat and eat and eat until there's no food left. Everything was getting better and now it seems to be getting worse. I feel so ugly, so alone, and now I am diagnosed with the most superficial disease ever. Cool man, I am a WINNER!!! I just want to crawl into a hole. The day started so well.*

I am fat. Aimless. Passionless. I used to be such a passionate and driven person. I used to love the world. My friends, myself, movies, acting, boys, I used to be passionate. I want my passion back. If I DID have this disease, disorder, or whatever I am supposed to be calling it, WHY DIDN'T ANYONE HELP ME?? Well, I guess my friends sat me down and talked to me, but my mom never said anything … wouldn't she have said something?

I want to be peaceful and happy, but I look pregnant. I have a double chin. I feel my thighs … they touch each other. They are short, fat stumps. I am broken inside and broken outside.

I stand in the mirror in defeat and hatred. I am told that what I am seeing is not real but I have two working eyes and they see me, they see pictures of me. I am fat. I am a failure. I am so fucking furious with myself for getting so fat. I had the good life. I was skinny. I was perfect. Life was good and I messed it all up. Either these distortions are getting worse or I am getting BIIIIIGGER.

February 8. *My eating disorder has turned on me. Stabbing my bony back with its painfully sharp knife leading blood trails in the form of tears everywhere I go. Furious at my only friend who has* *left me so empty. Today, my birthday, I switched the table and did what I needed to do for revenge: I ate, and ate, and ate like I hadn't eaten in a year…I was so alone. So scared. So cold. So confused. And now so fat.*

My eating disorder isn't going down without a fight. I hadn't expected a teenage girl fight with this bitch. I know that peace will not come without a death. This is war and either my disease is going down or I am. And when I say going down, I mean death. The two of us cannot … will not … live concurrently. I dedicate this new journal—this New Year—to the war, and to ensuring that I am not the one going down.

March 8. *During the past year, after discovering my eating disorder, I have never felt so alone. Like that feeling when I take a bath because I need to do something to relax, something to quiet my mind, anything to find comfort. However, I find myself resting in a lonely tub of water. Not feeling any better at all. And losing control of the only friend I have left … my eating disorder. I gave up everything for it. My passions, my interests all involved this damn disorder. I gave up my friends because they seemingly always want to go out to eat—temptation I didn't want. I've only had enough energy to pound through a workout and maybe enough oomph to research diet tips and read "fitness" magazines. I say "fitness" in quotes, because those magazines are not for athletes; they are not for healthy people. These magazines are weight loss magazines and powerful poison to an anorexic mind. Nonetheless, all of my relationships have gone to shit. I've stopped caring about them, and have begun to hate the relationships still floating around because they are with people who unconditionally love me. And knowing that they might take a stand against my disorder has instilled a fear in me I'll never really be able to express.*

Kristen and I met at a conference, and when I shared with her the purpose of this book, she asked me to please stop the presses so she could contribute her story.

Kristen, Age 22
March 14. *Did ok. What I ate: apple, diet coke, 2 tablespoons peanut butter, 3 cups of popcorn (air popped—no fat!), 4 cups of hot chocolate. I made it through the day. I feel really good. Really proud. My stomach feels flat—just like I like it. I didn't feel like I had to suck it in today. Yesterday was horrible—all that fat I ate.*

Such a loser. Today, I feel some hope. Maybe I can keep eating like this. Maybe I won't have to get fat. Maybe I won't throw up again. If I can just stick to this meal plan ... can I do it? Help me. Can someone help me???

September 24. *Today we went to LaSpada's sub shop. My favorite! I figured I would eat half and save the rest for later. Right away, I started worrying ... was I satisfied? Was I still hungry? Maybe I should eat the rest. I called my boyfriend and as usual it didn't go well. I tried to lie out in the sun for a while but was hot and uncomfortable and didn't like how my stomach looked in my bikini. I couldn't stop thinking about the second half of the sub in the frig. My mom tried to come out and talk to me but I wasn't listening. I was starting to think about bingeing and wondering how to get away. I told myself I would get out of the house, just to clear my mind. I would go to the drugstore for lipstick. I wandered around the store mindlessly, staring at the different colors of lipstick and not knowing what to buy. My brain started to feel numb and all I could think about was the yogurt store next door. I ended up buying 10 different colors and made a beeline for yogurt. I knew the kitchen was sparse at home—all I had was my sub. At first I thought I could just order a scoop but halfway through my order, I asked for 2 pints. I opened the pint and ate it on the way home. Now, I needed a pizza. I had to act casual and find out what time my mom was leaving. I stashed the other yogurt in the back of the freezer and went to talk to her. My heart was pounding the whole time—did she think I was being weird? Would she just hurry up and leave? I was off to the races.*

Unlike other diseases, eating disorders shroud their victims in a veil of isolation, secrecy and shame—which explains why only 1 in 10 people who suffer with an eating disorder ever seek treatment. Stephanie and Kristen are both in recovery, and have gone on to attain advanced degrees in psychology and mental health, where they are now in a position to help others. For them and many other young women, healing becomes possible only when they become willing to open up and allow family and friends in on the secret. Twenty-three years after she wrote about her struggle to overcome patterns of binge eating and purging, Kristen again turned to her DIARY to reflect upon the events that brought about a turning point in her recovery.

Kristen's Reflection, 23 years later

On September 25, 1989 I made a choice that altered the course of my life. I said, "yes" to the unknown—a life of recovery after 7 years of struggling with bulimia, alcohol and drug addiction.

Reading these diary entries now, I almost don't know this person. She is long ago and far away. Yet I have compassion. And, I have created another life so different from that one over two decades ago. It saddens me to remember; yet I know all of that made me who I am today. I believe that our challenges can make us into stronger and perhaps more interesting people. Without my struggles, I would not have the compassion I have today. I would not have chosen the line of work I did. I would not be where I am today. I was one of the lucky ones—first of all, I made it. Many don't. Some die, some return headlong into the obsession. Some dabble with recovery for the rest of their lives, never quite getting there. I was miserable enough and after two treatment centers, I was blessed with willingness. Willingness to do what it took to recover. Willingness to put my trust in my treatment providers. Willingness to do what was suggested. Willingness to eat three meals a day. Willingness to follow my aftercare plan. Willingness to have it be different than it was.

Recollecting those days, the understanding of my desperation comes flooding back. The embarrassment, the hopelessness, the lying, the manipulation, the fear, the disgust. What made me one of the lucky ones? Determined to provide this for others, I immersed myself in the field of personal growth, earning a Master's degree in mental health counseling, volunteering and working in treatment centers. As a therapist, I saw all types. I would see the light come on in someone's eyes and sometimes it would continue to burn brightly, then sometimes it would dull over and my heart would sink. I knew that true recovery was possible. And over and over, I watched people return to their disease. I understand their struggle. An alcoholic or drug addict can ultimately avoid their addictive substance; however, we need food to survive. People with eating disorders have to confront this fact continuously. They have to deal with and ultimately make peace with the fact that eating is essential for healthy living. It took me a long time to be comfortable with food. After putting my trust in my counselors, I slowly learned to trust myself and finally, to trust food.

I remember writing, "I don't know who I am. I don't know

What we call the secret of happiness is no more a secret than our willingness to choose life.
—Leo Buscaglia

where I am going. I am lost. Help me." I was seeking, searching, hoping. So lost. So alone. I kept my eating disorder a secret for so long. It wasn't until I collapsed one day in front of my roommate that people started to know. Finally, in my freshman year, I reached out for help and my mom found me an eternally patient and supportive therapist with whom I visited with some regularity throughout my 5 years at college. She tried everything to help me but nothing seemed to work. In hindsight, my inconsistent visits probably kept me alive.

On the surface, I appeared to be a "normal" college girl, but the emptiness I felt inside was extreme—like a black hole that continually sucked the life out of me. I would constantly compare my insides to others' outsides and come up short. Not pretty enough, smart enough, popular enough. My nose was too big, lips too small, legs too short … the list went on. If I couldn't be as pretty as the other girls I compared myself to, I could at least strive to be thinner. Since college is often a breeding ground for eating disorders, being the thinnest was an uphill battle. I was socially awkward, only comfortable with my best friends or when I was drinking and doing drugs, which became a regular occurrence.

As a therapist, I have counseled many parents who are trying in their own way to come to terms with their child's illness. It is heartbreaking to watch one's child (whether grown or young) struggle with an eating disorder. So often, friends and family members ask my advice on how to get their loved one to choose recovery. Sadly, there is no easy answer. There are no magic words. But that doesn't mean we can't do anything. I am eternally grateful that my parents were willing to confront my behavior. They educated themselves, talked to experts, read books, researched treatment centers and were involved throughout my treatment process. Even though they were divorced at the time, they put their differences aside and united in their efforts to help me. At the time of crisis, together, they did an intervention and presented me with an ultimatum. And although I was the one who had to say yes, without the early intervention of my parents, I wouldn't have started my recovery at such a young age and who knows where I might be today.

25 percent of college aged women engage in bingeing and purging as a weight-management technique.
—National Association of Anorexia Nervosa & Associated Disorders

Eating disorders often stem from a complex set of issues that involve the entire family—and as such, the individual's recovery truly is a family affair. In the diary entries that follow, shared by 16-year-old Nicole and 17-year-old Carrie, notice that both girls tried to hide their dysfunctional eating patterns from family members—and that both had a sister who knew something wasn't quite right.

Carrie, Age 17

May 20. I seem to be getting the "lonelies" when no one is around. My stomach gets all tense and I want to make myself puke. It almost calms me down.

June 4. I'm so depressed. God, I don't know what's happening to me. I can't study, I eat compulsively, and I change moods rapidly. Please help me. My throat's killing me. Yesterday I did so well! I don't understand why I do it—binge and then purge. Help ...

August 23. I really enjoy writing in this diary. I think it might not only help me express myself verbally, but also help me to understand and deal with my problems. So far I've diagnosed myself as having a neurosis towards dealing with eating, having anxieties about eating anything beyond full, and having a phobia of food. Well, at least I'm not psychotic—yet. I didn't quite make it today, but, I have now decided I don't like just chowing but simply eating a few cookies to satisfy the urge. Unfortunately, I ate too much at dinner and feared I'd lost control. I did work on my homework. I won't let myself sleep until it's done ... my sister goes back to college tomorrow—at least with her gone we won't have cookies, etc. around. I'll HAVE to learn how to control myself in front of her. She's definitely suspecting something's weird.

Nicole, Age 16

Dear Diary, It started about a month ago. I don't binge and purge all the time, or every day. Just sometimes. I know I have to stop. I also know what's causing it. I have realized it is men. In some way, I think by doing what I'm doing, I keep a part of myself a secret, something that no one can ever touch. When I met Tom and cared about him, I felt like I was losing control over my independence and myself. Well, I have this feeling again with Jack. I know its roots go back to Dad in some way. My sister caught me. Maybe by talking to her I can stop again. I don't want to be bulimic anymore. I also am tired of being there for everyone and never being able to have someone really care about me. I am afraid of relying on others. As I am writing this, weights are being lifted off my shoulders. I hope Mom or Dad don't find out, because I think I'll be able to stop on my own. If not, I will get help on my own. Everything is going too well for me now, and maybe for the first time, I have it all and *really don't know how to handle it. I really need help this time, but I'm not too far-gone to stop again without Mom or Dad knowing. Love, Me*

After reading Nicole's diaries, I was contacted by her younger sister, Sophia, who knew about Nicole's bulimia but didn't know what to do with that knowledge. Unbeknownst to Nicole at the time, Sophia was keeping a diary of her own, and wrote the following entry the very same day she discovered her sister's eating disorder—an event that had occurred 26 years earlier. Here is Sophia's entry, followed by her personal reflection.

Sophia, Age 15

Fuck, I hate my sister!! She is such a geek. I'm disowning her. I hope someone reads this so they know what she does:
1. Throws up after every meal.
2. Takes laxatives.
Nicole must have a mental problem because she's such a geek. I hate her and I don't care what happens to her. She can go to hell for all I care. She's such a fat goon!! Geek!! SLAP! She's such a selfish pig all she cares about is herself and drugs. Pot, cocaine, speed, booze and all her other crap. Fuck her—who needs her!!

Sophia's Reflection, 26 years later

It has been 26 years since that entry. My sister, Nicole, still has anorexia and is rail thin. She barely eats. She has been married three times and is addicted to painkillers. She lies a lot, and the drug use has made her paranoid. I like to think that if she had received the proper help, physically and mentally, that her life would have turned out differently.

I remember Nicole asking me to be her "lookout" so that she would not get in trouble for sneaking in late at night. Even though I was torn about it, I was determined to protect her from my parents. My loyalty was way off track. I wish I had confided in an adult (a friend's mom, a school counselor), someone who would have helped my sister—and me. It haunts me today to think that maybe, if I had risked her wrath and had someone help me open my parents' eyes, she would have gotten the help she needed and her life would be on the right track.

When confronted with a family member who is struggling with an eating disorder, parents and other loved ones may ignore their gut feelings, believe the lies their daughters tell them to throw them off the trail or buy into the hope the behavior is just a passing phase. Denial is a most reliable tactic of the FEARSELF. Mothers in particular may convince themselves that naming the problem will only exacerbate it by making it more real. In this excerpt from her book *Healing Your Hungry Heart*, author and therapist Joanna Poppink explained why she wholeheartedly advocates combating eating disorders head-on through education:

> *Sometimes parents are afraid that educational materials about eating disorders will stimulate an eating disorder in their teenager. Parents may be reassured to know that eating disorder education might be a wakeup call that jars the consciousness of young people in an early stage of an eating disorder. Through education, a young girl might recognize herself as being on her way to having a serious disorder. With encouragement and support from adults and peers in her environment she has a chance of redirecting herself before the disorder advances to relationship destroying and life destroying levels.*

Erin's eating disorder started when as a young teen she made a pact with a girlfriend to go on a month-long diet to lose weight. After a year or two of feeling unsuccessful at her attempts to restrict her food intake, Erin began throwing up her meals. What started as a seemingly harmless desire to eat less morphed into a full-blown battle with anorexia and bulimia that lasted more than half of Erin's life. The challenges of eating disorders are sobering as we take in the words of Erin.

"Starting the day I focused too much on what I was eating until just a few months ago, I have never really had a time in my life when I would call myself in recovery on my own without some kind of inpatient. It lasted for over 13 years, which was sad to me because I had participated in my eating disorder for longer than I had lived."

Erin T., Age 16
June 30. *I can't stand myself! I've let myself slip away and have become so fat. I was doing sit-ups tonight and every time I'd come up I'd get like 25 rolls in my stomach region. It's so incredibly sad!! But I'm going to try something I've never tried before, No carbs! And getting off my ass and doing something productive. I'll try running, sit-ups, push-ups and other exercises! Love, Self*

In one of her inpatient stays, she demonstrated a degree of objectivity that journaling alone makes possible. Erin wrote in the third person about the suffering she endured and the powerful steps she was taking along her journey back to wholeness. While her trials were far from over, her insights were seeds of truth planted in her heart. You'll notice Erin addressed her disorder by the name "ED-die"—the initials for Eating Disorder followed with a dash—and ending with the word "die." Many people struggling with disordered eating choose to give it a name other than their own as a way to distinguish the disorder as something separate over which they have the power to re-establish control. Here is Erin's reflection:

I am willing to witness my fears.
—Gabrielle Bernstein

Erin T.'s Reflection, *several months later*

When in the course of Erin's life, it becomes necessary for her to break free from ED-die's hold, and to finally assume that the Laws laid out by the Gods and Goddesses of Hollywood are false pretenses; the mothers, daughters, sisters, and girlfriends demand that she stand up, speak up, and fight for her right to be herself.

Life, Liberty, and the Pursuit of Happiness are three truths our Creator bestowed upon all humankind. Due to ED-die, they have all three been damaged, compromised, and nearly taken away. He has damaged Erin's Life by never allowing her to experience her teens, the feeling of falling for that first boy, or the satisfaction of completing her first year of college. Her Liberty has been greatly compromised by ED-die holding her captive to each and every command he laid forth. And her Pursuit of Happiness was nearly taken away, because he trained her mouth to smile so no one would know. ED-die quickly gained total and absolute control of every aspect of Erin. To prove this let the facts be submitted:

- ✸ *ED-die has long refused Erin of feeling things.*
- ✸ *ED-die has not only damaged Erin's Life, but also the lives of those she loves.*
- ✸ *ED-die has lied, cheated, and stole; and then told Erin to believe that's who she really is—the liar, the cheater, the thief.*
- ✸ *ED-die has infested Erin's mind, and declared himself the ruler of her world.*
- ✸ *ED-die has deprived Erin of many life experiences.*
- ✸ *ED-die has cut off Erin's emotions so they couldn't surface.*
- ✸ *ED-die has been redundant about "WE ARE ONE"!*
- ✸ *ED-die has forever kidnapped a little girl from childhood and*

molded her to be what he needed so he could survive, all because he is selfish.

⊛ *Without her welcome or invitation, ED-die has nuzzled his way into Erin's head, changing the way she thinks, and challenging her values. In every stage of these oppressions, Erin has fought tooth and nail with ED-die. But each and every time, she succumbed to ED-die's tyranny. Erin must, therefore, declare total, heart-wrenching separation from ED-die and name him as the Enemy.*

⊛ *Erin, therefore, solemnly declares in her handwriting that she is free and independent from ED-die's captivity. She is no longer in allegiance to ED-die. All ties are now totally dissolved. As the free, independent, powerful woman that she has become she is now able to do things according to her own will, just like all other free, independent people do. And for support of this Declaration, Erin pledges to stay honest, involved, and loving to the beautiful ladies of her Thursday night therapy group—so she can be persistent in recovery, putting one foot in front of the other, one day at a time. And finally succeeding!!*

Erin used her diary to become an objective witness to her own issues around food, instead of remaining a helpless victim of them. Addressing her enemy by name was another tool that helped Erin to distinguish her eating disorder as something separate from herself, which was essential in reclaiming the power she had relinquished to it. Observing her life from the point of view of the real Erin—her authentic, empowered, NATURAL SELF—allowed her to see a kind of director's view of the script in which she had once just acted out a part. In a sense, Erin recognized her CHOICES were clouded by the fog of the FEARSELF, and exacerbated by a lack of nutrition. She acknowledged her eating disorder was in fact a disease—and a tough one at that. With this in mind, she renewed the depth of her commitment to her support group and also went through a formal treatment program, where she worked with an individual therapist. At each turn she asserted her will to gain another degree of freedom from her eating disorder. By filling the empty space once occupied by her dysfunction, she began to see a vision of herself as being free and independent, which further reinforced the experience of peace she was creating. Alert to the tricks this disease may use to fulfill its twisted purpose, Erin sought the support of her parents who reminded her that in the presence of triggers or moments of weakness, they were just a just a phone call away and would help her make it through.

I remember one day, after immersing myself for hours in the diaries of girls like Erin who struggled with one type of eating disorder or another, I decided it was time for a break. On the way to my favorite coffee shop I listened to NPR and heard an interview with a woman named Catherine Blyth on the topic of her book, entitled *The Art of Conversation.* Catherine made some brilliant points about the importance of listening and—as her book title suggests—she described the "art" of keeping open the doors that make it possible to experience real connection with others. I was so excited about the points she was making that I sent her an email asking if she would like to contribute to this book by offering parents advice on how to better communicate with their daughters. Replying from her home in London, Catherine was eager to help, and long story short, I emailed a few entries of one of the diarists who wrote about body image and eating disorders. I heard back from Catherine a few days later and was touched when she told me the diary entries I had shared had inspired her to write about her own experience as an adolescent; as it turns out, Catherine also struggled with anorexia as a teenager. Her message is not only relevant to this discussion about body image, but it reinforces an insight central to this book as a whole. Here is Catherine's story:

> In my teens, my changing body seemed a threat as much as a promise. Meanwhile my mind was burdened by hormones and endless pressures. To pass exams, be popular, look right ... I felt an overwhelming responsibility to secure my future, yet had such limited freedom. My parents held the purse strings, and controlling my circumstances, my destiny, seemed impossible. Gradually, a desire to control food came to govern me. Could anyone have talked me out of my eating disorder?
>
> My parents talked around the problem, telling me I looked better, or worse, or not to be vain, or they couldn't understand, or I was irrational. Perfectly reasonable comments. Sadly, reasoning won't change a mind warped by hunger. I had plenty of insight into why I behaved as I did. It didn't make the rituals that shored up my walls any less addictive. A starving girl is down, self-obsessed. She wants to feel ... to think ... to be ... less. To engage with such a bleak point of view is difficult for any parent: for fear of endorsing it, according it too great importance. My parents didn't read up on the subject. They're traditional Brits, wary of spilling emotions, so

wanted this to be a phase I was going through, i.e., not their fault. In many respects, their predicament was an eerie mirror of my own: so much emotional responsibility, so little power. And I wanted to hear they loved me, not criticisms, not advice.

Reaching such a mind is easier by invitation than instruction. A parent's goal should be to send a loving message: that you're ready to hear your child. The easiest way is through active listening. So when they're talking, try not to interrupt, contradict, pose questions. Encourage the flow by nodding, murmuring, repeating their words if they trail off. Always ask at the end of a paraphrase whether you've understood correctly. By all means show sympathy, share similar experiences, answer requests for advice. But beware seeming to compete, or to dismiss their feelings, or suggesting you know best because you've been there, bought the detox, and realized cellulite is not in fact a sin.

To signal yours is a friendly ear, create opportunities for conversation to bubble naturally. Go walking, cook, chop wood or play computer games together (if you can hear above the noise). Ideal conversation-fostering activities are relaxing, raise serotonin levels, and create feelings of equality. Don't eyeball them, it's too intimidating. Instead, range yourself alongside your child—physically, metaphorically—and battle your own desire: to rule a child who is no longer available to be ruled, yet still needs your love and support. Accept it isn't a parent's job to be a psychologist, but to shine a brighter light, suggest other paths, not impose them.

I escaped my eating disorder by a practical route: a better hobby (writing), and eventually a passion for making food good. Now I love it, it loves me back. Perhaps if I'd led a more energetic life, with wider interests, food wouldn't have become my enemy. I regret it became such an instrument of hurt. But at least I learned that seizing life's pleasures is less a privilege than a duty.

Reading Catherine's story, I couldn't help but think about how much value this woman had contributed to others through her work—and what the consequences might have been if she hadn't managed to break free from the tyranny of the eating disorder that stifled her creative expression as a young woman. The faces of other wonderful human beings flashed through my mind, as did the words written by Portia de Rossi in her bestselling book, *Unbearable Lightness: A Story of Loss and Gain.* "I should've had my sights set on successful businesswomen and successful female artists, authors, and politicians to emulate," she wrote. "I squandered my brain and my talent to squeeze into a size 2 dress while my male counterparts went to work on making money, making policy, making a difference." I had to laugh as I thought to myself, what if Gandhi or Dr.

Does this hat make me look too TALL?

Martin Luther King had suppressed their contribution to the world because they were insecure about their looks? What if instead of channeling his energy, courage, and determination into abolishing slavery, Abraham Lincoln had squandered it obsessing about his looks? Thankfully for our nation, President Lincoln's perception of his intrinsic value went beyond his physical appearance.

In a larger sense, we are now engaged in another civil war—one taking place within our own minds, eating away at the soul of America's girls, and eroding our values as a society. As Lincoln said, "It is rather for us to be here dedicated to the great task remaining before us." Let us dig up the seeds of deception that give rise to our misperceptions about ourselves and replant them on hallowed ground that honors the SOULSELF in us all. If we could see ourselves from this larger perspective, issues around body image would appear infinitesimally small.

The Deception of Perception

I leave you, hoping that the lamp of liberty will burn in your bosoms until there shall no longer be a doubt that all men are created free and equal.
—Abraham Lincoln

Body image is almost entirely subjective, meaning that it is based more on our own perception than it is on objective facts. It is less like a still pond that clearly mirrors our reflection and more like a tide constantly shifting in response to changing thoughts and feelings. In the words of diarist and author Anais Nin, "We don't see things as they are; we see things as we are." As the following diary entry makes painfully evident, when our perception of our bodies doesn't match our expectations of what "should be," a vicious cycle is set into motion: guilt, self-judgment, and an ever-deflating sense of self-esteem.

Susan, Age 19

Why does this girl I see in the mirror continue to work so hard on becoming a healthy woman if she is going to fully, completely, and genuinely hate her reflection? When will the day come that I see the brave, ambitious, hardworking woman that I am look back at me? When will the day come that I can surrender these infected thoughts, send them off to space and settle into the faith I have in myself? I pray for that day every single night …

I am so ridiculously angry with myself. Why can I not move on from this? Why can I not seem to think or care about anything else? How can I let this be the first thing I think about when I wake up and the last thing I think about before bed? The only thing I see is my stomach. I look in that awful mirror and see my big stomach and as I draw my eyes down, I see my gigantic thighs; they are grossly touching one another. I like nothing that I see. It isn't until I finish looking at all of my fatness that I look into my pathetic face. My eyes are sad. They are disappointed and they hate the girl staring back.

Beauty is about perception, not about make-up. I think the beginning of all beauty is knowing and liking oneself. You can't put on make-up, or dress yourself, or do your hair with any sort of fun or joy if you're doing it from a position of correction.
—Kevyn Aucoin, Celebrity Make-up Artist (Earned $10,000 per make-up session)

Notice the deception of perception in the mind of this diarist as she agonizes over her physical appearance. The lies of the FEARSELF convince us that being overweight is the same as being unworthy; that our braces should keep us from smiling, or that our pimples are an unacceptable blemish on our character no one should ever see. When the perception of our bodies is tainted by the FEARSELF, we operate from the underlying assumption that looks determine our value, our ability to succeed, and even our right to be happy.

The life and death of singer and actress Whitney Houston provides a sobering example of the deception of perception. Even after exceeding the highest external standards of beauty and talent, she was still haunted by the same underlying question the diarists in this chapter struggled to answer: *Am I good enough?* Unfortunately for Houston, her answer to this question was ultimately a resounding *No*. Standing at the podium at her funeral, Kevin Costner, her co-star in the 1992 movie *The Bodyguard,* which catapulted Houston to the pinnacle of fame, recounted how the actress had nearly sabotaged herself out of the starring role. At the end of his eulogy, Costner reminded his former friend and colleague one final time of a truth which she—along with millions of other women—had clearly lost sight of. "Yes, Whitney," he said. "You are good enough." When our perception is cleansed, the lies of the FEARSELF are exposed, and we come face to face with the truth: Not only are we "good enough"; we are *magnificent, whole,*

Do you see an old woman or a young woman?

and *inherently lovable*.

The diary entries of a 17-year-old girl named Kim, who had long held the dream of winning a beauty pageant, reveal the constant battle between the SOULSELF and the FEARSELF. Along with such other appearance-driven pursuits as modeling, dancing, acting and cheerleading, beauty pageants are iconic representations of our culture's obsession with achieving physical perfection and, as such, can easily become breeding grounds for comparison and self-criticism. On the pages of her diary, Kim fights the good fight, and in the end emerges with her authentic self and dignity intact.

You alone are enough.
You have nothing to
prove to anybody.
—Maya Angelou

Kim, Age 17

May 26. *Mom and I watched the movie* Shrek. *It was so cute, and the message was a good one—about beauty. Beauty is only skin deep, kind of ironic since it is right before the pageant. I'm getting more and more psyched for the pageant. I'll show everyone. It means a lot to me and I really believe I can win that crown.*

May 28. *To be honest, I don't know what scares me more; winning or losing the pageant. If I win, will I do a good job? Will I have what it takes for Nationals? And if I lose, will I have the time and money to try again? What will everyone think? I'm so scared. I have literally worked my butt off, and dreamed about this since fourth grade. I just want to have that moment of accomplishment on TV where everyone I have ever known realized how capable I am. I'm trying to prove not just to the world, but also to myself that I am not a joke. I wasn't good enough to make varsity. I can't even leap right after four years of dance. I'm single and have various rumors I'm a ditz. I got dumped at homecoming. My dad hates me. I know being Miss Teen USA can't make me happy, but it would help. I overcame all this shit to achieve the biggest dream I've ever had. I hate feeling so conceited and competitive; I just can't wait until it's over so I can enjoy the summer. That's the thing I really want (after the title, of course). I was stressed all day, but talking to Tim and clearing the air with him was Chicken Soup to my Soul!*

P.S. I just have to be the best me I can be. I just called Erica to ask her how to remove cellulite. Her answer involved Velcro and a vibrator!

June 6. *Had my bikini wax today—ouch! Well, it wasn't that bad; pain is beauty. After that, I headed to Perfect 10 for my manicure and pedicure. That was cool. Twenty-four hours until my quest for a dream. I am together, happy and have family support. That* *feels better than any crown. At the end of the day, the sash goes on the shelf and the makeup washes off, so you have to be happy with yourself regardless. I am happy with myself. Whatever happens, happens. I am going to do my best, be myself and have fun. I have NOTHING to lose, only some sparkle to gain, but right now, there's enough in my heart to last a lifetime.*

June 7. *I checked in for the pageant and, oh god, was I intimidated. These girls are beautiful. I went to dinner and rehearsals, and "Swimsuit with Style." Yes, I want to win, but I can honestly say that any of these girls is qualified to win. I'm ready for whatever.*

June 8. *Well, I didn't win the pageant. I wasn't even in the top twelve! But I was the only loser not crying. I had to try and comfort some of the other girls. I did my best and I was proud of my performance. The pageant, on the outside, was beautiful, but a lot of corrupt stuff took place. For one thing, one of the contestants was caught making out with a judge's son. That's the 411. I'm out.*

There is a great scene in the movie *Shrek*, when the animated star makes the observation, "Ogres are like onions," because "both have layers." Shrek was right—and not just about onions and ogres. Human beings also have layers, and as Kim notes in her diary entries, external beauty is only skin deep. It doesn't reveal or reflect what's happening within our minds, hearts and souls, where happiness and sadness are actually generated. In her May 28 entry we see the FEARSELF creeping into Kim's thoughts, pointing out evidence of her limitations and filling her with anxiety. We also see that in the process of expressing her feelings, Kim allows herself to become vulnerable, and acknowledges her fear regardless of the anticipated outcome—winning or losing. Paradoxically, acknowledging our fears represents a giant step towards releasing them. This is just one of journaling's magical powers.

Immediately prior to and following the pageant, Kim's perception is once again realigned with her SOULSELF. She knows what's important; she is happy, she is secure in the love of her family, and she is committed to doing her best and having fun—a demonstration of the SOULSELF in action. As a result, when the winner was announced and it wasn't her, Kim was at peace—and was also in a position to extend that peace to the girls around her who were in tears. That she managed this feat with such grace amidst the largely superficial world of beauty pageants confirms Kim is now aware of the true source of her beauty—her authentic, Natural Self.

The Power of AWARENESS

When we regard our physical appearance with the awareness that we are more than just our bodies, the lens through which we perceive ourselves is cleansed. This awareness changes the way we talk to ourselves in the privacy of our own minds, which then opens up the possibility for outer change. I offer here my definition of AWARENESS, once again in the form of an acronym to make it easier to remember the richness of the word:

AWARENESS ...   AWAKE WITH ALL REALITY EXPOSED NATURALLY EXPRESSING THE SOULSELF

To be aware means to be AWAKE—another key word in our quest to become whole—thus deserving its own description:

AWAKE ...   ALIVE WITH ALL KNOWLEDGE EVIDENT

To be AWAKE is not the opposite of being asleep, but a state of being awakened in consciousness. The knowledge referred to in this definition does not come from books. It comes only when one resonates with the heart of the soul, the core of BEING. AWARENESS is the primary channel that tunes us into the root of the SOULSELF. It is through the power of AWARENESS that we are able to recognize the FEARSELF in all its various forms through the dramas and stories in which it shows up—as it is exposed in this chapter topic and all the rest to follow. AWARENESS also awakens us to the knowledge that change is possible and solutions exist that we may not have previously considered. Stephanie—whose earlier diary entries revealed in heart-wrenching detail her long-standing issues with body image and disordered eating—describes the changes that led to her recovery. As you read her reflection below, notice the role AWARENESS played in helping her redirect deeply ingrained patterns and release destructive habits.

> #### Stephanie's Reflection, 6 years later
> *I view my eating disorder much same way an alcoholic views their addiction to alcohol. I am always in recovery, and although I've coiled the problem like a snake, I understand that it can bite back at any time. When I feel anxiety or experience a major problem, my ego tells me that I am scared/sad/mad because I'm fat. I still struggle with negative thoughts, but rarely fall into dangerous behaviors. If I notice that I'm working out excessively or counting calories, or if my thoughts are lingering too much on my body, I immediately fall to my knees in prayer—then, I gently ask myself what is behind these thoughts, so I can get to the soul level. One of the first things*

I did was to stop reading fitness magazines and to start reading all of Marianne Williamson's books. A Return to Love *and* A Woman's Worth, *both by Marianne, changed my life. My favorite line is from* A Return to Love, *because it helped me realize the power of letting go. It goes like this:*

> *You spend your whole life resisting the notion that there's someone out there smarter than you are, and then all of a sudden you're so relieved to know it's true. All of a sudden, you're not too proud to ask for help.*

> *If I find myself thinking about what I ate throughout the day, or what I plan to eat the next day, I sometimes repeat a mantra to interrupt that process. When I was in the grips of the eating disorder, my thoughts and feelings would automatically trigger destructive behaviors. Over time I have developed an awareness that stops me from immediately reacting, and I now turn my attention inward to recognize what I am actually feeling and to understand why I am feeling that way. I defeated this "bitch"—as I referred to it in my diary—through journaling, therapy, yoga, mindfulness, and prayer. It really comes down to awareness; moment-to-moment awareness.*

KNOWING THE ESSENCE OF YOU

There is tremendous power in cultivating the kind of moment-to-moment awareness Stephanie speaks of in her reflection. It begins with the realization that in the very midst of making an unconscious CHOICE—whether to tell ourselves we are ugly when looking in a mirror, to binge on another donut, or to deprive ourselves of food altogether—the SOULSELF is calling us to make a higher CHOICE. The briefest pause is often all it takes to recognize we have other options. The power to effect change lives in the space between our thoughts; this is the gateway to the soul.

Creating Key Moments

Each one of us has the ability to transform any FEAR-SELF-driven experience into a KEY moment of deliberate change. Key moments are created by going within—if even for a split second—to unlock the grip of unhealthy habits and break destructive patterns from the past. Here, we recognize the power of CHOICE that is always accessible. By pausing to become mindful of the fact that we alone determine the direction in which we will proceed, we turn an ordinary moment into a KEY moment. Will we choose to thicken the fog and turbulence of the FEARSELF, or will we choose the path of the SOULSELF instead and break one more link in the chain that binds us to the ego's magic tricks of sabotage? When we become alive to the present moment, every aspect of our BEING—including our bodies—are *soular* powered, as we are renewed by the pulse of the Universe.

Our bodies are a place where we harbor emotional pain. By learning to focus our minds with attention and intention, we can release the deep-seated wounds that cause us to suffer. The following exercise is a daily practice to strengthen your ability to create KEY moments. It engages the Imagination aspect of your BEING. Starting with just five minutes a day may seem like a small and insignificant step, but in reality it represents a giant leap toward returning to the peace of the SOULSELF.

The next time you are experiencing an internal conflict, or feel the first grips of the FEARSELF beginning to take hold, pause for a moment and place your awareness on your breath. As you consider the CHOICES available to you in this situation, imagine in your mind's eye that there are two doors in front of you. The first door represents the unconscious habits of the FEARSELF; even as you look at this door you know exactly where it leads. The second door leads to the path of the SOULSELF, and it opens to a healthier CHOICE—one that leads to greater self-esteem, freedom, and authentic expression. Both doors are before you, both are locked, and you have just one KEY. As you contemplate your options, think about how many other girls and women are standing right now at a similar crossroads. What advice would you offer your sister, your best friend or your own daughter? Allow yourself to draw strength from these women, and know too that they will draw strength from the CHOICE you make.

Imagine placing your KEY into the lock and opening the door that illuminates your return to the SOULSELF. Take in the view and see where it leads. Notice how the destination feels ... Empowering? Exhilarating? Peaceful? And as you visualize yourself stepping through this door, know that by making this CHOICE, right here and right now, you are bringing yourself one step closer to the SOURCE OF UNIVERSAL LIFE—your SOUL—and you are also paving the way for others to follow suit.

All of the diarists in this chapter used journaling to create a KEY moment, to awaken to a new perspective, and to become more aware. Regardless of

SOURCE
OF
UNIVERSAL
LIFE
SERVING TO
EXTEND
LOVE
FOREVER

IMAGINATION

what their intentions were at the time of writing—whether to gain clarity on a particular issue or simply to vent their feelings on the page—AWARENESS emerged as a natural byproduct. The more AWARENESS we develop within ourselves and the more conscious we become of the CHOICES we make that affect the Body aspect of our BEING, the better we are able to support other women and teens who are struggling with similar issues. To be truly of service to them, we must be sure that our own inner teen isn't also trapped in the limitations of the FEARSELF.

If on the other hand we address only the symptoms and warning signs of poor body image and try to patch each one up superficially, we may well miss the deeper reality. The solution lies in our *willingness* to practice a new way of BEING. Because our bodies absorb the emotional wounds of our psyche, to effect change on a cellular level, we have to implement change at a *soulular* level. And if and when we realize we've made a CHOICE that has led us off course, our job in that moment is not to beat ourselves up with guilt and "should have's," but to gently let go, find empathy, forgive and recommit to the direction we know brings lasting peace. We are responsible for the way we talk to ourselves.

To the women and teens whose distorted body image generates an ongoing negative inner dialog, Joanna Poppink offered the following inspiration:

> *Stop immersing yourself in media bodies (in magazines, television, movies, etc.) and look at real people. On the sidewalks, in lines, in stores, on buses, in parks, look at people who do not measure up to your physical standards and who are walking with others who seem to love them. Look at women of substantial size who are holding hands with what appears to be a loved one or walking with an entire family, laughing, smiling, enjoying each other. Ask yourself, how is this possible? The answer could very well be that the negative critical stories you tell yourself about you are simply cruel and incorrect. You may have a better chance at happiness than you think if you start being more kind and generous with yourself.*

Whether we like it or not, the message we must seek to instill in our daughters, our sisters, our mothers and ourselves is in direct opposition to the message generated by the world of advertising and propagated throughout the media. Our culture has no authority to twist our bodies or our psyches to conform to a predetermined standard of beauty, nor does

AWAKE
WITH
ALL
REALITY
EXPOSED
NATURALLY
EXPRESSING THE
SOUL-
SELF

it have the right to infuse the notion into our minds and souls that our value is only skin deep. Every woman and every girl, by virtue of the fact we are here and alive and uniquely ourselves, is valuable beyond measure. As females, we represent 51 percent of the population. We have CHOICES and we have voices. Together we have the power to make an impact on the cultural landscape of our society.

Choices and Voices

Here is a list of things you can do *right now* to stop the madness of allowing body identification to represent true identification:

1. When TV and movie producers, advertisers, manufacturers and clothing companies seek to sexualize women and girls, use your voice to let our collective thoughts be heard and use the power of the Internet to create online petitions that promote social change.

2. Recognize the amount of time that our 8- to 18-year-old girls are already engaged with the media and refuse to add more fuel to the fire by buying fashion magazines.

3. Post a petition on change-making websites such as www.change.org demanding that our country impose the same laws already in place in much of Europe—laws which disallow critically underweight models to drape the pages of girls' fashion magazines. Write to the magazines' editors and demand that airbrushed photos be labeled as such. Join the conversation on www.mydiaryunlocked.com and use your own social media hubs to become a source of "soulcial" media to rally women to stand up and take action against those who continue to perpetuate misperceptions about females.

4. Seek out and join other groups who are raising awareness. One is The Representation Project, a movement that uses film and media content to expose injustices created by gender stereotypes and to shift the collective consciousness towards change. Search online for others.

5. Support companies with ethics and values that encourage the truth. The Dove Campaign for Real Beauty is a model of what it means to advocate for social change through its self-esteem programs. Visit www.mydiaryunlocked.com to learn about additional action steps

intended to disavow the forces of greed that seek to keep our SOUL-SELF in bondage.

Once we—as fierce, compassionate and conscious adult women and teens are AWAKE—we must claim our strength in numbers and seize the purchasing power we already possess to drive the force of change with our money and our mouths. Let's not stop at the notion of voting with our dollars. Let's teach the daughters of our society that while money may be one resource to effect change, tapping into the unlimited source of the human spirit and joining hands together with passion holds the only real power. Popular culture and mass media are a Goliath in fostering unhealthy body image attitudes. But just like Goliath, this culture has its weakness, for it is dependent on keeping us brainwashed and superficial. By seizing its weaknesses, we can claim our power as mamma bears no longer willing to see generations of daughters suffer. No longer will we continue the saga our own inner teens have replayed for years, jumping from one diet to the next, while our hearts have silently borne the weight of warped beliefs about our worthiness. This power does not start by fixing anybody else; it starts by first practicing these principles within our own hearts.

Together, we have the power to transform these values to ensure a safe world for ourselves and our daughters to be authentic—infused with health, happiness and joy.

The most common way people give up their power is by thinking they don't have any.
—Alice Walker

Living Life Unlocked

The Power of Self-Talk: Change "Am I Good Enough?" to "I AM Good Enough!"

Nature abhors a vacuum, which is why the decision to stop thinking negatively about ourselves must always be followed by a commitment to start thinking positively. There are many approaches to positive thinking, but the easiest I've found is to construct and apply affirmations in the following way: Start with I AM; not I will or I won't. The words I AM bring your desire to the present tense and position your mind to view that which you are affirming from the position of having already created it instead of gazing upon it on a distant horizon. This intensifies the power of the forces you set into motion the moment you commit to something you want. To AFFIRM is to:

AFFIRM ...   ACKNOWLEDGE FROM A FOUNDATION OF INTENTION REALIZED AND MANIFESTED

As Goethe revealed in his poem *On Commitment,* "Once you are committed ... a whole stream of events issues from the decision, raising in one's favor all manner of unforeseen incidents and meetings and material assistance, which no [woman] could have dreamed would have come [her] way." Example: "I am good to my body and my body is good to me."

Make sure your affirmation is inspired from your SOULSELF; that is, that it serves to create something to support inner resilience in one or more of the five aspects of your essential BEING. In their book, *The Healing Code*, Alexander Loyd and Ben Johnson explained that external possessions in and of themselves will never fulfill our desires at the level of the soul, and as such, the satisfaction we derive from them is short-term. When affirmations are used as a wishing well for material goods, the emptiness that inevitably occurs when spirit is absent from our goals will bring us back time and time again to the wishing well. If your desire involves something materialistic, look within to discover what quality or emotion would be present in your life as a result of possessing it, and focus instead on this essence. Keep the affirmations simple. It's as simple as that.

Practice each affirmation for at least 30 days—the amount of time it takes to change a habit. With each passing day, exercising all of your senses, step into BEING at one with your soul's desire so that by the end of the 30 days, your comfort zone will have expanded to embrace this positive attribute as a part of your Natural Self.

NATURAL
SELF

Chapter 3

The Mirror of Romantic Relationships

*When it comes to men who are romantically interested in you,
it's really simple. Just ignore everything they say
and only pay attention to what they do.*
—Message conveyed by Professor Randy Pausch to his
18-month-old daughter in The Last Lecture he delivered at Carnegie
Mellon University, just months before his death from pancreatic cancer.

Sarah, Age 16
*Now I'm going out with my best guy friend who has suddenly taken
an extreme interest in me, who I would rate the best looking guy
in the entire school. And I'm depressed because: I am now a victim
of the problems of relationships. I can't stop obsessing over whether
I'm good enough for him and feeling jealous of anyone who thinks
he is hot. I am paranoid of losing him.*

Crystal, Age 17
*I stayed in bed all morning because I was dizzy and tired. I felt like
throwing up. Can you really get pregnant the first time?*

Lynette, Age 14
*Danny told me he'd buy Camp Fire Nuts if I would be his girl-
friend. I said I would be his girlfriend until after he bought the
nuts. HA HA!*

Nancy, Age 16
*Not a day goes by when I don't think about you. My next step, at
least, is to stop saying your name. I don't know how to wipe my
slate clean. Not like you, anyway.*

Gina, Age 16
*So many people like the same guys it's not even funny. Plus, now
Katie likes Mike, and Donna does not like Bruce anymore, so she
says. Jody has started drinking again. Ken's parents are out of town.*

Party time. OH, we got one of those new video recorders [1980] so now I can record General Hospital. I won't have to miss a single soap opera!

Jessica, Age 18
The first time I meet a guy, or talk to him, or go out with him, or develop a crush on him, or kiss him, I immediately think of forever.

Janet, Age 17
I read the book "Jaws" today about sharks eating people. It's pretty hard for me to forget John. I keep telling myself not to even think about him anymore, but everything reminds me of him and how much fun we used to have. My thoughts are like sharks teeth, eating me alive. Before he left for college he told me not to be sad, just look back at the good times and be happy for them. I wish more than anything I could do that, but then I think of the future and it seems almost impossible that I can have that much fun again because no one will probably ask me out again. NEVER AGAIN.

New beginnings are often disguised as painful endings.
—Lao Tzu

If life is a series of lessons that guide us to blossom more fully into the truth of our BEING, then romantic relationships present some of the most challenging courses in its curriculum.

How well we are able to remain connected to our truth as we become intimately connected with another determines to a large extent how easy or difficult our personal relationships will be. No matter how winding or bumpy the road, relationships inevitably provide the opportunity to lead us back to the center of our own SOULSELF—where we remember both our truth and our destiny. The journey is not always an easy one.

Romantic relationships are mirrors that reflect with startling clarity the level of self-esteem and self-respect or self-doubt and self-loathing we carry in our hearts. Just as a magnifying glass placed between the sun and a scrap of paper on the ground sparks a flame, intimate relationships ignite the beliefs wc form about ourselves in our teen years and often carry into adulthood as unresolved teen fears. Through the bonds we create with others, our inner feelings are acted out as scripts on the stage we call life. Vested with the allure of romance, the dramas we enact in our intimate relationships can become so intense, they feel like they sear a hole in our heart, leaving us scorned and wary of being hurt again. So painful can these experiences be that at times we feel as parched as that scrap of paper—the heat-reducing us to a pile of ashes.

At 33 or 63, many still hold onto the pain of the 13-year-old still living inside. Yet as we learn to believe in ourselves, develop clear personal boundaries and come to know we are deeply worthy of love and respect, romantic love can be a blissful experience that multiplies the love and joy shared between two people. And even when loving another leads to loss, a foundation of self-love supports us in transforming the pain—like a phoenix rising from the ashes—into a new level of understanding and wisdom. Navigating intimate relationships inevitably involves challenges, but with AWARENESS and skill, we can embrace them as opportunities to become more authentically ourselves.

Anne Frank

January 22, 1944. *... The whole time I've been here I've longed unconsciously—and at times consciously—for trust, love and physical affection. This longing may change in intensity, but it's always there.*

In this chapter, we climb inside the hearts and minds of teens whose experiences with romantic love range from agony to ecstasy. Through their words, we may recognize our own longing for romantic love. And we may confront our own insecurities in relationships, lingering like a ghost of self-doubt, despair, a silent treaty of "settling" or even abuse that is cleverly disguised. In the presence of real stories told by our daughters and ourselves, we learn to embrace the power with which we are endowed by nature. We are made stronger and more compassionate by the pain we have endured. We gain the tenacity to hold our heads up high, put our collective foot down against needless injuries to the self-esteem of our daughters and ourselves and stand up for the personal empowerment of everyone, especially those who will bear tomorrow's children.

The diarists whose stories you'll read here explore the emotional peaks and valleys we encounter at every level of our BEING—our BODY, EMOTIONS, IMAGINATION, NATURAL SELF, and GENIUS MIND. On the subject of intimate relationships, however, none of these aspects is more relevant than the "E" that represents Emotions. From these diarists' reflections, we observe how the CHOICES we make—whether consciously calculated or in a moment of passion—may impose a life-altering change in direction that leaves a permanent imprint on the emotional health of the girls making them. Through their stories, we can better appreciate the toll that our

BODY
EMOTIONS
IMAGINATION
NATURAL SELF
GENIUS MIND

EMOTIONS

alliance with the FEARSELF—and its trademark limiting beliefs—takes on our well-BEING.

If the entries shared throughout this chapter appear to be skewed to sensationalize the dramatic, I assure you this is not the case. They are excerpts from typical teenage diaries, submitted in most part by grown women whose preserved written personal history demonstrates just how big a blow the feeling of rejection or unrequited love can deliver to our self-esteem. In addition to underscoring the pain of teenage heartache, the women whose stories are told herein also inspire hope, for today they are leading successful professional lives as PhD anthropologists, psychologists, engineers, managers and executive officers at companies like Facebook, Google and Starbucks—to name a few.

Limiting beliefs: Beliefs that either consciously or subconsciously block you from living authentically and reaching your full potential.

Rejection

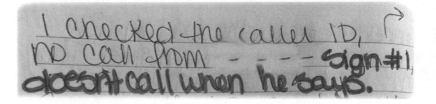

I checked the caller ID, no call from _ _ _ _ _ Sign #1, doesn't call when he says.

Sarah, Age 16
March 4. *Confession: I've never had a boyfriend. Adults always say things like, "You don't need a boyfriend at this age," but that is absolutely false. One glance at the lunch situation at school flooded with couples holding hands makes me jump at creating fake boyfriends to talk about. I mean, I get "Have you ever had a boyfriend?" quite a bit.*
October 11. *Now I am boy crazy and having fun with it. I've had this huge crush on this guy for like, five months. I would have seriously done anything in the known universe to have him be mine, and even when something really small happened, like he looked at me, it would make my whole day amazing. Then he started hanging out with this girl that I thought was a decent person until two "holdings" took place: they were holding hands, and I was holding back tears. I was miserable for weeks and swore that my life had no meaning since he was the only guy for me.*

When you acquire enough inner peace and feel really positive about yourself, it's almost impossible for you to be controlled and manipulated by anyone else.
—Wayne Dyer

Gail, Age 17

I know Pete is off limits. He's hot, popular; he's got a job. If I make drill team again, I might have a chance with him. I shouldn't even be worried about this, but I watch all the sappy movies and TV shows, I just want to be popular and fall in love. Jan just called and said that Pete was hooking up with beautiful Kerry. God forbid I can be happy. This always happens to me—I'll never find anyone.

Leslie, Age 17

January 19. I called Tim when I got home from choir practice tonight. "Of course, there's nothing wrong with you, I just don't see you as being the one for me," he said. Great. Exactly what I wanted to hear. Of course, I have to make it seem like it's no big deal. That can't help my self-esteem at all. I just want to be happy. Things should be so right for me, but I feel like everything is so wrong, and I'm slipping out of control. I just don't understand ...! I put on our song and cried.

January 25. Tears stream softly down my face. What have I done to deserve this? How can you be so cold? I thought you realized what you wanted. You give me so much emotionally and mentally that it leaves me in a state of bliss after I talk to you. You promised me it would never end! I thought that you were incapable of bringing me this much pain and loneliness. You're one of my absolute best friends, do you not understand that? Do you realize what I'm going through?

Haley, Age 15

September 28. I am so bummed I don't even know what to do! I love Joey so much it's not even funny! Today I went to the beach and I go up on the deck and Jessica, Debra, and Jill all were coming up the stairs at the same time and Jason said, "Joey, here comes your three girlfriends!" If he went for any of the other girls that like him I would be so fucking bummed! I will have to see if he changes seats in math class and lunch. I don't know what I would do. I'll write later. Love Haley

October 2. Today in math, Katie wrote something on Joey's shoe and he asked me to read it to him. It said, "Joey is a cutie—from all the ninth grade girls." Also, there is a picture of me that was taken at the beach and Katie asked him, "don't you think this is a good picture of Haley?" And he said yes!!!!! I was so stoked, but embarrassed. Please like me, oh please, oh please.

If someone is not treating you with love and respect, it is a gift if they walk away.
—don Miguel Ruiz

When people show you who they are, believe them the first time.
—Maya Angelou

It is not insult from another that causes you pain. It is the part of your mind that agrees with the insult. Agree only with the truth about you, and you are free.
—Alan Cohen

November 3. *Sorry I haven't written in a long time, dear diary. So much as happened. Joey and Jessica are going out and my heart is broken! I am happy for her but every time I see him my heart sinks. It hurts and makes me feel sad but I will get over it sometime. I liked Joey for nine months and I knew way down that I never had a chance. At the beach tonight, he said that I laughed like a hamster. Weird! This is how all love turns out. I like someone for too long, but he never likes me back. It bruises my heart for life and it makes me so sad! Why won't my wishes come true? I can't believe it's been one year of agony. Oh well, there will be other loves but none will be the same as his.*

If we consider these entries in the context of the Freeing Your BEING Compass, we can see how easy it is to allow our experiences in relationships to reinforce the anxieties, regrets and insecurities that make up the false beliefs of the FEARSELF. Sarah's loneliness causes her to filter the world to see nothing but couples, compelling her to make up a fake boyfriend to fit in. Then, in a strategy all too frequently retained by teen girls, she virtually admits she would forsake her own truth to have some guy be "hers." Likely because she has been conditioned to believe others have the power to make her feel inferior, Sarah doesn't realize her feelings of inferiority are generated within herself, and that by identifying, examining and changing her beliefs, she can change her experience.

In Gail's entry, we see a girl who doesn't feel good enough to attract the guy she wants unless she achieves a certain level of social status deeming her worthy. She probably isn't aware that 90 percent of the sappy movies and TV shows she admits to watching are written by men who were likely socialized to value women on superficial levels.

Haley's *all* and *never* thoughts reveal another unhealthy trait—that of *catastrophizing*, or taking a specific incident and generalizing it as if it were true for every situation, assuming it's far worse than it actually is, and has only a negative outcome. Teens are masters at this, but adults do it too. Words like *everyone, no one, always and never* offer clues we are immersed in this thought pattern. One of my own diary entries, written on the heels of a breakup, reads, "No one will *ever* ask me out again. NEVER AGAIN!!"… a poignant example of the *self* in FEARSELF, SEEKING THE EXPERIENCE OF LIMITATIONS FOREVER.

At some point in our formative years, most of us had experiences that caused us to question whether we are truly worthy of love. Sometimes, we

In 2011, only 11 percent of protagonists in movies are female. They are usually "body props," sex objects.
—The Representation Project

go on to attract partners who treat us with this same lack of dignity and respect. Thus, as others confirm our own false interpretations, a downward spiral of diminishing self-esteem is set into motion, which further multiplies our relationship challenges. Whatever limiting beliefs we formed, *at any age,* it is our responsibility to recognize, reject and dispel the smoke and mirrors from which they originally arose. Only when romantic or sexual love serves as an extension of the beauty found in our own souls, not a clouded perception that we are unworthy of love, can a relationship that involves sexual activity contribute to healthy self-esteem.

By the time I was in my mid-teens and ready to start dating, my father had been sober for five years. He went through rehab in the 1960s, before family dynamics were considered an integral part of the addict's healing process. Thanks in large part to the work of authors like John Bradshaw, Melody Beattie, Claudia Black and others, we now know that in any sort of unhealthy family structure, everyone in the family generally assumes a role that reinforces this unhealthy structure—a coping mechanism that helps us survive the situation psychologically, emotionally or spiritually.

When a piece of the puzzle changes, it changes the whole puzzle.
—*John Bradshaw*

I remember once seeing a *Far Side* cartoon picturing an *empty* auditorium behind a banner that read, "Welcome Children of Functional Families." The cartoon is funny, of course, because so few of us were raised in truly functional families. While there may not have been "tangible" problems such as physical abuse or alcoholism, shaming experiences come in many forms. It is often subtle, growing progressively worse as family dynamics deteriorate. Unless and until different CHOICES are made, our children and grandchildren perpetuate this dysfunction. The emotional aftermath of being raised in a troubled home can involve feeling shame, resentment, rationalization, hurt, anger and more; all of which create deep barriers to seeing ourselves and others as lovable, capable and worthy. I was no exception. Due in part to the negative messages internalized in my formative years, I entered my first romantic relationship emotionally empty and yearning for the love and approval I felt I had not received from my parents.

The only normal people are the ones you don't know very well.
—*Alfred Adler*

After we had been dating for a couple of months, I remember walking in the halls of my high school, when my boyfriend hollered "Hey beautiful!" from the rafters above. Dressed in typical North Dakota school apparel at the time—a flannel shirt and Wrangler blue jeans—and wearing half a smile and a red face, I glanced up, both flattered and mortified he had shouted it out for the entire world to hear. Reflexively, I shouted back. "I'm not beautiful!"—which of course only intensified my embarrassment. Though I was thrilled with the attention, deep down inside, my beliefs kept me from receiving the compliment, so I deflected it instead. Within a few months, my boyfriend learned of another girl who had a crush on him, and started spending time with her while continuing his relationship with me. My friends tried to tell me what was going on, but I tuned them out and instead tuned in to denial, sometimes even making excuses for him instead of acknowledging his behavior was inexcusable.

My heart broke open a little more as spring turned to summer, and those hot, humid nights were spent alone with the sound of the crickets that seemed to be screaming to awaken the part of me deep inside that knew he was with her. One day, he was supposed to call to set a time for us to go out that night. I had missed out on a day at the river swimming with my friends for nothing, as this was in the era before smart phones— okay, truth be told, it was before answering machines! While my friends were out roasting hot dogs, water-skiing and blasting the car radio with the doors wide open, I was sitting next to the phone, waiting. He didn't call … and didn't call. I washed my hair, turning the water off every three seconds to listen for the phone, and then dried my hair, turning the dryer off every three seconds to listen some more. I'm sure the gap of silence I held at each interval extended far beyond the actual length of time between rings on a telephone—a silence shouting out the desperation in my heart.

Finally, I decided to force myself to go out with my friends that evening. At 7 o'clock, I called home to ask my sister if my boyfriend had called. When she said "No," a pang in my chest caused me to drop the phone, its spiral cord dangling on the kitchen floor at my friend's house, my heart feeling as though it was dangling right next to it. I was having an anxiety attack, although I hadn't yet learned the term. It was the same feeling I'd felt since age four when my parents would fight after a night when my dad had been drinking heavily and I felt scared, hopeless, helpless, worthless and abandoned.

These emotions, I later learned, embedded themselves within my body, eventually hardening into beliefs that skewed my perception of others and myself. Just as quickly as my existence had been validated by my boyfriend's attention, it was now invalidated by his withdrawal of it. I mistakenly believed my worth was determined outside of me. My heartbreak was so intense that I tried my best not to feel it. Finally, one night I came home and mustered up the courage to admit a piece of truth to my dear, secret diary about what was really happening. I sat down and wrote this poem:

Probably

You said you'd probably call me tonight
And I knew once you did, I'd feel all right.
But I didn't think you'd forget so fast
While I hoped and prayed for a love that would last.
I waited and wondered and really felt blue
But I didn't dare leave—in case you'd come through.
Yeah, you've done this to me before
But I couldn't help dream that you'd knock at my door.
I guess "probably" has two different meanings.
I think it's "yes" and stay home in the evenings.
You think it's "no" and you're off the hook
And go out with your friends and your little black book.

Many years later, a friend introduced me to the following song, written by singer and songwriter Alanis Morissette, which so perfectly captures the roller coaster of romantic love and shows us how easy it can turn rejection from others into an excuse to reject ourselves.

So Unsexy (by Alanis Morissette)

Oh these little rejections how they add up quickly
One small sideways look and I feel so ungood
Somewhere along the way I think I gave you the power to make
Me feel the way I thought only my father could
Oh these little rejections how they seem so real to me
One forgotten birthday I'm all but cooked
How these little abandonments seem to sting so easily
I'm 13 again am I 13 for good?
I can feel so unsexy for someone so beautiful
So unloved for someone so fine
I can feel so boring for someone so interesting
So ignorant for someone of sound mind
Oh these little protections how they fail to serve me
One forgotten phone call and I'm deflated
Oh these little defenses how they fail to comfort me

More than 20 percent of teens have sex before age 14.
—The Representation Project

Your hand pulling away and I'm devastated
When will you stop leaving baby?
When will I stop deserting baby?
When will I start staying with myself?
Oh these little projections how they keep springing from me
I jump my ship as I take it personally
Oh these little rejections how they disappear quickly
The moment I decide not to abandon me.

I see my body as an instrument, rather than an ornament.
—Alanis Morissette

In the last two lines of the song, Alanis points us towards a powerful truth: The act of abandoning *ourselves* lies at the root of the pain we experience in relationships. For me personally, coming to the eventual decision that I would settle for nothing short of true love and healthy relationships gave me the strength to stop my self-abandonment and start standing up for myself. To bolster my resolve, I shared my insecurities with supportive friends. I began reading encouraging books such as *The 5 Love Languages* by Gary Chapman and *Hold Me Tight* by Sue Johnson, the co-creator of Emotional Focused Therapy. In my diary, I rewrote my desires as declarations. I meditated daily with the intention of becoming reacquainted with the real me. The KEY for me was changing my perception of what I believed I deserved in relationships and to then courageously practice communicating my truth on a daily basis. In other words, I became willing to risk the "comfort" of the status quo for the possibility of creating a more loving future. Thanks to the process of Emotional Focused Therapy, I was able to recognize my tendency to reach for emotional connection in ways that often masked underlying complaints or criticisms. With AWARENESS and conscious effort, I adjusted my communication to come instead from a place of love and a desire for a deeper understanding of my partner's needs. And I asked for nothing less in return. What I learned is that the moment I become willing to climb into the driver's seat and make a U-turn—a YOU-turn—in the direction of my true worthiness, emotional pain stemming from fear of rejection is dispelled in the same way darkness vanishes when a single candle is lit. I also learned that in relationships, there would always be opportunities (disguised as challenges) to get it right again and again. Maintaining harmony in committed relationships is a lifelong practice. Growth is measured not by a total elimination of discord, but in the process of reducing the time it takes to move out of a state of upset and back to a place of peace in a relationship.

Of course, keeping the flame that illuminates our worthiness aglow is a lot more difficult when we are both emotionally and sexually intimate with another, for these relationships stir not only our deepest hopes and desires, but also our deepest insecurities.

Misty, Age 19

It's the way the light catches
your eyes, sometimes.
The way I see your smile
that I rarely get to see.
So bashful to catch your stare
in a conversation,
you're so unaware that sometimes
I have no idea what you're saying.
So caught up in that trance
when you speak.
Yet so uneasy you'll catch on,
therefore I fidget with
whatever is around.
The way I felt your body
next to mine.
Although I wasn't touching you,
I was wanting to.
And that once in awhile
my heart drops
when you say my name.
The way you say my name.
I crave that.

As humans, we are both social beings and sexual beings. Sexual intimacy among individuals can be a natural extension of love, a means of communication, expression, and of course, reproduction. The fact that we are one of only a handful of species that experience sexual desire whether or not we as females are ovulating—known in the animal world as being "in heat"—provides one more indication that sex is as much a function of emotion as it is biology.

For some parents, a perfect world is one in which their precious daughter would have no sexual desire until her wedding day. At around age 25 or 30 she would marry a handsome prince who treats her like the princess she is and live happily ever after. Enter reality. In the early teen years, as our daughters' bodies begin to make the transformation from child to adult, hormonal changes activate sexual interest. Physically, their bodies are now mature to the point they are capable of bearing children. Emotional maturity, on the other hand, often lags far behind physical development and sexual desire. Scientific research has proven the teen brain is not fully developed in the areas of impulse control or using caution in making decisions.

To these considerations, add the influence of living in a culture entrenched in a "sex sells" mentality—in effect teaching our girls that sex equals love, happiness, power, popularity and attention. It teaches our boys that material possessions will get them laid—just as it assumes that is all they want. Understanding this equation, it becomes easy to see how romantic relationships can become a battleground for drama and dysfunction, devoid of real intimacy. It is relatively easy to get naked physically, but the emotional nakedness that accompanies the physical act has a much deeper and more lasting impact. When alcohol or drugs are involved, boundaries break down, inhibitions fall away, and the odds of becoming sexually active skyrocket. These same factors also play a role in sexual assault, which ranges from date stalking to actual rape.

Sex as "Power"

About 50 percent of rape victims are under 18 years of age when they are victimized.
—www.911rape.org

Nineteen-year-old Vicki had been dating her boyfriend Jim for only a couple of months when she captured in her journal the behavior that revealed a foreboding and volatile side of his character she had never before recognized.

> ### Vicki, Age 19
> **September 26.** *Hmmm … major breaks in Saga de Vicki. I met a new guy (another blond, pre-med) named Jim. He's fun and he took me to Homecoming. We weren't there long, but we were there long enough for Mark to see how good I looked. Everyone thought my boy was a hottie. Well, Jim and I are in that developmental phase. We'll see what happens. The other night we lied on the couch and did some stuff, mostly just cuddled and oh God is he fun.*
> **November 18.** *I haven't spoken to Jim in a week. I hope things are still cool between us, I like him a ton! I would be devastated if I lost him. I don't get this hot and cold thing.*

November 25. First of all, Jim and I couldn't be better. Turns out, he wasn't avoiding me, he was just busy.
December 12. I walked in on Jim cheating on me. For some ridiculous reason I forgave him.

Just before the New Year, Vicki was date raped by Jim. Although at the time she didn't write in her diary about the rape, she shares the following reflection about what happened that night:

Vicki's Reflection:

Up until the assault occurred, I believed that Jim was the most ideal and perfect man that ever existed; and even though he had ignored me, upset me, and even cheated on me, I never thought he was capable of physically hurting me. The night of the attack, he picked me up at my sorority house and took me back to his fraternity house to watch a movie. I think the first moment I realized something was wrong with him was on the drive. His fraternity house was on a one-way street, and he drove to it the opposite way. I kind of thought he may have been drinking, but it was pretty late so I really didn't pay too much attention to it. The next clue was that he went to the back of the house to park, which he never did before. Everyone on campus knew we were dating, so it wasn't like he was hiding me. When we walked into the house, this wave of emotion came over me. I just felt something wasn't right. I dismissed the feeling and told myself that I was just a little sick to my stomach or something. We walked into his room and sat on his bed to watch a movie, and when he locked the door, I became so uncomfortable that I told him I wanted to leave. I got up and he basically threw me back on the bed. I started crying and he didn't pay any attention to it. I tried to look into his eyes, but there was no connection any more, it was almost as if something had completely taken him over and he was a completely different person. I kept trying to fight back, but I finally gave up and shut down emotionally. I was paralyzed really, and numb. I just laid there in shock, trying to contemplate what was going on. And I basically laid there for hours—until the morning. I had no idea what to do. He drove me home in the morning, but we didn't speak at all. When he dropped me off, I knew that was the last time I would see him.

I filed a report, and my case went through the court system. While Jim was indicted on felony charges, the police department lost my rape kit and my case was never prosecuted. Because I never got that final closure from the ordeal, I carried blame around for years; blame for what had happened to me, and blame for impacting his future. I knew that the second I said something to the police, Jim's future—particularly his dream of studying medicine—would be over. In retrospect, this prevented him from being around patients who could have been vulnerable. Throughout all these years, I've always said that logically I understood that I didn't do anything wrong that night. But there has always been a disconnect between my head and my heart and I continued to search for answers as I wondered what I could have done differently. I am happy to report that I am now at peace, and I know that I did the right thing by reporting it. I protected other possible victims and not the one who committed the crime.

Nearly 1 in 5 American women experience rape at some time in their lives. Each year in the U.S., 32,000 rape victims become pregnant by their rapist.
—Based on statistics in American Journal of Obstetrics and Gynecology

According to Gavin de Becker, author of *The Gift of Fear: Survival Signals That Protect Us from Violence*, teenage girls are the most victimized members of the American population—and the least likely to report it. In his book, he empowered parents and teens alike to become highly attuned to their inner voice and intuition. These, he explained, are our most powerful allies in keeping us safe, and yet as girls and women we often override or disregard them in the name of being "nice." As she walked into her boyfriend's house, Vicki's gut feeling was so strong that she actually felt sick to her stomach, and yet she reasoned the sensation away and dismissed it from her AWARENESS.

This same attentiveness to intuition is what police officer Allison Jacobs tapped into when she knew in her gut something was not right about Phillip Garrido, the kidnapper of 11-year-old Jaycee Dugard, and took decisive action that led to Jaycee's rescue. Learning to pay attention to this inner voice of truth is the KEY to empowering our daughters and ourselves to do whatever is necessary to stand up for ourselves, physically and psychologically.

As a college student in my early 20s, I narrowly escaped being raped. I was returning home from a visit to see my parents when my airplane was caught in a winter storm in the skies above Minneapolis. After a harrowing flight filled with what felt like endless turbulence, we landed safely and were all sent to a nearby hotel to spend the night as the airport was shut down. Bonded together by our intense experience, a couple dozen passengers from my section of the plane planned to have a party in the room of a young man who generously offered to host us. I spent the evening talking, laughing and celebrating with perfect strangers who ranged in age from their 20s to their 60s. It all seemed so innocent. At midnight, as we were filing out the door, our host kept a conversation going with me. To be polite, I lagged behind the others who were already down the hall.

When the last person before me was out of sight, he grabbed my arm, closed the door, and threw me on the bed. Without speaking a word, our cordial young host turned into an animal. With great agility and strength, he magically removed his belt and pants while simultaneously holding me down. I entered a Zen-like frame of mind, and somehow stayed calm. Without raising my voice or sending any message that I perceived him to have any power over me, I began reciting a laundry list of reasons why he really didn't want to carry through with his plan. I said, "There's the police report, the trial, the mark on your record—all for a couple minutes of thrill." I don't know if it was my energy, my words or both, but he lost his drive and I stood up and ran out the door.

While I had enough AWARENESS to talk my way out of the rape, I did not have the courage or the follow through to report the incident to authorities. Looking back, I was still too young to appreciate the importance of reporting a rape or an attempted rape. This lack of action has always haunted me. How many others were lucky enough to get away? How many weren't? And how many others, like me, remained silent? If we add together the teens who are victims of rape or attempted rape, those who are targets of sexual harassment, sexting and date stalking, it becomes clear that available statistics merely scratch the surface of the real number of girls and women who are targets of sexual abuse. And while it's true that all such violations are damaging, sexual abuse at the hands of a loved one creates further confusion, as the child is betrayed and harmed by someone upon whom she is supposed to be able to trust and depend. When the perpetrator is somebody whose support a teen must rely upon, she may be too conflicted to share the secret with anyone in a position to stop it.

A couple of years ago, I met a young woman named Maureen at a coffee shop, where she gave me her diary that included the following entry. Maureen had written this immediately after her friend Kathy shared with her the details of having been sexually abused by her father when she was just 8 years old.

Maureen, Age 18

Dear diary, my best friend just told me about her incest as a child. I'm so furious right now. I'm writing her experience as she told it to me so I can get it out and keep me from burning up.

GENIUS
MIND

95 percent of college rapes in America are never reported to authorities. At the end of 2013, an estimated 180,000 rape kits remained untested in the U.S.
—jezebel.com

LITTLE

The little Madonna, so young, clean and innocent. Her skin is bronzed from the kisses of the sun. Her hair is a strawberry brown with shimmering flecks of gold on each strand. Possessing the quintessential naiveté, of her eighth year. He has chronic alcoholic breath and the strong, thick body of a man that uses his muscles with shameless and immoral pride. "Kiss me good night," is all she asked from him. His thin, purple lips parted as he pushed his pasty tongue into her small crimson mouth. She winced and pulled back in utter confusion. "Why is this happening" she wondered. He lies on top of her, breathing in short gasps into her ear; he penetrates her. She tries to scream but he stuffs his fist into her mouth. Finishing, he climbs off of her, leaving her in a puddle of humiliation and then covers her up as if to make it all right. Stroking her freshly bathed hair, he gets up and awkwardly strides across the floor to leave the room. Opening her eyes and drawing her body into a ball, she whispers, "good night, Daddy," and throws him an acid glance that hit his back as he leaves the room, satisfied for one more night. "What did I do to deserve this? Who can I trust? Will anyone believe me?" .... She lay there for hours searching for answers while drying her tears and feeling the shreds of her shattered heart.

As difficult as this is to read, I decided to include it because I was profoundly moved by how accurately Maureen was able to recount the emotional anguish her friend suffered as a result of being violated by her own father. Even more tragic for a victim of incest is the suffering that often continues long after the sexual abuse has come to an end. Low self-esteem is a common after-effect of such abuse, as many such girls retreat into FEARSELF-based behaviors such as depression, eating disorders, sexual promiscuity, hoarding, or addiction. These patterns may continue well into adulthood, and resolving them can be difficult until the girl becomes aware of the cause. As author Tara Brach shares in her book *Radical Acceptance*, "While there are times in our life we might have had no choice but to contract away from unbearable physical or emotional pain, our healing comes from reconnecting with those places in our body where that pain is stored ... No matter how deeply we have been wounded, when we listen to the inner voice that calls us back to our bodies, back to wholeness, we begin our journey."

As conscious parents and responsible adults, we owe it to all children to

The truth about childhood is stored up in our body, and although we can repress it, we can never alter it. Our intellect can be deceived, our feelings manipulated, our perceptions confused, and our body tricked with medication. But someday the body will present its bill.
— Alice Miller

be keenly aware of the signs or behavior changes that may indicate sexual abuse. We must realize that anytime incest is suspected, getting involved is absolutely the right thing to do. The website www.rainn.org is a great resource for victims of sexual abuse and those who care for them.

Even in the absence of any type of abuse, the spectrum of sexual activity among teen girls is vast and complex. There are girls who abstain from sex; girls who have sex with their one true love; girls who are sexually active; and girls who become promiscuous. Sometimes, the same girl weaves in and out of one or more of these roles. Interestingly, a study published in the journal *Pediatrics* concluded that teenagers who pledge to remain virgins until marriage are just as likely to have sex before marriage as those who did not make such a pledge. But because of a purposeful lack of sex education, the pledgers are much less likely to practice safe sex when they do have intercourse, resulting in a higher risk of pregnancy and sexually transmitted diseases. Contracting a disease that may be life threatening or increase the chances of certain types of cancer and infertility presents one set of grave problems. Getting pregnant creates an entirely different set of consequences.

10,000 teens contract sexually transmitted diseases every day in the U.S.
—CDC

Of 1,200 twelfth-grade girls in U.S. surveyed in 2012 by Seventeen Magazine and National Campaign to Prevent Teen and Unplanned Pregnancy:

96   percent have had some sort of sex education, including 70 percent who have learned about methods of birth control.

65   percent have had sex.

53   percent have had sex in the last three months.

46   percent of those who are currently sexually active had a partner who used a condom the last time they had sex.

19   percent have had sex with at least four different partners.

11   percent say they have been forced to have sex when they didn't want to at some time.

Teen Pregnancy

First, a piece of news to celebrate: The U.S. teen pregnancy rate has reached a historic low, declining 57 percent among 15 to 17 year olds since peaking in 1990. The National Campaign to Prevent Teen and Unplanned Pregnancy was set up in the 1990s, when they challenged the nation to cut the teen pregnancy rate by one-third. National Campaign CEO Sarah S. Brown wrote, "Thanks to countless people, social forces, effective programs, strong research, determined funders, and then some, the rate has been cut [by over] half. More teens are waiting to have sex; they also report fewer sexual partners and better use of contraception." Yes, there is more to do, and progress should not be confused with victory. The National Campaign reports that the United States still has the highest rates of teen pregnancy and birth among comparable countries. The teen birth rate in the U.S. is nearly one and a half times higher than in the United Kingdom, which has the highest rate in Western Europe, and nearly ten times higher than in Switzerland, which has the lowest rate. The U.S. teen birth rate is more than twice as high as the teen birth rate in Canada. Information available in the year 2014 provides the following window into the issue of teen pregnancy in the United States: More than 1,700 teen girls get pregnant *every day*. In the last eight hours, approximately 571 teenage girls have become pregnant. These are girls whose lives have been turned upside down—forever changed, no matter what they decide to do. Other relevant statistics tell us that of these 571, about 150 of them will have abortions, and 340 girls who will become teen moms (miscarriages and stillbirths account for the difference) *every eight hours* of every day. Most of these teen moms will be single mothers, as 88 percent of teen fathers do not marry the mother. While some of these new moms receive moral and financial support from their parents and their babies are welcomed into the family, most lack either one or both of these essential forms of support. In fact, more than 60 percent of teen mothers live in poverty at the time of their child's birth.

Maria, Age 16

June 10. *My babies are three weeks old. Yes, twins. Richard and I didn't really have a relationship. Just partied together a lot. We used condoms for the first month—but not after that, even though I didn't want to get pregnant. Once we were having fun, it seemed like too much of a hassle to use a condom. There was a lack of structure and nurturing in my home. I didn't really know what I was missing, I just knew I felt empty, and was desperate to fill that void. When I first found out I was pregnant, I started crying and I couldn't stop. When I told Richard, the first thing he said was to* *have the babies. I told him we don't have a relationship, so I said no, that's not going to work out. Soon after that, he was arrested for drugs, and is now in jail.*

Looking back, I realize that I didn't listen to anybody who tried to tell me not to hang out with certain friends, I just said, "whatever" and did it anyway. At the church I go to, there are a few girls who are pregnant. One of them is 15 and one is 16. The pastor asked me to talk to them. They were crying hard. I told them I know it's not easy to use a condom, but it's easier than raising a baby—or two. I had to drop out of school and get a job as a waitress to pay my expenses, but recently quit because I was too exhausted and ended up in the hospital. Most girls my age are worried about math tests, and I cry myself to sleep at night wondering how I will pay for diapers.

Only 2 percent of teen moms will graduate from college, a factor that alters their life trajectory in a way that diminishes—rather than expands—both their potential and their future opportunities. This is in part because even in the 21st century, mothers are still the ones expected to raise children—even if alone. Additionally, babies born to teen mothers are more likely to grow up in poverty or foster care, more likely to become victims of domestic violence, and three times more likely to become teen mothers themselves, thus perpetuating the cycle. The link between teen pregnancy and other critical social issues—from child abuse and neglect to school failure—is undeniable. We live in a society heavily invested in governing protections for a fetus, while attention to the basic needs of the babies and new mothers are too often ignored or minimized. To consider these problems in their entirety, we must also examine the subject of teen abortion.

Abortion

Karen, Age 17
October 13. *Went back to Mike's place last night and "fell asleep." Stayed all night. Now I am starting to worry. We talked about girls getting pregnant and what we would ever do if it happened to us. We didn't know.*
November 28. *Went to church. Every time I stood up I blacked out and almost fainted. Mom asked me if I could be pregnant because that was the first sign she had. I told her it was impossible. It can't really happen the first time, can it? I was shocked she asked me all*

One in three girls between the ages of 16 and 18 say sex is expected for people their age if they're in a relationship. —Teen Research Unlimited

the questions she did. When was my last period, etc.? Was sick all day but went bowling.

December 3. *Sue and I went out for breakfast this morning. I didn't eat between meals all day and I'm not going to until I lose this belly fat because my Christmas formal dress barely fits. Felt really sick and dizzy so I was in bed all afternoon.*

December 4. *I had the worst day in school I have ever had. I don't know why but I just kept crying and crying and felt so down. I get nervous in school now. Felt like throwing up today and have a bad cold, so mom sent me to the Dr. She said I better have a pregnancy test too! When I was in his office, I was really scared, but got up the nerve to ask him for a pregnancy test. After the test, he walked back in and said, "No wonder your pulse is through the roof! The test came back positive." He told me this without looking up as he wrote the phone number for an abortion doctor. He said that's what he would have his daughter do. I was in shock. I have a lot to tell Mike.*

Nearly 30 years after becoming pregnant at the age of 17, Karen reflects on her ultimate decision to have an abortion.

Karen's Reflections, 30 years later

Like so many couples, Mike and I didn't talk about the consequences of unprotected sex before having it. In fact, we didn't even think about it. It was as if we assumed we were in a group of people that had sex just for fun, and there was another group that had sex to have babies. In reality, of course, there are no separate groups. Personally, I didn't even know there were certain times of the month that increased the likelihood of pregnancy more than others. Even though I was seventeen, in the Bible belt town where I lived, I had never been educated about this basic fact. After we had sex for the first time, Mike pulled out the main reference book available at the time, Everything You Always Wanted to Know About Sex—But Were Afraid to Ask. There was a section on using the rhythm method of birth control. It said, "The big problem is that ovulation generally occurs fourteen days before the first day of the next menstrual period … but it can actually occur on any day of the menstrual cycle." It happened to be day fourteen for me.

Reading my diary brought me back to the roller coaster of fear and denial that I felt when I knew there was a possibility I may be pregnant. My entry about going bowling reminded me of my

In Mississippi, the state with the highest teen birth rate, 27 percent of children struggle with hunger. Mississippi rates number one in poverty in America.
—Gallup Study 2014

motivation behind it: I threw the ball as hard as I could, hoping it would cause a miscarriage. The next day, I tried to convince myself I was gaining weight from eating too much. When I came home with the fateful news that I was, in fact, pregnant, my parents were stunned. In the midst of many tears, my mom burst forth with a confession of having had an abortion after my older sister was born because they were too poor to have another child. Like the doctor, my parents felt that an abortion was the only option for me. They talked about how much education Mike had ahead of him to build a solid career (no mention of my education).

When I told Mike the news the day after finding out, the first thing he said was, "Let's see if there's an extra hanger in the closet." I was too sad to cry, and was not about to laugh at his miserable attempt at a joke. I was three for three on having others telling me what to do. What did I want to do? I was emotionally numb and my self-esteem was so low I didn't know what I wanted. I do remember lying in bed over the next few days and thinking of running away to another city and having the baby. I dreamed of having a girl and naming her Rhiannon, after the Fleetwood Mac song. With zero support on any level, the only way I felt I could have the baby was if I did it completely on my own. My mother made an appointment for the abortion. I began to worry. Will I ever be able to have babies after that? Will they shave my pubic hair, so when I take a shower in the locker room after P.E. all the girls will stare at me? What about the baby? Was it a human being? At home in my bedroom, I got down on my knees, and with hopelessness in one hand and helplessness in the other, I folded them together and bowed my head. As tears drenched with these questions spilled down my cheeks, I wept myself to sleep. At sunrise, I woke up with a sense of knowing, and called Mike to tell him the date and time of the appointment so he could be there with me.

After the abortion, my mother reassured me there would be lots of time for Mike and me to have babies, but we eventually broke up, and I kept the secret of my pregnancy locked up for many years afterward. Every year on what would have been the baby's due date, I grieved. "What birthday gift would I have given this year?" I wondered. Every Mother's Day, I looked in the mirror and silently said, "Happy would-be Mother's Day." I didn't write these feelings in my diary. But at the end of each day, I'd remind myself of how immature we both still were; I'd admit the truth that we were still too young to know what love was, and I'd recognize the reality that *our lack of education and financial resources would have kept us poor for years to come, burying both our dreams and our spirits. Today I have a wonderful family and successful career, and know in my heart that I made the best decision with the information I had and the guidance I received at the time.*

Like Karen, I also became pregnant as a teenager, and I too struggled with the decision of what to do. On the day I learned the truth, I came home and was surprised that my parents didn't yell at me when I told them. I was sobbing so intensely I couldn't stand up, so I don't think they dared. Even my dad had tears in his eyes, and my mom said she wished it were her so she could take away my pain. I searched my own heart for answers. When none came, I went to the public library and searched through *The Readers' Guide to Periodic Literature* (pre-Google—pre-computer) to find every article on the subject that I could find. The opinions were all over the map. There was the Roman Catholic position that declared the use of any artificial form of birth control as a sin because the sperm and the egg represent the beginning of life. Other sources encouraged each woman to consult with her own God to understand the truth of when life begins; then follow her inner guidance. I pored over each article until the classic bun-in-her hair librarian with wing-tipped glasses kicked me out at closing time. I walked into the dark night having searched for proof—for some kind of clarity that would make my decision easier. I found a lot of passionate opinions and judgments but uncovered no such proof.

For decades we have debated the same questions on the issue of abortion that still remain unanswered today. When does a soul enter a body? When does life begin? When does it end? Is there a beginning and an end, or does it just change form? What is the right thing to do? Who has the right to make the decision? Because there are no easy answers, there is no one person or group of people that can claim a stake of absolute certainty as to the moment it becomes unethical to abort a fetus because its life has begun. But of one thing we are certain: our teenage daughters' lives *have* begun and we are responsible for protecting and guiding them toward a safe and promising future.

This is a snapshot of my diary the day after I found out I was pregnant. And all the days after that for ten years to come. When I see these blank pages today, I mourn the toll taken by an unplanned pregnancy. I mourn for the emotional and spiritual emptiness that muted me from experiencing and expressing the richness of life.

I mourn for the pages never written by Maria, the single teen mother of twins; pages upon which she would share the fulfillment of her dreams of becoming a cosmetologist and raise kids within a happy marriage, setting an example of a love-filled family for her own daughters. Instead, her pen sits unused near a pile of tissues beside her bed after crying herself to sleep. She is alone with worry about how to feed and clothe the babies she loves.

If we are to mentor our young women to express their sexuality and pursue romantic love in ways that are self-respecting and healthy, then we as a society must not abandon our responsibility to educate them. We must not allow legislators to make laws on this subject with their head in the stars without the balance of keeping their feet on the ground. When, as parents, we cast the burden to teach our kids about sex completely on the school system, we neglect this essential and deeply influential responsibility. A page from the diary of 16-year-old Debbie makes this point clearly:

Debbie, Age 16
I talked to Emily today. I'd be a major wreck, but she is OK for now. One day at a time. Hope she gets her period soon. Her mom took her to the gynecologist last week for a pelvic exam, etc. In the Dr.'s office, Emily said she gets bad cramps before her period

and wondered if she could get the pill to help. Her mom said no, she didn't need it. When her mom left the room during the exam, Emily told the Dr. she was sexually active, but the Dr. couldn't give her the pill because her mom said no. Bummer. If only Ibuprofen prevented pregnancy.

Contraception and Prevention

In matters concerning intimacy and sexuality, a "Don't ask, don't tell" policy of not talking constructively and openly about these subjects undermines a girl's emotional development and her ability to navigate future romantic and/or sexual relationships. The reality is that human beings are sexual beings. We may not want our daughters to have sex, and it goes without saying we do not want them to get hurt, to get pregnant or to contract a disease. But we cannot prevent any of these things by sticking our heads in the sand. We've tried that for decades—probably centuries. In 1916, Margaret Sanger, the pioneer who popularized the phrase "birth control," was arrested for distributing information about contraceptives after seeing patients die from unsafe abortions. As a nurse, she had heard women ask their doctors how they could prevent unwanted pregnancies, and heard only one answer each time—to practice abstinence. She watched many of these same women die in childbirth following their next pregnancy. Nearly 100 years later, the fight for information continues, even though the majority of Americans wish that teens were getting more information about abstinence and contraception, not one or the other. In New Hampshire, where the teen birth rate is the lowest in the nation, state law requires comprehensive sex education that includes information on abstinence, condoms and contraception. In contrast, Mississippi, where abstinence is the state standard, has the highest teen birth rate. Too many abstinence only programs impose the danger of diminishing a girl's sense of self-worth by sending the message that if she does have sex before marriage, her moral purity will be lost and therefore her value diminished.

A sobering yet enlightening example of this was revealed by Elizabeth Smart, who was kidnapped from her home at age 14 and raped for nine months before being found alive. Speaking at a human trafficking forum, she shared about why she didn't run when her captors took her out in the open. In her religious upbringing, she had been taught that absti-

Our lives begin to end the day we become silent about things that matter.
—Martin Luther King Jr.

nence-only was the only acceptable approach to sexuality before marriage, and that one of her teachers even compared a girl who has had sex to a chewed-up piece gum, asking, "Who wants a piece of chewed-up gum?" So after Elizabeth was raped, feeling worthless and without value, she convinced herself no one would ever want her. Elizabeth thought, "'Oh, my gosh, I'm that chewed up piece of gum, nobody re-chews a piece of gum, you throw it away.' And that's how easy it is to feel like you no longer have worth, you no longer have value," she said. "Why would it even be worth screaming out?"

As revealed in the powerful documentary, *Let's Talk About Sex*, we are a society obsessed with purity and, as a result, we are creating the very problems we seek to avoid. We must be the change makers who help our girls make the safe journey into womanhood. To do this, we need to move toward a more realistic and common sense approach to sex education, and ensure birth control is available when it's needed. The results of this approach speak for themselves. A report published by researchers at the Washington University School of Medicine showed that when teenage girls in the St. Louis area were given no-cost contraception over a period of 3 years, abortion rates across the city dropped by 82 percent compared to the national rate. According to a nationally representative survey by The National Campaign to Prevent Teen and Unplanned Pregnancy, "Encouraging teens to delay sex and providing teens with information about contraception are seen as complementary, not contradictory strategies by most adults regardless of age, race/ethnicity, or geography."

By their 19th birthday, 7 in 10 female and male teens have had intercourse.
—Guttmacher Institute

Considering these statistics, if we as a society were to became advocates *for* responsible sex and contraception instead of opponents *against* sexuality and abortion, 571 teen pregnancies and 150 abortions would be prevented in the time it takes to complete an eight-hour shift at work, or 450 per day. And this level of prevention would continue *every single day.*

Ten Tips for Parents
Source: The National Campaign to Prevent Teen and Unplanned Pregnancy

1. Be clear about your own values and attitudes about sexuality.

2. Talk with your children early and often about sex, and be specific.

3. Supervise and monitor your children and adolescents.

4. Know your children's friends and their families.

5. Discourage early, frequent and steady dating.

6. Take a strong stand against your daughter dating a boy significantly older than she is.

7. Help your teenagers have options for the future that are more attractive than early pregnancy and parenthood.

8. Let your kids know that you value education highly.

9. Know what your kids are watching, reading and listening to.

10. Parents, learn the facts about contraception and prevention.

Most kids say they wish they were more knowledgeable about birth control. Although the majority of teens talk about sex with their friends two times more than they talk about it with their parents, a 2012 survey conducted by *Seventeen* magazine confirms that most would rather learn about it from their parents.

When sex-related questions arise, we would do well to remind ourselves that just because our daughters want to know more about sex and contraception doesn't necessarily mean they are having sex, nor does providing this information mean that we are pushing them towards it. Above all, we must do our very best to avoid conveying messages that encourage them to keep secrets or tell lies, especially about matters like sexuality, which may drastically impact their future. Particularly at this juncture in their lives when they need us the most (they may protest otherwise, but it's true), it is vital we leave open this critical door of authentic communication about sexuality between our daughters and ourselves.

Nearly 9 in 10 teens say that it would be much easier to delay sexual activity and avoid teen pregnancy if they were able to have more open, honest conversations about these topics with their parents.

Three-quarters of teens say that what they see in the media about sex, love and relationships could be a good way to start conversations with adults about these topics.
—The National Campaign to Prevent Teen and Unplanned Pregnancy

Healthy Romance: Soulful Communication

After studying and applying the philosophies of a wide range of relationship experts from across the globe and whose work has withstood the test of time, I've learned—sometimes the hard way—what works and what doesn't in nurturing loving relationships. From my research and experience, I've pulled together what I consider to be the most transformative statements for relational bonding and healing into a dialogue I call the Diamond Dialogue Model for soulful communication. These dialogues are designed to help see through FEARSELF-driven behavior between our loved ones and within ourselves. When each of the statements in the model is practiced on a consistent basis between two people with sincerity of heart, miracles become possible. Each expression can be used in sequence as a healing process or in random order, one by one, to maintain a healthy relationship.

Name
I'm Sorry
Tell me more
You could be right
Are we good?
I love you
Thank you
Silence

Diamond Dialogue Model

It is a beautiful thing when two hearts join in a soul-filled connection of mutual respect.

Name: Our name was the first word we ever heard, and it has been evoking emotional engagement within us since our birth. Dale Carnegie, the great human relations pioneer of the early 20th century, taught us that "remembering a person's name is to that person the sweetest and most important sound in any language." When you acknowledge another by name while looking into his or her eyes, you send a powerful message that affirms on many levels how important this person is to you. Far from a formality to be used only with acquaintances, a person's name holds the power of superglue for partners to focus attention on a conversation.

I'm sorry: We all make mistakes and have apologized at one time or another. The key to using the words "I'm sorry" to create a healing impact in a relationship is to make sure they are said with an energy of compassion and an attitude of "please forgive me." Only then is there an authentic effort to start fresh, to make a 180-degree turn back to more loving, SOULSELF-directed communication. In the ancient Hawaiian practice of ho'onoponopono, the kahunas—teachers of wisdom—advocated that families meet weekly to express concerns and prevent resentments from erupting.

Tell me more: If there's one lesson I hope you take away from this book, it's to be a good listener (first and foremost to yourself). What better words can express your genuine interest in another than "tell me more," followed by silence as you wait to hear the response?

You could be right: Would you rather be right or happy? In the long term, being right doesn't provide as much satisfaction as being happy or being connected. By acknowledging the other person could be right, you open your eyes to another way of looking at the situation. Whether you agree or not, there's a better chance of finding common ground when one is willing to see the other's point of view. Having a right-or-wrong mentality—a primary tool of the FEARSELF—can derail more meaningful conversations by causing us to lose sight of the love that binds us together, becoming lost in meaningless superficialities in which the focus is more on form than on content.

Are we good? In the third agreement in his amazing book of wisdom, *The Four Agreements*, author don Miguel Ruiz tells us, "Don't make assumptions." When we make assumptions in relationships, we may overlook that an issue or disagreement has not yet been resolved. Being brave enough to ask the question, "Are we good?" is an effective way of making sure there are no outstanding grievances or lingering resentments, while offering the opportunity to clean the slate.

I love you: Never underestimate the words "I love you." The diary entries in this book leave no doubt that as humans, we are very hard on ourselves. Even when things are going right, it's easy for self-doubt to creep into the psyche. How comforting to have a loved one steer us back on course by reminding us of the truth that we are lovable. The spoken words "I love you" have the power to open the hearts of both the speaker and the receiver. This phrase stands as a pillar of support as we face each

The Four Agreements:
1. *Be impeccable with your word.*
2. *Don't take anything personally.*
3. *Don't make assumptions.*
4. *Always do your best.*
—*don Miguel Ruiz*

day and each challenge. As an aside, it is every bit as powerful for children to hear these words spoken between their parents, as well as directly to them.

Thank you: It is said among many masters that gratitude is among the highest vibrations in the entire universe. As author Sarah Ban Breathnach puts it, "Gratitude is the most passionate transformative force in the cosmos." When you acknowledge your partner or child by expressing your appreciation, you are recognizing the love that they have extended to you, while also teaching them what you value—so more of the same can be drawn to you. This represents a complete circle of love that automatically guides us back to the core of the SOULSELF.

Trade your expectation for appreciation and the world changes instantly.
—Tony Robbins

Silence: Once the above statements are expressed, allowing a period of silence is important in order for each person to reflect on the emotions that have just been shared. How much time is spent in silence depends on how quickly each partner is able to absorb the dynamics of what transpired and to rejoin the other at the level of the soul. In silence, we harness our ability to remain open and available to continue the thread of meaningful conversation.

There are times when silence can convey a meaning most eloquently.
—Eleanor Roosevelt

The Diamond Dialogue Model serves as a good jumping-off point to make meaningful deposits into the emotional bank accounts of those we care about. The model is an equally valuable process regardless of age. The more frequently we incorporate this level of connection into our every-day communication, the better prepared we will be to *really* listen when our daughters or significant others seek our understanding when sharing something difficult. For parents and teens, issues around sexuality are often difficult to discuss, especially when what needs to be shared is controversial, or something that a teen fears will be met with disappointment or rejection.

Sexual Orientation: Same Love, Same Gender

Miranda, Age 16
I am in love and am so happy. I would love to tell my mother, but I don't know how she would react, and I don't want to let her down ... but I think a lie would be terrible so I will TELL HER if she asks. I wouldn't know how to start a talk like that. "Well Mom, we need to talk. I am gay."

Find out who you are and be that person. That's what your soul was put on this Earth to be. Find that truth, live that truth and everything else will come.
—Ellen Degeneres

In Norway, the native country of my ancestors, in an effort among publicly funded museums to be "deliverers of truth" and "put on display controversial subjects, things that are not said and are swept under the carpet," the Oslo Natural History Museum held an exhibition of gay animals in 2006. The exhibition revealed that same-gender sexual relations have been observed among 1,500 species, and well documented in 500 of those. What some cultures around the world have observed, science has now confirmed: same-gender attraction is a normal variant of sexuality.

While issues around secrecy and privacy make it difficult to arrive at an exact number, it is estimated that somewhere between 4 and 10 percent of our worldwide human population experiences some degree of attraction to people of the same gender. From a global perspective, attitudes towards same-gender relationships vary greatly. In general, Northern Europeans, who provide full equal human rights regardless of sexual orientation, represent one end of the spectrum. Countries like Russia, Saudi Arabia, Iran, Uganda and others in Africa—where same-gender relationships are punishable crimes that sometimes result in life imprisonment or even death—clearly represent the other. Here in the United States, levels of acceptance fall somewhere between these two extremes. In 2013, the U.S. Supreme Court ruled that a Federal ban of same-sex marriage is unconstitutional, and yet many states do not yet recognize same-sex marriage. While laws in the U.S. are gradually evolving to embrace a greater moral understanding in the direction of justice for all, heartbreaking stories of teen bullying, depression and suicide demonstrate that intolerance of individual differences still persists in our schools, in our communities and at home. A 2011 study published in the journal *Pediatrics* found that self-identified gay, lesbian and bisexual teens were five times more likely to attempt suicide than their heterosexual counterparts.

The following entries capture the emotional turmoil felt by many young women who are attracted to members of the same gender while being raised in a culture where heterosexuality is compulsory and expected. Their words describe the internal conflict that arises from the fight between the desire to fit in and the instinct to be themselves.

Christine, Age 18
This seems like a continuing soap saga but I have found out what the problem is. I am in love with Lynn—and I hate it and myself for it—so my ulcer is returning—full force. The nausea and all the

other good things that go along with it. The way she puts her hands on my leg in the car gives me an awesome feeling. She really does it for me. Robert doesn't, but I still don't quite know what to do. Every day I think something different.

Nikki, Age 16

Ellen asked me if I ever look at a girl and wondered what it would be like to be with her ... She completely opened the door for me. She made it comfortable for me to think about it and let it out. For the first time, I didn't feel like I had to block out my feelings because it's not the way it's "supposed" to be. I owned it, at least for a moment.

Nancy, Age 16

We rented movies tonight. One was Chasing Amy. *It's about a girl who is gay but falls in love with a guy. I was watching intently. Hello, this sounds like me and some of the people I've thought about as more than just friends. Junior year—Haley; Senior year—Carla. Actually, it goes back to fifth grade through ninth grade with Melanie. But, with her, it's different. With Melanie, I feel so open and honest when I talk to her. She knows a lot about me that others don't. We can talk forever and never run out of things to say. When I'm with her, I never want to leave. Sometimes we hold hands. Of course I make the initial move. Like if we are talking on the floor and her hand is out, I'll say something and then touch it and won't move. To me that's really intimate. It makes me want to spill my guts about how I feel, but I know I can't tell her.*

Suzanne, Age 19

April 11. *I still think I could live with Erica for years. Like make a life of it, but she doesn't feel that way. She is so cute right now. She's typing on my computer singing to the country music on the radio. She sang a verse to me. This is how I need to feel about the person I live with for the rest of my life. Unconditional love. Respect. Understanding. Someone I really want to hold in my arms all night. Wouldn't that be great? If I were a guy we would totally be planning our wedding by now. But she can't or won't live that way. We talked of living together after we graduate. Moving south somewhere together. It's love.*

April 25. *Erica had a date with Brad last weekend and I asked her what it was like to be with him. She said when she was with him she started to feel guilty and stopped him from moving forward. She* agreed with me that our souls belong together. But I don't have a penis. So society doesn't accept us. Too bad.

Erin M., Age 18

July 11. *Tonight I went out with Kevin. He is awesome to hang out with, but there's no spark. I don't feel anything when we kiss. I think about Kim and I wonder if I'm just trying to convince myself that I should be with Kevin. And I know I would feel something with Kim. But I know I'll never get the chance. So stop thinking about it, right? Not as easy as it sounds. When Kevin left, I talked to Kim for two hours on the phone. We talked about everything. She told me how much I mean to her. She said she couldn't explain it. It feels really good to know that someone cares for you that much. I'm not good expressing my feelings, so I just told her that I missed her.*

July 16. *I still catch myself looking at girls as much or even more than I do guys. What's the deal? Am I ever going to figure it out? That would be too easy. Tonight we all went to dinner at Applebee's and I was sitting to the left of Kim. We were talking and all of a sudden she put her hand on my leg and squeezed. It was brief, but enough to make me think. I'm still waiting for the opportunity I will never get, and even if I have something remotely close, I won't act on it. There's too much at risk.*

July 26. *Kim and I laid down in the spooning position, her on her side and me behind her with my arm around her side. She held onto my hand. I didn't want to leave, but I had to go on my date with Kevin. She told me she didn't want me to, which made me want to stay even more. But I got ready for my date and left for Kevin's just before 6 o'clock. I really love being close to Kim much more so than Kevin. But he is a nice guy and he really likes me. All I know is that I want to get as close to her as I can for as long as I can because it's so comforting. It's a good feeling to hold someone you care about. I wonder what she thinks about our relationship. I need to be careful, so I spend time with Kevin.*

August 1. *I'm scared to feel this way, but I'm not really attracted to Kevin. I think that I will always be attracted to women. It will really be hard to be married to a man if I'm always looking at women. I'm going to really have to be in love with him or be awfully miserable. Life is a crazy thing. The paths we choose change our lives.*

To understand the conditions of oppression or freedom in the organization of homosexuality is to deal with all the problems of human life and the struggle for dignity and freedom, love and hate, stigma, fear, secrecy, friendship, envy and power, political domination, and family loyalty and betrayal.
—Gilbert Herdt

The words written by Erin M. in her last diary entry are haunting. If we allow discrimination, intolerance or FEAR to strip even one young woman of her inherent freedom to choose her own path, then we have participated in a tragedy of epic proportions. If we allow cultural edicts to pressure our daughters into playing with dolls when they would rather be outside playing football, then we send them a powerful message: Who you are is not okay; there is something wrong with you. The gay and lesbian teens who internalize this lie are held hostage by the FEARSELF, separated from their pure and authentic expression. Ironically, those who judge others for being different and therefore abnormal often hold themselves equally captive by a smaller version of themselves. Their beliefs must also be driven by the FEARSELF, whether manifested as overt hatred or veiled behind self-righteousness or narrow-mindedness.

To justify discrimination against same-gender relations, some individuals and organizations cite a few hand-selected verses in the Old Testament; clinging to words written over 3,000 years ago allows them to literally remain in the dark ages. "Politicians who use the Bible aren't necessarily interested in the truth or the complexity of the Bible," said Robert R. Cargill, religious scholar at the University of Iowa. "They are looking for one ancient sound bite to convince people what they already believe." Verses in the book of Leviticus, which allegedly condemns same-gender relations as an abomination, makes the same declaration regarding the act of eating shellfish—and yet we would be hard pressed to find people picketing fishermen or threatening to blow up seafood restaurants for participating in this "abomination." The book of Deuteronomy, just two chapters later, mandates a social regulation instructing men to stone a woman to death on the doorstep of her father's house if it was determined she was not a virgin when she married. While the Bible has been used to support slavery and the oppression of women for centuries, if we are going to look to Christianity for clarity on the issue of sexuality, then we would do well to remember the KEY message imparted by Jesus was that of unconditional love. In fact, while there is no record of Jesus ever having referred to same-gender relationships, he specifically advised against judging others, commanding that we "Do unto others as you would have done unto you" … the very essence of The Golden Rule.

When Miranda was 27, she came out to her parents. The following excerpt, written by Miranda's mother, captures the internal struggles she experienced between her love for her daughter and her devotion to her religion.

There are too many kids out there suffering from bullying, rejection, or simply being mistreated because of who they are. Too many dropouts. Too much abuse. Too many homeless. Too many suicides. You can change that …
—Ellen Page

Miranda's Mother

When my 27-year-old daughter told me that she was gay, I was devastated. Not that I ever felt that I didn't love her, and I hope that she never felt that I rejected her, but it took me a while to process this information. I am a very religious person and had raised my children "right," or at least had tried my best. I felt guilty, like I must have failed in some, or probably many ways. I was saddened by all of the things I felt she was giving up, and the hardships I could see in her future. But most of all I was afraid for her; my religion teaches that homosexuality is a terrible sin. I had a stereotype of what a gay person must be, selfish, lustful, wicked, etc., but I know that my daughter is none of those things; she is a kind, loving, wonderful person! It felt almost like I had to choose between my child and my church. It has taken me a while to find a way to reconcile the two things that I am most passionate about in my life, my family and my religious beliefs. The older I get, the more I realize how much I don't know, but what I do know is that I love my child and I love my God. For now that is enough, I know that my path is to continue to love and support and believe in both of them. In my heart, I cannot feel there is a more beautiful expression of God than to unconditionally love and support your children.

Erin M., whose stories we read earlier, offers the following reflections of her teenage struggles around—and ultimate liberation from—issues related to her sexuality:

Erin M.'s Reflection—A Message to Teens

Always be true to yourself. I think the struggle that most of us have is to fit in with the crowd, society, and standards. The desire to fit in decreases as you get older, although it may never go away completely. You don't have to understand everything now. You don't have to know everything now. Part of life is learning and changing along the way. Just because you have friends or know of people that came out when they were 16 doesn't mean that you have to come out that young, or that you even understand feelings you are having. Heck, some people don't realize that they are gay until they are well into adulthood. Every person is different, and everyone's process and experiences will be different. Be patient with yourself. On the flip side, be gentle. Some straight people dislike gays because they feel like gay people "push it in their faces" and thus, they feel threatened. I'm not saying to hide or be ashamed, but try not to threaten others. If we can all live our lives respecting others, then people won't have a reason to hate.

I have not experienced the level of intimacy with a male that I have with a female. I only had a handful of boyfriends growing up, and most if not all, of them were because of outside pressures. In tenth grade, I dated a boy who was a good friend of mine just because my friends kept asking if he was my boyfriend. In my junior year of college, there was Kevin, who I dated as a cover up to dating Kim. In an odd twist, it was Kim's idea that I date Kevin, because she was concerned people would be suspicious about us. With Kevin, I enjoyed the company, but when it came time to kiss him, I felt like it was a chore. I was doing it for him—I didn't get anything out of it. No sparks, dizziness or butterflies. In my freshman year in college, I finally kissed a girl for the first time and I realized what so many people were talking about. And when I finally fell in love, love songs and love movies finally made sense. I could finally relate to the words and emotions that others were trying to convey. With the women I've dated, I have felt so sincere, so real. Now, looking back on the thoughts and feelings I had growing up, I can see where everything makes sense.

When I graduated from high school in the Midwest in 1996, I didn't know anyone who was gay, or at least if I did, I didn't realize it at the time. My parents didn't talk about it, my friends didn't talk about it, and it wasn't really on TV or in movies too much. Once, a high school coach told us female athletes to "beware" of the other athletes and coaches at colleges because the general idea was that most of them were lesbians. I never really knew what he meant by that, but it did put the idea in my head that being a lesbian was bad or gross or unacceptable. I went off to college, but remained in the Midwest. There I met a girl who had kissed another girl. Finally, I had someone to talk to. Also during college, Ellen DeGeneres came out, and all of a sudden being gay became something that wasn't so secret. It finally became a reality that I could also live with the truth of others knowing about me and that I wouldn't have to hide anymore. Of course, it was still very scary for me, because of the fear of losing friends or family, or being seen as different. My college had a group called "the 10 percent club," a reference to the statistic that ten percent of the population is gay. I was always curious and wanted to go to the meetings, but I was too scared about showing my face. What if more people found out? What if people started *calling me names? What if people didn't want to be my friend any-more? How would I handle all the questions?*

The summer after I graduated college, I finally told my mom that I am gay. Her first response was, "I've known for a while—probably since you were in high school." I said, "Really?" and thought to myself that if I could have told her then, I would have struggled much less. That evening, I went out with some friends to celebrate and felt like a huge weight had been lifted off my shoulders. I could finally be the person I wanted to be, without feeling like I had to change myself in order to fit in. Finally, I was free.

In his book *Same Sex, Different Cultures*, author Gilbert Herdt pointed out that much of our culture's sexual chauvinism is nothing more than leftover homophobia from the 19th century. In the same way we are unraveling our intolerance against minority ethnic groups, it is now time for us to recognize FEAR-based attitudes around same-sex attraction for what they are. Almost all of us have known someone who displayed same-sex tendencies—often from a young age forward. These friends and neighbors are neither bad nor wrong, nor does their sexual preference make them in any way less lovable than anyone else. If we close our eyes and picture someone we know who is of a different sexual orientation, we would be forced to admit there is no way to reconcile supporting laws that prevent her or anyone else from enjoying the same rights endowed to everyone. Embracing this truth heeds the call of the SOULSELF, for when this higher aspect of us is in charge, we are aligned with the desire to support equal justice and true empowerment for all.

Raising the Bar to Personal Empowerment

The root of powerlessness is lack of self-esteem, which is the belief we are unlovable or unworthy. A driving force behind this book is to provide a resource for women and girls to become connected to and emboldened by the truth of the personal power that exists within us all. By developing personal power, inner peace becomes not only possible but natural. Here's how to embrace the power vested in every one of us: Have the willingness to raise the BAR—BAR is my code word for:

Raise the **BAR** ...

BOUNDARIES, AWARENESS, and RESPONSIBILITY

Know Yourself—Know Your Boundaries

The first step in raising the BAR is to establish clear personal *boundaries*. Consider one of Shakespeare's most famous quotes, "This above all, to thine own self be true." One of the easiest ways to better know yourself is to notice how you feel in any given situation. As we face challenges in life, we must pay attention *from the inside out.* The NATURAL SELF aspect of our BEING, through intuition, helps us clarify our boundaries and distinguish healthy CHOICES from unhealthy CHOICES. In the story of Pinocchio, Jiminy Cricket reflected the boundary zone for Pinocchio's SOULSELF—to nudge Pinocchio to do the right thing whenever The Coachman steered him to the edge of the FEARSELF. In the same way, we all have a conscience that helps us navigate the waters of life, as our behavior within each aspect of our BEING flows between the banks of the FEARSELF and SOULSELF. During the teen years the search for self-identification is at its peak. This period of life represents an essential time of sorting out who we are, who we are becoming, and what is important to us in life and in love.

Kate, whose entries appear below, was the very first woman to send me her diaries in their hand-written, original form. She had been considering burning them but happened upon a post about my book on a media query website and seized the opportunity to help others. Her sense of humor shines through as she clarifies her boundaries about what she will and will not accept in a boyfriend.

When you hold yourself in esteem you radiate your own respect for yourself.
— Caroline Myss

Kate, Age 16
My Guy Requirements:
Can carry on a conversation without using "I" more than 50 times.
Has goals (going 30 days without a beer doesn't count).
Understands my indecisiveness and my thinking process.
Regularly challenges himself—not others.
Calls when he says he will call. Understands the word no. Respects my goals and doesn't get in the way of them.
Can watch the movie Titanic the whole way through once.
Ego smaller then Jupiter. Doesn't show off. This includes jumping into the river like Pocahontas.
Doesn't drive like a psycho.
Never touches me in a violent or possessive manner.
Does not kick the school mascot.
Knows how to play solitaire, because if he doesn't meet these requirements that will be his fate!

Other diarists share insights about the importance of establishing personal boundaries in relationships that were gained in hindsight:

Nathalie, Age 16

The hottest man came in to the restaurant tonight. At closing, he said, "this may seem a bit bold, but would you like to go out for coffee?" Not only did I go, but I let him drive. I do not know why—he seemed nice enough, but so did Ted Bundy.

Carol, Age 17

Mom and Tony went to Phoenix. I threw a party. Jack and I hooked up again—well, we fooled around for a while. He asked me if I wanted him to stop. I told him yes. I am just so emotionally weird. I like him so much. I am just scared for him to meet my mom; she would hate him because he's black. But I don't care about that. I just can't believe that I did as much as I did with him. It's not that Jack isn't the right guy; it's just that I'm upset with myself for going against my morals. I was one of those girls I swore I'd never become. I feel so bad. I can't go to the temple now.

Josie, Age 16

Here's what I want to say to Tommy: My body is not your walk in closet. Don't use me for your sexual needs. I want a real man, who isn't scared to tell people I'm yours. I want you to love me, and not in a sexual way. I want a relationship where we can walk in public and you hold my hand. I want people to know I call you baby, and that you call me baby, too. I want real love—emotional love. The love we have is sexual love.

These entries highlight everyday issues that force us to consult with our inner self to understand our own personal definitions of right and wrong. With every CHOICE made with respect to our own boundaries—not those imposed by others, but ourselves—we gain clarity, as Carol did when she stepped over the line of her own good conscience and felt the result. The common themes expressed by these young women served as lessons that help us to *know thyself*, so we can in turn be true to that self—the SOULSELF. All life is energy, and it is constantly being exchanged. When a young woman has the insight and courage to honor her personal boundaries and say no when she means no, she will no longer tolerate a partner who attempts to make her stray from her principles.

The second step in raising the BAR to personal empowerment is to deepen self-AWARENESS. The more attention we give to our inner thoughts, feelings and reactions, the more we sharpen the most valuable tool we have—AWARENESS, the state of being in which we are AWAKE WITH ALL REALITY EXPOSED, NATURALLY EXPRESSING THE SOULSELF. As you contemplate relationships—with yourself or someone you love, you can use the Freeing Your BEING Compass as a sliding scale to assess your proximity to the sacred space of the SOULSELF or the foggy fringe of the FEARSELF. For example, what messages are you receiving from your *Body* when you reflect on this relationship? Are you relaxed or tense? What about your *Emotions*? Do you feel happy, appreciated, anxious, frustrated? What are you *Imagining* for the future in your relationship? In a week? A month? A year? Thinking about the *Natural Self*, are you being "authentically you" in

THE FOG OF
THE FEARSELF

**GENIUS
MIND**

BODY
EMOTIONS
IMAGINATION
NATURAL SELF
GENIUS MIND

your relationships? Or are you compromising your truth to accommodate someone else? The KEY to healthy compromise is to notice whether you are left with an enhanced feeling of love or a feeling of regret because you have given up a part of yourself in the compromise. And what about your *Genius Mind*? What kind of thoughts are you telling yourself about how worthy or unworthy you are of respect in this relationship? What kinds of mind games are being played, if any? Make this AWARENESS check-in a regular practice to reconnect with yourself, and then share it with your daughters and your friends.

The third and final step in raising the BAR to personal empowerment is becoming willing to take full *responsibility* for our lives. Feigning ignorance regarding the role we played when things don't work out only results in another opportunity to repeat the lesson at hand. How else will we learn unless we objectively observe the actions that contributed to our own suffering? We not only owe it to ourselves to unveil this deeper truth, we owe it to our children to model acceptance of our own imperfections. When we stop wasting energy on blaming and making excuses, we unlock the power of responsibility—our ability to respond to circumstances in a mindful and inspired manner. As author and relationships expert Katherine Woodward Thomas wrote, "Until you take full ownership of all the ways you covertly colluded to create all the dynamics of the relationship, you can't access your own power to create a different experience and break those old patterns of love. You need to look at how you can show up differently in the future so you can trust yourself to never, ever do this again."

In 2012, *Seventeen* magazine and the National Campaign to Prevent Teen and Unplanned Pregnancy cosponsored a study entitled *Girl Talk: What High School Senior Girls Have to Say About Sex, Love, and Relationships*. In this study, high school seniors girls weighed in about lessons learned so far regarding relationships:

	Percent Agreeing
Don't do something that makes you uncomfortable just to please a guy.	82
Don't stress about falling in love; it will happen someday.	78
It is better to break up than stay in a relationship that's bad for you.	78
Don't worry so much about trying to impress boys.	78

No doubt the girls surveyed learned these lessons the hard way—and how wonderful if their wisdom finds its way to those who are encountering these challenges for the first time. Maria, whose story about becoming pregnant with twins when she was just 16, shares the following reflection to pass on a message of wisdom to younger teens:

> ### Reflection by Maria, Age 17
> *My message to teen girls is simple: Don't give up who you are just to be liked. All my friends were older than me, and there were lots of parties. I wanted to be like my friends, especially Bella, who I thought had it all. Now I realize I was really wrong to want to be like someone who I am not.*
>
> *To mothers of teen girls, I'd like to tell them to listen to your kids. Find out what is going on in their lives. Even if you are busy and have to work, try to have some time for your kids. At least make an effort to have a good relationship so they know you care about them.*

As parents, we want our kids' journey toward maturity to be as pure as possible—with as few detours as possible—so their sexual development unfolds innocently and organically. We want the channels of communication between us to remain open, so if and when they find themselves straddling passion and heartbreak, like the diarists who shared their stories here, we can remind them that more than any other type of other relationship, romantic relationships place us on the fast track to learning some of life's most important lessons. These relationships take bravery, and once we become skilled in the art of self-acceptance, they return love.

Living Life Unlocked

I commit to listening to myself and honoring *all* my feelings as I navigate the turbulent waters of romantic love. When an encounter with another causes me emotional pain, I remind myself that the power of self-acceptance lies not in the hands of another, but within the strength of my own heart.

When I am exploring my personal boundaries in relation to someone I love, I commit to check in with my heart and notice if I am feeling open or constricted; willing or hesitant. I will remember that anytime I am not at peace, I have, to some degree, formed an alliance with the FEARSELF. At these moments, I deliberately choose peace. Peace over seeking validation from another. Peace over my need for approval. Peace over my desire to be right. Peace over sacrificing what I know to be healthy personal boundaries in my romantic relationship. I remember my ultimate goal—in this and in every relationship—is peace.

Anytime I find myself behaving in ways that do not reflect the authentic expression of my SOULSELF, I breathe in the knowledge that, regardless of how far off course my CHOICES have led me, I have within me both the power and the responsibility to make a different CHOICE. Every step I take in the direction of my SOULSELF lifts the veil of FEAR and returns me to the power of true love.

Chapter 4

Teens and Parents—
Gateways to Accessing the
Inner Adolescent and Inner Mentor

If there is light in the soul,
there will be beauty in the person.
If there is beauty in the person,
there will be harmony in the home.
If there is harmony in the home,
there will be order in the nation.
If there is order in the nation,
there will be peace in the world.
—Chinese Proverb

Anne Frank, Age 15

No one understands me … Everyone thinks I'm showing off when I talk, ridiculous when I'm silent, insolent when I answer, cunning when I have a good idea, lazy when I'm tired, selfish when I eat one bite more than I should, stupid, cowardly, calculating, etc., etc. All day long I hear nothing but what an exasperating child I am, and although I laugh it off and pretend not to mind, I do mind. I wish I could ask God to give me another personality, one that doesn't antagonize everyone.

Linda, Age 19

Sometimes I feel like I don't know you Mama, and I know you don't know me. Sometimes I feel like we've never had a chance to meet. Who are you really? It hurts so much to admit the feelings of rejection and un-love.

Erica, Age 15

Seems like all Mom and Dad do is fight. I can't stand to be around them when they are together. And they wonder why I don't bring friends around more often. Duh.

Janet, Age 17

Julie's family gets in the same room and talks to each other. It's great.

Jessica, Age 18

It's complicated. Really complicated. I never thought growing from childhood to adulthood would be so complex. Lately I've been thinking far too much and I don't know what's wrong with me. All that my dad says is that I have issues. My mom doesn't even know much about what's going on with me. It's like I'm on this seesaw of emotions. I go up, and then I go down, up and down. It's as if the middle point of the seesaw is a giant monster controlling my thoughts and feelings. All right, I know I'm sounding a bit loony but I have to do something about the way I'm feeling. I can't help but think that my problems will never end. I need some freedom. Some spiritual liberation. I feel so trapped on the seesaw. I'm so mad I can't even cry.

Robin, Age 17

Went downstairs and Mom started going off about what a jerk Dad is by calling him a know-it-all. She told me she doesn't like Dad; she loves him like a friend or brother. But not sexually. It was weird when she said she loved him because she always dogs on him. She's still complaining about his drinking habits. I'm always hearing about my father the jerk or my brother, the secretive, nasty attitude boy. I just wonder what my mother says about me while I'm not here. Deep down inside, this saddens me more than anything.

Remember the last time you watched a baby who was just learning to walk? No doubt, Mom was perched somewhere close by, encouraging the unbalanced cutie pie to put one foot in front of the other and take those important first steps—giant leaps in the development of a human being. Even when her baby falls repeatedly in her attempts to move forward, Mom remains steadfast and faithful; the light in her eyes, encouraging words and outstretched arms all committed to ensuring her child's safe landing.

Natalie Fry

As pages turn in the calendar of this baby's life, more milestone events and accomplishments are celebrated, some more so than others. However, as children reach the age of puberty and the wobbling colts we once guided so easily start to behave more like wild mustangs, most parents will confess to feeling a sudden loss of direction. Parents are used to being in control and taking charge of their children who depend on them, but teenagers, whose search for self-identity and demand for independence is in full swing, are not so cool with having others in charge anymore. No longer children and not yet adults, teens are in a period of radical growth accompanied by driving curiosity and trial-and-error exploration.

The road toward individuality is a winding one that inevitably includes some turns in the wrong direction. But what else is new? As adults, we remember all too well the experiences we went through at that age, and yet we think that somehow we can prevent our daughters from making the same mistakes. For the most part, our efforts are in vain—especially if instead of supporting our girls in following their internal GPS we simply try to apply the brakes. Teen girls are testing their limits, just as they did when they were toddlers. The difference now is that in addition to learning to navigate new terrain, they must also contend with hormonal fluctuations, conflicting emotions, mood swings and peer pressure—all of which cloud their thinking. Experimenting in more adult settings with less adult supervision, the consequences of their actions can be far more serious.

It is one of nature's little ironies that we ensure the safety of our teens by keeping open lines of communication at the exact same time they are telling us to get lost. Unlike babies learning to walk, few teenage girls relish the sight of Mom's outstretched arms waiting to catch them if they fall. Although they still need her—in some ways, more than ever—the knowledge she is hovering like a helicopter nearby can send girls into a fit of rage. Mother's very presence seems to threaten the freedom they are fighting so hard to achieve. Of course, the girls are not the only ones in conflict.

As mothers, we are torn between the desire to encourage our girls' independence and our biological drive to keep them safe. So what happens when our daughters' need for autonomy and our mothering instinct to protect them come together under the same roof? Threads of this question emerge as a universal theme echoed in virtually every one of the volumes of diaries I have reviewed: the teen years are a time when our girls feel the least understood—and often, the most unloved—by their parents. By necessity, adolescence changes the relationship between mother and daughter. The girls whose diary entries you'll read in this chapter reflect the variety of ways they respond to this change. Some feel mothered to the point of being smothered, while others feel rejected or feel they don't know their mothers at all. Most feel their mothers don't know them.

In the face of our daughters' demand for greater freedom, we parents may find ourselves wavering between two extremes, each of which takes a toll: If we become hyper-vigilant or hyper-critical, we sacrifice precious intimacy in favor of monitoring or correcting their every move. If we view steps toward independence as a sign that we are no longer needed, we may make the mistake of withdrawing emotionally or physically. It is important to bear in mind that our goal is balance; to sense when a situation requires attention and when our daughters are best served by working things out on their own. This type of "give and take" demonstrates mutual respect—vital to the health of all relationships.

When our children sense our respect for their ability to lead the way, this empowers them beyond measure.
—Shefali Tsabary

Cultivating Mutual Respect

Parents often ask why I talk about the importance of respecting their teens, when it's the teens who need to be respecting them. The short answer is that gaining respect *from* your teens is found in demonstrating respect *for* them. As a parent, our respect for our teenagers is a *causal*, not a *casual* reflection of their respect for us. To teens reading this, take heart; mutual respect is a two-way street. The shortcut to getting the respect you desire is to earn it by paying due respect to your parents.

Below, Carol tells her diary how she really feels about her parents' lack of respect and regard for her, and their lack of involvement in her life.

Re·spect /ri'spekt/ to hold in high esteem; to honor the highest in each being; to be considerate.

> **Carol, Age 16**
> **December 22.** *We leave in the morning for Grandma's for the holiday. I am dreading the ride across the state because Dad's going to be smoking all the way and we're probably going to hear Conway Twitty sing Cowboy Joe songs the whole way and I'm going to have such a headache.*
> **December 23.** *We had to listen to terrible music on the radio— none of mine, and Dad's smoke gave me an awful headache. When I complained about the cigarette smoke, I was told I couldn't smell it in the back seat of the car. Yeah, right.*
> **January 6.** *Mom and Dad are going out of town this weekend. Mom kept asking me if I mind staying alone when they go out of town. I like it better than watching them stare at the TV all the time or having them argue and smoke cigarettes until the place is cloudy and my clothes stink. But it is a little embarrassing to admit to my*

friends that I'm all alone. Even though they act jealous and tell me I'm lucky that my parents trust me, I don't think any kid wants to be left alone.

Carol was dealing not only with a lack of respect from her parents, but a case of potential neglect. They smoked with her in the car, which is not just disrespectful but also physically harmful. They were autocratic in terms of not allowing Carol to participate in the selection of music for the trip. Back home, they flip-flopped from being domineering to becoming permissive to the degree of neglecting her by leaving her at home without any supervision.

My research on this topic led me to *Teens Today*, a study released by Students Against Destructive Decisions, which revealed a correlation between parental involvement and the incidence of high-risk behaviors in teens. The findings came as no surprise: high school students whose parents pay the least attention to significant periods of transition or rites of passage—such as puberty, changes at school and milestone birthdays—are five times more likely to engage in high-risk behaviors, and twice as likely to report daily stress and depression or boredom.

The U.S. Surgeon General estimates that living with a smoker increases a nonsmoker's chances of developing lung cancer by 20 to 30 percent.

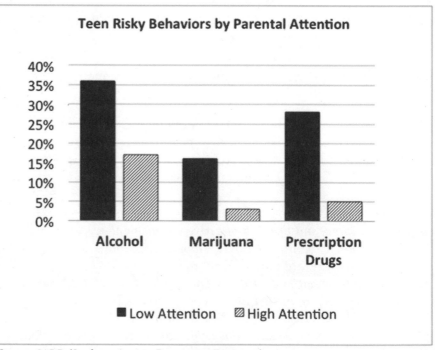

Source: SADD (Students Against Destructive Decisions)

As much as our girls may portray an image of independence, and to whatever lengths they may go to push us away, the truth is, they need to know that we are present and available—like an invisible safety net. If as grown women we are still licking unhealed wounds from our teenage experiences or if we are still too preoccupied in our own dramas, then our girls pay the price right along with us. Yet this is not a time to add a layer of guilt to those theatrics. It's an opportunity to learn to rise above them; to call upon our own inner parent—the wise heroine of the SOULSELF—to offer guidance and be the adult. Regardless of how much damage, neglect or criticism has been done to our relationship with our children, it's never too late to forgive ourselves or those who have hurt us so we can move forward knowing the present moment is the only time over which we have any control.

Mama Drama

Melinda's parents divorced when she was 10, and both quickly remarried. In the two years between eighth and tenth grade, her primary home shifted between each parent three times. As a sophomore, coming home with a crisp new driver's license in hand should have been a milestone to be celebrated. Instead, the tangled web of drama woven by her mother and step-dad overshadowed her accomplishment and her enthusiasm.

> ### Melinda, Age 16
> **March 13.** I overheard mom and step-dad, Todd, arguing about whether to get car insurance for me now that I'm driving. Todd said, "I'm worried about my money if she gets in an accident." Mom said, "I'm more worried about my daughter being okay." Then he said, "We'll just have another daughter." RIGHT.
> **March 15th.** Mom and I came home and Todd was plowed. They got in a big fight about him driving drunk—Mom lost.
> **May 26th.** Todd's gone again. He got drunk last night and picked a fight with Jacob. So my dear brother, Jacob, decided to go live with Dad. He is there for one month as a trial period. I am terrified he won't come home. We are so close now. I find myself calling him just to say goodnight, and driving by to catch him skateboarding. It seems as if everyone is leaving me.

When as mothers we allow ourselves to be treated with any form of

A child's capacity to self-love is directly related to it's parent's level of emotional integration.
—Shefali Tsabary

disrespect, we teach our daughters a dangerous lesson that this is how they can expect to be treated as well. Even when children are not in the room, and even if they never overhear a conversation like Melinda did, the energy of contempt is potent. It fills homes with a heaviness that cannot be hidden by a facade of happy pretenses. We may think we're glossing over our hostility, but it doesn't go undetected by our girls. Conflict between parents—particularly if kids are played like pawns, forced to pick sides, or cast in the role of referee—rocks the core of the safe haven that a home is supposed to be. In the midst of stormy family dynamics, it is no wonder Melinda felt lost at sea. Yet, as this next series of entries reveals, rigid, high-functioning families can generate just as much negative turbulence.

A prestigious academician, Colleen's father had high hopes for his daughter and was quick to speak out whenever he perceived that she was out of line. In her teen years, Colleen became passionate about all things fantasy and science fiction—particularly the TV series *Star Trek*—much to the displeasure of her parents, whom Colleen described as being "relentless perfectionists." The following entries are excerpted from the travel journal Colleen kept while she and her family lived in what she felt was a galaxy far away—Oxford in the mid 1970s during her father's sabbatical.

Colleen, Age 13

February 8. *Today Paul and I made a fort out of blankets, covers, chairs, suitcases, and a mini-table. It was shaped in a square, all roofed in, with an open patio in the middle. We used it a good lot until Dad came home and saw it as a mess. Lights out at 11:33 1/2.*

February 11. *The things I require from home for mental survival are letters and Star Trek. It's so hard without Star Trek. Tonight I cried myself to sleep. It's not the kind of thing I can confide to anyone. Dad teases me continually about it. Paul stabs, teases and insults me. Mom is sick of what she thinks is a fantasy carried too far. The kids at school think it's silly, and laugh at it. The only person I really could ever mention my passion for Star Trek was Vivian, back home. She didn't make fun of me, tease me or stab me about it. This journal is the only place I can let it all out. I hope Star Trek is still on TV when I go back to the U.S. If not, I'll crumble. Lately, things that I really enjoy make me so sad. Maybe it's because I'm getting to be a teenager. I just have to drop it, though, because Mom can't be talked to about such subjects because she has no patience and is sick of them; Dad's impossible, and Paul's just a kid. If Hotsy were* *here, I'd talk to him. Even though he is a cat. I feel lonely in this apartment. Lights out at 10:22 1/3.*

Although Colleen's parents never blatantly steered her away from her dreams, they didn't encourage them either. Fortunately, Colleen's passion for science endured, and turned out to have very practical applications. Gleaning the best of her father's positive attributes and seeking therapy to overcome his negative ones, she now enjoys a rewarding career as an author of academic computer science books.

Like Colleen's dad, Linda's mom seemed to know just who and what she wanted her daughter to be—to the extent she paid little attention to who Linda actually was or what she wanted.

Drawing from Linda's diary. Age 16

Linda, Age 16

October 21. *Here's the message I get from my mom. "Smile, smile, smile. Don't frown. If you frown, I'll have to notice you and stop what I'm doing and ask you what's wrong. And if you tell me, I might have to comfort you, or think about your pain, or extend myself to you. I don't have time for frowns. I am too busy. So, smile, smile, smile and eat your cookies. And we will go on as we always do, pretending all is well with our world."*

October 22. *I feel closed in and tight and rigid. My hair is swiftly pulled back and my blouse buttoned up to my neck, choking me with your purity and modesty and morals. I hate being here, smiling into your self-*

You taught me to be nice, so nice that now I am so full of niceness, I have no sense of right and wrong, no outrage, no passion.
—Garrison Keillor

made mirror. I would run away in a minute if I could think of any place to go. But I am afraid to hurt anybody's feelings. I am afraid to cause trouble and cry out loud, I NEED HELP TOO. Because no one will listen to my words and their meaning. I want to be able to breathe deeply again and feel whole within myself, and not so fragmented.

Linda's story reminds me of Neil, the lead character in the 1989 film *Dead Poet's Society*, whose passion for acting was met with stern disapproval by his father, who wanted his son to be a doctor. In the movie, Neil decides he would rather end his life than conform to his father's expectations of what he should do with it. While this is just a fictional example, it has serious implications in real life. Something special indeed dies inside our children when we insist on molding them to fit an image we have created instead of allowing them to discover their own rhythm and pursue their own unique desires. Imposing our will upon our daughters may ensure they survive, but the real question is, will they thrive? That we as a society have learned to content ourselves with mediocrity makes it clear why there are so many people walking the earth, in the words of Thoreau, "living lives of quiet desperation." Fortunately, through grace and action, Linda escaped this fate, and her life today is representative of the movie's deeper message—*Carpe diem:* seize the day. Looking back on her diary entries three decades later, Linda offers the following reflection:

Linda's Reflection, 30 years later

As a teenager, I felt I was not a real person with my own thoughts. I was just someone who was supposed to do what my mother told me to do, look the way she wanted me to look, and feel nothing. In my family I was never ever allowed to "need" anything. They all looked to me to fill a need in them. After my first year of college, I entered a dark period. I had a lot of pent up anger and pain because I had been shut down so much that I didn't know how to express myself—or even that I could. I told my best friend that this was no way to live and I'd give it a year, and if I couldn't get or be helped, then I was going to figure out a way to end my life. She was upset and wanted to counsel me—she was studying to be a nurse. I told her I needed someone who didn't know me and had at least a degree in psychology and was older than me. I took action and began therapy. They took me seriously and insisted on seeing me every day the first week or so. With that much attention focused on me, I began to turn my life around. As a young adult, I continued to heal and began to love and accept and forgive myself. I immersed myself in self-help books, counseling, and prayer therapy that taught me to focus within and receive guidance. Being grateful, I learned, is the starting point for creating change.

 Today, I'm comfortable in my own skin, and continue to listen to my heart and follow my own path. My wish is that between parents, mentors and teachers, all bases would be covered so our kids would know they are loved and they have a unique gift to share with the world that no one else can—themselves.

Parents' expectations of who their children "should" be can overshadow and interrupt the process of children's discovering for themselves who they are. Day-to-day logistics and petty disagreements, if we permit them, can consume so much of our attention we lose sight of the big picture. Remembering the old adage that our job as parents is to work our way out of a job helps us keep things in the proper perspective or, as author Stephen Covey puts it, "begin with the end in mind."

Keep the End in Mind—and Mind the Path

Allison, Age 17
I told my dad about that minor car accident I got into at the parking lot at Starbucks a few weeks ago. He got so upset. I didn't dare tell him about all the other things I'm worried about … this whole thing with my insurance and my teeth and my new antibiotics and how I haven't been keeping up with my thyroid medication. I wish I could, but you can't tell your parents everything anyway. No one really does, that I know.

Sherry G., Age 16
Here I am somewhere between old and young, and those I hold dear are nowhere to be found in my worst moments of fear. I feel lost to nothingness in the winds of change that make no sense. Lost between old and young. At dinner, I got drilled about holding my silverware wrong.

Cara, Age 17
My car quit and Dad had to push it—with me steering—to our house. He was so mad at me. He thinks I'm a bad driver because the battery died. Mom just stared at the TV when we came in. I'd

To be yourself in a world that is constantly trying to make you something else is the greatest accomplishment.
—Ralph Waldo Emerson

Always be a first rate version of yourself and not a second rate version of someone else.
—Judy Garland

Shame, blame, disrespect, betrayal, and the withholding of affection damage the roots from which love grows.
—Brené Brown

want to know what my kids had done during the day. We got our report cards and I got four A's and one B. Could be better but I was satisfied. All Dad cared about was that his day was disrupted by the dead battery.

ACKNOWLEDGE
FROM A
FOUNDATION OF
INTENTION
REALIZED AND
MANIFESTED

A dead battery is a lot easier to recharge than the spirit of a girl who feels dejected by the lack of her parents' love and attention. Cara has the impression her parents are more interested in TV than they are in her, while Allison's dad may have missed a crucial opportunity to forge a deeper connection with his daughter and respond to potentially serious worries regarding her health. These entries make a troubling point. Too often, parents take for granted that kids know how much we love them, and lose sight of how important it is to frequently express and AFFIRM that love. How tragic it is when more time is spent correcting table manners or coordinating carpools than guiding, reassuring and respecting them as they make the transformation from little girls to fearless young women. In the end, girls hear what's *not* right about them, and love is not received, despite our good intentions.

To parent with the end in mind is to think beyond managing daily tasks; to seize every opportunity to equip our daughters with a sense of resourcefulness described by Arianna Huffington in her book *On Becoming Fearless*: "When there are dead ends there are also U-turns, and if we don't panic, bridges can appear—we just need to trust that there is a way. And there is *always* a way. That knowledge is a gift of fearlessness we can model for kids." Inevitably, some of the roads a young girl takes will lead to dead ends, but if she is confident within herself, she will find the resources to make a U-turn—or maybe even to build a bridge. With practice and experience, she learns to respond creatively, no matter which way the road turns. As adults, we can help teens develop this degree of inner confidence by focusing more on encouraging their efforts than on rewarding their achievements.

Encouragement vs. Praise

There is a subtle yet powerful difference between encouragement and praise. In our eagerness to enhance confidence, we may lavish our kids with praise; the idea being that praise builds self-esteem. At first glance, a phrase such as "You were the best piano player at the recital" may seem a generous form of recognition. In its purest form, praise is a way to acknowledge a specific job well done. However, praise can lead to undue pressure if our kids misconstrue it to believe that only by performing well—or worse, that they must perform better than others—can they earn our approval. The message we unwittingly send to our children is that they are acceptable only when behaving in a certain way. Does this mean we should abandon all compliments and disregard signs of progress? Absolutely not. Just be mindful to avoid conveying the message that the praised behavior must be present for our teenager to feel loved and accepted. How do we do this?

Well-timed words of encouragement that acknowledge our daughters' efforts—*regardless* of the outcome—are carried well into womanhood as a valuable life skill that helps them soar. Encouragement may be offered by saying, "your commitment and passion for the piano came through so clearly at the recital today." The key difference is encouragement focuses on the *effort*, the level of dedication we bring to any endeavor, which is something that is within our control. Praise places the focus on the ultimate *outcome* of our effort, which is often beyond the realm of our control. Self-esteem is fostered by the knowledge we did our very best; it is not contingent on being the very best. As parents, we must be ever mindful of how easily our voices are internalized by our children. Girls who are *encouraged* by parents learn to be self-accepting and hopeful; girls who are routinely criticized grow into adults who lack confidence.

encourage: en·cour·age [en-ker-ij] to support or inspires confidence; origin: denoting the heart as the seat of feelings

Criticism and Judgment

Anne Frank, Age 15
June 13, 1944. *Dearest Kitty, ... What's so difficult about my personality is that I scold and curse myself much more than anyone else does; if Mother adds her advice, the pile of sermons becomes so thick that I despair of ever getting through them. Then I talk back and start contradicting everyone until the old familiar Anne inevitably crops up again: "No one understands me!" This phrase is part of me, and as unlikely as it may seem, there's a kernel of truth in it. Sometimes I'm so deeply buried under self-reproaches that I long for a word of comfort to help me dig myself out again. If only I had someone who took my feelings seriously. Alas, I haven't yet found that person, so the search must continue.*

January 12, 1944 (recalling her schooldays). Dearest Kitty, every morning when I heard footsteps on the stairs, I hoped it would be mother coming to say good morning. I'd greet her warmly, because I honestly did look forward to her affectionate glance. But then she would snap at me for having made some comment or other and I go off to school feeling completely discouraged. On the way home I'd make excuses for her, telling myself that she had so many worries. I'd arrive home in high spirits, chatting nineteen to the dozen until the events of the morning would repeat themselves and I'd leave the room with my school bag in my hand and a pensive look on my face. Sometimes I decided to stay angry, but then I always had so much to talk about after school that I forgot my resolution, and want Mother to stop whatever she was doing and lend a willing ear. Then the time would come once more when I no longer listened for the steps on the stairs and felt lonely and cried into my pillow every night.

Who among us has not fallen victim to the inner critic whose scolding and cursing voice we hear far more clearly than those of anyone in our midst? This is the expression of the FEARSELF trying to engage us in its snare of self-judgment and shame, taunting us with questions that elicit our deepest insecurities: "Do I matter? ... Am I good enough? ... Am I lovable?" This voice begins lecturing at a young age and, if left unchecked, may continue through adulthood. As Anne Frank's entries suggest, an effective way to combat this interrogation is to first learn to identify its influence, and then offer ourselves *words of comfort* to dig out of self-induced desperation. The physical act of getting our feelings out of our bodies and down on paper helps by making them tangible and therefore more manageable.

In his book *Mindsight*, author Daniel J. Siegel, M.D., explained, "Journal writing activates the narrator function of our minds. Studies show that simply writing down our account of challenging experiences can lower our physiological reactivity and increase our sense of well-being—even if we never show what we've written to anyone else." Monique turned to her diary to address her feelings of being judged, and she had the strength to acknowledge herself for her efforts.

Monique, Age 18

I'm doing the best I can and I wish people would just appreciate that. I know my dad has high hopes for me and only wants what's best. But I feel as though I'm being chastised all the time. If my dad can't see how hard I'm trying, I just wish he would leave me alone. Here I am, a freshman in college, living at home, working hard and trying to get good grades this semester. I'm trying to keep my checking account balance high, I'm babysitting, I'm doing home-work (most of the time) ... I do my best.

Janet, Age 17

September 8. *We practiced with sparklers for our pom-pom per-formance this coming Friday. I'm excited about it. Came home and mom and dad were arguing. When they aren't fighting, they're talking about something I'm not interested in, and if I ask a ques-tion, they don't hear it. Oh well, if they heard me, they would just criticize whatever I say. I have a really bad headache.*

September 12. *We performed tonight during half-time at the foot-ball game. I was really nervous right before we performed. Mom and Dad didn't like it at all, I could tell. They didn't say anything about the routine or my performance afterward. Well, I was pretty bad, I guess. My sparklers were the first to go out. But it was fun, and we got a lot of positive feedback from others.*

Like Monique, in high school I never felt that my dad noticed the good in me. Every time I heard him put others down, even though he wasn't talking about me, I was convinced he also criticized me when I wasn't around. I felt I could never live up to his standards. My sparklers' going out during the drill team performance was symbolic of the little spark of my spirit extinguished with each judgment I received from my parents. Granted, I was a sensitive child, but even kids with "thick skin" are not immune. Children are profoundly vulnerable to criticism directed at them by their parents. Dr. John Gottman, the nation's leading relationship researcher, conducted studies and concluded in his "magic relationship formula" that healthy relationships maintain a 5:1 ratio—namely five pos-itive interactions, (such as listening with kindness and empathy) to every negative one, (such as lack of interest or expressing anger). "Negative actions have a lot more ability to inflict pain and damage than positive things have to heal and bring you closer," he noted. While Gottman's studies focused on couples, my meta-research affirms this ratio is relevant in any relationship. This is not surprising given the fact we have evolved based on our ability to react to that which threatens us. As author Rick Hanson put it, the brain is like Velcro for the bad, but Teflon for the good. When wounded or emotionally unhealed parents take their frustrations

*Take in the good, a dozen seconds at a time.
—Rick Hanson*

out on their children in the form of physical, verbal and emotional abuse or neglect, the effects can be downright tragic.

If you are a teenager living under the shadow of your parents' negativity, reflect on the Freeing Your BEING Compass to sharpen your AWARENESS of the ever-present CHOICE to be your own best friend or your own worst enemy, and remember which direction leads you back to your SOULSELF— to peace. A lack of support, the presence of hostility or even abuse from others does not mean that you are not deserving of love. *True* friends, *mature* adults and *nurturing* family members see mistakes as lessons being learned. They can see through your pain and respond from a higher place that prevents the igniting of hostilities. Experiment with the tools provided throughout this book, and be watchful of your own inner critic. Today, we know it is within the power of the brain to build new neural structures and reverse the evolutionary tendency to attach to fear-based thoughts. As you see from the diarists, you are not alone in being hard on yourself. Even as the outside world may use outdated standards to measure true accomplishment, you can be the change you want to see by acknowledging yourself for doing your best. And remember, your parents are people too, with an inner critic in their heads—and they also thrive on encouragement.

Abuse

I am deeply saddened by the number of diary entries I've received from women who spoke not only of growing up in households where they felt criticized and discouraged, but also of environments where overt abuse took place within the family. More so than contributors on any other subject matter, the diarists who were victims of abuse—whether they suffered the direct blow or watched it happen to someone they loved—struggled over whether to share their stories or keep them locked away. Some didn't want to relive past pain; others were conflicted about turning over information about their own parents, even if their names were changed.

Let me be clear that children and teens who experience rejection or betrayal in their environment are not to blame for the circumstances in which they suffer. As minors, they are never at fault for neglect or abuse inflicted upon them by their parents or anyone else. We do not act differently until we know differently. We cannot make new CHOICES until we

Cells that fire together, wire together.
—Adapted from Donald Hebb

Ditch your inner critic and wake up your inner superstar.
—Amy Ahlers

are aware there are new CHOICES to make.

After two years of internal struggle over whether they should make public the pages of their diaries, Hallie and Annie bravely submitted these entries, revealing what really went on behind the white picket fences surrounding their teenage homes.

Hallie, Age 14

Dear Diary, he's only 4. Why does he have to get beaten for just being a kid? Daddy came in and saw the pillow foam all over the floor. Bobby didn't do it, we all did. But us girls, we never get it as bad as Bobby. Even when he came back and saw that we'd cleaned it up, he still had that look in his eyes, that glassy, distant look that scares me to death, especially when he's drinking. Just as the belt came down across his back, I knew Bobby's spirit took shelter in another place and time, at least I hope it did.

Annie, Age 16

I awaken with tears in my eyes to the dull sounds of screaming and hitting that pulls the family apart. I have the urge to run into some dark little corner of my mind and retire there. Leave my body a lifeless shell.

Even after reading these entries and a dozen more like them, I still clung to an idealistic hope that Hallie and Annie represented a shrinking minority, and that child abuse was on the decline. But then I went on a family trip to Universal Studios in Florida, and there in the world of fantasy, I was awakened to a disturbing reality: not only are kids still being abused, they are maltreated in plain sight for all the world to see.

On this brisk Thanksgiving Day, as my daughter and I were waiting in line to select a magic wand at Ollivander's Wand Shop in the Wizarding World of Harry Potter, I saw a mother in front of us squeeze and twist her kindergarten-age son's neck to the point his face turned reddish blue as he gasped for breath. He had simply stepped out of the perfect single-file line in which she had ordered him to remain, and now her hand marks left a bright red imprint where each finger had squeezed. I watched him breathe as hard as he could to fight back tears that I'm sure would get him in more trouble if they were to escape down his cheeks. As I began to talk to the mother about it, she grabbed her son, yelled at me to mind my own business and fled into the crowd. When I came home, I did some research on the frequency and impact of both abuse and physical or corporal punishment, and the statistics I uncovered were alarming. In the United States, we lose five children every day—the worst record in the industrialized world—to abuse-related deaths.

In one year, 3.4 million reports of child abuse are made, involving 6.2 million children, some 750,000 of whom are confirmed as indeed having been abused. Sadly, the biological mothers of these children made up the largest percentage of all perpetrators. While the connection between child abuse and adult mental disorders has been clear for years, studies like the one by Tracie Afifi, PhD reveal an increased risk for mental illness among participants who sometimes or very often experienced acts of physical punishment in general, including spanking, pushing, grabbing, shoving, slapping and hitting children.

In an article entitled "Hitting Your Kids Increases Their Risk of Mental Illness," *TIME: Health and Family* writer Bonnie Rochman summarized the findings as follows:

> *Across the board, people who'd experienced these forms of physical punishment were more likely to experience nearly every type of mental illness examined. Their risk of mood disorders, including depression and mania, was 1.5 times greater than people who hadn't been slapped or grabbed. The risk of depression alone was 1.4 times greater, which was the same rate for anxiety. People who'd been physically punished were 1.6 times more likely to abuse alcohol, and 1.5 times more likely to abuse drugs.*

Why do those of us who don't inflict physical punishment on our kids need to be reading this? Is it "none of our business," as the mother in Florida told me? Physical discipline and abuse is everybody's business for a number of moral and ethical reasons; primarily, because it hurts children. In addition, kids who experience abuse and neglect are more likely to be arrested, both as juveniles and as adults, and are more likely to commit violent crimes. In an era when it's commonplace to hear news of mass murderers raging through schools and malls, leaving shoppers, movie goers and innocent first graders dead, it seems clear the time has come for the age-old passage, "Spare the rod, spoil the child," to yield to wisdom and common sense. It is up to us to hold the light and change the laws for those still living in the shadows of dangerous parenting patterns. One respectful action at a time, one signature at a time, one voice at a time, one

There can be no keener revelation of a society's soul than the way in which it treats its children.
—Nelson Mandela

Physical punishment should not be used on children at any age under any circumstances.
—Tracie Afifi, PhD

In 37 countries around the world, children are protected by law from corporal/physical punishment of children by parents. The U.S. is not one of them.

smart-phone snapshot or video at a time to document live public child abuse, we can heed our social responsibility and stop the growth of violence at its very root—in the home, where peace always begins. I'm talking about real peace, not the appearance of peace manufactured in the homes of mothers who sacrifice their own needs, their own authentic desires, or their own responsibilities to themselves for the sake of their families … and suffer in silence as a result.

"It's a Mom Thing"

Although they are often masked as "supermoms," women who do everything for others and nothing for themselves commit a different form of violence—violence against the self. As noble as it may appear, it's not a healthy model to teach our girls that they are any *more* or *less* important than anyone else—even their mothers. Everyone deserves equal rights. A common theme that emerges in virtually every workshop I facilitate with mothers is one of over-compromising; of sacrificing self-care in the name of caring for others. For some women, this pattern of behavior is so pervasive they have come to accept it as the norm. When questioned about the message their self-sacrifice conveys, most answer with some version of this all-too-common reply: "It's a Mom thing," they say with a smile.

Let me clarify: self-sacrifice is *not* a Mom thing. Whenever there exists a feeling of loss or depletion; or of abandoning our own needs or values for the sake of pleasing another, it's a FEARSELF thing. This is not to say you won't stay up all night to care for your sick child because you need sleep. Caring for a sick child is a heart-expanding, altruistic experience. But if your family goes out on an adventure in which you'd like to take part, but you stay home instead to do their dirty laundry and feel resentment about it later, know that you are probably "giving" from a state of lack that further diminishes your self-worth.

To wear with pride a badge of self-denial by declaring that martyrdom "is a Mom thing," is to miss the point of motherhood. The real "Mom thing" is to teach our daughters how to care for themselves, in body and in soul, by *modeling* that self-care. To truly empower our daughters, we must change the ways we've diminished our own value—whether we've tolerated condescending backtalk or name calling, remained a silent victim of a drunken partner, or turned the other cheek when suspecting a cheating

See if you can give yourself gifts that may be true blessings, such as self-acceptance, or some time each day with no purpose. Practice feeling deserving enough to accept these gifts without obligation—to simply receive from yourself, and from the universe.
—Jon Kabat-Zinn

spouse. Pretending to live a happy dream is not a beneficial standard to uphold for our teen girls. In whatever ways we've abandoned ourselves, the journey to reclaim our wholeness begins one courageous step at a time. When we are willing to assert from the proverbial mountaintop, "Not in my house!" to anyone who attempts to discredit our worth, we break the emotional chains that keep us bound in unhealthy relationship patterns. When we empower ourselves, we empower our daughters, who empower their friends, and eventually their own daughters and sons. Truth is contagious. Confident mothers and empowered daughters are bound to occasionally have their own versions of what is true for them. Being able to work through disagreements in a supportive and bonding way is a powerful way for each to become more in touch with the SOULSELF.

Your greatest contribution to helping other people live their destiny is for you to live your own.
—Alan Cohen

Pressing "Pause": Respond vs. React

The fight-or-flight mechanism, which triggers within us the impulse to criticize or even attack, evolved over millions of years as a means of alerting us to impending danger. In our hunter-gatherer days, the impulse to react as quickly as possible was vital to our survival. And even though we no longer have to defend against the daily threat of being mauled by a hungry tiger, disagreements and power struggles between parents and teens can evoke similar sensations.

responsibility: "response-ability," the ability to respond with wisdom instead of react with thoughtlessness

Parents have the responsibility to demonstrate what it means to take the high road during heated discussions. Training the mind to respond instead of react is key. By decoding the two words respond and react, I hope to clarify the range of CHOICES available in each and every dialogue.

When aligned with the SOULSELF as we interact with others, we naturally increase our capacity to RESPOND—to:

RESPOND ...   REFRAIN AND ENTER A SILENT PAUSE IN ORDER TO NURTURE A DECISION

Pausing, even briefly, opens the possibility of staying calm and provides an opportunity to view the situation through the eyes of our wiser, more centered self that sees beneath the turbulent waves of emotion on the surface, to the deeper need being communicated.

When we are motivated by the lower self—the FEARSELF, we are quick to REACT—to:

REACT ...   RACE TO EXERT ANY CONCLUSIONS TRIGGERED

Refrain &

Enter a

Silent

Pause in   **VS.**

Order to

Nurture a

Decision

Race to

Exert

Any

Conclusion

Triggered

Reactions are usually rooted in old programming, unconscious assumptions and repeated habits and patterns whose effectiveness or relevance in the present time we have never stopped long enough to question. Anytime we feel our emotional "buttons" being pressed, we know with certainty that the FEARSELF is at the helm, eliminating our ability to pause and impairing our ability to think clearly. Deep and conscious breathing in moments like these allows us to better manage our emotions and opens the space for their transformation. It may also help to visualize a pause button on a remote control and mentally press that button.

Colleen—our science-loving, Trekkie diarist—launches a perfect opportunity in the following entries to explain how such a transformation might have played out had her father responded instead of reacted, as he obviously did in the stories she shared upon first arriving in England.

Every time you are tempted to react in the same old way, ask if you want to be a prisoner of the past or a pioneer of the future.
—Deepak Chopra

Colleen, Age 13

August 14. Mom and I got caught in the rain and we were sopped. We looked funny. Dad "ha ha'ed" and "I told you so-ed" us. Hit with the reality of being here, I started to freak out. What will school be like? Will I go to a rigid old school, or a new open school? Will I have to dress like a jerk? Will there be *Star Trek?* Friends? Neighbors? A yard? Lots of homework? Books? Stores? I wonder. The wind is howling and blowing and moaning and then howling again. I'm scared.

Anne Frank

January 6, 1944. ... I need my mother to set a good example and be a person I can respect. But in most matters, she is an example of what not to do ... I imagine a mother as a woman who first and foremost possesses a great deal of tact, especially towards her adolescent children—not one like Momsy, who pokes fun at me when I cry.

After already feeling ridiculed for being caught in the rain, Colleen was no doubt hesitant to share her internal storm. What if she had been met with compassion about her miserable experience? Perhaps the stage would have been set to express her fears, which would have been understood by her parents, who would comfort her. Even better, what if her parents had anticipated what a big change this was for a young girl and had asked if she had any questions about the move? This kind of proactive thoughtfulness extended by parents contributes rich reserves to the bank account of emotional bonding and connectedness.

Colleen, Age 13

Important announcement! On this day, I shrunk my braces! I dropped them in boiling water two or three times, hoping to sterilize the germs. OOOps! They shrunk. Dad yelled his head off at me. I cried forever, dripping like a faucet. Mom asked why, and I said I was tired of being pushed around. Dad yelling, Paul whining and griping, Mom either just here in body, or yelling, and me always in the middle getting zapped, unless I'm yelling back. Mom and I discussed it and I went back to bed. Lights out at 11:30 1/4

To this day, there is a part of Colleen that smiles when she thinks about the determination and resourcefulness she summoned to solve the problem of ridding her braces of germs. Having just learned the scientific facts about using boiling water to eradicate bacteria, she was eager to put her new knowledge to good use. What if her parents had paused and gathered their wits enough to recognize the well-meaning intentions behind what she did? What if, instead of lashing out in anger, they acknowledged her for possessing these qualities? Of course there is the issue of money lost, but that's where gentle redirection can be addressed—*after* acknowledging their daughter's willingness to apply her newfound skills. This type of response represents a new way of seeing, and a new way of stepping back and looking at how automated our programmed reactions to our kids are, and how those reactions impact their self-esteem.

Ultimately, every bit of frustration and condemnation is a direct reflection of our proximity to the foggy fringe of the FEARSELF; and each burst of empathy and intuition, to the sacred space of the SOULSELF. Life is a journey of learning to understand and to love, not to control or manipulate. Pressing our internal pause button allows us to connect at a deeper level with what's really going on and address it from a state of calm. By checking in with ourselves and remembering that each moment holds the possibility to engage with kindness and respect, we open the door to authentic, soul-to-soul communication.

Kindness is a language which the deaf can hear and the blind can see.
—Mark Twain

The ABC's of Conversation

Any healthy conversation must follow what I call the **ABC's** of conversation. We must be:

AWARE OF BEING CONSCIOUS

... ABC

When we are aware that we are communicating consciously, we sharpen our ability to choose what we say and how we listen to what others say. Communication is much more than a means to relay information from one person to another, as the word suggests; it is also one of the primary ways we *commune* and connect with another person. The words we choose when engaging our teens in conversation can either evoke defensiveness or promote understanding. The approach we take has a great deal to do with whether we encourage our teens to open up or shut down.

commune: com·mune [v. kuh-myoon] to share one's thoughts or feelings with profound intimacy

In just about every conversation, "I" statements—such as "I feel frustrated/confused/hurt"—are easier for the listener to hear because they convey the idea that we, the speaker, have taken responsibility for and ownership of our emotions. In contrast, "you" statements—such as "you are making me angry"—assign blame to the other person for the way we are feeling. Whenever we feel misunderstood or unheard, it's best to consider the possibility that perhaps *we* may not have expressed ourselves clearly. "Let me rephrase that" is a lot more useful than "You don't understand." Blaming the other person for a breakdown in communication does nothing to repair it. A transformative application of this idea arises when a daughter is having a pre-teen or teen moment in which she communicates with a sassy, negative, disrespectful or back-talk attitude. Take a deep breath, and state the truth: "I feel disrespected and hurt by the way you are talking to me right now. I want to enjoy my time with you, and that's not possible when either of us is being mean to the other. I'm not willing to be treated that way." Even if your daughter doesn't come around that instant, you are planting seeds that can only grow into a higher level of respect in the future. Plus, you have just modeled what it looks like to stay in your own power and refuse to create more distance in your relationship.

The most important key in conflict resolution is remembering that we often have no idea about what someone else is experiencing, even when that someone is our own daughter or our own mother. To better understand one another, we first have to become humble enough to admit we don't understand. This means we have to listen. True listening is different from the simple act of hearing the words spoken by another. An encouraging note about empathetic listening is that it is a discipline that becomes stronger and more effective with practice.

Listen is an auspicious anagram of the word silent.

I have decoded the word *listen* to better understand its power. When we truly LISTEN, we:

LISTEN ...   LET IN SILENCE, TOTAL EMPATHY AND NON-JUDGMENT

This level of listening escorts us behind the scenes of our dramas and conflicts, to the state of BEING where solutions become possible. AWARENESS of listening skills can be enhanced by taking the Listening Quiz written by Kathryn Kvols, creator of the Redirecting Children's Behavior course.

How Well Do You Listen?
By Kathryn Kvols, Author and Founder of the International Network for Children and Families (INCAF). Adapted for parent/teen relationships.

Listening Quiz

What kind of listener are you when it comes to your teenage daughter? Take this short quiz to find out your listening style.

1. **When my teen talks to me, I typically ...**
    a. only respond if it affects me directly.
    b   listen to the first part of what she says, so I get the gist. After a bit, I tend to get distracted by whatever's on my mind.
    c. stop what I'm doing and listen intently.
    d. stop what I'm doing and look into her eyes while I listen.

2. **When it comes to the tone of voice my teen uses ...**
    a. I don't notice different tones.
    b. I take notice when she says something in a whiny or angry tone of voice.
    c. I try to listen for the total message, including the words she says and the tone of her voice.
    d. I can know how my daughter is feeling by the tone of her voice, even if her words say the opposite.

3. **When I communicate with my teen at home, it's usually ...**
    a. yelling, from across the room.
    b. at normal volumes, but I'm usually doing something else at the same time (multi-tasking).
    c. while we are looking at each other.
    d. face to face, at eye level.

4. **How many times do I have to ask my teen to do something before she does it?**
    a. My daughter seldom does what I ask.
    b. It may take several times, but eventually my daughter gives in.
    c. I may have to repeat myself once or twice, but not often.
    d. One time.

5. **How true is the following statement: "I have to yell to get my teen to do what I ask."**
    a. Always true
    b. Usually true
    c. Sometimes true
    d. Seldom true

6. How frequently do I empathize with my daughter?
   a. Hardly ever, I've got bigger problems.
   b. Only when I agree with what she is saying.
   c. I usually empathize with my daughter.
   d. I try to get into my daughter's shoes and make sure she feels understood.

7. Does my daughter feel free to come to me to discuss uncomfortable issues, like friends, peer pressure, sex, and difficulties at school?
   a. I don't even want to know ...
   b. My daughter would probably not want to talk to me about that stuff because she knows I'd flip my lid or she wouldn't want to add to my worries.
   c. My daughter might be reluctant to share these things with me, but I know she would.
   d. My daughter often comes to me with personal issues like this, because I listen to her, empathize, and try to be supportive.

Scoring

If your answers were mostly As, then you are not listening at all. You dismiss most of what your daughter says to you, so you shouldn't be surprised if she ignores what you say to her. Take some time to reevaluate the kind of relationship you'd like to have with your daughter, and consider taking a parenting course to build your listening skills and reconnect with your kids.

If your answers were mostly Bs, then you may be pretending to listen. You are too busy in your mind thinking about something other than what your daughter is saying to you, yet you appear to be listening by offering an "uh huh" or "I understand" scattered in the conversation. Your objective is to make your daughter feel like you're listening so perhaps she will leave you alone to finish what you're doing. She probably mirrors the behavior you model, making it a challenge to get her to listen to you. Brush up on your listening skills to make communicating with your daughter less challenging.

If you answered mostly Cs, you are an attentive listener. You are fully present to your daughter. You are not only listening to what she is saying, but you are also attuned to her body language and the tone of her voice. Your objective is to "be there" for her. Find out how to improve your already stellar listening skills!

If you answered mostly Ds, then you are an empathetic listener. Empathetic listening is the capacity to recognize and share feelings that are being communicated by your daughter. This is the deepest level of listening and requires one to suspend all judgment. Your objective is to really "get" what your daughter is trying to communicate so she feels heard, accepted, and understood.

One of my favorite problem solving formulas I learned during my years assisting in The Dale Carnegie Course and I've used it in many situations with great success. Written by Dale in 1936, this straightforward series of four questions paves the way for a meeting of the minds.

No problem can be solved from the same level of consciousness that created it.
—Albert Einstein

1. *What is the problem?*
2. *What are the causes of the problem?*
3. *What are the possible solutions?*
4. *What is the best possible solution?*

When disagreements begin, mothers and daughters can sit together, mindful of the message encoded in the word LISTEN, and remember that the KEY components of silence, empathy and non-judgment increase the chances of resolution. A sure way to close the door on a conversation with a teenager is to start a sentence with, "You need to …" Instead, try, "Do you want to hear a story about what I did at your age?" Then, be candid and weave your message into your true story.

Ask vs. Tell

The series of books on *Positive Discipline* written by Dr. Jane Nelsen have held a spot on my bookshelves for years. One day, over lunch with her at a parenting conference, she offered the following advice for communicating with teenagers: "Stop trying to 'stuff in,' and learn how to 'draw forth.'" Asking something of our kids invites their cooperation in a way that telling them something cannot. For example, LISTEN to the difference between the following two phrases: "Stop fighting with your brother," and "How can you and your brother solve this problem?" The first is punitive, while the second is empowering. Asking questions engages our kids' creativity and places the focus on solutions, whereas making demands calls attention to wrongdoings and sends the message that they are at fault.

Fault is an "F" word that serves to blame, shame or defame another for making a mistake. The target—the one being blamed—simply represents the situation or the dynamic at hand. As such, finding fault has no place in family discussions. Particularly when raising teenagers, it is vital to remember that mistakes are part of the growth process. Teens must likewise consciously practice restraining from finding fault in the misbehaviors of parents and siblings. Mistakes are errors to learn from and move on, not a reason to sentence others to emotional imprisonment. Our efforts to discipline teens are far more effective when we strive to allow consequences to serve as resources for problem solving over punishment. Aligned with the SOULSELF, we take in the information as just that—information—without making assumptions. There is no judgment, no knee-jerk reaction or verbal counterattack. We simply express our truth, RESPOND from that truth and allow the love that exists between us to flow.

Researcher and storyteller Brené Brown, PhD has created something she calls the Wholehearted Parenting Manifesto that applies beautifully to all relationships, including the ones with ourselves.

If we allow a child to experience the consequence of [her] acts, we provide an honest and real learning situation.
—Rudolf Dreikurs

Wholehearted Parenting Manifesto
SOURCE: *Daring Greatly,* by Brené Brown, PhD

⊛ *Above all else, I want you to know that you are loved and lovable. You will learn this from my words and actions—the lessons on love are in how I treat you and how I treat myself.*

⊛ *I want you to engage with the world from a place of worthiness. You will learn that you are worthy of love, belonging, and joy every time you see me practice self-compassion and embrace my own imperfections.*

⊛ *We will practice courage in our family by showing up, letting ourselves be seen, and honoring vulnerability. We will share our stories of struggle and strength. There will always be room in our home for both.*

⊛ *We will teach you compassion by practicing compassion with ourselves first; then with each other. We will set and respect boundaries; we will honor hard work, hope, and perseverance. Rest and play will be family values, as well as family practices.*

- *You will learn accountability and respect by watching me make mistakes and make amends, and by watching how I ask for what I need and talk about how I feel.*

- *I want you to know joy, so together we will practice gratitude.*

- *I want you to feel joy, so together we will learn how to be vulnerable.*

- *When uncertainty and scarcity visit, you will be able to draw from the spirit that is a part of our everyday life.*

- *Together we will cry and face fear and grief. I will want to take away your pain, but instead I will sit with you and teach you how to feel it.*

- *We will laugh and sing and dance and create. We will always have permission to be ourselves with each other. No matter what, you will always belong here.*

- *As you begin your Wholehearted journey, the greatest gift that I can give to you is to live and love with my whole heart and to dare greatly.*

- *I will not teach or love or show you anything perfectly, but I will let you see me, and I will always hold sacred the gift of seeing you. Truly, deeply, seeing you.*

Making Peace with Our Parents

I'll never forget the day I left for college at age 18. I stood by my car, which was filled to the brim with books, blankets and my stereo, and prepared myself to say goodbye to my parents. My mother had to prompt Dad to give me a hug and tell me he loved me, which he did, dutifully. At this, I rolled my eyes, tossed my hair, and shifted my weight from one leg to the other, a bit turned off that he had to be told to make even a token gesture of affection. My perception was that he just wanted me out of there so he could go on with his day, like usual. It was many years later that my mom told me the truth about that day. After I pulled out of the driveway, listening to the song "*Carry On*" by Kansas on the radio, my dad went back into the house and sobbed like a baby for the remainder of the day, and for much of the next week or two. Watching his youngest child leave the nest was much harder on him than I ever imagined at the time.

Twenty-eight years later—Father's Day, 2004—I sat next to my dad, then terminally ill and under hospice care. As we talked and held hands, I saw in his eyes the love he felt for me, which for so many years had gone unexpressed by him and unrecognized by me. Now I knew it had always been there. I understood that if only he had been born in a different generation, had a different upbringing, or had made different CHOICES, he might have been better able to share the love that was deep within his heart. I forgave him for not being who I thought he should have been. More importantly, I forgave myself for holding onto a past that never was what I thought it was. In that moment, looking into his eyes and feeling his carpenter's hands, calloused from decades of working hard to provide for his family, my heart opened up to a deeper understanding of one of my favorite poems:

Forgiveness is the key to happiness.
—A Course in Miracles

If I Had My Child to Raise Over Again

If I had my child to raise over again,
I'd finger paint more, and point the finger less.
I'd do less correcting and more connecting.
I'd take my eyes off my watch and watch with my eyes.
I would care to know less and know to care more.
I'd take more hikes and fly more kites.
I'd stop playing serious and seriously play.
I'd run through more fields and gaze at more stars.
I'd do more hugging and less tugging.
I would be firm less often and affirm much more.
I'd build self-esteem first, and the house later.
I'd teach less about the love of power,
And more about the power of love.
It matters not whether my child is big or small;
From this day forth, I'll cherish it all.

SOURCE: 100 Ways to Build Self-Esteem and Teach Value,
by Diana Loomans

From this heart space, I was able to revisit and reframe the poem, *No Mistakes*, that I'd written three decades earlier:

The Inner Coach

It's OK to make mistakes
When trying out new things;
To share my gifts with all the world
And feel the love it brings.
My inner coach is telling me
You are a part of the team,
And now it's time for you to share
And manifest your dream.
My friends are all supporting me
They help me feel so strong.
There never is a question now
Of "Where I do belong?"
I know now that I have the courage
To do so many new things
I'm always loved just the same
With all the magic that real love brings.
—Janet Larson

What can you do to promote world peace? Go home and love your family.
—Mother Teresa

My courage is reflected in my commitment to remain AWARE of fears when they arise as anxiety or regret or are cloaked as anything that might sabotage my greater good. I know I am loved because I have made the CHOICE to meet those fears with a response of love. My own inner coach, parent and mentor is the voice of love itself.

Living Life Unlocked

I commit to transforming my inner critic to an inner coach; my inner adolescent to my inner mentor. I do this by first becoming a "bird in the corner" of my own mind—by becoming the observer of the thoughts in my head from a heightened perspective of a bird flying over them from above. I gain AWARENESS of the negative programs and outdated beliefs that have been running my life and sometimes ruining my life. When I become that bird who watches my every move with clarity, I welcome the knowledge gained from the vantage point of the bird's eye view. I embrace the power within me to rise above the petty differences that arise between my daughter and me or my mother and me as I soar to a new level in our relationship—one filled with compassion and understanding, one that isn't afraid to experience the ebb and flow of the natural space that sometimes comes between us and inevitably brings us closer together. I realize that when I offer gifts of love to her, I offer them to myself.

Within me resides the discipline to mind my mind as I learn to listen, to pause before I REACT, choosing instead to RESPOND with purpose and conscious intention to nurture the results I desire, as only a loving parent (or daughter) can do. I take care of myself, and I take a stand for what I believe in, knowing my mind is a part of the Divine feminine mind, and when I give birth to the freedom within me, I give birth to the possibility of freedom for all.

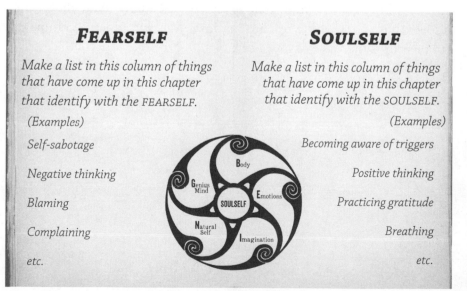

FEARSELF

Make a list in this column of things that have come up in this chapter that identify with the FEARSELF.

(Examples)

Self-sabotage

Negative thinking

Blaming

Complaining

etc.

SOULSELF

Make a list in this column of things that have come up in this chapter that identify with the SOULSELF.

(Examples)

Becoming aware of triggers

Positive thinking

Practicing gratitude

Breathing

etc.

Chapter 5

From Bullying to Bonding and BEING Ourselves

*Be yourself and you will find, who minds doesn't matter
and who matters won't mind.*
—Rachel Simmons, *Odd Girl Speaks Out:*
Girls Write about Bullies, Cliques, Popularity, and Jealousy

Janet, Age 17

I'm so thankful to have Julie as a friend. She understands me and she really gets my jokes when everyone else just gives a blank stare. It's like we have the same mind.

Leslie, Age 17

Throughout my entire elementary, middle and high school years, I've always felt like the odd girl out. The pressures to be popular, beautiful and dateable are enough to make any girl crazy—but I also lack a solid group of friends. There is a lot of drama, jealousy and backstabbing with my girl friends, especially when it comes to boys.

Kayla, Age 17

My friend, Lisa, is begging me to hook her up with Bruce. I told her he drinks, cusses and is sexually promiscuous. She still wants him. I can't let her do that. I know what he would do to her. But she still wants him. She thinks she can change him. That scares me. I'm worried about her, she's my friend, and I know how much her future means to her.

Elisha, Age 16

All they want is gossip. Gossip they can tell others about just so they can have a conversation. It's wrong, it's all so wrong. Why should people be used like that?

Jen, Age 16
Here's my day, summarized in this poem:
They say that I am twisted
and that I am a freak
do they really not know me
or judge me because they're weak?
They tell me that I'm crazy
and that I don't belong
I cannot help but wonder
if maybe they aren't wrong.
They don't even know me
but they judge me just the same
they see me as abnormal
and think ridicule is a game.

Regardless of age, once our primary needs of food and shelter are met, all human beings share the same basic needs: We need to feel we belong, feel we are loved and feel we are valuable; and we need freedom to experiment and explore and express ourselves. While our first experience of these needs being met or unmet occurs within the context of our nuclear family, as our social circle expands to include not only home but also school, community and—importantly—friends, we rely on our social network to meet more and more of our basic needs.

Thankfully, we do not embark upon the voyage into adulthood alone, but rather in the company of trusted others—some of whom we have known since infancy—who make their own journeys alongside us. In adolescence, as teens grow more independent of Mom and Dad, friendships assume a new priority—for at this stage of our development we look not so much to our parents to influence our evolving identity, but to our peers. The experience of being liked, accepted and understood by people our own age is crucial to building a healthy self-concept and high self-esteem. For teenagers and adults alike, the trust and intimacy shared between close friends is a source of emotional support that makes us more resilient when faced with the stresses of everyday life.

From the stories of the diarists in this chapter we witness the heartwarming power of friendship and the heartbreaking agony of bullying. We glean insights and strategies for managing and maintaining friendships and for protecting ourselves against rivals, without causing unnecessary pain or harm to others or ourselves. Ultimately, we realize the most important relationship we will ever have is the one with the person looking back at us in the mirror, and we learn to become a more loyal friend to ourselves.

The Heartwarming Power of Friendship

The power of friendship was made evident in a study conducted by the University of Virginia, in which students were outfitted with heavy backpacks and told to walk up a steep hill. Participants were given measurement tools and asked to indicate the steepness of the hill they had climbed and the heaviness of the weight they were carrying. When they did it alone, the backpacks felt heavier and the hill was estimated to be steeper than when they participated in the experiment with a friend. As Liz and Amber note in their diaries, having someone to lean on does more than lighten our load; friends allow us to more fully enjoy the richness of life.

It was only a sunny smile, and little it cost in the giving, but like morning light it scattered the night and made the day worth living.
—F. Scott Fitzgerald

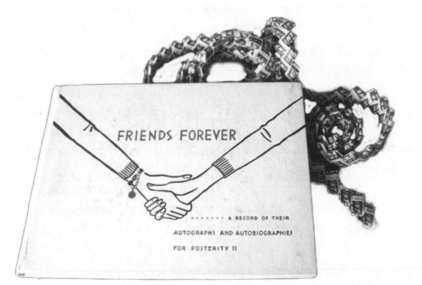

Memorabilia saved by a diarist. Gum wrapper chain exchanged between friends.

Liz, Age 16
I talked to Nicole for a long time tonight like an hour and a half. It's cool because we were talking about old stupid stuff and just cracking up. And I shared with her about mom and her boyfriend, Jim, and

how sad mom is that he still hasn't come back, and how she tries to be strong in front of me, but I know it's tearing her apart, so I feel torn apart. And I told her about how scared I am that my brother's school may be incapable of handling his needs. She just listened and reminded me that everything happens for a reason. She quoted Erma Bombeck, who said that worry is like a rocking chair: it gives you something to do, but never gets you anywhere. I know I'll be okay. I know it. I have a lot to live for. My talk with Nicole helped remind me that I am not alone, which was my biggest fear. And I think she needs a friend just as much as I do right now.

Amber, Age 17
May 8. I'm still sad that Jen moved away. I really miss her, but this is a good time for me to build new friendships. I am also getting a chance to concentrate on myself and discover what I want in a friend. I've learned a lot from Jen, and now it's cool learning how to be more independent, so in a way, I'm still learning from her!
May 20. Melissa and I are becoming buds. Yesterday I went to Target and she was "randomly" in the same aisle! I needed a friend like her. I'm so thankful!

> *My friends have made the story of my life. In a thousand ways they have turned my limitations into beautiful privileges and enabled me to walk serene and happy in the shadow cast by my desperation.*
> *—Helen Keller*

Liz and Amber were fortunate to have the friendships they had, and wise beyond their years to be grateful for the experience. Because friends reflect our sense of belonging and acceptance, the relationships we develop with our peers have a huge impact on our self-esteem. And yet, in the same way a loyal friend can lift our spirits and bolster our confidence, a breech in trust within that friendship can undermine our confidence or even send us plummeting into anguish and self-doubt.

The lessons in the diary entries in this chapter reveal the range of touching and troubling experiences girls encounter when navigating ever-changing relationships with peers.

The Heartbreaking Agony of Bullying

Over the following pages, we witness the raw devastation felt when a once trusted ally turns adversary, a bully emerges out of the blue to threaten an unsuspecting target, or a teen becomes a target of a social media hate campaign. The insidious gnawing away at the foundation of one's sense of self-worth from relentless bullying is tragic for the bullied target. It is mind-blowing to imagine the callous indignity emerging from bullies who we could only hope would have a stronger sense of character and be raised in a supportive environment in which values of respect toward others would be ingrained in their hearts. The headlines of far too many newspapers reveal the jaw-dropping "is this for real?" behaviors of some teenagers acting out in a most hateful and desperate act of intending to bring others down.

What makes someone vulnerable as prey and what drives a teenager to become a malicious predator? What does it take to break the hardened shell of a bully who—until the veil of superiority is exposed as the self-doubt that it truly is—only laughs and scoffs at anti-bullying programs and goals? What is it in a society that cultivates the possibility for kids to become coldhearted and for the culture to allow the violation of its children? Through the entries to follow, we will explore these issues as the raw truth is exposed.

Voices of the Bullied

Tammy, Age 14

I wish I could read Joni's mind to know what kind of a mood she will be in ... whether she will think I'm worth being around or not. Just because I have people to spend time with one day doesn't mean they will be around the next.

To describe teenage social life as volatile would be a huge understatement. From day to day and even hour to hour, a girl's social status can rise or fall drastically as alliances shift among friends. Sometimes she feels included and accepted; at other times bewildered, as though the rug of belonging was pulled out from underneath her. When a teen's daily life brings repeated encounters with enemies known or unknown, the peer group to which she turns for emotional sustenance has the potential to become a source of emotional toxicity that can lead to significant psychological and even physical damage.

As parents, we are well aware of looming dangers such as school shootings, terrorist attacks and similarly random acts of violence. However, a far more insidious form of violence often goes unrecognized while it is being inflicted upon our teens, despite the fact that it takes place in our own communities and in many cases right in our own homes. The most frequently occurring form of violence among school-aged kids in America is not carried out with the use of guns or bombs, but with mean-spirited words and acts of aggression, exclusion and bullying that are perpetrated between peers.

In my self-esteem workshops for girls, I make it a point to ask how many have experienced being bullied firsthand and am continually amazed at the number of hands that fly up around the room. Even at the "Brownie" level of Girl Scouts (first through third grade), most girls have already been the target of threats, teasing and put-downs. Sadly, statistics released by the National Center for Education confirm that my findings among Girl Scouts are far from unique: Each year, over 3.2 million school-aged children are bullied, and each day, approximately 160,000 teenagers skip school because of it. A study published by the *Journal of the American Medical Association* found that nearly a third of children in sixth through tenth grades had either bullied someone else or been bullied themselves.

For the sake of definition, bullying refers to any aggressive or mean-spirited behavior intended to hurt, harass or humiliate another person. While it may take the form of physical pushing, shoving or hitting, the most wounding assaults do not involve the use of fists, but of words. Entries like those that follow were common in virtually every one of the thousands of diary entries within the hundreds of teen diaries I have reviewed. Sometimes the verbal warfare erupted out of jealousy or as an attempt to jockey for social status. Other attacks were aimed at singling out some feature of the target—her weight, appearance, accent, race, CHOICE of friends, extra-curricular interests, academic performance or sexual orientation—for the sole purpose of attempting to make her feel inferior.

Charlene, Age 13

I have some "friends" who always make fun of my appearance. I think true friends are not supposed to make fun of me, and I don't really need that type of friend. When I look in the mirror I see myself as ugly because of all the years that people have called me an ugly, fat bitch. I may always look happy, but deep down inside I am sad.

Elise, Age 16

All I ever see is the world laughing at me. Making fun of me because of my math grade (which mom is gonna kill me for) or because I did something stupid, or because someone was talking bad about me, or because I'm short! You know what ... I can't control those things. But when all I hear are negative things about me, how can I possibly think that my life has value? How can I say that I have people in my life who care about me when all they do is make fun of me? Okay, so I'll admit, they're not all like that. But where's my ray of light? There's no silver lining to this cloud, and I feel that when I stick up for myself, I just get more miserable because then people hate me. Or they tease me even more. So my choices in life are either: a) "I'm miserable and let people walk all over me" .... or b) "I'm even more miserable and have no friends." Wow, man I have a hard decision to make! I mean, I can't even have real relationships with anyone. So I guess I'm picking option b. Yay—what fun for me. I wish with all my heart that people would love me for who I am, instead of pointing fingers at my flaws and telling me that I will never be good enough. If I had a place to run, I would.

Katy, Age 12

Dear Journal, I don't want to go to school ever again. I hate it! I hate the work and I hate the people and they hate me. The other day these boys came up behind me while I was putting my books in my locker. They called me names and asked me why I even bothered to show my face at school because no one wanted to go to school with a lesbian. I tried to ignore them because I was afraid of what might happen if I stood up to them. When I went to leave, they pushed me against the wall. Then they slammed my locker shut on my hand, breaking my finger. I held back tears while I watched them run away laughing.

82 percent of LGBT (Lesbian, Gay, Bisexual, Transgender) students report being verbally harassed (name calling, threats, etc.) because of their sexual orientation.
— Gay, Lesbian, & Straight Education Network

"Emotional" bullying—the name-calling, ridiculing, threatening, ostracizing, or gossiping about another—depicted in these entries is by far the most common manifestation of harassment among teen girls. Through these acts, the bully seeks to enhance her own social standing by damaging the reputation of her target. And as the diary entries in this chapter attest, the emotional wounds inflicted by words can be far more hurtful than cuts or bruises.

Handle them carefully, for words have more power than atom bombs.
—Pearl Strachan

Gossip as a Form of Bullying

Mikaela, Age 16

Girls call me a whore and slut. The guys call me ugly and fat. They all say that nobody would want to date me and that I am the worst thing ever created on this planet. They compare me to a whale and *call me a lesbian. It is really hurtful. I hate myself and I always wonder why was I even born.*

Taylor, Age 16

The popular kids at school continue to harass me. I wish I cared less about what they thought of me so I could concentrate on myself. I wonder if the rest of my life will be like this. A bunch of cliques that band together. That's why people hate high school. I can't wait to be done with it.

In her book *Odd Girl Out*, Rachel Simmons makes the distinction that gossip "crosses the line and becomes bullying if it damages friendships and causes people to dislike someone." Clearly, those who bullied Mikaela and Taylor crossed this line. What these girls may not realize, however, is that those who mock and exclude them do so because they themselves are insecure. A bully is an instrument of FEAR. This insight is revealed in my acronym for GOSSIPING:

GOSSIPING ...

Gestures **O**f **S**preading **S**tories **I**gniting **P**ersonal
Insecurities **N**ative to the **G**ossipers

Gossiping is like a hallucinogenic drug that makes you think you are better. The gossipers seek to expose the weaknesses of others as a way to keep their own insecurities hidden and protected. The following poem, which was written, appropriately enough, by someone who wished to remain anonymous, articulates both the destructiveness of gossip and the madness of trying to feel better by trying to make someone else feel worse.

Nobody's Friend

My name is Gossip.
I have no respect for justice.
I maim without killing.
I break hearts and ruin lives.
I am cunning and malicious.
I gather strength with age.
The more I am quoted,
The more I am believed.
My victims are helpless.
They cannot protect themselves against me
because I have no name and no face.
To track me down is impossible.

The harder you try,
The more elusive I become.
I am nobody's friend.
Once I tarnish a reputation,
It is never the same.
I topple governments
And wreck marriages.
I ruin careers and cause sleepless nights,
Heartaches, and indigestion.
I make innocent people cry in their pillows.
Even my name hisses.
I am called Gossip.
I make headlines and headaches.
Before you repeat a story, ask yourself:
Is it truc?
Is it harmless?
Is it necessary?
If it isn't, don't repeat it.
—Author Unknown

In earlier times, gossip was passed along by word of mouth or, at worst, as handwriting on a bathroom stall. Today, in stark contrast, gossip magazines and 24/7 cable news networks feed on the intentional fabrication of stories and twisting of facts, which serve to amplify another's hateful words. They do this to play on the fear-strings of their audience, who feel compelled to keep glued to their source because they think they are being educated with dangers and warnings that will keep them safe. Ultimately, it's all done under the fog of the FEARSELF with the underlying goal to sell advertising and increase profits. When this industry goes out of business, rest assured it will be a sign we are on the right path of creating a saner and more nurturing environment for our kids—modeling the bully-free zones we desire for them in every venue of life, whether school or home. News sources and networks engaged in such practices are poison to the love and care of everyone's soul. Allowing children and teens to be within earshot of such negativity is nothing short of offering them a model of bullying that has become socially acceptable. Do a little homework. Look at fact-checker websites to see the number of infractions committed by your news source. Then, do the real work of checking in with your internal home—the compass of your own soul—to see if the spirit in which

**THE FOG OF
THE FEARSELF**

these messages are conveyed aligns with the values you want to impart to today's children, who are in the midst of constructing a foundation for how to be in this world.

Add to this the platform of the ethers of the Internet, where gossip and hateful messages quickly spread like a virus. According to bullying statistics issued from the White House, in 2010 approximately 2.7 million students were involved in cyberbullying activities, as either perpetrator or target. Devastating messages like "I hate you. You should kill yourself" are casually tossed around by girls hiding behind electronic devices that can connect to everyone and everything—*except* the human heart.

Cyberbullying

Among teen and tween girls, who spend an increasing amount of time "plugged in" to the Internet, social media sites have become the method of CHOICE for broadcasting disparaging remarks and opinions that most teens would never have the courage to say face to face. These online formats give teens the false impression they are operating in their own private little world where their words and actions have less severe or immediate consequences. Many sites actually allow questions and comments to be posted anonymously—providing a toxic cover for those who are driven to perpetrate these online attacks. As a result of yet another veil added to the illusion of detachment that the computer screen already offers, anonymity ignites online exchanges that may escalate quickly, and the aftermath can be emotionally devastating—and sometimes deadly. Cyberbullying dispels any residual excuse from the past that "kids will be kids," as the cruelty is documented and the effects are very real.

> ### Erica, Age 13
> *Just received this email from Hannah:*
> *Dear Erica,*
> *I HATE YOU!! YOU HAVE THE NERVE TO TELL JULIA YOU WERE GOING TO EUROPE BUT NOT ME? HOW DARE YOU! JERK! Just kidding. I'm so jealous of you. Sorry, my caps lock was on. Talk to you soon!*
> *Your friend, Hannah*

If Erica felt confused by the mixed messages in her friend's email, it would be easy to understand why. Sharing emotionally charged feelings like hatred and jealousy electronically leaves the door wide open for "virtually" every possible interpretation. Gone are all the cues we use to read between the lines of human communication—body language, tone of voice, facial expression—leaving us with only cold, hard words on a screen.

While researching the role that social media now plays in acts of hostility and bullying among teens, I happened to attend a daylong retreat with mindfulness Zen master Thich Nhat Hanh. He made the point that the advancement of technology and telecommunications has ironically led to a regression in our ability to truly communicate. I understood him to mean that our communication skills have diminished not only because of the lack of face-to-face time with people, but also because the impersonal nature of our communication allows immature, often thoughtless messages—like the one from Hannah to Erica above—to be sent in the absence of visual or emotional cues from the sender, and to be received without any visual or emotional feedback from the receiver. Further complication results when a written communication like "I HATE YOU!" is followed up with "Just kidding!" In this case, what the sender is really doing is hurting someone and then attempting to deny her right to be upset about it. This is a super-manipulative thing to do, because it not only lets the one who made the remark off the hook for taking responsibility for her actions; it also sets her up to dismiss or ridicule the recipient's lack of a sense of "humor" should she dare to speak out or complain.

It may be difficult to understand why a teen would provoke a peer to the point of anguish, but it's vital to seek this understanding. The more insight we have into the factors that compel some girls to act out aggressively and underhandedly against one another—whether online or in person—the better able we will be to sidestep these attacks and not take them quite as personally when they do occur.

The Psychology of the Aggressor

To the outside world, the bully may project an image of confidence, but more often than not, she is plagued with feelings of loneliness or inadequacy on the inside. It is ironic, to say the least, that some teens are compelled to single-out, humiliate and exclude others in the cruelest of ways for the very reason that they themselves are desperately lacking a sense of belonging. The need to be included, to feel important, and to be a part of something greater than oneself can lure kids into cliques, or—in the most extreme cases—to become part of a gang. Both provide a sense of identity and offer the promise of validation, acceptance and support. Teens form these alliances not necessarily because they agree with them but because they are desperate to fit in, to gain popularity, or to protect themselves against the ridicule of others.

Frank Peretti, who was born with a birth defect that left him physically disfigured, was the target of merciless ridicule throughout his early childhood and teenage years. Now in his 50s and a best-selling author of several novels, he has turned his focus to an in-depth study of the effects that bullying and emotional abuse have on children. His book *No More Bullies: For Those Who Wound or Are Wounded* explores the dynamics of aggressive behavior among children, concluding that kids who pick on other kids do so because "they have a deep troubling need of their own"—be it at school or at home.

Beneath the bully's tough persona is a person who attacks because she feels powerless, threatened or lacking in confidence. Capitalizing on another's perceived weakness is a convenient way to shift the focus away from the experience of her own perception of inadequacy. In many cases, "mean" girls have been treated disrespectfully by peers, siblings or even parents and are seeking to rebuild their self-esteem by chipping away the self-esteem of others. As the saying goes, there are two ways to have the tallest building in town. One is to build the tallest building; the other is to tear all the other tall buildings down.

We Live What We Learn

> *Facebook, 2013*
> *"nobody cares about u"*
> *"i hate u"*
> *"you seriously deserve to die"*
> *"Yes IK I bullied REBECCA and she killed herself but IDGAF."*

In a heartbreaking and highly publicized case of cyberbullying that occurred in Florida in 2013, authorities discovered the above messages on the Facebook page of Rebecca Sedwick, after she took her own life one month before her thirteenth birthday. Following the investigation, two girls aged 12 and 14 were arrested and charged with aggravated stalking. That these girls were the perpetrators of cruel and heartless cyberbullying is without question. A deeper and more insidious problem was later revealed, however, when not long after 14-year-old Guadalupe Shaw was arrested for aggravated stalking, her stepmother, Vivian Vosburg, was arrested on suspicion of child abuse and neglect. The Sherriff's office was tipped off about a video—also posted on Facebook—that showed Vosburg beating two young boys in the face, cursing them as they screamed and cried. In a news conference, Sheriff Grady Judd said, "This clearly indicates to us that this appears to be a normal way of life. They're laughing and cussing and throwing the F-bomb around, and then they're posting that conduct for all to see."

Where could a child such as Guadalupe have possibly learned to become part of a campaign that would ultimately end the life of another child? While we may never know for sure whether her merciless bullying of a peer was a result of having been emotionally or physically abused by her stepmother, we certainly know that violence begets violence, and this is how the cycle continues. Aggression and hatred only perpetuate more acts of aggression and hatred. The key to breaking this deadly cycle is to place a primary focus on building the self-esteem of every teen—those who are bullied *and* those who do the bullying. Regardless of how it appears, all bullying is a cover-up for insecurity. Hostile, underhanded, or cruel behaviors are *always* rooted in the FEARSELF.

While some parents neglect or abuse their role as caretakers of the souls of their children, others fail to model the virtues of standing up to protect an individual who truly needs a dose of mature interference or mediation.

FRAGILE
EXPERIENCE OF
ANXIETY OR
REGRET
SEEKING
EVIDENCE OF
LIMITATIONS
FOREVER

When Bullying Occurs at Home

While we normally think of bullying as taking place primarily among peers, our exploration of this topic would be incomplete without noting the results of a study on sibling bullying published in 2013 in the journal *Pediatrics*. The research indicates that sibling aggression is related to the same serious mental health effects as peer bullying. I'm not surprised to learn that being the target of aggressive or mean-spirited behavior is equally harmful whether it takes place inside or outside the home. But what is perplexing to me is the notion that we ever assumed kids should be immune to behavior intended to hurt, harass, or humiliate them just because the perpetrator was related. After all, isn't home the one place we are supposed to be safe?

> ### Kiley, Age 13
> *My sister keeps saying she wishes I was never born. She just uses me for practical jokes. It hurts so bad. Yesterday she pulled my hair so hard my head was bleeding. From behind her newspaper and coffee, my mom just says to work it out. Here I am in my room again feeling lonely. The only thing I want is for someone to just sit and listen.*

Kiley's family is like many who ignore fighting between siblings—failing to discern when conflicts are "typical rivalry" and when they have escalated into harmful bullying. The conclusion in the *Pediatrics* study is clear: "The mobilization to prevent and stop peer victimization and bullying should expand to encompass sibling aggression as well." This study makes it clear that parents must be as vigilant in bullying detection and prevention at home as they wish school administrators were when their kids are at school.

Whether at the hands of peers or siblings, the teen initiating the bullying and the teen allowing herself to be bullied are both temporarily lost in a FEAR-based emotional fog that blinds them from seeing just how valuable and precious each one of them is. This is the same screen created by the FEARSELF that prevents us from asking for help when we become the target of another girl's jealousy or aggression, and it is the FEARSELF that keeps us from standing up in defense of other girls who become such targets—sometimes even when we consider those girls as friends.

THE FOG OF
THE FEARSELF

The Role of the Bystander

The following diary entries are painful to read, for the wounding that occurs when one friend is betrayed by another goes so much deeper than the initial hurt, rejection or sadness. Far more destructive is the embarrassment, humiliation and shame that a girl suffers as a result—and almost always in private.

Sarah, Age 16

May 28. At the lunch tables, slutty girls tried to make me feel inferior for not having experienced a relationship. My friend, Tina, didn't stand up for me whatsoever as they gossiped away. Anyway, I made up a story about when I went to camp and met a guy named Tim. Their mouths agape, I walked away seeming like a decent girl. When I get a real boyfriend, I plan to use the Tim story to tack onto the real boyfriend and then I can shed the fake boyfriend tales altogether. I'm emotionally shackled.

June 1. I'm also wearing an emotional shackle put on me by Tina. She went to a college party and met this "hot college guy" and is now rubbing it in my face.

Although she may not be aware of it in the moment, a girl who witnesses a physical or character assault on another girl plays a crucial role in the outcome of the situation. A high school sophomore who feels genuine loyalty toward a longtime friend may be faced with a difficult conflict when the group makes that friend the focus of gossip or excludes her when they sit down to lunch. If she believes that her continued acceptance within that group requires her to also turn her back on her friend, she may blindly follow the actions of the group and, in the process, lose sight of what truly matters.

If we could watch the inner thoughts of someone witnessing such an injustice unfold in slow motion, we would see her making a CHOICE that takes her away from the truth of the SOULSELF, her SOURCE OF UNIVERSAL LIFE SERVING TO EXTEND LOVE FOREVER, and becoming more enmeshed in the FEARSELF as a result of betraying her friend. Even if she tells herself that turning away was nothing more than a casual gesture, it is a CHOICE with which she will have to eventually come to terms, for it didn't occur only at the lunch table, but in the very core of her BEING. The pang of guilt we feel when excluding another merely reflects the pain of abandoning our own true self.

As we contemplate the role we choose to play in any act of aggression, it is essential to realize that there is no such thing as an "innocent" bystander, because our very presence in the situation functions as a gesture of silent approval and encouragement for the bully. In fact, research has shown that bullying occurs more frequently in the presence of bystanders because

It takes a great deal of bravery to stand up to your enemies, but a great deal more to stand up to your friends.
—J. K. Rowling

There is no gesture more devastating than the back turning away.
—Rachel Simmons

to some extent the aggressor is emboldened by having an audience, which of course only escalates the encounter. Similar observations have been made in studies of group behavior: The more people who observe a person being attacked without help, the less likely it is that someone will come to their aid. If on the other hand one person alone witnesses the attack, the odds of that person's getting involved increase dramatically. To immunize ourselves from this vicious mob mentality, we would do well to consider deeply what the situation looks like from the target's perspective. Mikaela, whose entry about being bullied we read earlier in this chapter, courageously offers us exactly that.

> ### Mikaela, Age 16
> *For all of the people who are bystanders or think it's ok to bully other people: It is not ok to hurt other people mentally, emotionally, or physically no matter what. Why do you stand there and watch someone bully another person? Why do you bully a person? Are you that insecure about yourself that you have to put other people down to make you happier? Is it the fact that you have problems in your own life that you don't know how to deal with so you hurt others to get rid of your pain? If you bully someone, try to find out why you do and get therapy or talk to someone you trust! Please stop hurting other people. Kids kill themselves because of the rude things you say to them. When is enough, enough?*

The world is a dangerous place, not because of those who do evil, but because of those who look on and do nothing.
—Albert Einstein

The solution, of course, is not to compound aggression with more aggression, and it's certainly not to cower passively on the sidelines, but for each of us to learn to clearly assert our true opinions and wishes when our inner compass nudges us to go north instead of south.

The Target, the Bully, and the Balance of Power

Between the poles of passivity and aggression lies a sweet spot of assertiveness that affords us equal access to both our power and our peace of mind.

Passive behavior is marked by withholding our feelings and ideas, and metering our responses according to what we think will win us the approval and acceptance of others. As a young teen, I was the poster child for passivity. I was the person who apologized if someone else bumped into me. I did far more listening than I did speaking—and not because I didn't have anything to say. In retrospect, I would have been the perfect target for mean girls and bullies, had I been unlucky enough to encounter more of them. The only time I felt bullied was in seventh grade when a few of my friends ditched me at a movie theater. I had been beaten up by a couple of girls at a softball game the year before, but it didn't hurt like being the sole girl excluded from a group. Why? Because at a deeply buried level, I was haunted by the question, "If my own friends don't like me, who does?" It wasn't until I was an adult that I learned to become more assertive. As I practiced speaking up in situations where I would have otherwise remained silent, it occurred to me that being passive was a little like the tale of *Goldilocks and the Three Bears*; metaphorically speaking, passive behavior is the chair that is "too small," because in the act of holding back our true feelings and perspectives, we diminish our own self-esteem as well as our ability to connect with and contribute to others. Passive behavior indicates self-esteem is lacking, and the potential for being intimidated by someone more aggressive.

Aggressive behavior, at first glance, is easily mistaken for confidence, but the key difference between the two is that aggressive communicators rely on insults, threats, sarcasm and double-teaming to bring about their desired results. When we communicate our needs with aggression, we do so at the expense of the feelings of those around us, often violating others' right to be treated with dignity and respect. The rush of a sense of power experienced when we lash out with aggression might cause us to feel important in the short term, but in the end, seating ourselves in this "chair that is too big" alienates us from others and ourselves.

Assertive behavior is the chair that fits "just right," in the sense that it is a manifestation of true inner worth and self-confidence. Assertiveness is the sweet spot of high self-esteem. To communicate assertively is to engage the fullest expression of the Natural Self by freely sharing our feelings, thoughts, ideas and opinions in a direct way that honors our perspective without diminishing the perspectives of others. When we are assertive, we are able to stand up for ourselves and others when appropriate, and in a way that is neither too overbearing to be tolerated nor too timid to be taken seriously. To be assertive is to have the ability to defend our values and rights—without infringing upon those of others. Implicit in our BEING when we communicate assertively is the knowledge that everyone deserves to be treated with respect. The balance of power has been achieved. All are empowered.

The following acronym used in assertiveness training courses is useful to remember any time we are confronted by the aggressive words or behavior of another, whether it's directed toward us or toward someone we care about: Stay *CALM—Cool down, Assert yourself, Look them in the eye, and Mean what you say.* Consider the following statements: "Today is not a good day to tease me," or "If you want me to respond to you, please speak to me with respect." Notice that each one directly conveys a message, without being antagonistic or making ourselves an easy target. Of course, the words we use are only part of the equation. To be truly effective, we have to put every aspect of our BEING behind the words; to speak like we mean what we say and to walk like we have a purpose—after all, we do.

Several years after she wrote in her diary about being targeted by an emotional bully, Gina beautifully articulated her newfound ability to stay CALM, and described the wisdom she gained as a result of the experience.

> ### Gina's Reflection, 7 years later
> *You can think of it like this. Can anyone touch your insides, literally? Can they physically stick their fingers down your throat, or use some other treacherous tool to dig deep at your soul and make you feel bad? No. Generally speaking, the majority of the time we are not in danger of people coming at us with fingers ready to dive down our throats. But somehow, these people still make us feel bad. How? Because we are giving them the right to hurt us. Why would you want to give someone that power? I eventually realized that absolutely no one could make me feel any less than who I was, unless I gave them permission.*

One's dignity may be assaulted, vandalized and cruelly mocked, but it can never be taken away unless it is surrendered.
—Michael J. Fox

As Gina describes, when the hurtful words or actions of another don't hurt, it's because we are clear within ourselves that they are untrue, so they have no sticking power. It's as simple as that. And when words or actions do hurt, we can be sure we have allowed someone else to edit the secret internal script that we know to be the truth about ourselves. Jack Canfield, my longtime mentor, has a great way of illustrating this point. "If I tell you that you have green hair, but you really don't, do you feel bad?" he'll ask. "Of course not," comes the obvious response. Because we *know* the color of our hair, so there is not one iota of doubt within us to lure us into feeling bad as a result of having been told that our hair is green. The same is not true about some of the other things people say to us and about us, however, and our reactions often have less to do with their words than with how close those words come to piercing a core insecurity. As a case in point from my own experience, when kids capitalized on the rhyming potential of my name, chanting *"Janet Janet came from another planet,"* my reaction varied from laughing with them or feeling berated, depending on the level of my self-esteem at the time.

In her book *Bossypants*, actress Tina Fey shares about a time when an angry co-worker at *Saturday Night Live* called her a "cunt." Her "weird reaction," as she put it, was to simply state, "No, you don't get to call me that. My parents loved me. I'm not some adult child of an alcoholic who is going to take that shit." By standing up for herself, Fey demonstrated that it's what *we* hold to be true about ourselves that determines our self-concept—and consequently trains other people how to treat us. After drawing that line in the sand, Tina was never called that name again.

Being Your Own Best Friend

We reclaim personal power and strengthen our immunity against all forms of bullying when we can look in the mirror and acknowledge that if we are not our own best friend, we are our own worst enemy. This message is as humbling as it is liberating. Anytime I feel put down by another, anytime I have allowed someone else's fears, insecurities or opinions to redefine my self-concept or rock my self-esteem, I need only remember that for their words to hurt me, my agreement with them is required—and this is something which I alone have the power to grant or to withhold. Likewise, their lack of words—such as a lack of response to my text messages or not liking my posts can only invalidate me if I incorrectly think such responses are necessary to prove I am worthy. I become my own best friend by noticing and giving attention to one good thing about me at a time.

Each time I trust my inner source of power and summon the internal voice that reminds me that I am valuable and worthy of respect, I come to understand a little bit more that hurtful words and actions directed at me by another are never really about me at all. They come from the pain and insecurity of someone who has temporarily lost sight of her internal worth and has, for the moment, fallen prey to the notion that wielding power over me will again validate her. When I can see this struggle for what it is, as two shining souls temporarily lost in the clouds of the FEARSELF—reading from its limiting script, playing out its painful dramas, perhaps even exchanging roles of target and bully in different scenes—I begin to see that every aggressor is in fact a teacher. That nasty bully stood before me to show me where I had weaknesses in my own self-esteem. She showed me places where I needed to grow to be a stronger, more loving person to myself. She took on the role of villain to show me where I was choosing fear over love.

The sooner I reclaim the AWARENESS to validate what I know to be true about me when I am centered in the core of my soul, the sooner I can step out from my role as a bystander who silently watches as I put myself down, and become an upstander, who—like Katy—rises out of the shadows of the FEARSELF to take a stand for that which is real and pure within each of us.

Not only immunized from, but emboldened by, the bullying she once endured because of her sexual orientation, Katy—while still a teenager—took a stand by initiating a petition on www.change.org and demanded the Motion Picture Association of America change the rating of the documentary film *Bully* from R to PG13. With that single action, she increased AWARENESS about the insidious nature of this issue tenfold, as the movie became available to more widespread viewings in high schools across the nation. Here is Katy's reflection on her earlier diary entries:

Awake
With
All
Reality
Exposed
Naturally
Expressing the
Soul-
Self

Katy's Reflection, 6 years later

I grew up living with my mom, my dad, my grandma and my little sister. We went to church every Sunday when I was little, my sister and I took dance classes and figure skating lessons, my mom was involved with everything I did in school and I had plenty of friends. My family is extra loving and my parents encouraged my sister and I to do anything we ever wanted to.

Being gay was never really something we talked about at home, we didn't have any gay or lesbian friends or family members, but as far back as I can remember my mom always told me everyone was equal no matter what. She would say it doesn't matter what color someone's skin is or what religion they are or who they love, everyone deserves to be treated equally. For a long time I didn't really know what she meant so I rolled my eyes and nodded my head and said, "okay mom."

When I was in middle school I had a crush on a girl. I told my best friend and she told the rest of the school. I was bullied on a daily basis for something I was taught didn't matter.

I didn't tell my parents about being ridiculed because I was afraid of what they might think and who they might tell. In fact, I even lied that I broke my finger in gymnastics. I didn't know of any other lesbian students and there were no out lesbian adults in my community so I felt alone and I had no resources to go to for help. After eighth grade my parents moved me to a private school because, even though they didn't know why, they could see I was miserable. I had their support without realizing it.

At my new school, I became part of the community. I made friends who became my support system, kind of our own little family. With their help I gained the courage to come out to my parents just before turning sixteen. My parents were both as loving and accepting as anyone could be. The bravery I learned from my new found friends not only helped me in being comfortable with myself but it also gave me the strength to speak out and stand up for what I believe in. With the support of my family I was able to start and win multiple anti-bullying and LGBT equality campaigns.

After sharing my story through national television, news and media outlets and gaining celebrity support from people like Ellen DeGeneres and obtaining signatures from over half a million people the MPAA agreed to give Bully the PG13 rating it deserved. Now over 1.8 million students across the country have seen this film and joined me in speaking out and taking a stand against bullying. Law-makers on a national level have also been inspired by Bully and the story I told to make the film accessible to those who needed to see it most. I am so thankful for having the family I have and the love and support that they give me. I couldn't be living in New York and going to college next year without the support from my wonderful family. This past year my mom even traveled the country with me during a two-month period where I was advocating for anti-bully-ing and LGBT equality campaigns, and it truly shows how much she accepts and loves who I am.

The kind of strength summoned by Katy must be practiced, but once we find the courage to stand up for ourselves, standing up for others becomes a natural extension. Sometimes it takes going face to face with someone who seems intent on convincing us of our unworthiness, to reclaim the knowledge we are unconditionally worthy.

If we take Katy's example to heart, perhaps the next time we're faced with rudeness from another, or an encounter of short-temperedness at

The tide of history only advances when people make themselves fully visible.
—Anderson Cooper

Nothing others do is because of you. What others say and do is a projection of their own reality, their own dream. When you are immune to the opinions and actions of others, you won't be the victim of needless suffering.
—don Miguel Ruiz

home, we can pause and wonder what pain our antagonist is feeling that would trigger such an attack, and in so doing, keep our own inner adolescent at bay. And maybe, just maybe we can be present enough in the moment to hold back a reaction of revenge, and instead pause long enough to recognize that this person is currently out in the stratosphere of the FEARSELF, believing some kind of lie about herself, and trying to take it out on us. We can inquire within about the lesson this encounter holds for us, as we see her before us now as our teacher, presenting us with the opportunity to see the situation from the only place of truth, the SOULSELF, where only love abides. By approaching this situation with a conscious level of AWARENESS, we recognize that what could have degraded into an incident of bullying can transform into an experience of bonding, and blossom into an opportunity of BEING our highest self. What a beautiful choice-point for friendship to bloom—with others and with ourselves.

Living Life Unlocked

One of the easiest ways to become more assertive is to practice it in front of a mirror and role-play a scenario in which you'd like to see yourself RESPOND with more self-confidence—perhaps a situation in which someone frequently attempts to belittle you. Repeat the same scenario five times. Why five? Each time, you will practice responding with confidence by placing your AWARENESS on a different aspect of the five components of BEING, beginning with *Body*, and progressing through each one.

For *Body*, consider that your body language speaks volumes. Be honest about your starting position, and make adjustments to your shoulders, posture, facial expression, etc. to communicate self-assurance. Next, act out the same scenario and explore the *Emotions* that well up in this situation. Consciously practice a more empowering expression of your feelings to convey a sense of inner strength. Keep practicing until you convince yourself of your own strong foundation in a sea of emotions. The next "take" of the scenario puts the first two together while keeping your *Imagination* focused on a positive outcome for all involved. Visualize not only your ability to turn a potentially damaging exchange of energy around for the good, but also imagine in detail the follow through—the experience of walking away having accomplished your mission in this situation. The fourth time, practice being your *Natural Self* with authentic and well-deserved personal power. Don't worry if the first few times you don't come off as empowered. It took a while to lean into your FEARSELF for protection, and it may take some practice leaning into your SOULSELF with conviction; but rest assured, that's where real power comes alive. Last but not least, engage your *Genius Mind* to rally the power of your thoughts by trusting your own inner guidance. Harness the discipline of the mind to act and speak with focused intention—to be the wind beneath your own wings and become your own best friend.

Repeat this exercise as needed in different situations. When you can face any situation with every fiber of your BEING aligned with your truth, nobody can succeed in an attempt to bring you down. You, however, will succeed at rising to your fullest potential.

The world is but a canvas to our imagination.
—*Henry David Thoreau*

BODY
EMOTIONS
IMAGINATION
NATURAL SELF
GENIUS MIND

Me with my friend Mary, who wrote the poem at the beginning of Chapter 3. Laughing, hair blowing in the wind ... that's what friends are for.

Chapter 6

From Addiction to Awakening

Self-acceptance comes from meeting life's challenges vigorously. Don't numb yourself to your trials and difficulties, nor build mental walls to exclude pain from your life. You will find peace not by trying to escape your problems, but by confronting them courageously. You will find peace not in denial, but in victory.
—J. Donald Walters

Misty, Age 15
My mind is now medicated. A band-aid over a deep wound.

Tracey, Age 13
My teachers seem to be suspecting that I'm smoking weed, but so far haven't followed up on their hunches.

Emma, Age 16
Once again, Todd showed up drunker than shit. Ten bucks says mom will take him back and everything will continue to be fucked up.

Cha, Age 13
I was standing in the school bathroom between classes today, thinking about drugs after having done LSD last night. I started having a conversation in my head about it and went into a panic attack because I wasn't sure if I'd actually spoken my thoughts out loud with others around to hear. No one ever said anything, so I guess it was just in my head.

Sophia, Age 15
There is such a large communication gap between my parents and me. I never thought there really would be, but there is. First of all, my mom tells me not to drink, but she drinks, so I don't think she is one to talk.

Toianna, Age 18
In elementary school, the teachers saw my dad in black outs plenty of times at evening events and couldn't miss the gaseous fumes on his breath. He was slurring his words so people could barely understand him when he convinced my fifth grade teacher to hold me back. Like it was my fault that I was failing, not that Dad kept Mom and me up all night with drunken ramblings. Now, in high school, I'm an honors student by day and budding drunk by night.

If the experiences shared throughout this book weave together the issues most frequently encountered by teen girls, I'm convinced that the misuse of alcohol and other drugs is one of the most common connecting threads. Even if its abuse occurred two, three, or even four generations back, unless wounds have been healed and patterns redirected, alcoholic homes continue to inflict emotional harm upon their family members. Every day, on average, about 8,120 individuals age 12 and over try drugs for the first time, and 12,800 try alcohol. That's almost 15 per minute—24/7. By the time they graduate from high school, 70 percent of teens have tried alcohol and 44 percent have tried marijuana. Advertisements on TV and images on social networking sites would have us believe that partying is all fun and no risk. Yet the truth is, family dynamics, genetic predisposition, depression and other co-occurring (also called dual diagnosis) mental disorders can dramatically escalate a teen's chance of becoming snared in the claws of addiction.

It can be tempting as parents to compare our kids' experimentation with alcohol or drugs with our own, but the fact is that today's drug world is different than the one in which we were raised. The potency of heroin and marijuana has skyrocketed since the 1960s, while prescription painkillers are now manufactured in a way that is much more dangerous to the brain when misused. A frightening 25 percent of heroin users are likely to become addicted. The 2014 heroin overdose of celebrity Philip Seymour Hoffman stirred a wake-up call on the surge of heroin use, the dangerous reality of drug mixing as well as the deadly odds of receiving a higher purity rate or a toxic Fentanyl-laced supply. In other words, there exists today a greater potential for instant dependency that could lead to long-term addiction or overdose.

American teenagers experiment with drugs at a higher rate than teens in any other country in the world. Few do so with the intent—or even the

The CDC has tracked a tripling of drug-related deaths since 1990.

thought—of becoming addicted. Yet the looming fact that 95 percent of adult addicts began using as teens leaves parents struggling to understand whether their daughters' curiosity about drugs and alcohol is a normal and passing phase or a sign of an emerging crisis. While there is no disputing that adolescence is an experimental phase of life, we cannot overlook the fact that certain drugs take over the CHOICE-making part of their adolescent brain—still very much under construction. Decisions made today can have an effect on the rest of their lives, which is why it is difficult for parents to strike a balance between involvement and trust as we watch our babies play with fire.

When celebrity Lindsay Lohan, whose life has been laced with drug and alcohol scandals, was asked by Oprah Winfrey during an OWN interview what her drug of CHOICE was, Lohan said it was alcohol. Despite the fact that its use is deeply woven into our culture, alcohol is very much a drug. In fact, it's a drug that kills more teens than all other illicit drugs combined.

In this chapter, we explore the range of ways alcohol and other drugs, including prescription medications and inhalants, impact the lives of teenage girls—from casual experimentation to full-blown abuse. Making sure our daughters understand the dangers of these substances represents only the first step in teaching them to steer clear of their abuse. The real work lies in teaching them to draw upon the resources of their own true essence—their spirit *within*—for courage and confidence, instead of seeking a false sense of security through the artificial cloak of alcohol (a word whose root meaning, as synchronicity would have it, is derived from "essence or spirit.") For teens, tools and skills are presented to help navigate social situations in a way that makes abstaining from these substances a natural CHOICE. Insights shared by those who have experienced addiction first hand are offered to prepare teens and parents for the challenges these issues pose, to recognize potential warning signs, and open up lines of communication with those at risk. The difficult journeys these diarists have travelled impart universal lessons about letting go, choosing in the direction of our highest good and loving ourselves enough to be authentic in the presence of others. For adults, the stories told by the teen girls on these pages may help us see through the smokescreens we use to hide our own addictions, even if they are non-substance related, such as obsessions with food or work, negative thinking and, yes, our tendencies to worry or

What is addiction, really? It is a sign, a signal, a symptom of distress. It is a language that tells us about a plight that must be understood.
—Alice Miller

become consumed with thoughts about our children. If a parent's addiction is drug or alcohol related, the lack of stability in the family becomes evident, as is reflected in the following diary entries and insights.

When Parents Are Alcoholics or Addicts

Sherene, Age 19

Every time I saw my stepfather drunk and standing over me with evil in his eyes, I swore that I'd never drink, but last night I got drunk for the first time. I'm 19 years old and never thought I'd do something so stupid. I wish I hadn't done it. I was drinking vodka and everything was fine, then I woke this morning without any clothes, in a place I've never been, and the guy says we had a great time. I only wish I could wash this shame and guilt off of me. I wish I could wash this mistake from my memory.

Shame is the intensely painful feeling or experience of believing that we are flawed and therefore unworthy of love and belonging—[that] something we've experienced, done, or failed to do makes us unworthy of connection.
—Brené Brown

There is an old saying that familiarity breeds contempt. In this case, familiarity also breeds repetition, for as much as Sherene despised her stepfather's drunkenness, and no matter how much she vowed not to repeat it, his was a behavior she knew. The discomfort and shame she felt inside herself afterward was also paradoxically within her habitual comfort zone, making it a familiar behavior to return to time and time again.

According to the American Academy of Child & Adolescent Psychiatry, one in five adult Americans have lived with an alcoholic relative while growing up. Kids who are raised in an alcoholic home are three times more likely to be abused and more than four times more likely to be neglected than those from non-addicted families. But even in the absence of physical abuse, and even if these teenagers do not themselves become addicts, they are still raised under the influence of shame, low self-esteem and shaken confidence. The dramas and traumas surrounding addiction create a turbulent aftermath that affects children as much as the addicts themselves. Dysfunctional relationships, sexual promiscuity, eating disorders, depression, anxiety and experience of trauma and other mental disorders are just a few common patterns that emerge in children of alcoholics. And even if they've seen the dark side of drug or alcohol abuse and vowed never to repeat it, statistically, they are still four times more likely to succumb to addiction—and run a higher risk of engaging in other destructive behaviors as well. Also, they are more likely to marry an addict.

The last few lines of Sherene's entry reveal a host of seemingly unrelated issues that, in actuality, share alcohol as a common denominator. According to the *Journal of Marriage and Family*, teenage girls with a prior use of alcohol and/or cigarettes increased their risk of early sexual experience by 80 percent. Similarly, a report by The National Campaign to Prevent Teen and Unplanned Pregnancy concludes that under the influence of alcohol, condom use declines. And as blackouts, guilt, regret and promiscuous sex send girls on a downward spiral of shame, they may continue abusing alcohol in an attempt to distance themselves from the very feelings triggered by their alcohol use, perpetuating a destructive cycle. By this time, a girl's self-esteem is all but shattered.

While family history plays a significant role, not all teens who experiment with drugs or alcohol grew up in homes marked by substance abuse; conversely, not all who were raised by an addicted parent grow up to abuse substances. Some, like me, find other ways to cope with residual feelings of anxiety and only sparse crumbs of self-esteem.

When as a young adult I started my career as a human resources consultant, my life was organized around fulfilling two intersecting intentions: my need to prove myself worthy and meeting my boss's demand for more billable hours. With my home apartment less than a block from the office, it was not uncommon to find the nighttime security guard standing on the sidewalk at midnight, watching me make the walk from the office back to my apartment complex. My career had just begun, and I was already showing signs of becoming a workaholic. Picking up a copy of Claudia Black's book about children of alcoholics, *It Will Never Happen to Me*, I saw just how much my childhood experience matched the description she shared in the book, down to the roles family members adopt and the typical problems they carry into adulthood. The two overarching messages in families overshadowed by addiction, she explained, are DON'T TALK and DON'T TRUST.

Having learned early on that home was not a safe place to share my feelings, I taught myself to suppress them instead—a trait that would later translate into an ability to ignore my body's signals of exhaustion. As I read further, I felt Claudia had been a spy in my heart: "Children of alcoholics don't perceive others as resources, therefore, they live life alone," she explained. "Being isolated with feelings of fear, worry, embarrassment, guilt, anger, loneliness, etc., leads to a state of desperation, of

Note to teens: No matter what anyone says, know that your parent's drinking or using is never your fault. Even if it's the voice in your own head telling you this, it is simply not true.

being overwhelmed … they learn how to discount and repress feelings, and some learn simply not to feel." Emma, who shared in an earlier entry that she fully expected her mother to repeat the saga of allowing her alcoholic step-father to return home, essentially became the victim of a parent who chose not to set responsible boundaries that would ensure a healthy and safe environment for her daughter. We know the addict does not have the faculties to make appropriate CHOICES, but nonetheless, the mother is culpable in keeping Emma in this toxic situation. Her mother may rationalize her actions by thinking she is modeling loyalty or compassion, but in fact she is teaching Emma that exploitation and abuse—evident in the cycles of taking the addict back—is acceptable in relationships. It is a clear example of why children of alcoholics or drug addicts often lack boundaries so vital in the development of high self-esteem.

In my case, I experienced a fog of anxiety for which I had found a fitting term in a college psychology class: "impending doom." Weary of the toll my workaholism was taking on my personal life, I began attending Adult Children of Alcoholics meetings and workshops, where I gradually learned to access and express my feelings. In my late 20s, during a weekend-long inner child workshop, long-suppressed feelings of helplessness came to the surface, inspiring the following poem:

You Make the Call

We went out for ice cream
My dad and me
He sneaked and had a drink
Not thinking I could see.
When we came back home
I was standing in the hall
"Did he stop for a drink?
You make the call."
She looks in my eyes
Waiting to hear
I look in his
and I scc a tear.
My knees start to quiver
My heart starts to race
I'm caught in the middle
As I look from face to face.

I start to get dizzy
And I fall on the floor
You see I'm only five
So I can't walk out the door.
—Janet Larson

Affirmation of Serenity

Even though my father took fiercely to heart the courage and wisdom expressed on his homemade plaque of the Serenity Prayer, and stopped drinking for good when I was 10 years old, the foggy feeling of my dysfunctional ID—Impending Doom, with me since childhood—remained. Getting my feelings out on paper during that pivotal workshop increased my level of AWARENESS and led me to reflect on what I consider the three key words on that plaque—*serenity, courage and wisdom*. These concepts, I realized, are valuable not only for those facing drug or alcohol addiction, but for everyone whose addictive thoughts, habits or actions keep them living life at a more shallow level than the calling that lies waiting, deep within their heart. My desire to align all aspects of my BEING with the SOULSELF inspired me to personalize my own Affirmation of Serenity:

> *May I become still long enough to gain clarity about the truth of who I am, and to let go of everything that is not true about me. In that recognition, may I remain focused as I move in the direction of my highest good with ease and strength. Even though I may be in the midst of fear or pain, my true compass—my heart—will always lead me back on the path back to my soul. Should I become confused along the way, may I be graced with AWARENESS so clear that I step into that place of stillness where no choice needs to be made, for truth lives there, and I know what to do.*

These insights came after many years of self-inquiry and introspection, yet my hope for teens reading this is to convey the understanding that if your parents are struggling with alcohol addiction, it's likely they are too besieged with shame and low self-esteem to manage their own affairs with confidence—let alone to teach their children what it means to summon the courage to change. Most likely, they are projecting feelings of inadequacy onto others—often their own kids, and sometimes even strangers.

I remember a story my mother once shared with me about an alcoholic named Ann, who ran out of gas one day as she was driving home. This was BCE (before cellphone era), so she walked from her car to the nearest house to ask if she could use the phone to call for help. In the distance between the car and the house, Ann began telling herself all the reasons the homeowners would not let her use their phone: They would say she smelled of alcohol. They would be worried because she looked so disheveled. They would be suspicious of anyone who would let their car run out of gas, etc, etc. She arrived at the house and knocked at the door, which was promptly answered by a smiling woman. The first words spoken came from Ann, who—entrenched in the illusory attack and defense mindset symptomatic of the disease of alcoholism—yelled, "I DIDN'T WANT TO USE YOUR DAMN PHONE ANYWAY!" and stormed off alone back into the night.

Just as Ann was too preoccupied with her own insecurities to register the smiling face of the woman who greeted her at the door, most alcoholic parents are too consumed with indulging, managing, denying or hiding their addiction to provide children with consistent validation that they are intrinsically lovable and capable. As a result, many children of alcoholics find themselves at a pivotal point in their lives, lacking the foundational knowledge that they are enough; that they have what it takes to reach their full potential and to overcome whatever obstacles may lie in their path. If they are fortunate, these kids have learned about the dangers of drinking by watching their parents, and they avoid it. Unfortunately, the numbers reveal that many are not so lucky. Like Misty, whose diary entries appear below, some turn to booze to numb feelings of inadequacy or to bury residual pain from past emotional traumas.

Teen Drinking

Misty, Age 16
June 23. *The booze drowns the taste of salty tears on my tongue. It numbs the muscle that beats slowly beneath my ribs. It burns deep into the place that I pretend does not exist. I don't wanna face the tomorrows. I can barely escape the yesterdays. I am bruised and disoriented and still the cloud thickens.*
June 30. *I let the alcohol pump slowly through my veins. Clouding my mind and making it easier for those harsh words to roll from my tongue. Once where that bitter taste eased my conscience and drowned my fears now only intensifies them. Allowing me to hate*

you and everyone who tries to comfort me. Let it be that way if it's the easy way out of hurting myself. Let it be known that I can't stand this existence anymore.

The desire to suppress painful feelings drives teens and adults alike to use mind-altering substances to the point of becoming numb. My acronym for the word NUMB is:

Nobody Understands My Being

This definition underscores the mistaken belief at the heart of our instinct to isolate, or numb out, at precisely the moments when we are in greatest need of support. The paradox, of course, is that the experience of sharing painful feelings with someone who cares *enhances* the possibility of becoming more self-empowered without the numbing effects of alcohol or any other substance; for when we unite in the truth with another human BEING, both cannot help but be healed and lifted into a more powerful presence of love.

Misty had enough clarity to see that alcohol was clouding her mind, but she had not yet reached a level of AWARENESS to understand the answer to her problem rested in her reaching out to accept help from those attempting to comfort her. Of course, this answer only works if those who reach back to help (usually parents) do so with authentic motivation in their minds and unconditional love in their hearts. In this context of giving and receiving help, I define HELP as the:

Healing Essence of Love's Presence

Too many girls do not feel the extension of even one of these gestures, much less both. Whether real or imagined, they see their parents as either too caught up in their own lives, too much in denial, or too attached to molding their daughters' personalities into what they—the parents—think they should be, which may have been the reason the girls became ensnared in the clouds of unreality to begin with! Even well-intentioned, loving parents are in an uphill battle because of the misperceptions and self-doubts that leave many teenagers not feeling safe enough at home to express their authentic hopes, doubts, flaws and fears. This is why it's so critical they have a place where they can express all of their feelings.

In her mid-teens, Diana dared to ask the kinds of big questions young girls are bold enough to ponder, in spite of the fact that her mother responded with small answers. Diana's perception that her relationship with her parents consisted of little more than instructions on "what not to do, how not to do it, and who not to be" fueled her growing desire for freedom and drove her into greater secrecy about how she was spending her free time.

Diana, Age 15

January 4. *Lately, when Mom asks me where I am going, I lie automatically. It's sad that I don't even feel guilty. Often, I'm out drinking, but sometimes I'm just spending an evening out driving around with my friends. But I can't tell her that. I would be grounded.*

January 11. *I wasn't supposed to date before the age of 16 but for some reason Mom let me. Now I think she is sorry. I guess that leads up to what just happened. Last Friday night was the Sadie Hawkins dance. Dave, Carol, Jack and I had some whiskey and 7-up. I was so drunk. The last thing I remember was reaching for the glass. We shouldn't have gone to the dance. But it's too late now. Mr. Forbes, our principal, caught me, and Dad came and got me. But my problems were just starting. I was suspended from school Monday. I had to talk to Mr. Forbes. I started crying and lying that it was my first time drinking, and that I had only had two beers, and I don't know what else. I cannot go to any school activities until after January 28th, the end of the semester. Also, I am grounded for two weeks. Mom seems to think Jack is too old for me, which is crazy. I could have access to anything I wanted without him. Not to mention I happen to be in love with him. We are very close and I think we share something very special. I can just hear Mom if I told her that. Anyway, she doesn't like him too much right now. But, hopefully, things will work out.*

January 15. *Everyone keeps saying, "It probably taught you a lesson." Well the only lesson it taught me was not to get caught next time.*

January 16. *Being grounded, I have a lot of time to think. How I wish I could remember every possible minute of my life! When I'm 36, will I remember when I felt depressed or happy, or sad? Will I remember how I felt when I looked out the window yesterday and saw the snow and the cold? Will I remember how excited I felt right before I went to the Homecoming dance? Life is passing so fast. What is its purpose? Does anyone else wonder about these things? Did my mom ever have questions like this before all of her thoughts* were focused on how things look to other people in the outside world?

January 29. *I just had a long talk with Mom. It is going to take her a long time to trust me again. Not just drinking and Jack stuff, but me in general. It's all so weird. My Mom really doesn't get it, and she doesn't get me.*

Anne Frank

Sunday, Sept 27, 1942. *... Mother and I had a so-called discussion today. But the annoying part is that I burst into tears ... It's obvious that I'm a stranger to her. She doesn't even know what I think about the most ordinary things.*

Many years later, Diana—now herself a mother of two daughters—reflects on her relationship with her mother, and how her addiction to drugs and alcohol began as an attempt to fill the void she felt at home.

Diana's Reflection, 37 years later

Regarding my problem with alcohol, I wish someone had stepped in to help me realize it was a problem sooner. I went through years of hell before going to AA. If my mom had ever wanted to hear the truth about me, instead of being so concerned about what other people thought, it would have been better for all of us. My mom felt that if she didn't address it, it didn't exist. One of the most typical responses from my mom was, "Diana, stop talking nonsense."

Growing up, there was no instruction or example about how to be happy from the inside out. I have made sure to teach my own daughters to prioritize happiness. My Dad was a good man, but not strong enough to stand up to my mom. In my effort to be happy, I turned to alcohol and pot.

I continued to drink while I finished school and worked on other aspects of my life. At the age of 21, after a very serious car accident (not alcohol related), I decided that I would figure out how to be happy. I quit drinking with the help of AA and it was the best decision of my life. I have created a world I love, filled with happiness and loving people surrounding me. While my mom has never changed her approach and is still very unhappy, my attitude toward her has changed. I'm able to see her history of growing up with very strict parents, and having had difficulty with change.

What I wanted from my mom, and didn't receive, was what I made sure to give my kids. Honesty, support, and lots of listening

Never compare your "inside" with somebody else's "outside."
—Unknown

Let the alcohol level get below the ears and then you can start hearing.
—AA saying

without judgment. My daughters have never felt foolish or stupid talking to me about anything. I listen, and even if I have thought, "oh, you will feel differently when you are older," I don't say it. I never make them feel silly about their views, ideas or plans. As a mother, I have learned that you don't have to let children do whatever they want to have a good relationship. You don't have to be best friends. That can come later. What you have to do is listen, listen, listen. Spend time together without asking too many questions. In situations when you are going somewhere or doing something together, that's when real life stuff comes up. Don't force it, and be ready and open when it comes. Even when I am busy, I stop and talk. It's that important. If my teenagers need help, I am there. Today, I consider that from my mom, I actually learned how to become a really good mother. I am at peace, and satisfied with my life and my decisions. Everything I went through led me to a wonderful place.

The Value of Straight Talk

One of the most powerful universal truths about adolescents is their zero-tolerance policy for adult hypocrisy.
—Dr. Michael Bradley

As parents, our success in helping our teens steer clear of alcohol abuse hinges on our ability to recognize the dangers of the mindset Diana saw within her own mother—"Mom felt that if she didn't address it, it didn't exist." While it can be tempting to avoid uncomfortable subjects, what we don't know about our daughters' experimentation with alcohol *can* hurt us—and them. Demands, commands and all-out wars against alcohol are likely to be counterproductive to our ultimate goal of raising girls who respect themselves, know their boundaries, and develop both refusal skills and a healthy AWARENESS of moderation in all things. In fact, maybe you've noticed that parents who approach the topic of alcohol with an attitude of strict authority seem to raise the kind of kids who jump at the first chance to experiment. Teenagers, more than human beings of any other age, are up for a power struggle and are ready to rebel nearly every time they feel their freedom being compromised.

Susie Walton, my own parenting mentor, ingrained in me this old saying: "Rules without relationship equals rebellion." The more you catch your kids doing something right, the less you'll catch them doing something wrong. Voice your positive observations of right action, instead of taking them for granted. For example, "You did a great job listening to your instincts and getting out of a shaky situation." Love expands the relationship, fear contracts it. My interviews with diarists have confirmed I wasn't alone in experiencing how the power of the fear factor instilled by parents may have robotically kept us from drinking in high school. In the long run, however, fear-driven behavior is not really powerful at all. This is why those motivated by fear sometimes head into a whirlwind of parties once off to college or away from home.

Does that mean we should be permissive to every whim and desire voiced by our teenagers? No. In Diana's case, a sequence of unfortunate events both preceded and followed the Sadie Hawkins dance. First and foremost, there was no strong foundation or indication of a healthy bond in the parent-teen relationship to begin with. Second, there appears to have been no clear conversation about family values and expectations regarding alcohol use. Next, when she did get caught drinking, there was a lack of genuine curiosity and no concern about her health and safety from her parents. "What happened? What did you learn? What can we do differently as a family?" are a few questions they might have asked. Consequences may still have included grounding or other restrictions, but the primary focus would come from a loving, rather than a threatening place. Placing too much emphasis on lost trust may come off like a guilt trip, and create even more separation. A targeted discussion addressing where responsibilities and agreements fell through the cracks helps both sides clarify and renew a commitment to responsibilities. Remember to decipher the word responsibility. In this situation, what needs to happen for each person involved to be *able to* RESPOND differently in a similar scenario? Lessons of self-management, problem solving and negotiation were missed in what could have been a powerful course correction and an opportunity for a connection.

This is what makes teenagers such powerful teachers on our own path to inner peace. It was so easy to coax them back up after they stumbled and fell as toddlers. Now, stumbling and falling may manifest as breaking agreements or experimenting with alcohol or other drugs. As parents, we are thrust into the advanced class on how to remain composed and present during this turbulent developmental stage of our kids' lives. It is our curriculum to deepen our practice of the virtues of patience, understanding, fairness, consistency, follow-through, forgiveness, unconditional love, balance and, yes, even laughter. Radiating such qualities doesn't mean we move passively through these years, it means we embrace every twist and

FRAGILE EXPERIENCE OF ANXIETY OR REGRET

REFRAIN AND ENTER A SILENT PAUSE IN ORDER TO NURTURE A DECISION turn as we ride the roller coaster of our lives. We do it with our seatbelts securely fastened to the center of our soul. We do it with our hearts and minds ready to use every stomach-churning experience as an opportunity to maintain the loving connection we celebrated so many years ago when that innocent baby who at times veered off track made it safely back into our arms.

It's true that in today's lessons, our lectures about things like alcohol abuse are likely to be met with eye-rolling and feigned listening; and it's also true that an open dialogue offering practical, real life strategies for navigating the challenging situations our girls are likely to encounter has a far greater chance of capturing their attention. Role-playing various scenarios is a great way to prepare for situations our daughters are likely to encounter at one point or another.

When my friend Kathleen's 15-year-old daughter Megan asked to go to a friend's party where Kathleen suspected alcohol would be available, she used the leverage of her daughter's desire to go as an opportunity to test her refusal skills. Role-playing the part of a sophomore boy, Kathleen used a variety of tactics—first to persuade her daughter to drink, and then to accept a ride home from someone who had been drinking. In the end, this dialogue did more than help Megan prepare for these situations in advance; it also brought to Kathleen's attention a fact that her daughter hadn't before shared: she'd been offered alcohol before—as well as cigarettes and marijuana—the first invitation dating all the way back to the beginning of eighth grade. Unbeknownst to Kathleen, Megan had already developed some pretty solid refusal skills on her own.

When Kathleen shared this story with me, I asked her if she would revisit this subject with Megan, this time making a list of all the responses the two came up with. The conversation that followed was educational, enlightening and at times even comical. Kathleen knew her daughter was not exactly a wallflower, but the assertiveness she demonstrated when role-playing ways to refuse alcohol both surprised and delighted her. What follows is a list of all the responses Megan came up with, both to being offered a drink and to accepting a ride from someone whom she suspected had been drinking. Note that these refusals are organized by the degree of their escalating intensity:

Strategies for Saying "No" When Someone Offers You Alcohol

Just say KNOW.
—David Sheff

- ⊛ "No, thanks."

- ⊛ "Not right now."

- ⊛ "I'm not drinking tonight."

- ⊛ "I'm not really a fan of alcohol."

- ⊛ "Maybe later; I'm pacing myself."

- ⊛ "And show up to my volleyball (cheer/softball/soccer, etc.) game tomorrow morning hung over? No thank you!"

- ⊛ "My mom has a Breathalyzer at home. I know; she's crazy!"

- ⊛ "Wow; you make 'drunk' look pretty darn attractive, but I think I'll take a pass."

However, because teenage parties aren't exactly organized by guest list, and because the possibility of parents coming home early or the police being called in response to a neighbor's complaint can create a need for a hasty Plan B, it's likely that at some point our daughters will be offered a ride home by someone who has been drinking. To this scenario, Megan and Kathleen came up with several possible responses. Some were polite refusals ("No, thanks. I already have a ride;" "I'm not going straight home; I'm staying with a friend"); others were crafted to blatantly point out the foolishness of making such a CHOICE: ("Get in the car with you, in your condition? No thanks; I'd like to live to see my 16th birthday.").

This twenty-minute talk accomplished a lot more than giving Megan some creative ways to sidestep potentially dangerous situations involving alcohol. It also sent the unspoken message that her mom is AWARE of the pressures of being a teenager; she understands that the waters are not easy to navigate. Most importantly, Megan understood that regardless of the situation, her mom is always on her side. Kathleen also took this opportunity to state her values with regard to underage drinking. She is not a mother who lives with her head in the sand, but one who knows where to draw the line in it. Understanding it is within a teenager's job description to test boundaries, she made it clear that the privilege of going to dances and parties comes with the responsibility to refrain from doing anything illegal—including drinking as a minor or taking drugs. Once an acceptable boundary has been crossed, teenagers are often compelled to reach

AWAKE
WITH
ALL
REALITY
EXPOSED

beyond the new line, most likely into riskier territory. Kathleen had read statistics and reports like the one by *The Partnership* at www.drugfree.org that disclosed these facts:

> *Just as research shows that parents who discipline by hitting or degrading their child have children at an increased risk for substance abuse, permissive/lenient parents who allow their children to do what they want when they want (because they either don't want to deal with a child's behavior or they don't want their child to be angry with them) also place their children at increased risk ... The more exposure to drinking in adolescence and parental acceptance of substance use, the higher the risk of later problems with alcohol and other drugs.*

One thing for parents to keep in mind, however, is that the urgency of the present moment, usually the upcoming party, is sometimes all a teenager is able to focus on. It is, therefore, up to us to help our girls think logically about the results their actions will have, long after the fact. Knowing that no serious discussion of teenage drinking would be complete without addressing the real dangers and consequences of alcohol abuse, Kathleen—once she sensed that the lines of communication on the subject were open—shared with Megan the following compelling reasons why it's in her best interest to avoid alcohol:

While 80 percent of teenagers have tried alcohol by the time they graduate from high school, the majority are not regular drinkers.
— The Monitoring the Future Study, the University of Michigan

- ✪ *To maintain self-respect. According to teenagers themselves, the most effective way to persuade them to avoid alcohol is to appeal to their self-respect; to let them know that they are too smart and have too much going for them to rely on a crutch. Teens also are likely to pay attention to ways in which alcohol may lead to embarrassing situations or events that could damage their reputation or cause a rift in important relationships. For example, when word gets out that a teen is a drinker, a very common consequence is for other parents to limit their child's contact with that person.*

- ✪ *To avoid a potentially life-threatening danger. According to the CDC, in 2011 nearly one million high school teens drank alcohol and got behind the wheel. That a primary cause of teen deaths is caused by motor vehicle crashes involving alcohol is only one factor that makes alcohol dangerous. Drinking also makes a girl more vulnerable to sexual assault and unprotected sex. And while our teens may genuinely believe they wouldn't engage in hazardous activities after drinking, the fact is that because alcohol impairs judgment, someone who is under the influence is less likely to consider high-risk activities to be dangerous.*

⊕ *To stay out of trouble with the law. Because alcohol use under the age of 21 is illegal, getting caught can get a teen into potentially serious trouble with the authorities and could delay getting a driver's permit and license.*

⊕ *To avoid falling victim to a family history of alcoholism. If there is a family history of alcoholism, your child bears a higher risk of developing a drinking problem.*

⊕ *To ensure healthy brain development. The adolescent brain may be particularly susceptible to long-term negative consequences from alcohol use. Alcohol consumption while the brain is still maturing may trigger long-term biological changes that may have detrimental effects on the developing adolescent brain.*

One further note for us as parents is that it's vital to make sure our own behaviors reinforce the same message we are sending our children—that moderation is essential and that alcohol is never an acceptable remedy for solving problems or escaping a bad mood or a difficult situation. Remember that each CHOICE we make takes us in the direction of *freeing* our BEING—BODY, EMOTIONS, IMAGINATION, NATURAL SELF, and GENIUS MIND—or in the direction of *repressing* it. To determine which way we parents are headed, we can simply notice the purpose behind each action we take. If there is drinking at a party, what role is the alcohol playing? If the idea is to get drunk, we are headed down a slippery slope that will diminish our discretion and our ability to enjoy the evening, and perhaps even place us in harm's way. If, on the other hand, the idea is to have a drink or two over the course of a night while conversing, laughing and playing games with friends, the alcohol is secondary to socializing, and we will likely create a much more enjoyable (and safer) experience.

BODY
EMOTIONS
IMAGINATION
NATURAL SELF
GENIUS MIND

The following quiz, adapted and reprinted from *Young People and AA*, printed by Alcoholics Anonymous World Services, Inc., may help to bring to light answers for both parents and teens:

Score-It-Yourself Quiz for Teens Who Drink

⊕ *Do you drink to overcome shyness and/or build up self-confidence?*

⊕ *Is drinking affecting your reputation?*

⊕ *Do you drink to escape from study or home worries?*

✪ *Does it bother you if somebody says maybe you drink too much?*

✪ *Do you have to take a drink to go out to date?*

✪ *Do you ever get into money trouble over buying liquor?*

✪ *Have you lost any friends since you started drinking?*

✪ *Do your friends drink less than you do?*

✪ *Do you drink until the bottle is empty?*

✪ *Have you ever had loss of memory from drinking?*

✪ *Has drunk driving ever put you into a hospital or a jail?*

✪ *Do you get annoyed with classes or lectures on drinking?*

✪ *Do you think you have a problem with liquor?*

✪ *Do you drink when you get mad at other people, your friends or your parents?*

✪ *Are your grades starting to slip?*

✪ *Did you ever try to stop drinking—or drink less—and fail?*

✪ *Have you ever had a drink in the morning before school or work?*

✪ *Do you lie about your drinking?*

✪ *Do you get drunk when you drink, even when you don't mean to?*

✪ *Do you think it's cool to be able to hold your liquor?*

Unless their parents are alcoholics, teens are bound to notice that in most adult social gatherings where drinks are being served and consumed in moderation, the focus is not on the alcohol or its effects any more than is an appetizer or dessert the purpose of the gathering. Alcohol itself is just a substance. But as the great psychologist Carl Jung, one of my favorite leaders in the field of psychology, wrote in a letter to Bill Wilson, co-founder of Alcoholics Anonymous, that his experience with many alcoholics, (and one in particular about whom he was speaking in his letter), "His craving for alcohol is the equivalent, on a low level, of the spiritual thirst of our BEING for wholeness." I believe this thirst has two parts. The first, arising out of a deep sense of hopelessness plaguing most addicts, is a longing to connect with one's authentic self. The second reflects our need for genuine connection with other human beings. For far too many people, the attempt to quench this thirst for wholeness extends beyond the use or abuse of alcohol and reaches into the depths of other drugs, some of which present different, and sometimes more dangerous, risks than alcohol abuse.

Drugs and Addiction

Claire, Age 16

After skiing today, we went to Steve's room and drank beer before I took three Valium. Next, we went to some friend's hotel room and I had two more beers, one joint and two glasses of V&O. Not surprisingly, I fell asleep in the guys' room. When I woke up, Jane, Liz, Cathy and I went to the store and I was so fucked up! Jane and I ran arm in arm and we talked about old times. On the way back I fell down and crushed both of my knees. They're in pain. I was in hysterics—totally bawling. I asked for Richard or Tom (I don't remember). Then in the morning I woke up and couldn't figure out what happened to my pants!

Claire's Reflection, 25 years later

I used a lot of drugs and alcohol in high school. There wasn't much parent supervision, and my group of friends wasn't involved in enough activities to keep out of trouble. What is truly frightening is this lethal combination of drugs and alcohol I was doing. The fact that I was able to come out of it with only a foggy memory and sore knees is amazing. I was a recreational drug user, not an addict. I quit using cocaine in high school after I read a public service announcement in a teen magazine that highlighted using cocaine even one time could cause a heart attack. That article literally scared me straight. I never used coke again. I stopped smoking pot the day I graduated from college. I knew that I wanted to go into the world with my head on straight. Unfortunately, my drinking continued. I was not an alcoholic, but I was a binge drinker. I drank to excess for too many years. I am lucky that I wasn't raped or killed, given some of the less than brilliant things I have done—including driving drunk and having one-night stands. Now, I know what to look for with my own children if they go down that slippery slope. I don't think it ever crossed my mind that something terrible could happen. I was just young and incredibly naïve. Whenever I see a story on television about parents losing a child to binge drinking, date rape, etc., I think, "There by the grace of God go I." It really could have been me. I know now that I was way too young to have been on a loosely supervised ski trip with boys and girls. I thought I

An alcoholic will steal your wallet and lie to you. A drug addict will steal your wallet and then help you look for it.
—David Sheff

was so grown up at sixteen. I was not even close. I should have had a more watchful eye on me.

Marijuana, prescription drugs, ecstasy, inhalants, cocaine and heroin are just some of the drugs our teens are using. Other "designer" drugs popular among teens are Smiles, Molly and Bath Salts (no, not the kind you put in your bath) and others. Due to the number of deaths associated with sudden sniffing death syndrome (SSDS), the Council on Drug Abuse (CODA) has declared inhalant abuse, especially in children and teens, an "alarming issue." The practice of combining alcohol and prescription drugs as Claire described in her diary entry and later reflection, is not uncommon among teenagers.

A government study reveals that Americans, who constitute less than 5 percent of the world's population, consume approximately 80 percent of the world's opioid supply.

Another variation of teenage use of pills is known as "pharming." During pharming parties, teens dump into a big bowl a collection of drugs such as Xanax, Vicodin, Valium, Percocet, Adderol, Ritalin and Oxycontin, obtained, most likely, from medicine cabinets at home. Partygoers take the drugs at random, often not knowing what they are taking, or the potential side effects of combining these medications. The blinding perception of adventure hides the potential danger—especially of opioids like Oxycontin, whose maker admitted to misleading doctors and the public about its risk of addiction and was forced to pay $600 million in fines. Without the guiding feminine principals and moral compass that protects and cares for others, the health care industry that is designed to nurture our health can lead us into an epidemic of greed-based addiction.

Even when taken innocently—perhaps after a sports injury or accident—this pain medication has the potential to lead down an insidious and treacherous path of addiction, especially for teenage girls. Often, health insurance benefits that helped to pay for the drug prescribed for a physical injury runs out; yet dependency has already run rampant, even after the physical injury has healed. And because heroin, also an opioid, happens to be much cheaper than Oxycontin, some addicts turn to this street drug because it provides a similar high. Just as prescriptions for all types of opioids have skyrocketed, the use of heroin has reflected the increase. In fact, four out of five new heroin users have abused painkillers.

Prescription painkiller overdoses send a woman to the ER every 3 minutes in the U.S.
—CDC

Whether the addiction began in an attempt to have fun or to ease pain, the fact is that prescription opioids now kill more people than heroin and cocaine combined. Every day, 42 women die from a drug overdose—and nearly half of those overdoses are from prescription painkillers. A true addict in need of a fix will do anything to get the drug—including sell her own body—an act that introduces a whole new level of life-threatening dangers.

Drugs are like hijackers who take over brain circuitry.
—Brian Johnson

Painkillers And The Heroin Market

A growing number of people are using heroin in recent years, in part because it can be cheaper and easier to find than opioid painkillers purchased on the black market. Most heroin users were first hooked on prescription opioids, which generated $11 billion in 2010 for the pharmaceutical industry.

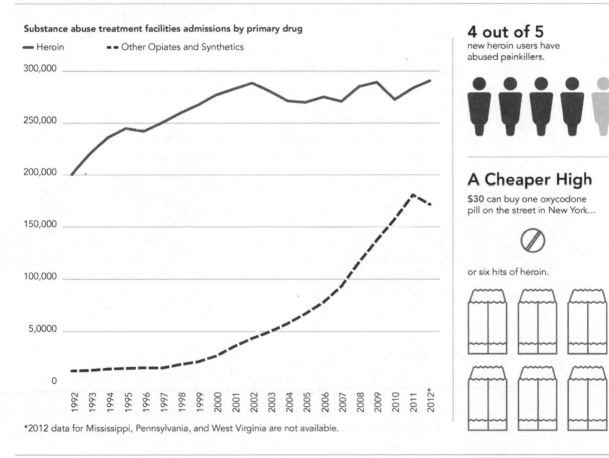

Substance abuse treatment facilities admissions by primary drug
— Heroin   ▪▪ Other Opiates and Synthetics

*2012 data for Mississippi, Pennsylvania, and West Virginia are not available.

4 out of 5
new heroin users have abused painkillers.

A Cheaper High

$30 can buy one oxycodone pill on the street in New York...

or six hits of heroin.

THE HUFFINGTON POST
* Adapted for Grayscale

Sources: SAMHDA, Los Angeles Times, Frost & Sullivan

Reprinted with permission.

A 2012 documentary featured on NBC entitled *Sex Slaves: Addiction*, brings to light that girls who are addicted are sometimes sought out by drug dealers and pimps looking for those in desperation to take advantage of—and to gain even more control over by introducing them to methamphetamines, or meth. Meth is especially dangerous due to the unsurpassed surge of dopamine that hits the brain and causes extreme pleasure. Tragically, as the brain becomes used to receiving these large doses of dopamine, it stops producing its own. This means that when the addict stops using meth, the withdrawals are horrific and may lead to an inability to experience pleasure at all.

The earlier a girl starts using alcohol or other drugs, the higher her chances of developing an addiction. In light of the fact that kids who start drinking before age 15 are four times more likely to develop alcoholism than if they wait until they're 21, it's no wonder that Cha, whose entries and later reflection are printed below, became an addict.

> ### Cha, Age 9 (yes, age 9)
> *It's Labor Day weekend and my mom has been downstairs watching the Jerry Lewis telethon all day while my older sister and I were trippin' balls of LSD and trying to hide it from my mom. The night ended with us in the bathtub with terrible stomach cramps, drinking orange juice, trying with all our might to get tired enough to sleep. I have my ballet lesson tomorrow so I really want to sleep.*
>
> ### Cha, Age 12
> *My mom bought alcohol for my sisters and cousins and their friends. She said she was tired of fighting about it, and figured they would just get it elsewhere, and would rather have them drinking at our place than out and about.*
>
> ### Cha, Age 13
> *Jessica came over and I pretended to hide smoking weed from my mom for her sake because I was afraid of what she would think of my mom for allowing it, or that she would tell her parents my mom allowed it.*

Years later, Cha wrote a reflection about the underlying causes that contributed to her experimentation and later addiction to drugs.

Reflections of a Former Addict

Cha's Reflection, 35 years after first taking drugs

My sister, seven years older than me, was very developed, and started attracting boys/men to her by age 14. She and my mom went around and around over issues not atypical for adolescence. Now I look back to those times and remember the days my mom tried to be the authority figure she should have been. A time before she gave up. She had grown up in a poor family in Arkansas. Never having witnessed courage, strength or will, she had no well from which to draw anything different. My father was not really a part of my life as a young child. He was a truck driver who used to visit on occasion when passing through town.

At age 7, I was sent along on dates between my sister and her boyfriend, who was in his late teens. My mission was to spy for mom, but I was hip to the notion they were doing something different, and I certainly did not want to be excluded. I'm sure my sister's boyfriend was all about getting in her pants, so getting me high was probably used as a distraction from what they were doing. So while I learned my basic multiplication tables after daybreak as a second grader, I smoked weed in the back seat of a car at dusk.

By age 10, I was becoming aware of my own sexuality. I became infatuated with one of my sister's boyfriends. He gave me pot and LSD and began touching me, and at some point, attempted to have penetration sex. I did bleed, so I'm pretty sure my hymen was torn at that time. I have to tell you that thinking about that really grosses me out. I try not think of that as the time I lost my virginity—in all reality it probably was. But today, I resent him even more because he was the first one who shot up my sister and brother with drugs— and they are still bound by addiction to this day, 25 years later, which breaks my heart.

Coming into my own teen years, I became more interested in sex and drugs and partying. There was never a time that I consciously thought of drugs as an escape. It's just the way it was; it's what everyone around me knew and did. There were always older boyfriends that would well be considered sex offenders for their association with us girls. At the time, I felt I was fairly picky about who I slept with—unlike my older sisters. I guess it's all relative, because I had a dozen partners at the age of 14. That was the age at which I met my oldest son's dad. He was 10 years older, and an ex felon (petty theft). We clicked immediately, and within a year of meeting him I left home with him. I told my Mom I wanted to go and she said, "Well you are probably going to whether I say yes or no, so you might as well." (As I type this, it is hard to wrap my mind around that concept of allowing my daughter who is almost 14 to leave town with a man in his 20s.) We ended up in Colorado, staying with an odd couple and doing more cocaine. The wife had an addiction to rock cocaine, and it was enough of a turn off for me to see her picking at her hair and jonesing (craving her next fix) the way she did that I only smoked it once or twice. Thank goodness.

But eventually, I started using, snorting pure grade meth, and before I knew it I was hooked. When we didn't have money for the meth, it was really bad ... I was going through a pretty heavy withdrawal, and my addict boyfriend was a real asshole to me. I hated my life, I missed my family, my friends, and I missed my boyfriend who was all wrapped up in his own addiction, thinking only of himself. He shared needles and didn't even care if he got hepatitis or anything else. We did a lot of stealing during that period, and long story short, one time there were lots of cops outside my window. I panicked, got dressed and went to a window on the opposite side, crawled out and bolted. I hid in the bushes for a long time and finally escaped. Under assumed names, my boyfriend and I fled to Truckee, California, where he left me when our drug dealers harassed us for money we owed them. We got back together just before my 18th birthday. At 19, I became pregnant with my oldest son. I smoked some pot still, but not with the frequency that I did pre-pregnancy, and did no other chemicals while pregnant. The birth of my son changed me in a profound way. I wanted so much more for him. Sadly, I would never achieve it being with his father. At 25, I'd become too "grown up" by not wanting to do dope with him and wanting to move on. He found a 17-year-old girl to be with, and I quit my job, took my piece of shit car, my son in the back, and moved back to Kansas—home. A job at a call center helped me begin to raise my son on my terms, in a drug free environment. My current husband and I became clear that drugs were not a part of how we wanted to continue, so I believe ... if memory serves me right ... the last time I used any chemicals was in 1997, many years ago.

The stories of teen drug addiction are as heartbreaking as the recoveries of the lucky ones are inspiring. Christina Huffington, in *The Huffington Post*, wrote:

> In the end, every addict's story is the same. At first, the substance—whether it's drugs or food or sex or alcohol—works perfectly. It erases the boy who broke your heart, drowns out the voices saying you will never be enough, numbs the fear that suffocates you—until, first slowly and then all at once, it stops working and all you're left with is pain a hundred times worse than what you were trying to forget.

Daughter of Arianna Huffington—an iconic model of self-empowerment, Christina serves as an example that no matter the background or social status of a teenage girl, no one is immune to the indiscriminate claws of addiction. In her article, she shared about first trying cocaine at age 16, then finally seeking help and getting sober at 22. Huffington came forth with the details of her struggle with addiction in hopes of letting others feel less alone and to encourage them to ask for help, as she did.

One of the most important resources we can give girls is to help them understand the price of these soul-stealing fears. To live in fear is the worst form of insult to our true selves.
—Arianna Huffington

Gateway "Drugs"

Christina was right. Choosing a path of drug use to escape pain inevitably leads us further into pain. Anytime we seek internal fulfillment through external means, we set in motion a fundamental disconnection from our Natural Self. Sometimes it's not until drug use has escalated out of control that we realize just how disconnected we've become. Looking at our actions in hindsight, however, it's easier to recognize the pivotal CHOICES that led us to the end of the road—psychologically, physically, and spiritually.

We often hear that marijuana is a gateway drug to heavier drug use—yet many teens don't try pot for the first time unless they have first been drinking. In fact, I think the only reason I accepted a "community" joint that was being passed around at a KISS concert I attended in college is because I'd been to a pre-concert party where I'd imbibed a few strawberry daiquiris. However, after reading the stories of countless girls who have abused any form of chemical substance, I began to reflect upon the real triggers that lead down the road to addiction. I've come to the conclusion the real "gateway" is not a substance at all, but a mistaken belief—or a whole succession of them—of somehow being unworthy, not enough or alone. The CHOICES that lead most teens into drug or alcohol dependency are not driven by a desire for euphoria or to get a "buzz" on, but to compensate for deep-seated feelings of inadequacy or self-consciousness. In other words, they are looking to an external source to fill an emptiness they perceive within themselves. This point was driven home for me in another story my friend Kathleen shared with me.

The act of role-playing possible strategies for refusing alcohol and other drugs with her daughter Megan opened a more honest discussion between the two about the topic. Kathleen was pleased when Megan came home one day and shared some additional insights she learned at a school assembly on drug and alcohol prevention. The presenter, Megan explained, began the lecture by drawing a circle on the chalkboard. This circle represented a healthy, non-addicted person; a person who feels comfortable enough in her own skin to socialize with others without needing a chemical high to "loosen up." When this person consumes alcohol or other drugs, the "buzz" she feels is in addition to or an extension of the state of comfort she was already feeling. When the high wears off, she experiences the low that normally follows all chemically induced highs, but eventually returns to her previous self-esteem "set-point."

The presenter then drew a second circle on the board, but this time filled it in with dark spots. This circle represented a girl plagued by feelings of inadequacy—not just the garden variety of negative self-talk that, as far as I can tell, is nearly universal. The darkened areas of this circle represented the loneliness, the emptiness and erosion of self-confidence caused by comparison, insecurity or the stress of trying to "measure up" or fit in. When teenage girls have accepted an underlying limiting belief, such as "I'm too boring just as I am" or "I'm not brave enough without alcohol," and they reach for a drink or smoke weed, they are *not* doing it to enhance their enjoyment of the moment, but to drown out their pain and discomfort. The teen (or adult, for that matter) whose inner "circle" of self-esteem is swallowed into this black hole of self-rejection is more prone to become dependent—in other words, to compensate for what she believes is an inherent deficit or shortfall within herself. When the high wears off for this person, the painful emotions that had been temporarily numbed by the chemical return—and they may be stronger than ever. And then what happens? She craves the next high. Thus the cycle of dependence or addiction is set in motion, despite the fact it only compounds the problem and

You are only as sick as your secrets.
—Addiction recovery slogan

drives her even further into darkness and despair.

Where There Is a Will, There Is a Way

Special alert to anyone reading this and struggling with an addiction: *You deserve to be healthy and happy.* There is hope for everyone who has the desire to change. Addiction is a disease, but it's a treatable one. If we are willing to unravel the outdated and flawed programming we've constructed to shield us from rejection or protection, we can find the courage to let down our guard, to ask for help, and to connect authentically with those around us. When we dispel the myth that sharing our secrets will make us unlovable or unacceptable in the eyes of others, we come to understand this truth: *Vulnerability is the new power.* Shedding our illusions of isolation and loneliness and standing united with others who share similar struggles reduces our need to make ourselves "comfortably" NUMB and makes us less susceptible to the inner triggers that fuel dependency on external substances. Asking for help is not a sign of weakness; it is an invitation to connect. Connecting with others *who deserve our trust* is a powerful declaration that we are ready to correct the destructive urges that keep us from turning to sources of actual nourishment—friends, family, loved ones, community, support—in favor of securing the next "fix." As Christina Huffington noted in the article quoted earlier, "Addiction lives in darkness, it feeds off our secrets and it thrives in the shadows." The moment we are willing to take our addictions out of the darkness and re-examine them in the light of day, we take a pivotal first step towards recovery. This degree of surrender demands a great deal of courage, but it is this leap of faith that brings about the experience of grace, which a great many former addicts describe.

So significant are moments of grace in generating a shift in perception and direction that I've created an acronym to help break down exactly what occurs in these transformative moments: **GRACE** is the:

GENUINE RECOGNITION AND ACCEPTANCE OF OUR CONNECTED ESSENCE

. . . GRACE

It is *genuine* because there is no more sincere or authentic act than surrendering our will to the intelligence that orchestrates the very pulse of life, from the tiniest organism to the largest galaxy. *Recognition*, or *re*-cognition, is the mind's remembrance that even in our illusion of isolation we

I have met brave women who are exploring the outer edge of human possibility, with no history to guide them, and with a courage to make themselves vulnerable that I find moving beyond words.
—Gloria Steinem

Better keep yourself clean and bright; you are the window through which you must see the world.
—George Bernard Shaw

are still inseparably linked to the Source. Our *acceptance* of the fact that we are one with the same intelligence that has the power to heal anything restores our understanding that we are *connected* with the *essence* of the life force itself. Even for those who feel like they are drowning in a sea of blackouts, one moment of clarity can be enough to turn the ship of self-destruction around. By slowing down, even slightly, our tendency to reach outside ourselves for this connection, we catch a glimpse of a light that shines on a new possibility. If in these transformative moments we can gather the presence to recall the meaning of the five words that make up the gift of GRACE, we will realize that maybe, just maybe, we are not all alone in our pain. By challenging the messages ingrained in our heads that convince us that happiness can be found in artificial pacification, we take a giant step toward true healing. GRACE is a blessing from the universe that has allowed many to rise out of the hell of addiction, to restore self-respect from the inside out and to use their experiences in service to others. And it is available at every moment.

For today, all you need is the grace to begin beginning.
—Julia Cameron

Three Steps to BEING in the Moment

There is a close link indeed between this long-held tenet of Alcoholics Anonymous and the practice of mindfulness. It's been nearly a century since AA cofounder Bill Wilson convinced Emmett Fox, a leader in the New Thought movement, to share his "one day at a time" motto to thousands of 12 Steppers at Carnegie Hall during the 1930s, and this brilliant behavioral technique is still helping millions. Rather than dwelling on unbearable regrets from the past or bearing the burden of thinking about how to stay sober for the rest of one's life, Fox taught his listeners to place their focus instead on the "here and now"—to take one step, one moment, one day at a time. This same message is at the heart of the practice of mindfulness; a skill that, like cooking, is easily learned with practice.

When I cook a new dish, I experiment with different recipes a few times, select what I feel are the best ingredients from each, and make the dish my own. I approach my personal growth in much the same way. I learn as many tools as I can to help stay in touch with my natural sense of aliveness, my own inner truth. Then I blend the best of each and make the practice my own. This has developed into a three-step process that for me has evolved into a daily ritual I practice and recommend as a tool for living in the moment.

In the first step, I carve out 15 minutes a day to consciously align all aspects of my BEING—my BODY, EMOTIONS, IMAGINATION, NATURAL SELF, and GENIUS MIND—with my SOULSELF. The first few minutes are dedicated to internally or mentally scanning my body—otherwise known as doing a progressive muscle relaxation exercise. In this phase, I get comfortable, with my spine as straight as possible, and then follow the flow of each muscle group from the top of my head down to my toes, almost as though there were an imaginary scanning device that catches and releases any tightness in my body the moment I become aware of it. (I know I hold tension in my jaw, because it starts to shake when I mentally pass through that area!)

In the second step, I focus on nurturing my expanding AWARENESS. I start by replacing anything that is *in tension* with *intention* to BREATHE through it. My definition for the word BREATHE in this context is to use the breath to create a:

BRIDGE TO RECONNECT YOUR ENERGY AND TRUST YOUR HEART ESSENCE

... BREATHE

As I focus on my breathing I observe my thoughts as if I were a bird perched in the corner of my mind or, as some describe it, as if my thoughts were leaves floating down a river, and I am sitting on the riverbank watching them go by. I notice my feelings, letting them come and letting them go. Within a few minutes, I become aware of a vibration of energy flowing through me, like you feel after rubbing your hands together, back and forth, and then stopping to feel the sensation generated in the space between them.

The third step is to connect to the energy that animates both my body and my mind—which is my own combination of breath AWARENESS and mindfulness. I switch up my practice based on my intention at that particular moment. If my goal is to quiet my mind, I repeat a phrase or mantra, like "I am at peace." When I am seeking guidance regarding a certain situation, I may recite, with a receptive attitude, a request I learned years ago from *A Course in Miracles:* "What would you have me do? Where would you have me go? What would you have me say, and to whom?" Sometimes I just sit quietly; other times I prefer to be led by a guided meditation by Deepak Chopra or Deva Premal or by an affirmative self-hypnosis audio I wrote and recorded using audio recording software on my computer. By

As long as I am breathing, in my eyes, I am just beginning.
—Criss Jami

doing these things, in the span of a quarter of an hour, I have recalibrated my compass and have brought my attention to the present moment by engaging all five aspects of my BEING. This practice is a sort of homemade blend between mindfulness and cognitive behavioral therapy (CBT).

I thought my practice was homemade, until my research led me to explore Dialectical Behavior Therapy (DBT). Developed in the late 1980s, DBT combines practices similar to those inspired by my own intuition, while focusing on acceptance-based interventions to encourage the validation of patients who were regularly invalidated in their formative years. It also combines CBT, which supports us in changing the thoughts and feelings that cause psychological problems by becoming aware of them, with mindful meditation, which takes us to a deeper level of conscious AWARENESS from which we can more easily access intuition and other inner resources. In 2014, a meta-study (a study of a number of studies) at The Johns Hopkins University concluded that mindfulness meditation may be helpful in reducing anxiety, depression and pain. Dr. Madhav Goyal, who conducted the study, wrote, "Clinicians should be prepared to talk with their patients about the role that a meditation program could have in addressing psychological stress."

In his book, *A New Earth: Awakening to Your Life's Purpose*, Eckhart Tolle offers a similar practice we can use in moments when we notice a compulsive need arising from within:

> *Stop and take three conscious breaths. This generates awareness. Then for a few minutes be aware of the compulsive urge itself as an energy field inside you. Consciously feel that need to physically or mentally ingest or consume a certain substance or the desire to act out some form of compulsive behavior. Then take a few more conscious breaths. After that you may find that the compulsive urge has disappeared—for the time being. Or you may find that it still overpowers you, and you cannot help but indulge or act it out again. Don't make it into a problem. Make the addiction part of your awareness practice in the way described above. As awareness grows, addictive patterns will weaken and eventually dissolve. Remember, however, to catch any thoughts that justify the addictive behavior, sometimes with clever arguments, as they arise in your mind. Ask yourself, who is talking here? And you will realize the addiction is talking. As long as you know that, as long as you are present as the observer of your mind, it is less likely to trick you into doing what it wants.*

If at first glance it seems like a huge leap to relate a simple practice of mindfulness to a complex problem like addiction, look again. Spending 15 minutes in daily mindful AWARENESS holds within it a seed that will eventually bloom into longer periods of sustained AWARENESS, because each moment spent being mindfully aware of the present instead of reinforcing an addiction strengthens our ability to navigate similar circumstances in the future. When we are suffering and feeling weak or vulnerable, the ability to stay present to that experience is the key to allowing it to pass through us. Uncomfortable though compulsive or painful feelings might be, if we can learn to observe them—to be informed by them rather than being affected by them—they come and go like any other experience. It's when we struggle to deny, suppress or dismiss them that these feelings become stuck, and keep us stuck along with them.

Mindfulness is best practiced during moments when we feel relatively calm and at peace. As we learn to observe the thoughts that arise about things that have little or no emotional charge, we train ourselves to become more present and conscious—rather than reactive and unconscious—when feelings of craving or compulsiveness arise. In recovery, these are referred to as HALT moments. As soon as we become aware of a desire to use, we take it as a cue to HALT; to observe what is going on in our bodies: Are we *Hungry, Angry, Lonely, Tired?* In the space between our thoughts and our response to those thoughts, our mindfulness muscles are strengthened.

Anyone, addict or not, can benefit from becoming more mindful of HALT moments, for unaddressed physical or emotional needs leave us vulnerable to relapses of all kinds—whether it's a relapse into chemicals or into a less authentic expression of ourselves. BEING present to what is happening within our bodies and minds gives us greater power over the CHOICES we face in every moment. The decision to drink or take drugs brings us deeper into the FEARSELF, while the opportunity to remain present through fleeting moments of weakness takes us one step toward the SOULSELF, and a giant leap toward wholeness. As parents, we need not wait for a child to hit rock bottom before we intervene; on the contrary, the earlier we intervene, the easier the recovery. This is especially true for teenagers. It is a myth also that the addict herself has to *want* our help to benefit from it. Generally speaking, they simply can't see the depth of their own addiction, and in some cases need to be coerced into treatment.

Many mothers and fathers wish they had seized the opportunity to do something before their child turned 18, when parents no longer have any legal influence over a child. But no matter what has or has not been done up until now, don't get caught up in the FEARSELF. Feelings of self-blame or guilt on the part of the parent are counter-productive. Stay focused on what can be done in the present to help keep the addict moving toward a clean future.

Treatment and Recovery

From the meta-research I've done on addiction and recovery in adolescents, it seems that at least two forms of treatment are required to increase the potential for lasting sobriety, and these two foundational components can be used in any combination. The first addresses the individual's connection with her own soul, commonly achieved through interventions such as CBT, mindfulness meditation, yoga, counseling and hypnotherapy. These practices can lead to the identification of the underlying experiences, emotions and beliefs that give rise to addictive behavior, but they must also be combined with a second form of treatment, which address the addict's connection to others. Through group support programs, such as those offered through AA or more secular organizations like Women for Sobriety, teens learn to build new self-esteem–enhancing social networks. This latter component of healing—connecting with others—is every bit as essential as the first, for addiction forges destructive ties while destroying healthy ones, and it's almost impossible to "pull out of it" by going it alone. Because many addicts have at least one underlying mental illness or learning disability, these must also be treated if sobriety is to be maintained. A program that focuses only on the chemical component is not addressing the problem at its source and is inviting a relapse. The research also indicates that loving and compassionate positive reinforcement works, and that negative reinforcement does not work.

The most effective form of treatment is one that brings into view the whole picture—the individual's relationship with her community as well as her relationship with herself—body, mind, and soul. The word yoga comes from a root word meaning union—often defined as the union of these three aspects. Tommy Rosen, a pioneer in Yoga and Recovery, advocates a combination of yoga, meditation and diet to help break what he

An addiction is the experience of a part of your personality that is completely under the control of external circumstances. Healing an addiction is one of the greatest spiritual accomplishments.
—Gary Zucav

37 percent of alcohol abusers and 53 percent of drug abusers also have at least one serious mental illness.
—Journal of the American Medical Association

calls the "forcefield of addiction." In his web-based interview series, *Recovery 2.0*, he explained that because the ancient tradition of yoga is designed to bring our AWARENESS to what is happening in both body and mind, it can help to restore mindfulness, even in someone who is accustomed to using alcohol or drugs to "check out."

Breathe, relax and feel the body receive its own truth.
—Danna Faulds

My yoga teacher, Sara Tobin, shared the following thoughts with me about why yoga is so effective in its ability to interrupt compulsive behaviors:

> *Through the movements of yoga, we naturally tune in to how and where emotions and stress are being held in the body. As we develop a consistent yoga practice, our awareness deepens, allowing insightful changes to occur both physically and emotionally. Through this deep awareness we recognize where our habitual or compulsive patterns are stored in the body and how they affect our overall health. Conscious breathing or connection with the breath creates movement which allows the release of stuck patterns and offers space for new openings to occur. Yoga literally helps us get our "issues out of our tissues."*

It seems that nothing short of a truly holistic approach has enough momentum to guide a teenager out of the state of disconnection and isolation created by drug addiction. One missing component, and even a teen who has made significant strides toward recovery may disappear back into her private oblivion. In the span of time I have devoted to writing this book I've come across some heartbreaking examples of this, including an interaction I had with a college student I'll call Jenna. After learning about the *My Diary Unlocked* project through word of mouth, Jenna contacted me via email with the following message:

Jenna, Age 19
Hello, Janet; I am 19 right now and have overcome a crack addiction, and have kept a diary throughout my battles with recovery. In these journals I wrote poems about other issues I was facing, such as self-mutilation and other mental health issues, living in a single parent home, small town life, and of course my drug addiction. I was hoping to publish my work eventually and would like to see something like that done. I am willing to speak to you more regarding this issue.

When I followed up with Jenna, she fell silent. My emails to her were returned with an automated message that delivery has failed; the recipient cannot be found. I never met this young woman, and yet I am haunted by concerns about her whereabouts and wellbeing.

We all know that children don't come with instruction manuals, and very few of us have it together on all levels before we make the decision to become parents. Sometimes, our best intentions to guide and protect our children are overridden by fears so paralyzing we simply put our heads in the sand. But of all the issues facing our teenage daughters, the most dangerous one to deny is the abuse of drugs or alcohol. Knowing the potential for life-long damage that could have been avoided had a parent stepped up to the task of intervening, I've decided that DENIAL needs its own acronym: It's the:

DENIAL ...   DECISION TO EXCLUDE AND NEGLECT INSIGHT, AWARENESS AND LOVE

Fortunately, resources now abound that offer parents and other concerned adults prevention tips and warning signs of alcohol and drug abuse—to help us become more attuned to the risk factors that may lead to potential addiction.

Prevention Tips

Here is a recap of solutions to prevent a teen's innocent experimentation with alcohol or drugs from escalating into a long-term addiction:

- Establish a loving, trusting relationship with your child.
- Make it easy for your teen to talk honestly with you.
- Talk with your child about alcohol facts, reasons not to drink, and ways to avoid drinking in difficult situations.
- Keep tabs on your young teen's activities, and join with other parents in making common policies about teen alcohol use.
- Develop family rules about teen drinking and establish consequences.
- Set a good example regarding your own alcohol use and your response to teen drinking.
- Encourage your child to develop healthy friendships and fun alternatives to drinking.
- Know whether your child is at high risk for a drinking problem; if so, take steps to lessen that risk.

- Know the warning signs of a teen drinking problem and act promptly to get help for your child.
- Believe in your own power to help your child avoid alcohol use.

Although some of the following signs may simply reflect normal teenage growing pains, others may indicate a growing problem. Most experts agree that a drinking problem is more likely to exist if you notice several of these signs at once, if they occur suddenly, or if they are extreme in nature.

Warning Signs of a Drinking Problem

- *Mood changes: flare-ups of temper, irritability, and defensiveness.*
- *School problems: poor attendance, low grades, and/or recent disciplinary action.*
- *Rebelling against family rules.*
- *Switching friends, along with a reluctance to have you get to know the new friends.*
- *A "nothing matters" attitude: sloppy appearance, a lack of involvement in former interests, and general low energy.*
- *Finding alcohol in your child's room or backpack, or smelling alcohol on his or her breath.*
- *Physical or mental problems: memory lapses, poor concentration, bloodshot eyes, lack of coordination, or slurred speech.*

Kids at highest risk for alcohol (or drug) related problems are those who:

- *Begin using alcohol or other drugs before the age of 15.*
- *Have a parent who is a problem drinker or an alcoholic.*
- *Have close friends who use alcohol and/or other drugs.*
- *Have been aggressive, antisocial, or hard to control from an early age.*
- *Have experienced childhood abuse and/or other major traumas.*
- *Have current behavioral problems and/or are failing at school.*
- *Have parents who do not support them, do not communicate openly with them, and do not keep track of their behavior or whereabouts.*
- *Experience ongoing hostility or rejection from parents and/or harsh, inconsistent discipline.*

Source: *Adapted from "A Message to Teenagers...", and has been reprinted with permission of* Alcoholics Anonymous World Services, Inc.

CONSTANTLY
HAVING
OPTIONS
IN
CREATING
EXPERIENCE

Addiction is a medical condition.
—Dr. Nora Volkow

Is Addiction a Choice?

The power of personal CHOICE has emerged as an underlying theme in relation to every topic explored throughout this book. CHOICE is the key dynamic in the Freeing Your BEING Compass. CHOICE is the force which at any moment can turn an ending into a new beginning, and it determines whether we are at war or at peace with ourselves. The ultimate gift of being human is having the ability to make CHOICES that alter our own destinies.

So now we must ask ourselves: What is the role of CHOICE in the life of an alcoholic or drug addict? Are these simply people who have "made their bed, and now need to lie in it," as the saying goes? I would argue that while our CHOICES—often made while in the thick fog of the FEARSELF—may lead down a road to chemical dependency, no one *consciously* chooses to become an alcoholic or drug addict. Teenagers like Diana, Misty, Claire and Cha drank and used drugs with the goal of feeling better, not to become addicts or alcoholics. Often, the impulse to use in order to escape painful feelings is not even conscious enough to be subjected to any degree of mental consideration. It's unlikely that this behavior is preceded with a thought such as "I think I'll develop a drug or alcohol addiction to fill this hole in my heart and numb my feelings." As Cha told us, once addicted, this thought process wasn't even on her radar—in the very same way that most smokers are not consciously aware of the hidden anxieties or unmet needs that cause them to light up. In fact, the National Institute on Drug Abuse (NIDA) sponsored a study at the University of Pennsylvania revealing that biological triggers in the addict's brain responded to drug-related images in just 33 milliseconds—so quickly that the patients were not consciously aware of seeing them. Combining this science-based information about how the brain's hardware functions together with the principles of the SOULSELF is important in determining how we judge those with the disease of addiction, and how we weave together this complex tapestry to create the best strategies to address drug treatment.

I discovered the HBO series *Addiction* one day while visiting my local library. In it, the mother of an addict shared something that will stay with me always. She said, "Society looks at addicts as druggies, junkies, felons. We look at our children and we see cowboy boots and ballet slippers; we see Christmas mornings and birthday parties. We hold forever in our hearts the first instant we held them in our arms and looked into their infant eyes. We can build a better system or continue to bury our children."

When a friend of mine, whom I'll call Denise, confided in me that she had recently been awakened to the reality of her daughter's drug addiction, the desire to believe the stories and excuses offered by her child was undeniable. She recounted those early days of her daughter's addiction:

> When Chelsea came to our cabin with friends to spend the fourth of July, I found needles in the pocket of her shorts. She said they belonged to her friends. I believed her even though she had needle marks in her arms. She said those were from giving plasma. I wanted so badly to believe Chelsea was not an addict or was not using drugs that I bought into these excuses. After a series of events, including a second DUI, a number of forged checks on our accounts, the service of subpoenas to appear in court to testify against drug dealers or people accused of crimes related to drug use, I finally admitted what I had suspected, but didn't want to believe—my daughter was addicted to drugs. Her life had been derailed. Even though Chelsea had been to treatment three times prior to the second DUI, she still did not think she had a problem. After the second DUI, my husband and I took a hard line. We cut her off from financial support and told her she could no longer live at home. This, among other things, made her finally realize she had a problem. She agreed to treatment and this time, she took it seriously. She wanted to get better. Two years later, she seems to be doing okay.

Denise tells me that she still worries constantly about her daughter. Every time the phone rings at a late hour, or every time she sees the call is from Chelsea, she wonders if it will be a call to tell her that there has been a relapse. Denise's word CHOICE that her daughter's life had been "derailed" reminds me of an analogy about an addict standing on a train track. The train is coming, and too often, parents think they must sacrifice everything for the life of the addict. But in reality, as the story goes, all the sacrifice (the exhaustion of all the parents' financial and/or emotional resources) does is leave the parent "dead" and the addict moves on to another train track. What is the proper balance between supporting addicts and enabling them? There is no one-size-fits-all response to these situations. Sometimes the tough-love approach, like the one my friend Denise finally resorted to, is what is needed. So many factors are involved that each situation must be weighed on a case-by-case basis. Parents or caretakers must go within their own inner BEING for the answer.

On a national scale, we often forget this personal face of addiction. We view it instead as a moral failing, in spite of undeniable evidence that addiction is a disease. If a person who has been diagnosed with diabetes eats a candy bar, no sound-minded doctor would recommend kicking that person out of the hospital. If a chemo treatment failed to eradicate a person's cancer, she would not be barred from the clinic, and yet health insurance coverage for addiction recovery is limited based a similar line of reasoning. Author David Sheff, who in my eyes is as powerful a champion for recovery as Gloria Steinem is for women's rights, explained this problem in his book, *Clean*:

> *The war on cancer has been a multitiered assault that has focused on education and prevention, changing public policy, and improving treatment—all toward the goal of decreasing the number of cases of cancer and saving the lives of the afflicted. The war on drugs has focused on interdiction, arrest, prosecution, and eradication (which has been largely ineffective—America spent a record $100 million to eradicate poppies in Afghanistan in 2008 …). Despite this investment, in 2013 opium production in Afghanistan reached a historic high. If we're finally going to effectively take on America's drug problem, we must end the war on drugs and declare an all-out offensive—against addiction. Like cancer, addiction is a disease that must be conquered.*

A person who had cancer would never be evicted from treatment after five days or a month, but would instead receive the needed care. Whether in an inpatient or outpatient program, addiction treatment takes time measured not in days but in months, and sometimes in years. As someone who has been repeatedly denied health insurance for a pre-existing condition—a mark on my forehead, I can only imagine the added frustration and stigma that addicts and their families must endure when treatment for their disorder is denied. Rather than receiving care for their medical—and treatable—condition of addiction, they are labeled, penalized and largely rejected by the American health insurance system.

In our neighborhoods, schools and workplaces, we judge those with alcohol and drug problems much more harshly than we would someone with another type of ailment. As a society, we impose the ultimate judgment by locking them away rather than getting them the help they need.

Considering that our prisons are bursting at the seams and that drugs are the number one cause of crime, it seems only common sense to take heed of the message from Dr. Redonna Chandler of NIDA, whose research supports the fact that 5 million of an estimated 7 million Americans who live under criminal justice supervision would benefit from drug treatment intervention. The fact that fewer than 8 percent actually receive such treatment leaves me impassioned for the day we wake up and realize that taking care of the other 92 percent is the most logical way of creating a kinder and safer nation.

Contemplating the issues related to substance use and abuse provides us with some of the richest lessons available in terms of aligning our values—both individually and collectively—with the SOULSELF. And while the journey through addiction and recovery is far from an ideal path of personal discovery, many who have traveled it look back on their battle with addiction from a vista far above the darkness they once fumbled through blindly in search of themselves. From a more awakened state of consciousness, they can retrace the steps—sometimes taken a day at a time, sometimes a moment at a time—that led them to a place of wholeness they had never before experienced. At times, their journey may have included steps taken backwards in the direction of the FEARSELF, for anxieties and regrets from deeply ingrained habits can easily lead to a relapse. Drawing on inner resources, using tools learned in recovery and relying on the loving support of family and community, addicts like Cha managed a graceful turnaround back in the direction of her truth.

The beauty of the revelations and insights gained by these diarists and their parents is that they are rooted in universal principles such as the power of humility, of self-review, of listening to body and mind with acute and present AWARENESS, of knowing what is within our control and what is not, and of relinquishing our attachment to a specific outcome. In essence, they offer us a template for a healthy way to live each day of our lives. I cannot help but wonder the growth that would be possible for all of us—teen and adult—if we had the courage to examine our fear-based impulses and triggers as rigorously as the addicts whose stories are penned in this chapter did through the process of recovery. What if we all committed to living our lives in an ongoing state of "recovery," to being ever aware of those moments we drift away from the truth of our BEING, and making gentle course corrections to get back on track? To the teens who managed this feat while caught in the grips of a drug or alcohol addiction, I feel deep and heartfelt gratitude. You are our teachers, and your hard-earned lessons were learned by slowly forging a pathway to peace while in the throes of chaos and self-destruction. It is my hope that all of us develop the mindfulness to remain on the transcendent path that led these girls back to themselves.

Living Life Unlocked

Whether the stories in this chapter spoke to you as an addict or as an advocate for preventing addiction in teens, the following action steps will support you in becoming a force of clarity in our emerging *soul*ciety:

Commit to set aside 15 minutes a day for 30 days to do the **3 Steps to Being in the Moment** (mindful meditation practice) described in this chapter.

Do five yoga sun salutations a day, preferably in the morning. With each breath and each pose, focus on the natural balance of effort and surrender. For more detailed instructions, you can find videos on the Internet to follow along with; just search for "yoga sun salutations."

Take out a sheet of paper or a diary and write at the top of a page: *5 reasons I forgive myself.* You don't even have to know what the five reasons are ahead of time. Use the exercise to trust in the process of the here and now, and write whatever comes to mind. Be open to letting the reasons flow spontaneously … one moment at a time.

Chapter 7

SAD:
from Stress, Anxiety and Depression
to Possibilities for Being at Peace

You do not know the weight of this self you are carrying
until you put it down.
—Zen

Misty, Age 19
My memories have been buried. Burned. I did it to myself with matches onto my skin to see how it felt. Tracing those veins down … down around my wrist, to my elbow. Guiding me … showing me where to cut … along the dotted lines. Rip me open … dissect me … expose me … remove my spine.

Monique, Age 18
I'm in emotional hell. I called Laura. She didn't pick up. I left her a long whiny message about how depressed I was to be back at school. I'm usually very pro-school. Pro-knowledge. Pro-education. Pro-everything. But this morning I felt like Pro-shit.

Wanda, Age 16
I feel so lost. Everything is always hazy, and I'm always shaky. When will I be able to catch my breath? Why do I have to worry and stress about every little thing? I'm tired of losing control, shutting down, panicking, and losing sight of reality. Anxiety, you are my devil.

Janet, Age 17
I was hoping that when I woke up my headache would be gone, but it was worse. I had to read aloud in class. I was so nervous my head was throbbing. I am beginning to do poorly in school. Sometimes I worry about nothing.

Elisha, Age 15

The past will always be with me, I can't forget it. It's like a shadow following my every move. Glaring at me with its evil eyes; while I sleep, eat, walk. It's with me no matter what. Please can it leave; please can it be separated from me.

Elise, Age 17

Last night I wrote this ... but I'm better now.
My heart cries with everything I have within me
begging to be heard
begging to be listened to
everywhere people walk around me
they stop to stare but never listen
they never hear the pain
the night comes and I'm all alone
shivering in the darkness I beg for help
but there is no one here
all the light is gone
I sing myself to sleep with the screams
the silent screams that cause me to fall
every last one of my waking days
hurt ... and frustrated.

The adage that "the only thing constant is change" has been handed down since the days of ancient Greece. From Ophelia to Hermione, we've seen the changes a girl makes as she courses her way through tragedies and triumphs in her life. For a teenage girl, change can be good—even exhilarating. It is when she must adapt to the unfolding of her personal circumstances without first gaining the skill set that will help keep her anchored to her genuine, Natural Self that suffering may begin. Most adults still struggle to navigate the forces of change with some measure of grace; but this is a task even more difficult for an adolescent, whose proximity to a changing world is the only constant she knows.

A look at the numbers of teenagers affected by psychological and emotional challenges echoes a message central to theme of this book: More than ever, you are not alone. Five times as many teenagers experience mental distress today than they have across past decades dating back to and including the Great Depression in the 1930s. The U.S. Surgeon General reports that 10 percent of children and adolescents in the United States suffer from emotional and mental disorders serious enough to impair their

They must often change, who would be constant in happiness or wisdom.
—Confucius

day-to-day lives at home, in school and with peers. Nearly half of college students report having felt depressed or anxious to the point they couldn't function. There is a difference between sadness and depression, and between occasional worry and longstanding anxiety.

It is estimated that half of all serious adult psychiatric illnesses, including depression, began by age 14. Considering that mental illness affects over one in four adults in America every year, the impact caused by emerging mental disorders during the critical years of adolescence is staggering. In the U.S., $34 billion was spent in 2010 on psychotropic medications—those affecting one's mental state—with an increasing number of teenagers adding to this number every year. Finding a balance between prescribing medication for those who really need it and treating those who may respond better to therapy and other alternative treatments in lieu of pills is a constant challenge, and an issue that becomes more charged when the patient is a minor. The unquestionable fact is that the mindset needed to bring about real solutions to mental health challenges—that of transparency, acceptance and thoughtful consideration of available treatments—is still sorely lacking in today's society. The misconception that raising the subject of mental illness is a sign of weakness, or an invitation for it to take a foothold in our lives, may lead us to avoid the topic. However, by ignoring it, we arm it with the power to hijack virtually every aspect of our BEING. Parents and family members with a misplaced focus on the stigma of outer appearances over internal peace may inadvertently establish priorities that sabotage the health and well-being of their children. Day in and day out, newspaper headlines of the frightening and increasingly tragic ways our teens deal with emotional pain make it clear appearances are not the reality.

Why is the inner world of a teenager's life so critical to her psychological well-being for years to come? How can it rock her core emotional stability, despite the absence of genetic conditions that might otherwise predispose her to developing such challenges? After years of poring over diary entries written by children and teens and interviewing those who are now adults, it's clear to me that in the face of real *or perceived* threat, children become stripped of the gift endowed by nature—that of remaining comfortable in the skin of their own inner truth. A teen who is a witness to or a victim of disrespectful treatment, poverty or other unstable situations—and yet who must still depend on adults for her survival—is pulled

Depression is the most unpleasant thing I have ever experienced ... It is that absence of being able to envisage that you will ever be cheerful again. The absence of hope. That very deadened feeling, which is so very different from feeling sad. Sad hurts but it's a healthy feeling. It is a necessary thing to feel. Depression is very different.
—J. K. Rowling

Never judge your family's interior to another family's exterior.
—Unknown

away from the present moment to devise a plan of self-protection for her future. Over time, conditioned to remain mentally on guard, she becomes susceptible to chronic fear-based issues like depression and anxiety as she learns to filter her experiences through her FRAGILE EXPERIENCE OF ANXIETY OR REGRET.

In this chapter, we meet teenage girls who have encountered some of life's more wounding and difficult challenges, which led them beyond stress and anxiety and into the personal hell of depression and self-harming. Many emerged from these emotional low points with new insight to guide them out of the crater of despair and back to a meaningful life. From their diaries and later reflections—and from the contributions made by experts in related fields of human suffering and human potential—we learn what it takes to create and maintain a healthy home environment where emotions are expressed in healthy and life-supporting ways. Parents, mentors and teens gain tools to strengthen the foundation of present-moment AWARENESS, which guides us out of pain and guilt, grief and loss, and back to the peace of the soul.

Can we expect to be happy all the time? No. But when our experience of despair or sadness is seen in the broader context of our connection with our SOULSELF, we can more easily find peace in the midst of our sorrow. Teens whose attention is consumed by animosity at home, unhealthy peer influences or a growing burden to conform may often push darker feelings further into the shadows of despair. Only when we begin unlocking these emotional layers through honest discussion and acceptance will we break free of an epidemic attempting to eat away the soul of individuals and the fabric of a safe and healthy society.

What is the source of our first suffering? It lies in the fact that we hesitated to speak. It was born in the moment when we accumulated silent things within us.
—Gaston Bachelard

SAD ... Stress, Anxiety and Depression

Stress is caused by being 'here' but wanting to be 'there.'
—Eckhart Tolle

As the saying goes, "life is not what happens to us, but how we respond to things that happen." Unhealthy stress is a manifestation resulting from a lack of available emotional tools to RESPOND to the events of our lives. A certain amount of stress can be good, when it is harnessed as energy to be used for a more enthusiastic expression of oneself. But when the adrenaline produced in our fight-or-flight response is combined with toxic thinking, stress can become paralyzing. Roni Cohen-Sandler, PhD, author of *Easing Their Stress: Helping Our Girls Thrive in the Age of Pressure,*

Natalie Fry

shares the following insights regarding the effects of stress and pressure on teenage girls:

> What I learned from my research is that all stressed-out girls, no matter their specific issues, are prone to becoming estranged from their inner lives. What I mean is that even teens who are driven to achieve are so busy living up to others' expectations that they either don't develop or eventually relinquish their own goals. They are so focused on achieving external emblems of success that they don't get the chance to figure out what really excites them and gives them pleasure. They barely know who they are or who they want to become. More troubling, when accomplishments lose meaning, teens begin to feel bored and empty, states that I believe are related to the prevalence of serious problems such as depression, cutting, and eating disorders among young women today.
>
> When a healthy method of coping with stress or trauma is not a part of a girl's experience, when her inner experience and

outer reality become disjointed, the weight of the disconnect often mutates into anxiety, depression or both.

Stress

Melissa, Age 19
Despite the fact that I was infinitely happier to be at Mount Holyoke than I was last year, I had a very difficult time falling asleep Thursday night. With the knowledge that I would indeed be getting a car also came the anxiety of getting behind the wheel again. Even with my driving lessons this summer, I was nervous. Between that, and thoughts of everything I had to do before classes, I was extremely restless.

Our greatest weapon against stress is our ability to choose one thought over another.
—William James

Going off to college brought Melissa face to face with circumstances that forced her out of her comfort zone. Moving to a new place, learning to drive, and anticipating the challenge of a curriculum with so many unknowns are common milestones most teenagers will reach at some point along the road to adulthood. Melissa took a powerful step toward getting the jitters out of her body by writing them down on paper. Journaling about changes and the feelings they evoke is in itself a proven method to begin to regain control over the situation at hand. An effective next step after writing a list of stressors is to follow up by adding a list of confidence-building affirmations. This serves to keep our level of tension from escalating into potentially self-esteem–damaging stress or anxiety. Writing helped Michelle to manage her stress, see the bigger picture, and to think about her upcoming challenges in a way that made them feel more manageable.

To experience peace does not mean that your life is always blissful. It means that you are capable of tapping into a blissful state of mind amidst the normal chaos of a hectic life.
—Jill Bolte Taylor

Michelle, Age 17
I am taking my SATs in a few weeks. Isn't it amazing how one test taken during the course of your teenage years can so influence your entire life? I disagree with a test of this nature. I think that if it is true that all humans are created equally with the same brain capabilities, then why don't colleges give them a chance to get in by interviewing the person, not by the test that is supposed to measure what you have learned in life. Who knows the true amount of knowledge that a person has acquired in life? And how can that be measured? As I ask these questions ... I try to laugh to hide the tears ... I am so stressed.

This same kind of proactive or solution-based approach to handling the small stuff while it's still small may have helped Angelica from becoming overwhelmed.

Angelica, Age 17

I'm tired. I'm stressed. Everything in my life should be fine, but to me it seems all-consuming and it's about to eat me alive. I'm scared, and I certainly don't know what to do. I'm sick of being alone. I don't know why the small things are bothering me. What is my problem? Do I need help? All night I was thinking about who and what could possibly help me. When you don't know what's wrong, how can you ever expect to make it right? I feel like I'm bugging everyone. Why am I not good enough? Or if for some reason I am, then why don't I feel like I'm worth anything?

While Angelica's stress reflects her very personal experience of loneliness and self-doubt, Alison's feelings express the collective stress triggered by an event experienced by millions.

Alison, Age 16

September 11, 2001. *Today, the most horrific sight to ever grace my vision appeared. Mom woke me up to tell me news that I still can't believe. Two hijacked planes crashed into the WTC twin towers. I sat looking at those beautiful buildings with goddamn airplanes in them. It was like a movie. Airplanes with innocent people used as bombs. Then a plane crashed into the Pentagon, which come to find out was headed for the White House. The whole country has stopped. Things are so screwed up. It's a nightmare. It's awful. No school today.*

September 16, 2001. *A lot of shit has happened this week. All this terrorism stuff sucks. It's really scary. I have never seen anything like this. I'm feeling really stressed and insecure, no real reason why, but it seems like I have a lot of trust issues. I'm scared of getting hurt.*

Though Alison couldn't understand her post 9/11 feelings of insecurity, the work of Heartmath, a nonprofit research and education organization teaching people how to self-regulate emotions, explained clearly the power of collective stress. Rollin McCraty, PhD, research director of the Institute of Heartmath, conducts scientific studies on the intelligence of the heart. In the documentary *I Am*, he shared that studies by Roger Nelson, retired from Princeton and head of the Global Consciousness Project (GCP), have shown that the presence of strong emotions—especially the collective emotions like those experienced across the globe on 9/11—cause electronic devices programmed to generate random numbers (much like tossing coins) to suddenly begin generating numbers that are *not* random. That is, by the mere presence of strong emotionality, an order to the numbers generated on all 65 devices around the world emerged, proving his conclusion that the heart emits electromagnetic fields that change according to one's emotions. Tom Shadyac, producer of *I Am*, underscored this finding, explaining that when the collective mind becomes highly focused, it has the power to change our physical environment. At some level, Alison was in tune with the power of this invisible collective mind.

We often don't make the connection between our personal experience and societal stress when those in our own inner circle of family and friends are not affected. But anyone who is old enough to remember 9/11 undoubtedly felt, as Alison did, the common thread that binds us to the human race as a whole.

Anxiety

If you want to conquer the anxiety of life, live in the moment, live in the breath.
—Amit Ray

Jenny, Age 15

Dear Diary, I can't help but write even though I have nothing to say. My overall feeling right now is anxious/nervous butterflies. I feel like I'm slipping away from everything and I'm holding on for dear life; while at the same time trying to do a one-handed push-up. Just to stay on track I have to fight so hard. I feel like I have some good qualities but not enough to be anyone worthwhile. Love, Jenny

Anxiety is often described as the experience of having excessive, irrational FEAR and dread. Jenny's description reminds me of my own bouts of anxiety which so paralyzed me with FEAR that I would pinch myself to keep from totally losing it, leaving black and blue marks covering my thighs for days or weeks at a time. For me, the pinching wasn't a self-harming action, but a "hang on for dear life" impulse; one in which I thought I was alone in experiencing, until I began reading other's stories.

"Nervous" was the only word I knew to describe the panic and anxiety I experienced during my formative years. One of my first memories in life is what I now know to be an anxiety attack. I was about five years old, and my parents had dropped us kids off at another family's house across town where we joined their kids and teenage girl babysitter while the adults went out for a night on the town. When the older kids were asleep, I began shaking and sobbing, curled up in a ball. The babysitter brought me out to the front porch, took me in her arms and asked what was wrong. Unable to put words to my feelings, I continued to cry, and though soothed by her tenderness, I felt there had been a big mistake; that I didn't belong in that situation, in that dirty house with older boys cussing and being brutal to each other. As anxiety continued to get a stronger foothold on my emotions, I began to wonder if maybe I had been born into the wrong family. I also felt the dread of knowing the fighting that was sure to come in the middle of the night when we would be back at home. I shook until there was not an ounce of energy left in my body to make so much as a twitch, and fell asleep in the arms of a girl I had never met, and would probably never see again.

Women are 60 percent more likely than men to experience an anxiety disorder over their lifetime.
—National Institue of Mental Health

By the time I was a young adult, I had experienced many more anxiety attacks. The worst of the worst came after a breakup with a boyfriend. Even though I'm the one who ended the relationship, the emotional vacancy, the cheating, and verbally abusive treatment I'd received left me feeling as abandoned as I had felt on the front porch of the house so many years earlier … as alone as I felt in college as I neared death in the hospital with no one at my side. My most haunting thought in the midst of my attacks is that I was sure to end up a bag lady. The darkness I felt at times led to a succinct description of my identity—Impending Doom.

The tides had turned for the better in my relationship with my parents, and this time I was able to land on the doorstep of their snowbird home in Florida to begin to heal from what I believe to be a nervous breakdown that set me on the journey to the SOULSELF. Wanting to extend comfort to me as much as they could, my parents helped me find a therapist and let me take the car to the beach, where nature wrapped her arms around me as I relearned to let go and BREATHE into the pulse of the ocean's waves. Never knowing when the darkness of panic would consume my being, mealtime never failed to provide drama. I love to eat and wanted to eat, but in the midst of anxiety and depression my stomach was locked up tight, and the thought of going to the usual early bird dinner at the Greek Pappas restaurant where my parents dined every night threw me only deeper into hell. Crying weak and helpless tears, I fought to remain

BRIDGE TO
RECONNECT YOUR
ENERGY
AND
TRUST YOUR
HEART
ESSENCE

curled up in the familiar ball I'd formed at age five. This time, though, my dad was there—with tears welled up in his own eyes—as he pulled on my arm and begged me to come to dinner. The days he didn't give up, I'd sit at the table, surrounded by senior citizens making more noise than toddlers. The clanging of silverware and banging of dishes added sound effects to the war zone in my mind as the knots in my stomach grew bigger and the pounding of my heart beat faster.

Welcome were the days—usually after a therapy session—when I was relaxed enough to not only order the early bird special, but to have a couple of side orders to boot. We all breathed a sigh of relief when I was able to take in nourishment. During that period, the library was a great refuge for me. It was there I ran across the painting, *The Scream*, by the Norwegian artist Edvard Munch, and felt I was looking in the mirror right to the core of my feelings. Inscribed below the painting was the artist's diary entry from January 22, 1892, describing his inspiration for the work:

> *I was walking along a path with two friends—the sun was setting— suddenly the sky turned blood red—I paused, feeling exhausted, and leaned on the fence—there was blood and tongues of fire above the blue-black fjord and the city—my friends walked on, and I stood there trembling with anxiety—and I sensed an infinite scream passing through nature.*

Edvard Munch

Slowly and surely, I stayed on the path to healing, using many of the tools I'm sharing with you now.

Signs of Anxiety

Physical-based:

- ❂ Feeling a fullness in the throat or chest
- ❂ Having difficulty catching your breath
- ❂ Feeling like your heart is pounding
- ❂ Feeling dizzy or lightheaded
- ❂ Sweating or cold, clammy hands
- ❂ Feeling jumpy
- ❂ Having aches, tense muscles or soreness
- ❂ Feeling extremely tired
- ❂ Having trouble falling asleep or getting a good night's rest

Source: www.maketheconnection.net

❂ **Emotion-based:**

- ❂ Feeling restless
- ❂ Feeling on edge or keyed up
- ❂ Being angry or irritable
- ❂ Worrying about everyday decisions for several days in a row
- ❂ Fearing that something bad is going to happen
- ❂ Feeling doomed
- ❂ Becoming easily distracted
- ❂ Having difficulty concentrating
- ❂ Feeling like your mind goes blank
- ❂ Finding it hard to do your work or normal activities

Post-Traumatic Stress Disorder

A close cousin of anxiety is post-traumatic stress disorder (PTSD). At MayoClinic.com, PTSD is defined as a mental health condition that's triggered by a terrifying event, with symptoms that may include flashbacks, nightmares and severe anxiety, as well as uncontrollable thoughts about the event.

My experience of being at the mercy of Category 4 Hurricane Iniki, the most powerful hurricane in recorded history ever to strike the state of Hawaii, resulted in many months of sleeplessness and hyper-sensitivity; the slightest sound of a breeze rustling through the trees was enough to startle me AWAKE. Serendipitously, during the hurricane, I was a guest at the bed and breakfast owned by Shakti Gawain, the author whose book *Creative Visualization* I'd found years earlier during my time in Florida. Using the process of visualization for 30 minutes every day was instrumental in helping me to release the powerful emotions I experienced during the hours when 145 MPH winds ripped the roof from over my

Anxiety is excitement without enough oxygen.

IMAGINATION

head and I remained crouched in a closet with other visitors to the island. The riddle that begs the question, "Imagine you're trapped on a deserted island—how do you get off?" is solved with a common-sense answer that must be converted to common practice. The answer? *Stop imagining.* The mind can only focus on one thing at a time, so replacing bad thoughts with good ones unlocks the power of Imagination to be used for good as it lets go of FEAR. I later coupled this force of visual imagery with hypnotherapy, a method of deep relaxation that invites focused attention, allowing the Imagination and Genius Mind aspects of BEING to reconnect to a healthier and balanced reality. Far from stage hypnosis, which has made it difficult for some people to take it seriously, hypnotherapy has been used as a therapeutic method to treat both psychological challenges and physical pain.

In *Psychology Today,* Harvard psychologist Deirdre Barrett explained that being in the deeply focused state brought about by hypnosis "is not therapeutic in and of itself, but specific suggestions and images … can profoundly alter [clients'] behavior. As they rehearse the new ways they want to think and feel," she explained, "they lay the groundwork for changes in their future actions." Personally, I've used hypnotherapy with profound success to relieve my PTSD, to let go of negative habits and to transform anxiety to confidence. Now whenever I experience the first inkling of anxiety, I recognize it as a warning signal that an old belief system has surfaced that is not in alignment with my Natural Self. Using the audio software program on my laptop computer, I literally rewrite and record a new script preceded by a guided relaxation and breath-AWARENESS exercise to engage all of my five senses. Within days or weeks at most, I have not only let the negative pattern go but have empowered myself by bringing my vision into alignment with the place within me that takes action under the sole direction of my authentic self. Teenagers who experience anything from test anxiety to phobias, a lack of self-esteem to PTSD, may benefit from this process when they recognize they have stepped out from the calm center of the SOULSELF and entered the storm of fear-based thinking. Credible therapists and professional audios are available to those who do their homework through proper research and inquiry.

If PTSD is a cousin to anxiety, then (speaking from experience) depression is its close, yet evil, stepsister. While not always occurring hand in hand, where you find one, the other is often not far behind.

Depression

Sherry G., Age 19

When did I stop
Searching for four leaf clovers,
Wandering the shores
For shells and treasures,
Writing short stories
Bringing characters to life,
Calling my grandmother
To tell her I love her,
Believing in people
Listening to the wind,
As it talks to the water
Wondering about the stars,
Riding my bike
Eating cake,
Smiling at people in traffic
Taking pictures with old-fashioned film,
Watching the sunset
Visiting the sick,
Roller skating
Just to go round and round,
Feeling complete
Feeling so free …,
When did I stop being me?

Natural
SELF

Sherry's words vividly capture the gloom that is the hallmark of major depression. For her, the disconnection from her Natural Self came like a slow burial, causing her to doubt whether she would ever feel like herself again. Depression is an insidious disease that often sneaks in silently under the radar of an otherwise play-acted happy life. And because the arrival of each new emotional low point occurs slowly and over time, it's often hard to put a finger on the exact moment when—as Sherry expressed—"I stopped being me."

The slow infusion of negative thinking, unhealthy beliefs and emotional suffering is a trademark strategy used by the FEARSELF to keep us living within the boundary of its limitations. As long as we remain comfortably (or uncomfortably) NUMB to its presence, we remain powerless to break free. In her next entry, Sherry creates a first important clearing in the fog of her pain and shame, as she allows herself to explore their underlying cause.

Sherry G., Age 19

Silence in words not spoken
Screams the obvious
From a make-believe reality
Pretending things never happened to me …
Will the smile be natural again?
Someday will I forget the pain
Forever real as rain?
This stormy February I hide my face …

Motivational author Louise Hay tells us that one probable cause of depression is feeling anger we believe we do not have a right to feel. In Sherry's case, the trauma of having been abused as a child caused her to turn her anger inward, leading to the onset of depression. For the next diarist, depression manifested as feelings of emptiness and hopelessness, causing her to lose touch with the sense of optimism that she once had as a younger child.

Linda, Age 19

Saturday, wild winds blowing. Cold day. Where is spring? I feel sad and can't put my finger on why. A lump in my throat forms when I look through this diary. So many embarrassing, painful, and sad feelings written on these pages. My therapist suggested I ask myself the question, "What do I want?" this week. The answer is, "I want to feel happy, I want to feel calm, I want not to be lonely or left alone. I want to feel good about myself. I want to be in the sunshine, I want to try out a new living situation. I want someone who loves and cares about me, I want to love and care about somebody. I want people to want to see me and hear me. I don't want to hide. I want to like myself; I don't want to punish myself. I want to be able to breathe deeply again and feel whole within myself, not fragmented. I want to be able to depend on someone I love, I want to have someone to depend on me. I want to face my fears, my pain, my hurt, my brother, and my life. Knowing how I feel now, often so dead and defeated, only makes me feel sad to think how optimistic and ambitious I used to be. Always thinking a miracle was just around the corner; that something will happen to change my life.

Writing in her diary, Linda became aware of the vast gulf that had developed between the optimistic girl she once was and the desperate young woman she had become. Looking back through my own diaries, I read that same desperation between the lines in many of my entries. For me, depression grew like *The Blob* in the 1958 movie of the same name. The blob—for those too young to remember—was an amoeba-like alien that got bigger and bigger until it took over everything. Depression, the metaphoric blob in my life, had so radically taken over my thinking process that I actually came to believe the turbulent long-distance relationship with my boyfriend John, who had moved away to college, was both its cause and its cure.

Janet, Age 17

October 28. John called me tonight! First time since he dumped me for Paula. I was so shocked. He was disappointed I didn't come to see him when I was in town. He is coming home this weekend and asked me out for Saturday night. I'm in such a state of shock I can't study for my English Literature test so I'm not going to school tomorrow. He said he misses me and is coming here just to take me out! My depression instantly went away.

October 31. It's Friday and John came home today but I didn't see him. I'm so scared for tomorrow. What will I do if he doesn't even call me? That would be typical for him to do based on history. I'm really scared. I wonder if he is out with Paula tonight.

November 1. I stayed home all day to wait for the call from John about our date tonight. Was really worried because I didn't hear from him all day, but then he finally called at about six. He just talked for a while and then he said he better go. I said, "I thought you asked me out tonight." He said, "I thought that was for Saturday OR Sunday." But I know we decided on Saturday, and I told him so. So he came over, but then he had to leave for a couple hours to go to a party. We were sitting on my steps and Paula drove by. Then he sat and told me how much he loves me. He is mixed up, and I'm mixed up too, now. Maybe I'm the kind of person that likes to have her ego stepped on because I put up with anything, and then I get so nervous and depressed I can't think or go to school. To think I was so excited that I couldn't go school on Friday, and now I'll miss much of the coming week due to my depression. I hope I change and learn to accept changes even if I don't like them because right now it's really hard for me to do, and I feel like I'm going nuts.

Reading this now, it's no wonder I felt like I was going nuts, because I was in no way accepting reality. What my intuition was telling me in my heart was being denied by the fears in my head—a concoction ripe for the onset of both anxiety and depression. How I wish someone had said, "Look at the red flags, girl! LISTEN to your heart!" I may not have listened, but at least a seed of truth would have been planted. Instead, clouded by a thick fog of naiveté, I chose to deny the information that my boyfriend's actions were speaking louder than his words. Blinded to the facts of the situation, I slipped into an abyss of depression that led me even further from reality. I began to neglect the people and activities that were a true source of joy in my life, and placed my happiness on the altar of a relationship that there was no hope of sustaining. For me, the darkness of depression grew much worse before I was finally able to admit how much I had been kidding myself, and to notice the emotional price I was paying by doing so. Like the girls whose diary entries follow, few were the days when I found reason to feel any measure of excitement. Little did I know, I was not alone in my experience.

Don't turn away.
Keep your gaze on the
bandaged place. That's
where the light enters
you.
—Rumi

Lauren, Age 16
All I want to do is go to bed and not get up until I feel normal. That could be awhile ... but I don't care. I don't care about school, I don't care about friends, I don't care about being happy. My birthday was on Thursday and it was supposed to be MY day ... not anyone else's, and I was supposed to be happy. But was I? No. I'm tired of being sick, and I'm tired of feeling like I can never get out of this pit that I am in. The sad thing is that nobody notices, or if they do they don't care enough to do anything. I'm tired of being the girl next door. Obviously this image isn't working for me ... I feel like I need to be somebody, anybody else. I just wish that I was invisible, because that's how I feel ... at least then I would have a good reason why I have no friends. Why do you all hate me? I just wish I could talk to someone.

Jenny, Age 14
Why am I so mood-swingy, diary? So depressed? Why do I judge people the second I see them? Why do people hate being my friend? Why does everyone even waste their time being my friend? Then on top of that, why don't I even want to tell my parents hardly anything? Why can't I SHUT-UP and be happy with what I have and think about other people for a change? Because I'm a selfish

BITCH. There's one answer. Why aren't I nice and sweet and funny and cute? Why? Because I'm a wannabe-ugly-flat-fat-assed-BITCH. Because I'm just worthless shit to everyone including my incredibly ugly, dirty, disgusting self.

Monique, Age 19

5:05 P.M. exactly. I've discovered the pinpoint of my anxiety and depression. Few people ever do, or so I'm determined to believe. Most people live their lives wallowing in self-pity and depression and die not knowing where it stemmed from or why they had it. I know why I had it.

I just realized that ever since I started working at "Worst Neighborhood School," I have been experiencing a case of fear, paranoia, anxiety, shame, and depression. I knew before I worked there, that I was no one special. That I was no queen bee. That I for sure was a nobody. After a few weeks of my new job, I also felt that the children, the adorable, hellish angels were tormenting me to no end. I know they're just kids. I know they haven't yet experienced enough of the world to really know what to say and what not to say to adults, and how the world works. But they spoke the unspoken. They talked to me truthfully and were brutally honest about it. I know that because they are small children, I should remain unaffected by it all. I started becoming mad with paranoia that what the kids blatantly said aloud ... was precisely what every adult was probably thinking of me, but they were too nice to say anything about. I started to take everything they said seriously. I started to dwell on it. I could no longer look them—or anyone else in the eye. And for some reason I felt this extreme hatred emitting from society, people, kids, my parents ... everyone! As if me, looking the way I did was somehow wrong. I'd like to shout, "I'VE DONE NOTHING WRONG!" Because I haven't. So what if I don't look like her. Or act like her. I'm me. Duh. DUHHH! I thought for a brief moment, a wave of realization came crashing through me ... I have nothing to be ashamed of ... I've done nothing wrong.

Although each of these girls has a different story, all of them share depression as an underlying theme. In an article posted on Daughters.com, Arianna Huffington faults what she calls "soul-stealing fears" for the fact that so many teen girls descend into low self-esteem and depression, and she asserts that helping our daughters understand the real cost of fear is one of the most important resources we can give them. "To live in fear is

It takes courage to grow up and become who you really are.
—e. e. Cummings

the worst form of insult to our true selves," she wrote. "By having such a low regard for who we are—for our instincts and abilities and worth—we build a cage around ourselves. To prevent others from shutting us down, we do it for them. Trapped by our own fears, we then pretend we're incapable of having what we want, forever waiting for others to give us permission to start living. Pretty soon, we start to believe this is the only way." The diary entries in this chapter are clearly consistent with the fear-based mindset that Arianna describes. Even Anne Frank, with whom it is almost impossible to associate the word cowardice or fear, hinted in her diary as to the ways big and small that she was not being true to herself, exposing from a different angle the connection between fear and depression:

Anne Frank, Age 14
I'm currently in the middle of a depression. I couldn't really tell you what set it off, but I think it stems from my coward-ice, which confronts me at every turn.

It's not always easy to recognize, as Anne did, when our daughters are suffering from depression. Merging my own experiences as a teenager with descriptions of the behavioral and emotional changes that may signal the presence of depression, I summarized the most common among them in the following list.

Warning Signs of Teenage Depression

- Sadness
- Helpless or hopeless feelings
- Irritability or anger
- Lack of interest or withdrawal from activities
- Crying easily
- Avoidance of friends and family
- Low self-esteem
- Self-critical attitude: focus on personal failures
- Suffering school performance
- Neglected physical appearance
- Feelings of guilt or worthlessness
- Difficulty concentrating and making decisions
- Changes in eating habits; weight loss or gain
- Slow or rapid movement
- Alcohol or substance abuse
- Difficulty with authority
- Risky behavior
- Suicidal thoughts or actions
- Self-harm, such as cutting, burning, or excessive piercing or tattooing
- Self-Harm: Cutting

Self-Harm: Cutting

Even more disturbing than unlocking the diaries of teens who have lost the spark of their child-like nature to depression is reading the words of those who resort to cutting and other forms of self-harm in an attempt to cope with emotional trauma. Unfortunately, this manifestation of depression is on the rise among adolescents. In the U.S., it's estimated that one in every 200 adolescent girls between the ages of 13 and 19 regularly cut themselves. Self-harming is becoming so commonplace that it is sometimes referred to as the "new-age anorexia." For those who find it difficult to understand why a teen would seek to self-inflict physical pain as a way to soothe emotional pain, Misty's entry below provides a window into the desperation that drives these acts.

> ### Misty, Age 15
> I long for your approval,
> and long for your embrace.
> Your words put me on trial,
> as if I am some disgrace.
> I know that I'm not perfect,
> but I try so hard for you.
> All I want is your respect,
> and for this aching to be through.
> Can't you see I'm hurting?
> Or don't you even care?
> To ease this inner pain, I bleed.
> and you're still unaware.
> I've scarred myself,
> little do you know.
> I have built walls around myself,
> so my pain will never show.

When Lucie Hemmen, PhD, author of *Parenting a Teen Girl,* introduced the topic of "cutting" in one of her lectures, some parents assumed she meant cutting classes at school. Jaws dropped when these parents discovered the word's actual meaning. It is an alarming fact that more and more teenagers are cutting themselves, burning their skin or engaging in other forms of self-injury as a way to make physical, and therefore more manageable, their painful or uncontrollable emotions. As Dr. Hemmen explained:

> *Cutting is a coping mechanism, which means it is a way to regulate feelings. Unfortunately, it "works" in that teens report it makes them feel better. They feel like that they can control it, keep it secret, see and feel a "result," and express emotions people don't seem to like, especially anger and sadness. To make things worse, the brain wires quickly for this behavior, creating a stress + cutting = relief circuit that becomes harder and harder to break over time.*

The urge to cut can be especially compelling in the absence of more effective coping strategies for dealing with stress, and as Elise's entry demonstrates, it is an addictive behavior that's difficult to break free of, even when a teen understands its harmful effects.

> ### Elise, Age 16
> *I'm just calling out for someone to save me, but I feel like no one cares. You know, my mind is in many places right now. I really want to just come to school with cuts and bruises and have people pretend like they care for once. I'm hurting so much that I think even fake sympathy would be better than nothing. It's scary ... I thought that I was over all of this. I thought that I could be a whole, happy person and that most of my pressures were gone. I switched friends, I read the Bible ... I don't involve myself with things that will never work out. I was free. I put my past behind me. Now I feel like certain parts are being brought up again. I've never wanted to hurt myself since last year. I've never wanted to cry myself to sleep every night, or fallen asleep immediately from all the stress in my life since then. I have never felt so alone ...! All I want to do is lock myself in my room and never come out.*

Elise's desire to reach out to others who can help her to understand her pain is a healthy one, and yet this impulse is immediately countered by the desire to lock herself up in a room and "never come out." The desire to isolate exposes a potent way the FEARSELF keeps us trapped in a cycle of depression—by tricking us into believing we lack the motivation, the ability, or the worthiness to take actions that will move us back in the direction of inner peace. Even if we are aware of available resources, unless we also have the discipline to take one step at a time, procrastination can sabotage forward movement. This is why baby steps are so critical for a person who is depressed. There is a time to allow ourselves to fully acknowledge the depth of our suffering, and there is a time to feel our fragile emotions, *and* to take action anyway. Very different are the experiences of taking a step forward with an attitude that "I have to take this action in order to fight against my depression," and "I am feeling depressed, and I am going to take this action anyway, in order to see how doing so may change my experience."

Key to overcoming any negative emotional state is realizing that even in the midst of a moment of weakness we still have the ability to take baby steps that gradually return us back upon the path to the SOULSELF. We can make the CHOICE to reach out to a friend, to allow ourselves to have a good cry, to do some form of physical exercise, to read something inspirational or funny, to write in a journal, or to put our problems on pause and just take a nap. All of these are much healthier alternatives for releasing emotional stress than self-harm, substance abuse, and other low ranking coping strategies, because they all have the ability to slow down impulsive behaviors and redirect our perspective. Healing from depression almost always involves setbacks, but true breakthroughs occur once we understand we can use stumbling blocks as stepping stones to shift our state of AWARENESS and redirect each aspect of our BEING to align with our higher good.

By continuing to watch the emotions, the sadness, the thoughts that come to mind, and by practicing the discipline of separating those things from our definition of ourselves, we can in fact remain in charge as the master of our own ship, even when the seas get stormy. Just having the willingness to press the reset button in our mind unlocks a door that reveals the next logical step, so we needn't feel pressure to change everything all at once when our strength is already compromised. As Elise eventually discovered and pointed out in her reflection below, if it weren't for the trying experiences she had as a teen, she never would have grown into the woman she is today.

SOURCE
OF
UNIVERSAL
LIFE
SERVING TO
EXTEND
LOVE
FOREVER

Writing saved me from the sin and inconvenience of violence.
—Alice Walker

Elise's Reflection, 12 years later

Life is constantly changing, and my feelings of depression have ebbed and flowed since my early days. It is a battle but is one that can be overcome; I haven't wanted to hurt myself in years. The peace that I have now during bad days comes from staying true to who I am. Sure, there are people who don't like me—but there are also people who love my dry humor, tiny stature (small but powerful), the way that I don't always catch on to jokes and how I laugh at some of the most inappropriate times. Just remember that everything happens for a reason and that trials only make you stronger. I

Now, as I look back on my life, I can honestly say I wouldn't change it. The pain and suffering have brought me psychological understanding and spiritual strength. I still feel the pain when I reflect on those experiences, but while once they would throw me deeper and deeper into anxious despair, now they feed my desire to keep growing.
—Marie Balter

know how horrible I used to feel, but without those feelings I wouldn't have gone away to college. If I hadn't done that, I wouldn't have met my best friends, wouldn't have met my husband and wouldn't have gotten the job I have now (the other school I was considering didn't offer the major I ended up selecting). My background has made me tough and has definitely prepared me for whatever is next in my life.

Central to the lifting of Elise's depression was her discovery that the challenging situations of her life had come bearing the gift of wisdom. For author David Fitzpatrick—whose depression was so severe that even as an adult he still regularly cut himself with razor blades—honesty was a catalyst. In the final pages of his memoir *Sharp*, Fitzpatrick described the experience of catching the first glimmer of light that emerged from within the dark fog of his mental illness.

> *The veil, the damp, gauzy veil that had separated me from the rest of world forever was disappearing. I could feel and see parts of it still hanging around the fringe but it was leaving. It was going away …*
> *I think the veil lifting was hope settling in around me, finding a space inside a really depressed guy's body, and asserting itself. Also, honesty was a huge component—to admit that I was 40 years old, and did I really want to be hurting myself, and have that veil around me for the rest of my life? The veil lifted when I started to believe in my possibility of a decent life for me, even a hopeful one.*

Having found a space within where he could be honest with himself, Fitzpatrick began to experience the gradual melting away of the veil—the disconnected state of being which throughout this book we've referred to as the FEARSELF. Once realigned with truth, his authentic journey out of depression and back to health was under way. Jenny, whose earlier entries seethed with self-hatred, charted a powerful path out of the darkness of depression. Her reflection offers hope and encouragement for anyone to follow in her footsteps.

Jenny's Reflection, 15 years later

I cried when I read back over my diary entry 15 years later, because I can't believe I ever felt so worthless. And yet, I remember those moments like they were yesterday. Here I am now—a self-employed author, speaker and business coach living in New York City, surrounded by friends and family, and sharing my ideas with the world in the hopes of inspiring and uplifting others who are feeling stuck or unhappy. I made it out of the darkness, and my heart goes out to others who are still there. Stay strong—there IS light ahead. You WILL find your path.

I've cried myself to sleep many times in my life, often "without reason" because I couldn't pinpoint what was wrong. Sometimes I still can't. My diary entries reminded me of every night I laid my head on a pillow soaked with tears ... where writing it all down—every high and low and tortured thought—felt like my only salvation. I don't want any of us to feel that despondent ever again. And if—by some unfortunate cognitive error or faulty intellectual logic—we do, I want us to have the tools to fight our way out and thrive. For me, getting my physical fundamentals in order was key to making it out of the darkness: developing a regular yoga and meditation practice, making sure I get outside each day, taking energizing walks through the streets of New York, getting plenty of sleep, and fostering meaningful connections with friends and family. Ultimately, all of this rolls up to self-acceptance and self-compassion: I am at my best when I can accept who I am, flaws and all, and take action in my life from a loving place. This is like building a muscle and it doesn't happen overnight—for me it comes with practice. None of us is perfect—in fact, our beauty is rooted most deeply in our very imperfections and vulnerability. It always helps me to remember this, and to know I am doing my best every day to be of service to myself, my family and my broader community. I want us all to live BIG ... unapologetic and unafraid. Those of us who survived those tumultuous teen years were able to seek out the tools to pull ourselves out of emotional ruts. I am fiercely committed to make those tools even easier to find and accessible for both teens and adults.

Healing Depression: A Guide for Teens and Adults

As a layperson who has researched and experimented with everything from traditional psychiatry and psychotherapy to mindfulness, hypnotherapy and other alternative approaches for healing depression and anxiety, I have found that a hybrid of all of the above—tailored to suit each unique individual—to be the most effective. The more options we avail ourselves of, the greater the likelihood we will find one that resonates. The use of anti-depressant medications falls within these available options, of course, and yet is a topic surrounded in controversy, particularly as it relates to treating teen depression.

Whenever I hear people judge another person's use of antidepressants, my guess is that the one passing judgment has probably never sat with a suicide note in one hand and the means to commit it in the other. The use of medication to treat depression is a decision to be made consciously and with the affected teenager, her family and the caregiver's full knowledge of the possible risks and benefits. Just as there is a wide range of causes of mental illness, there is no one-size-fits-all treatment for it. Also to consider is the fact that a treatment which proves helpful in one phase of life may not work as well at another time—even for the same person. This is why I gravitate to the idea of having an abundance of tools, resources and practices available for treating mental illness or to support someone who is simply going through a difficult time.

At certain periods in my life, I have found a small dose of anti-depressant medication to be beneficial for lifting my mood to a baseline level of functioning where I could finally catch my breath, see things from a new perspective, and begin making CHOICES that realign my psyche with the positive flow of life. Ultimately, I believe that whether I'm taking a pill to open my neural pathways, breathing fresh air while taking a walk in the morning sun, or seeing a therapist to help me unlock the barriers created by childhood programming, the bottom line is the same. Whatever means best supports the cells of my body and the pathways of my brain in realigning with the truth of my soul—to *be* in the place where I know I am an inherently worthwhile BEING who deserves love—is what sets me free. Everything else is in the details.

My soul is where being is.
—Mariel Hemingway

Our brain functioning is just as much a part of our human nature as our bodies. Yet, much like the condition of addiction, we remain closed about mental health issues at a time when opening up about their prevalence is key to overcoming them. In her documentary, *Running from Crazy*, Mariel Hemingway shares her history of depression as a celebrity who has been haunted by seven suicides in her family, including that of her grandfather, Ernest Hemingway. Her hope is to open the door for others to feel supported in speaking out and getting help.

One of the biggest breakthroughs in my own experience of healing depression came while listening to Eckhart Tolle's lecture series *The Journey into Yourself*, in which he shared a process for moving through intense emotional pain. He explained that when we let go of resisting our feelings, down to and including the muscle contractions and tension in our bodies (how did he know what I was doing in the clutches of my anxiety?!), we "allow the pain to force [us] into utter and complete presence." What is so powerful about this message—and I know because this advice was pivotal in supporting me in coming out of my depression—is that it is the opposite of putting on a happy face, or faking it 'til you make it (which, by the way, has its own merits in certain conditions, but clinical depression is not one of them). When I gave even my darkest feelings permission to exist instead of fighting against them, when I surrendered to the moment and allowed everything to be exactly as it was, I had a profound experience of inner peace.

This shift in sensory perception is identical to the one I experienced when I was in Hawaii when Hurricane Iniki struck. After hours of being terrorized by what sounded like a freight train running over my head and the wind tearing through the house and tossing furniture around like playthings, there was a sudden break in the chaos as we passed through the eye of the storm. The calm brought with it a profound sense of peace and somehow I knew that even though the hurricane was not over, I would be okay. Sure enough, when we passed out of the eye of the storm and winds again began to rage, I carried that field of comforting AWARENESS with me.

Never having lost the symbolism of that experience, to this day, as a figurative anchor, anytime I need to reposition my own inner eye to the calm center of my soul, I still recall the sensation of having been at the core of one of the fiercest storms in a century. In fact, this same symbolism of a whirlwind of FEAR encircling and temporarily obscuring the peace of the soul is at the heart of the Freeing Your BEING Compass that is so central to this book's message. A hurricane is a force of nature, but it pales in comparison to the innate power of a human being to move through a personal storm and transform its potentially destructive energy into a source of strength. The following reflection written by Sherry, whose diary entry of hopelessness and emptiness opened this discussion, is a beautiful example of harnessing the potential that underlies any difficult time and consciously resolving to transform it into love.

AWAKE
WITH
ALL
REALITY
EXPOSED
NATURALLY
EXPRESSING THE
SOUL-
SELF

Sherry G.'s Reflection, 32 years later
When my spirit buckled and my anger welled to a breaking point,
I felt a surge of strength and understanding in my soul, and knew I
HAD to hang on to my light, my strength, my joy, my hope ... and

my passion for life itself ... for looking for a four leaf clover, for feed-ing the seagulls by the lake, for talking to a stranger in the park, for painting, writing, dancing, for taking time for me. It has at times been a difficult yet continuous journey to stay in that positive place of self-awareness—but now I keep a steady guard of honoring my soul even in the face of external circumstances that might otherwise affect my spirit and my will.

Sherry's description of holding onto her light in the midst of darkness reminds me of a giant rubber band, stretched to its maximum; its pow-erful energy capable of being released in the direction of FEAR or faith. In a single moment, Sherry experienced the co-existence of both emotions, and this was enough to open the door. With each bit of space we make for conscious AWARENESS to enter our hearts and minds, we crack open the door to a new way of looking at ourselves and our lives. As this door of perception opens, we see new opportunities and resources we didn't notice before. Maybe there's an exercise class that no longer sounds quite so daunting. Maybe the fresh oxygen to the body inspires a desire to con-nect with a classmate, to take on a bigger challenge, to learn something new ... with each consecutive step forward, a soul once in hibernation reemerges back into the full vitality of life.

Depression is nothing more than believing a stressful thought.
—Byron Katie

While baby steps are what lead most people on the path out of depres-sion, sometimes this transformation occurs in a flash of insight. For a woman named Byron Katie, the emergence out of her "dark night of the soul" happened in such an instant.

The Work of Byron Katie

From her own powerful experience, Byron Katie, whom *Time* magazine has called "a spiritual innovator for the new millennium" created a simple yet life-changing healing process known as The Work. The founding prin-ciples of The Work, as outlined in her book, *Loving What Is*, align so beautifully with the message of the power of AWARENESS brought to life through the diary entries in this book, I was delighted when she agreed to share it here as a tool for reframing the beliefs that lead to depression.

At the center of the impulse that drives us to use coping strategies that end up causing more harm than good is a story we tell ourselves and then experience as reality. In fact, once we convince ourselves that it's true, we see all of life through the filter of that story, no matter how fictitious or outdated it may be. As everyday CHOICES are made from the perspective of this lie rather than from our own inner truth, we become more and more disconnected from our Natural Self—sometimes to the point of feeling we no longer know ourselves, or we feel guilty for living a dishonest life.

Don't believe everything you think.
—Wayne Dyer

The transformative power of The Work lies in the questioning of beliefs. As Katie says, "All you need is a pen and paper, and an open mind." In the same way that writing in a diary supports us in gaining important insights about ourselves, Katie finds that writing the answers to the four questions of The Work allows us to identify our stressful or negative thoughts. The act of writing them down on paper stops them from spinning around in the mind and allows us to examine them and, ultimately, resolve them.

With a receptive mind, our natural responses to these questions expose our hidden beliefs while offering a process to undo fear-based thoughts. As a larger truth reveals itself, a light shines on previously uninvestigated thoughts, many of which have climbed into the driver's seat of our minds, where they have been secretly operating the steering wheel of our lives. When the mind has the presence to question itself, it stops resisting *what is;* it stops attaching itself to thoughts such as "I can't do it," or "This shouldn't be happening." Hidden beliefs that create depression and emotional upset become exposed for what they are. The moment we begin to inquire, new options flood in, because the intention to understand the truth from a childlike state of wonder yields insights that are nothing short of brilliant.

After answering the four questions, we turn the original statement around. The turnaround is a way of experiencing the opposite of what we believe. Often there are three turnarounds—a turnaround to the self, a turnaround to the other, and a turnaround to the opposite. This loosens the grip on the belief we have so firmly held—even though that belief undermines our happiness. Each turnaround is supported by three examples of why it is as true as or truer than the original statement. The examples need to be specific and genuine. When we find them, we deepen our realization that the original thought is just one way of seeing reality and a way that doesn't serve us.

For the sake of illustration, let's do The Work using as a basis the content from two actual diary entries from this chapter. Please note, however, that the answers provided are examples, not the actual words of the diarists.

The Work
by Byron Katie

The Work	Janet	Lauren
Judge Your Neighbor Worksheet (Example here: One belief at a time). ***Write down a stressful thought.***	My boyfriend is unloving to me.	Nobody cares about how I feel.
Question #1: *Is it true?* (Yes or No)	Yes. (Move to #2.)	Yes. (Move to #2.)
Question #2: *Can you absolutely know that it's true?* (Yes or No)	No. (After contemplation, I realize I don't absolutely know for sure.)	No. (I discovered that there are some friends and family members who might care about how I feel.)
Question #3: *How do you react, what happens, when you believe that thought?*	I feel depressed. I feel sad and self-pitying. I get angry at my boyfriend. I become a victim. I start to think that I will never find anyone who understands me.	I feel alone, unloved and misunderstood. I feel a heaviness in the pit of my stomach. I feel hopeless.
Question #4: *Who would you be without the thought?*	I would be happy and independent.	I would feel lighter. I would be grateful for what I have.

Turnarounds: Specific, genuine examples		
Turnaround	**Janet**	**Lauren**
A) Turnaround to the self	I am unloving to me.	I don't care about how I feel.
Find three examples of how this turnaround to the self is as true as or truer than my stressful thought. (Only one example is shown in this illustration.)	I sit by the phone all day instead of being with my friends and enjoying myself.	I don't ask others to celebrate my birthday with me.
B) Turnaround to the other	I am unloving to my boyfriend.	I don't care about how others feel.
Find three examples of how this turnaround to the other is as true as or truer than my stressful thought. (Only one example is shown in this illustration.)	I am not honest with him about how I feel.	I don't really listen to them when they tell me about their problems.
C) Turnaround to the opposite	My boyfriend is loving to me.	People do care about how I feel.
Find three examples of how this turnaround to the opposite is as true as or truer than my stressful thought. (Only one example is shown in this illustration.)	We spent a lovely day together at the zoo last week.	My friends and family did their best to make my birthday special; we had dinner and a cake.
Note: More detailed instructions, Worksheets, examples and videos are available free of charge at www.thework.com, including topics for teens and adults.		

The Work helps us to understand that it is not people who upset us; it's what we *believe about people* that upsets us. Examining our stressful thoughts and reactions to those thoughts enables us to piece together our role in the situation. By taking complete responsibility for our feelings and actions, we free ourselves to lead the lives we have always wanted, whatever the people in our lives do or don't do. Once we as parents become fluent in turning our beliefs around, we can pass this skill on to our kids.

The Power of Parents

"Out of the mouths of babes" comes the realization of just how great an influence we as parents and other concerned adults can have on teen girls. This reflection from Jenny, who successfully navigated the web of teenage depression, offers both sound advice and hope to parents who now find themselves called to support their girls in doing the same.

> ### *Jenny's Reflection, 15 years later*
> *I wish for every parent to know how important it is to give your children the space to figure things out AND let them know that you love them unconditionally. That who they are is already enough—beyond what they do or accomplish. Support them, encourage them, cheer them on, and don't give up even if it doesn't seem to be working. Your voice makes a huge difference and they will carry it with them in their darkest moments. And don't be discouraged by the fact that your daughter may be snubbing you when you speak; it's probably a front to keep up an image. Be assured your love is sinking in somewhere, even if her ego seems to shut it out at first. And even though you can't prevent the painful feelings she has, you can certainly shine a bright light to help lead the way through them.*

Forging a relationship with our daughters based on compassion, empathy, courage and the other SOULSELF-aware qualities that Jenny so beautifully describes requires us to model for them what it means to live in balance with the various aspects of our own BEING. The more we align our thoughts, emotions and actions with our true Natural Self, the better equipped we will be to support our daughters, sisters and friends in the event that depression or other forms of mental illness enter the picture.

As adults, we are the mirrors into which our girls look for validation and confidence as they grow into fully developed and autonomous young women. If we as mothers are mired in unhealed emotions from our past, the reflection we offer them is a distorted one. Instead of the clarity and light of the SOULSELF, our daughters see only our defenses and barricades. How can a teenage girl learn to treat herself with empathy if she is raised with a lack of understanding and compassion? How can she secure confirmation of her own inner truth if there is nothing or no one with whom to resonate?

As each of us becomes willing to peel back the layers of limiting beliefs and self-sabotaging patterns to face our own shadows, we pave the way for the next generation to charge forward in their own self-exploration. When we become vulnerable enough to share our own truth, we extend this openness as an invitation for our teens to follow suit. The more willing we are to step into our daughter's reality when she needs us to understand, the more we learn to recognize and welcome those raw, rare moments when there is an opening to sit cross-legged with her on the floor, looking eye to eye—tears or no tears—and let it all out, together. We stop trivializing her concerns with blanket "You'll be fine" statements that suffocate her self-expression and close down the possibility of true connection. As we awaken to our full potential as parents, teachers and mentors, we are better able to remain present, even when her call for help is camouflaged and delivered as a personal attack on us, for we know that when she is hurting, she sometimes lashes out at those who love her most.

Studies have shown that if a child has even one person who understands her as she really is, her potential for self-acceptance skyrockets. The responsibility rests on all adults to step up to this challenge. True, it is ultimately the responsibility of each teenage girl to love herself and know she is worthy, but especially in the face of mental illness, it's up to us to create an environment of acceptance and support that inspires healing and self-love. Only then, with our collective loving arms, will we weave a safety net strong enough to catch our girls when they go off course. Imagine the transformation in our society when we succeed at unraveling the web of anxiety and depression in a way that nourishes the souls of those trapped in its threads. Let's start now.

Setting an example is not the main means of influencing another, it is the only means.
—*Albert Einstein*

Living Life Unlocked

Whatever the cause of emotional anguish—whether a limiting belief or a painful experience—know that as long as you have the ability to make new CHOICES, you also have the ability to change the way you feel. There are 1,440 minutes in every day. That's 1,440 opportunities to use the present moment to take actions big and small to lift you out of the fog of depression and realign with the truth of your BEING. Dance. Play music. Shoot baskets. When you are down, reach out for someone to talk to. Visit the school counselor. If you are in despair, call a hotline. Ask to see a therapist—you never know when financial assistance may be available until you ask. When no one is around to empathize with your pain—instead of telling yourself you shouldn't be feeling it, surrender your resistance and allow yourself to let it be as it is. Practice giving empathy to yourself. Search for inspirational quotes on the Internet. Write down your favorites and post them on your mirror, or on the ceiling above your bed so you see them first thing in the morning. Read books about self-esteem and personal growth. Create associations or triggers that draw your attention back to the present moment. For example, every time you see a red car, or every time you receive the first in a thread of text messages, notice any tension in your muscles, then take a deep breath and let it go. Know that becoming more aware of your body's sensations is intricately linked to expanding your ability to hear more clearly the nudges of your SOULSELF. Above all, know that you are lovable just the way you are, no matter who says anything to the contrary. You are capable of feeling better and creating a new and happy life … and you deserve it.

Chapter 8

Through Grief of the Dying to the Truth of Living—on Death and Suicide

There are things that we don't want to happen but have to accept,
things we don't want to know but have to learn,
and people we can't live without but have to let go.
—Author Unknown

Chloe, Age 13
My mom just told me my dad died in a car accident, and I felt a nuclear bomb explode in my heart.

Melissa, Age 15
It wasn't just a lump they found in Mom's breast—it was cancer.

Jennifer, Age 16
Today is one year since my father died. It seems like it's been forever, and then again it seems like yesterday that he would come home and pick me up; I'd tell him about school and maybe sit on his lap, then laugh and have fun at dinner.

Toianna, Age 20
In my Sylvia Plath period, I never did try to stick my head in the oven, but I did wake up most days of my senior year in high school trying to come up with at least one reason not to kill myself.

Kyra, Age 16
Up until now, all my entries have been so girlish and silly. At least it seems that way when I learned today that Bradley committed suicide.

Celeste, Age 11
I never got to say goodbye to my sister. I was too upset when she left for not letting me come with her. Little did I know my life would be saved by not being in that car.

Life gives us lessons in death, and death gives us lessons in life. Next to birth, death is the most significant event any of us will ever face. Coping with this transition—whether it means accepting our own mortality or enduring the loss of a family member or a friend—is difficult at any age. For teenagers who feel as immortal as the sun and stars, however, the loss of a loved one may trigger their first experience of having the world as they know it turned upside down. Regardless of whether death occurs by accident, illness, suicide, violence or war, the stages of grieving are consistent—and as Mavis Staples noted in her song *You Are Not Alone*, "every tear on every face tastes the same."

When a death occurs not from accident or illness, but because someone has taken his or her own life, another layer of trauma and confusion is understandably added for those struggling to answer the haunting question, "Why?" The teen years are already demanding, filled as they are with pressures and expectations imposed both from the outside and from within. The aftermath of facing a serious loss can send a teen's self-esteem and sense of security plummeting. In the absence of coping skills, dark thoughts and volatile emotions may pull her farther away from the SOUL-SELF and into the realm of dangerous behaviors. For some, when the scale of hopelessness tips heavier than the AWARENESS of available resources, the result may be suicide. Even worse, a teen's final act of violence may be carried out in the form of rage against innocent others in classrooms, shopping malls or similar public places—a deeply disturbing trend that is on the rise.

The diarists in this chapter help us make our way through the daunting task of facing the death of a friend, family member or peer. Exploring the factors, both accidental and intentional, that bring a life to an end brings us full circle to topics touched on earlier in this book—abuse, depression, bullying and abuse of drugs or alcohol. From a report by Mothers Against Drunk Driving (MADD) we learn that about every two hours in the U.S., underage drinking contributes to the death of a teenager—whether by auto accidents, murders, suicides, alcohol poisoning or other related causes. Add to this the average of twelve young people between the ages of 15 and 24 who commit suicide every single day. We must acknowledge the heart-wrenching truth of just how many young lives are claimed by senseless and preventable acts. As we hear the stories of those who have lost a loved one, we gain wisdom to help our daughters and ourselves more easily cope with death and to move forward with life while honoring the necessity of each stage of the grieving process. The diarists who have bravely bared their hearts on these pages give us new insight on this delicate and often-hushed topic, bringing to light that the mental and emotional well-being of our children is a goal that must be placed among the highest priorities in our homes and in our society. Simply broaching the subject of death or suicide is an important first step to breaking down the barriers that may keep our daughters from seeking the help they need to heal trauma or emotional pain. Yes, the subject of death raises more questions in the hearts and minds of teens than any adult has answers for, yet we cannot let this be an excuse to dismiss the conversation. We may not have all the answers, but BEING fully present with our teens, soul-to-soul can help all concerned to more easily accept that death is an inevitable part of life—even those deaths for which we are not at all prepared.

When Death Occurs Suddenly

On Labor Day of my first weekend away at college, the sound of the telephone broke the silent hum of the fan under which I was lying on my dorm room floor to beat the summer heat. Along the Missouri riverbanks on highway 1804 (named for the year Lewis and Clark logged in their diary as having passed through on their great expedition west), there had been a terrible automobile accident claiming the life of Charmaine, my roommate Julie's younger sister. Within an hour, my bags were packed and I was headed for the train station to go and mourn the loss with Julie and her family. While I did whatever I could to be supportive of the family as they went through the surreal motions of funeral planning and comforting younger siblings, inside I felt NUMB. I simply couldn't imagine being in the shoes of someone in the immediate family and facing such a devastating and sudden loss.

In the days following the funeral, after friends and family members had left to carry on with their lives, Julie and I returned to our freshman year of college with heavy hearts and mounds of make-up schoolwork. Studying Humanities and watching the summer leaves turn bright colors and fall from the trees, we had a newfound perspective on life and death. The night of the first winter snow, Julie and I each woke with a start at 3:00 a.m.—both having had dreams of Charmaine. We rose from our beds,

Snow Angel

spontaneously threw on our winter coats and ran outside, plunging into the newly fallen snow glistening under the lamppost and made snow angels in celebration of what we felt was Charmaine's presence.

Julie and I have remained lifelong friends, and while I was in the process of compiling the diaries of the women whose stories are told throughout this book, she recalled that her youngest sister Celeste had written about Charmaine's death in her diary. Celeste not only shared her entry from back then but also reflected on how the impact of losing her big sister continues to influence her life to this day.

*Death ends a life, not
a relationship.
—Mitch Albom*

Celeste, Age 11

My life has changed this week. It started out to be a great Labor Day weekend. On Saturday night, Charmaine had a party with a dance and lots of friends in the haymow of our big red barn. Sunday morning, she was on her way to a beach party down the road from our ranch along the Missouri river when she was killed in a car accident by a drunk driver. Today, less than a week later, my house is full of strangers bringing plates of food and my mom is gone to the hospital to be with my older sister Vanneisa, who survived the accident but is still having lots of surgeries. I went to the backyard and was laying face down in the grass and crying so hard that my nose started bleeding. Julie, home from college, found me curled up in the grass and took me inside, hoping to make me feel safe again.

Losing her sister at the age of 11 certainly shook Celeste's sense of security, but as we will learn from her later reflection, this experience ultimately gave her a better understanding not only about death, but also about life. That Celeste was able to extract wisdom from this early wounding event is thanks in large part to the passing of time. Of course time in and of itself does not heal wounds—it is what we do with that time that heals. Teens who are still in the wake of death's immediate aftermath—such as Sherry, whose father died suddenly from an illness, and Dawn, whose close friend was killed in a motorcycle accident—reveal the intense confusion that each faced when trying to make sense of these unexpected losses.

Sherry D., Age 13

The day before yesterday my dad died suddenly of a brain aneurysm. I would have written sooner but I've been busy. I still don't believe it happened. Even as I am writing this I can't picture it really happening. I think when I go home he'll be there, but he won't. He's gone forever. I guess it's not going to hit me until I go to the funeral. Then it's going to shock the hell out of me. I don't know what my dad did to deserve this. How about my mom—she thought she would die before my dad since she has cervical cancer. There are so many people at my house. They are all telling me that everything is going to be okay. But it won't. I hope I start to understand the situation soon. Love, Sherry

Dawn, Age 17

Rest in Peace Nick ... we all love you! Okay ... a lot to talk about ... I actually don't remember much about today, it's kind of a daze. All I could think about was Nick's family. This morning I heard the answering machine clicking and I realized someone called. Then I heard, "This is Michelle"—and I almost hit stop because I thought that it was for Mennonite or sewing women calling for my mom, but I decided to listen to it anyway. Well she went on saying she was calling for the prayer chain, because last night Nick was in a motorcycle accident—so I was thinking, "Okay he's paralyzed, at most" ... but then the message went on: "... he was killed." I almost threw up when I heard the news. Is this the same boy who was here all summer, who I've been drooling over for the past two years, who is only 19??! Nineteen is too young. He was too sweet. He had his whole life ahead of him ... work and love! In choir, I read a note Tracy wrote about it, about him being in a better place, that he is never gonna be in pain or have to worry about anything. I started bawling after reading it. I'm crying as I'm writing this. Why did he get picked to die? Maybe if he were wearing a helmet. Maybe if he wasn't going so fast. Maybe if there hadn't been a fence there. But life isn't based on maybes. Death is final.

While Dawn is right that physical death is indeed final, all that we learn from those we love while they are with us—as well as from the process of grieving them when they are gone—remains with us throughout our lives. Over 30 years after losing her older sister Charmaine, Celeste reflected on the lessons learned as a result of the experience and the ways in which her life was forever changed.

Reflection by Celeste, 30 years later

I was eleven when my 16-year-old sister Charmaine was killed in a car accident. Two young women had been drinking all night long on the Montana state line and had stolen a pickup to go home. Driving 80 MPH on the wrong side of the road that beautiful Sunday morning, they collided head-on with the car my cousin Pam was driving. My sister Vanneisa was in the middle and Charmaine was by the passenger door. Shortly after they left for the party we got a phone call and my parents raced out of the house. It was several hours later when my father and his brother came into the kitchen. My uncle finally said the words. There had been an accident and Charmaine didn't make it. Pam was hurt, but OK. Vanneisa was on her way to a big hospital and was going to have to have surgery on her heart, lungs and leg. What I remember is that in that moment it was as if we were all children—my dad, my uncle and all of us kids. The men were as cracked open as we were. We all felt helpless. I kept thinking, "What are we gonna do?" Over and over. I wanted to make my dad answer, but I didn't dare ask because I could tell he was just as scared. There was nothing we could do. No fixing it. No going back in time, no way to undo it. Even my dad could not fix this one. I was so confused. I couldn't believe that this could happen. As the days and weeks passed, I needed my parents so badly, but they were lost in their own grief and trying to understand it too. My mom was gone for months to be at my sister Vanneisa's side in a hospital in Billings, Montana, as Vanneisa fought for her life. It really was a miracle that she lived.

After thirty-some years, we are all still finding our way through it. I try to imagine what life would be like if the accident would not have happened. I think Charmaine would have been an artist. She whittled wood into little men, sewed her own pretty clothes and made jewelry. She had beautiful hands and golden hair. I still cry when I think of the moment I heard the words. I don't know if it is because I miss my sister or that her absence is a reminder of how fragile life is and of what we have to lose. I do know that my deep appreciation for relationships and my awareness of the limitations of time were born from that tragedy. What a strange gift. My sister's death made me so much more connected to life. Every day I wish she were here to grow old with us. And every day I try to breathe it all in.

That death has the ability to connect us more profoundly to life is one of the great ironies of being human. As we who survive the death of a loved one reach new milestones and face life's twists and turns, we cannot help but imagine how those we've lost would have responded ... the advice they might have given ... the conversations that might have been.

Preparing for the Inevitable

While the sudden death of someone dear denies us the opportunity to ask pressing questions or say any final goodbyes, knowing ahead of time that a loved one's passing is quickly approaching leaves this door wide open. When Kimberlee learned that her father was dying, she seized the opportunity to more fully express her love for him. Confirmation of her father's love for her before he died is unmistakable in the entries below:

> **Kimberlee, Age 16**
>
> *February 8.* *Dear Diary, I came home and my dad had a red rose and chocolates and a year's subscription to two magazines for me, and he said they were my early Valentine's Day presents. Why he gave me this stuff early I have no idea.*
>
> *February 10.* *At 8 a.m., I took my dad to the hospital because he couldn't breathe. He's in intensive care. I love him so much, more than anyone. If he needed to have a heart to live, I would gladly give him my heart. I hope he gets better. I can't believe all the things that are happening. My dad is almost about to die. He has been on a respirator (which is a machine that breathes for him) since yesterday. And the doctor says things look really bad. You should see him. It is so hard for me to look at him.*
>
> *I wish I could explain how I feel right now. It's the worst thing I ever saw or will probably ever have to go through. I don't know how I will live without him. I have always been with him. He watched me grow from a baby to 16 years old, and now he's in the hospital fighting for his life, and I know he's so, so scared. He can't talk at all but last night he tried to say, "I love you," to me. I know it hurt him to try to say that with the tube down his throat. Then he told me to go home, and I was scared because I thought it was because he was going to die, and when I left I cried so hard. He is suffering so badly. And last night, I was sitting with him and we were holding hands and I said, "I love you more than you could even imagine," and he stared at me and nodded his head and then later I said, "you're the greatest, Dad," and he looked at me and stared right*

into my eyes for so long. And I knew he felt so much love for me at that moment.

February 24. *My dad is still in the hospital. The doctor said he wasn't going to make it. He is becoming incoherent now. That means he doesn't recognize me or anyone else because he can't get enough oxygen to his brain. Yesterday he was pretty high on all the medication they are giving him to sedate him, and he can't talk because of the tube going down his throat and into his lungs, but he asked me to take him home. Over and over he told me he wants to go home. I felt like dying. I told him he couldn't go home yet because he can't breathe on his own. He looked at me and then made a strange face like someone stabbed him. We gave him a pencil and paper because he wanted to tell us something but we couldn't read what he spelled out. He got mad that we couldn't read it.*

February 27. *A lot of things are happening. I can't talk about all my feelings, it would take too much writing. This morning a few minutes after 8 a.m., my dad passed away in the hospital. I was at home. Linda said that he just closed his eyes and went to sleep, then a few seconds later, a nurse came in and told her that he had passed away. When I got to his room and saw him, it reminded me of the first time I saw a dead person when I was in 6th grade. This girl in our class … her dad died and our whole class went to the funeral, and when I walked up to the casket, he was just lying there all peaceful looking. When I looked at my dad lying there with all the tubes removed, I just got this strange feeling, the weirdest feeling I ever had and I also had a feeling of deep loss. My heart felt weird, like it was breaking slowly, but barely holding together, so it felt really tight. My whole chest felt tight.*

Though there is always more we wish we had said and done while our loved ones were still alive, Kimberlee's diary serves as a living testament to her love for her father, and his for her. Although it has been over 25 years since his passing, this reflection is a comforting reminder of the special connection between them.

Kimberlee's Reflection, 25 years later

My dad is my hero and always will be until the day I shut my eyes for the last time. I know his love for me is never ending and it will be with me all of my life, watching over me, watching me become someone that he can be proud of. And my love for him will follow him always. I can still remember the sound of his voice, how he said "g'night, love ya" each night, his cough ... I have the same cough (minus the emphysema, I don't smoke), and I have the same stubborn attitude. I think about him so often and I wish I had just 15 minutes to see him, touch him, and hug him, again. All I can do is carry his love through me to my children. Sometimes we get out his briefcase from when he was a sharpshooter in World War II and when he was a sheriff and look through all of the goodies in it—purple heart, bronze star, etc. He used to let me look through it with him—under his supervision—about once a year. I still have everything in there that he kept in there, including his last pack of cigarettes he was smoking. Weird to hold onto things like that, like they MEAN something.

Sentimentality aside, I feel like my relationship with my dad ended sort of unresolved. I know we were able to bond in the hospital when he was dying but he couldn't speak, so I filled in the blanks with all my regrets of how I had shut him out so many times over the previous years. I just don't want the same thing to happen between my children and me. I would be devastated if they ever shut me out of their lives like I did my dad. I was all he had. :(

As difficult as watching a parent's health decline must have been for a 16-year-old girl, I know that making the most of the time we have with family and taking every opportunity to say "I love you" makes us a little more prepared when the time comes to let them go.

A few months before my mom's passing, I had flown to North Dakota where she was having emergency heart surgery to save her life. Relieved the surgery was a success and yet also aware of the fragility of her condition, I used the time we had together while she was recovering to engage her in many deep conversations about our family history. As is the case with what is likely buried in the psychological closets of most families, our conversation brought back proud memories as well as the skeletons of experiences I would have preferred to forget. I shared with her that one of my intentions in writing this book was to show readers that by turning over the rocks hiding the dark side of the history of our lives, we open the possibility for the light of truth to heal the imperfections—to understand them for the gifts they behold and the insights they reveal. It was then that my mom took a deep breath, held my hand and disclosed for the first time the beatings my father suffered as a child, a piece of the family puzzle that explained so much about the complex nature of my father. It was this thread of history shared in the context of seizing a moment that may never come again that exposed intergenerational truths and gave me a deeper understanding of my dad's inner struggles.

As we shared our beliefs about life and death, I reminded her of the profound effect that *Life After Life,* a book by Raymond Moody I'd read in high school, had on my perspective about death. I told her how, because of that book, I'd made a special point to speak with my Grandma before she died about the near-death experiences it described, and the sensation of peace and calm and light felt by so many. I shared with my mom how that conversation with my Grandma had opened the door for her to tell me about similar accounts she'd heard from loved ones in her life, including my Grandpa. While dying in her arms, drifting in and out of sleep, Grandpa had shared with her that he was having conversations with his brother Chris, who died before him, and that Chris was comforting him in a way he'd never experienced. This sharing led us to a deeper discussion of philosophies of life. Mom and I discussed the morals—and lack thereof—in today's society, and laughed about respective childhood memories.

While I was grateful I had the opportunity to share this level of communication with my mother, it wasn't until after her death a few months later that I realized what I wish had transpired in those last talks. In particular, I wish I had thanked her for not judging me when I became pregnant as a teenager. Having read so many diaries and heard the stories of so many teen girls living in unwed-mothers shelters where I had conducted self-esteem workshops, it is difficult to understand how I could have overlooked the tremendous gift of love she extended with her unconditional acceptance of me in that situation. As I grew older and became a parent myself, I was able to become more detached and neutral about what my parents did and didn't do. I saw just how many times I had judged my mother—and my father, who had died a few years earlier. I realized that rare is the parent who is all good or all bad. Sometimes, a parent offers support when we least expect that parent to come through, and sometimes a normally supportive parent misses the mark and is not there when needed. Although forgiveness had occurred on all sides, it wasn't until after each of my parents had passed that I recognized the love that was there all along; this realization brought about even deeper levels of love and healing.

The line dividing good and evil cuts through the heart of every human being.
—*Aleksandr Solzhenitsyn*

As kids, it's difficult to see past our unrealistic expectations that our parents should be perfect. When we are later able to acknowledge their limitations, we are presented with the opportunity to take our relationship with them to a more authentic level where unconditional acceptance abides. Of course, this doesn't necessarily mean we agree with all of our parents' CHOICES, but rather we come to accept that they were not—nor could they have been—any different than they were. After navigating countless twists and turns in her experience with her mother's breast cancer, Melissa was finally able to find that acceptance in her heart.

Melissa, Age 15

November 3. *I have complained so many times about so many things—stupid things that don't matter. But NEVER again. One of my worst fears, and the subject of several nightmares, is Mom dying. And just now, I found out how close that nightmare came to becoming a reality. It wasn't just a lump they found in Mom's breast—it was cancer. But she is going to be OK. If it had spread, not only would she have had to have a mastectomy, she could've died. God, I can't ever imagine that. It's like in one moment, all the complaints I have ever had are negated! Because without Mom, nothing would matter. I realize now how truly fragile life is and I will never take it—or Mommy—for granted ever again.*

December 15. *Mom just said she couldn't wait until Christmas is over. How sad that she is so tired and sick that she feels this way. I'm starting to realize the great effect that the chemo has had on her.*

Melissa's Reflection, 16 years later

Many years have passed since that day in November when at age 15 I learned my beloved mother had breast cancer, yet I still remember it like it was yesterday. It turns out, my parents had kept her condition a secret from me until she was getting better. They told other people how serious it was, but not me. When the cancer came back 7 years later, I naively assumed she would be okay, as she had been before. Once again, I was very much kept in the dark about how advanced the cancer was—so much that a couple of months before her passing, I went on a two-week summer vacation to London. I returned to find Mom had completely deteriorated and she died six weeks later. After her death, my relatives and family friends told me they had known for quite a while how sick she was, and they had encouraged her and my father to be up front with me. I understand that, as before, their instincts were motivated by love and a desire to protect me. But I regret they didn't trust me to handle what was happening—especially because I made certain choices based upon the assumption I would have all the time in the world with my mother. If I ever have to deal with a serious illness, I would be up front with the people who are close to me, particularly any children I might have. I would never want them to be as blindsided as I was when I discovered just how gravely ill my mother was.

Melissa's description of how it felt to be kept in the dark about the severity of her mom's cancer brings to light a dilemma many parents face when deciding how transparent to be with children regarding situations they believe will be deeply unsettling. When under the pretenses of protecting our kids from pain we withhold information, we run the risk of creating distance between family members—even when our intentions are exactly the opposite. To deny our kids the opportunity to share in life's trials as well as its triumphs is to deprive them of vital opportunities to understand the situation more fully, to extend compassion, and to come to terms ahead of time with the possibility of loss. Further, sheltering our teens from life's challenges may come at the cost of eroding their trust in us to be forthcoming in other important matters. Although we don't intend it, our attempts to spare them fear or anxiety can end up shaking the very emotional stability we so dearly want to remain steady.

In truth, those who keep secrets are modeling a pattern of relating that blocks a healthy exchange of real life concerns, leaving the door open for further communication breakdowns. Learning to have age-appropriate conversations on everything from the birds and the bees to life-threatening illnesses is a crucial trait to inspire healthy adult and parenting relationships—now and in the future. Resources abound on websites like www.kidshealth.org that model ways to initiate conversations on sensitive topics. To build closer connections, truth must always remain the guiding principle, for every truth told invites deeper discussions about other issues we hold close to the heart.

Though we may never know whether Melissa's mother realized the impact of withholding from her daughter vital information about her health, we do know that this decision taught Melissa valuable lessons which will serve her for the rest of her life. Healing occurs any time we use our experiences to learn, grow, and elevate our AWARENESS in the direction of wisdom. The expanded AWARENESS that came out of Melissa's grieving

The ultimate lesson is learning how to love and be loved unconditionally.
—Elisabeth Kübler-Ross

the loss of her mom is now sealed in her heart—and is brought back to her mind every time she unlocks her diary.

Melissa's Reflection (continued)

I loved my mother, even as a teen. She was a supportive and loving woman. Though she's been gone for more than 10 years, her influence continues to guide and strengthen me. I cherish the following excerpts from a goodbye letter she wrote to us kids, and keep it folded safely within my diary:

Dear Melissa, Good health, both emotional and physical, is the NUMBER ONE essential in life. Please never take it for granted. With it, all things are possible. Without it—nothing is important. We all make mistakes and should not be too hard on ourselves when we do. Hopefully, we learn from them and grow with the experience. Failing is part of living in a world composed of human beings and not of saints. All we can do is try our best and strive to help make life a bit brighter for others and ourselves. A smile, common courtesy and lending a hand to someone in need goes a long way. Try hard not to be too sad when I'm gone. We've all got to go sometime and for sure, I've been luckier than the vast majority of the folks on this "ole" planet. A zest for life, and living it to the fullest, never left me and I hope it will never leave you. Have all the fun you possibly can. It's all we take with us when it's time to go. Love you forever, Mom

Sometimes the dying live more fiercely and wisely than the rest of us.
—Julia Cameron

...You don't know what you've got until it's gone...

Oh, Mom.   I ♡ u. — I Miss u.

An estimated one in seven children, like Melissa, will experience the death of a parent before the age of 20. Even more tragically, according to a report in *USA Today*, each year some 90,000 parents in the U.S. will confront the profound suffering that follows the death of a child. Add to these statistics the number of friends and extended family members who pass during the regular course of our lifetimes, and it becomes obvious that our culture as a whole is in need of an education about how to grieve these losses in a way that ensures a happy and peaceful future.

On Grief and Grieving

"Good grief!"

To weep is to make less the depth of grief."
—William Shakespeare

Most of us have heard this expression before, but probably not as a means to convey that yes, indeed, grief is good. In fact, we are more likely to consider this phrase an oxymoron—putting two words together with opposite meanings. And yet, genuine grief is a powerful and necessary part of regaining our emotional balance after the loss of a loved one. In the uninhibited expression of our most painful emotions, we can find ease and comfort in the midst of our mourning. To remind myself of this, I created an acronym that redefines GRIEF as:

GRIEF ...   GOING RIGHT INTO THE EMOTIONAL FEELING

As they say, the only way out is through, and this is the message we must model for, and teach our children about, grieving. GRIEF is not to be suppressed but embraced, as a reflection of the connection we shared with the departed one.

I will not say, do not weep, for not all tears are an evil."
—J.R.R. Tolkien

Although the grieving process looks different for everyone, Elisabeth Kübler-Ross, the legendary pioneer of research on death and dying, identified five stages that reflect common experiences shared by people across nearly all cultures. In *On Grief and Grieving*, the last book before her own death which she co-authored with David Kessler, she noted how those we have lost continue to impact our lives: "The person you were is forever changed. A part of the old you died with your loved one. And a part of your loved one lives on in the new you." For some, the part that lives on inspires them to live more deeply and to serve others more fully. Perhaps this is why September 11 has become a federally recognized National Day of Service in the U.S., with tens of millions of people volunteering their time in service to others.

While Kübler-Ross developed her "five stages of grief" based on her studies of patients facing terminal illness, these stages are relevant to anyone experiencing a catastrophic personal loss, rejection or tragedy.

The Five Stages of Grief

1. Denial: "This can't be happening to me."
2. Anger: "Why is this happening? Who is to blame?"
3. Bargaining: "Make this not happen, and in return I will _____."   *... Fill in the blank*
4. Depression: "I'm too sad to do anything."
5. Acceptance: "I'm at peace with what happened."

Experiencing any of these emotions in relation to loss is both healthy and natural, and to the extent we allow ourselves to express them fully, we permit "time to heal all wounds." Contrary to popular belief, you do not have to go through each stage in order to heal—nor is it likely you will experience them in a neat, sequential order. It is also true that not everyone who grieves goes through all of these stages—and that's okay. The important thing is to allow your feelings to unfold without worrying about what you "should" be feeling or which stage you're supposed to be in. Kübler-Ross herself never intended for these stages to be a rigid framework that applies to everyone who mourns. As she wrote about the five stages of grief, they "were never meant to help tuck messy emotions into neat packages. They are responses to loss that many people have, but there is not a typical response to loss, as there is no typical loss. Our grieving is as individual as our lives."
—Adapted from www.helpguide.org

People are like stained-glass windows. They sparkle and shine when the sun is out, but when the darkness sets in, their true beauty is revealed only if there is a light from within.
—Elisabeth Kübler-Ross

Regardless of what type of loss we've endured, the process of grieving comes in layers; milestones such as birthdays or anniversaries can create unexpected setbacks. Those who have lost a friend or family member to the tragedy of suicide are dealt a double blow of emotions to process and grieve.

Suicide

Kyra, Age 16
August 26. *After registering for classes yesterday, I was in my car, happily listening to* Foolish Games, *by Jewel, on the radio. I was off to do errands at the church, the bank and video store. While*

driving, I saw a truck like Tom's parked on the curb next to the bluffs. I slowed down, and sure enough, it was my boyfriend, Tom, walking into the street to stop my car. "Kyra, something terrible has happened," he said. I almost smiled because I thought he was going to say something like, "I'm grounded for a year," or "I can't see you anymore," and was just overreacting. Nothing could have prepared me for what came next.

"Bradley committed suicide."

I didn't understand what he said. It was so foreign, like another language.

I screamed, "WHAT?"

He said, "I'm sorry, go on to the church." He slammed the door and walked away. I sat in my car for five minutes, stunned, then went back home. By the time I got out of the car, I was bawling. My mom saw me, and cancelled her next appointment when I told her what happened. This is something no one should have to deal with. Especially a bunch of 17 year olds.

This is a guy I dated in middle school and went to formal with before I started dating Tom. I spent the night at his house two times. I saw him every day at school. I just can't believe this. It is beyond anything I've had to deal with before.

This is for TV and movies, not real life. Things like this aren't supposed to happen. This has been the worst fucking month of my life. If only he had told someone. If only someone had known.

October 25. It's been two months since Bradley took his own life. These sixty days have forced me to do a lot of changing and soul searching. I cry every day about different stuff. College, Tom, Bradley, but most of the time I don't know why I'm crying. My relationship with Tom is so different now. Sometimes he'll not want to talk to me or he'll not want me to come over and I end up feeling rejected and then I have to just be really sensitive and figure what mood he's in. Usually he's thinking about Bradley. It makes it hard sometimes having to figure that into the picture. I love Tom though, and I'm willing to try my best to be a support for him.

December 29. Tom and I have had a few ups and downs. We went on the ski trip together. I think we spent too much time together because by the second day he started getting really sensitive about everything, even jokes. That's how it's been since Bradley died. It's kind of like we have two relationships: There's the one where Tom wants Kyra to have sex and go to the movies and dinner and make-out and eat family dinners like a normal relationship. Then there's *the Tom and Kyra who get depressed and cry and push away from each other about Bradley and then open up and talk about him. It's hard to get used to the two levels, but I will.*

Kyra's Reflection, 13 years later

It has been years since high school ended. While the parties, classes, the fun times and the fights with friends are all a blur, there are a few events that stand out. The exact details of the days following Bradley's death and the emotions that came along with the suicide of my friend remain crystal clear.

It's funny the things that make me think of Bradley. For years, almost anything could trigger it. A beautiful sunset that I realized Bradley would miss, a new song on the radio or a new TV show I thought he would like; a party he would miss, prom, graduation and even my wedding, years later. I always focused on all the things I knew he would miss. For a long time I thought maybe I was weird or overly sensitive to still think about him so often. I recently found out that if I am weird or overly sensitive, so are a lot of my classmates.

Last year was my ten-year class reunion. I brought up that one topic everyone seemed to shy away from. Everyone I spoke with had Bradley on their mind, and had for years. Somehow the pain caused such a deep cut in people, those who were close to him and lots of people who weren't close to him at all. On some level I felt that taking his life was a selfish thing. On a mental level I knew this, but in my heart, it took me a long time to realize it. For about ten years, I blamed myself, and that guilt held me a prisoner of my past.

Through the years, I was haunted with guilt about spending so much time with Bradley's best friend, Tom, my boyfriend at the time. I knew Bradley had been through a difficult break-up before his suicide, and I felt like I should have pushed Tom to spend more time with him, instead of with me. I kept hearing the voice of Tom's mother, whom I overheard at the funeral making a comment about how "Tom just hadn't had much time for Bradley with how much time he spends with his girlfriend—[me]." That nailed guilt into me so deeply that I couldn't let it go until about a year ago. I think a big part of letting go of it was finally realizing I wasn't alone in feelings of remorse or my wishing I had done some things differently; that other people who weren't even close to him felt similar emotions. I have also learned to not take things so personally and to put less weight in the offhand comments that others say—in this case, Tom's mom.

So, while Bradley's death still sits heavy with my classmates and me after eleven years, I am finally learning not to tear up when I hear old songs he liked or new ones that I think he may have liked. I know I will never be "over" my friend's death. For so long, my sadness over his death blinded me to the fact that he wasn't just the victim; he was troubled, and he caused a lot of pain in others as well. I hope Bradley found peace, and I hope his family, friends, ex-girlfriend, and everyone who knew him will one day find something passable for peace as well.

My life has a few black spots. Bradley's death remains one of the darkest. If I took anything from his seemingly senseless suicide, it would be to really appreciate life. It is the memory of Bradley that helps me to remember the fleeting nature of life. I have tried over the years to find the reason for his death. I know this may seem a strange goal, as there appears to be no actual reason for someone to kill oneself. It makes me feel better to think that something so tragic happened for a reason. If I settle on something, it would be that he affected the 750 people at his funeral in such a profound way that they became better people. Maybe those 750 of us who cared about him learned to live better lives. I know for some this may have taken a while. Like Tom, who shut off his emotions, and me, who put on a mask that I felt I was expected to wear, yet anguished in private. Or our friend Pete, who refused to mention Bradley's name unless crying while drunk, or Bradley's ex-girlfriend, who wore her mask like a shield, and as far as I know, has never removed it. But eventually, I hope all the many that were hurt will heal from those emotions. Heal so their souls don't forget, but still heal.

Jack Canfield, a pioneer in the field of personal growth and my mentor for nearly 20 years, read Kyra's diary entries and later reflection. To her wish that those affected by suicide will one day have access to tools to help them move through GRIEF and sadness and eventually back to peace, he offered the following insight about the path toward emotional healing:

Jack Canfield on Loss
One of the hardest things to deal with when someone commits suicide is our own guilt. "If only I had (or hadn't) said something to them. If only I had spent more time with them. If only I hadn't been so selfish. If only I had noticed. If only I had reached out sooner, more often, or at all." The truth is, with the exception of

bullying, cyberbullying and physical abuse that may contribute to another person's taking his or her own life; we are not responsible for another person's behavior. They are. All the "could haves," "should haves" and "would haves" that cross through our minds are only useless mental processing that just keeps us stuck in the past and most often robs us of our present. There is nothing we can do about the past except learn from it and release it. The problem is that most people don't know how.

In my 40 years of experience with coaching clients and workshop participants, I have come to realize that every one of us is always doing the best we can to meet some basic need with the current level of skill, information, resources, awareness and tools we have. This is true at all ages, but especially during the teenage years, when our emotional development is still very much under construction. In this situation, Bradley had the need to end his pain and suffering. Lacking the necessary psychological tools and processes that are now available in classes on psychological education, self-esteem curricula and group counseling, and the awareness that all feelings, no matter how painful, will eventually pass, Bradley turned to one of several coping strategies used by teenagers; alcohol, drugs, sex or suicide. He was doing the best thing he knew to do to alleviate his suffering. His actions were not the fault of Tom or Kyra or any of Bradley's other friends. None of them had these skills or resources either. Fortunately, today there are more resources available to teens. There are online forums and websites, suicide hot lines, classes on raising self-esteem and learning how to talk about and release difficult and painful feelings. There's Oprah's network, Dr. Phil and a host of other TV shows that show us we're not alone in our suffering and offer resources, books, audios and websites that pave the way back to emotional health.

However, even with all of that, people still commit suicide. If it happens, even once we realize we are not responsible—we did not pull the trigger, we did not drive the car off the cliff, and we did not force pills down the other person's throat—we still have to release our grief. We still have to let go and move on.

I have found some processes that are fairly simple yet profoundly effective to help accelerate the process of letting go. The first is The Work of Byron Katie [described in an earlier chapter]. Questioning the painful beliefs—such as "Bradley should not have killed himself" or "I should have been able to stop him from committing suicide"—can help release feelings of responsibility for the

Let it be.
—John Lennon

I don't let go of concepts—I meet them with understanding. Then they let go of me.
—*Byron Katie*

actions of another. For more examples of The Work, read Katie's book, *Loving What Is*, or visit her website at www.TheWork.com and watch the videos of Katie taking people through the four questions.

The Total Truth Process

Jack Canfield

A second powerful technique is one that I've been teaching for nearly 40 years. The Total Truth Process is a six-step process for releasing the negative emotions of anger, fear, guilt and grief and returning to peace, love, forgiveness, acceptance and appreciation. The process can be done verbally (talking to the person who has committed suicide out loud by imagining them sitting in an empty chair facing you) or by writing out the steps in the form of a letter. However you choose to do it, here are the six steps, using Kyra's experience with Bradley's suicide as an example:

The 6 Steps of The Total Truth Process

1. **Anger**
   (Start by telling the person who has died everything you are angry about.)
   "I am angry that you killed yourself. I'm angry that you are no longer here to have fun with. I'm angry that you left me alone without you. I'm angry about all the guilt I've been carrying around. I'm angry that I couldn't concentrate in school for months after you died. I'm angry that you took the coward's way out rather than having the courage to reach out for help. I'm angry that you didn't ask me to help you!"

2. **Hurt and Sadness**
   "I feel hurt that you didn't trust me enough to reach out to me. I'm sad that you are not here to enjoy playing music with. I'm sad that I'll no longer be able to talk with you about the things we shared." Etc.

3. **Fear**
   (There are two kinds of fear to address here—fears about the welfare of the other person and fears about ourselves.)
   "I'm afraid to think about how much pain you have been in.

I'm afraid your soul is not at peace. It scares me that I will never know what happened to you. I'm afraid I'll always feel guilty about your death. I'm afraid I'll never be able to be totally happy because of what happened. I'm afraid someone else I love may commit suicide. I'm afraid now that you've done it I might even consider it."

4. **Remorse and Regret**

   "I regret that I didn't see the signs or realize how much pain you were in. I regret not reaching out to you more. I regret that I didn't tell Tom to spend more time with you. I am sorry for how much emotional pain you must have been in. I am sorry we didn't have counselors and therapists and more conscious parents available to us back then. I'm sorry you took your life."

5. **Wants and Desires**

   "I want you to know how much I miss you. I want you to know that I and all of your friends cared about you, but we didn't know how lonely and unhappy you were. I want you to be happy wherever you are. I want you to know there were 750 people at your funeral who cared about you. And wherever you are, I want you to know you are not forgotten."

6. **Forgiveness, Appreciation and Love**

   "I forgive you for taking your life. I forgive you for messing up my mind and my life for years. I forgive you for _____ " (and here you can add anything else he may have ever said or done that you may have resented him for). *"I appreciate all the good times we had together."* (Be specific and mention positive memories, positive qualities he taught you, gifts he gave you, etc.) *"And finally, I want you to know that I love you."*

"Take your time as you do this process," Jack concludes, "and allow yourself to feel the feelings as you speak or write the words. The more in touch you can get with your feelings, the more complete will be the release. For more information on The Total Truth Process, read Chapter 29 in my book, *The Success Principles*."

The Total Truth Process is one of the most powerful tools I have found to resolve unprocessed emotions from the past. Layer by layer, this process leads us through and beyond anger, guilt, sadness and fear and back to the SOULSELF, where real transformation becomes possible. After years of practicing and teaching this technique, I have found it has evolved from a step-by-step regimen into a reliable means of shifting the understanding of a situation—a shift that seems to happen, as Jack would say, "auto-magically." Not surprisingly, this was one of the first tools I reached for when I was ready to begin unraveling the emotions my ex-boyfriend's suicide had triggered within me.

Even though we were no longer dating when Jim made the CHOICE to take his own life, I still found a way to feel guilty about what he had done. We had remained friends after the breakup, and at the tail end of a trip back to San Diego after I had moved to Hawaii, he asked if I'd come over for a visit before my plane left to go back to Honolulu. Not knowing what his intentions were to have me over, and running short on time anyway, I declined the invitation. When I got back to Hawaii, Jim called to tell me how disappointed he was that I didn't make time to see him. He was a musician, and although I had no way of knowing this at the time, it turns out that he had written a song about me ... about how courageous I was, and had wanted to sing it for me in person. That phone call was the last time I ever talked to Jim; he hanged himself in his garage two months later.

I carried this image in my purse for years to spot check emotions behind non-peaceful emotions.

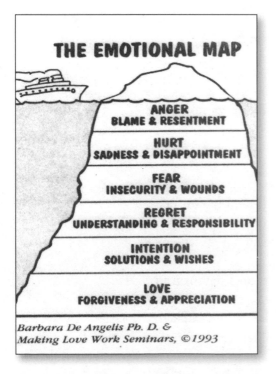

Barbara De Angelis Ph. D. & Making Love Work Seminars, ©1993

When I did The Total Truth Process about this incident, the first emotion that came up was anger. Why didn't he just tell me that he'd written a song for me and wanted me to hear it? He was depressed and chose self-pity and rejection instead of making a clear request for support. I can only assume that he had hit such an emotional low that the healthy CHOICE to reach out for help was simply out of reach. Despite the fact that many people begged him to seek therapy, he thought he should be able to pull himself out of it. Being extremely opposed to anti-depressants, he ruled medication out of the question as well. As I went deeper and processed through each emotion from anger about his stubbornness to acceptance of his free will, I was reminded of the "iceberg model of emotions," a term coined by author Barbara DeAngelis.

For those who are grieving, anger and guilt are the

more obvious emotions visible on the surface; yet as we go deeper, beneath our defenses, we get in touch with more vulnerable feelings like sadness, hurt, fear and remorse—as well as desire, forgiveness, love and appreciation. Our sincere desire to seek the *total* truth of the situation acts like a fire that melts through feelings we may have numbed, out of self-preservation. Once that ice melts, our AWARENESS returns to the very core of our BEING, we understand the incident from a much larger perspective, and we are free.

Doing this process in relation to my ex-boyfriend helped me understand the difference between the things I can and cannot change. Realizing he made the CHOICES that led him down the path of self-sabotage and destruction allowed me to begin letting go of my guilt. Gradually, I was able to release my list of reasons of why I was to blame for the fact that he tied a rope around his neck and climbed on to the orange five-gallon bucket we often used to collect rainwater. In my cloud of guilt, I felt as if I had been the one to buy the rope, tie the noose and kick loose the bucket from underneath him. The fact is, the night before he killed himself, *he* chose to drink and drive, resulting in a car accident and a DUI. *He* chose to let that be the straw that broke the camel's back in deciding life was not worth living. *He* chose not to consider whether he may have a chemical imbalance. *He* chose not to seek counseling for his depression. *I* chose to make it to my plane on time. The Total Truth Process brought me back to a place of genuine love, compassion and forgiveness, both for myself and for Jim. Still, the experience changed me, in ways both big and small and for many years to come, underscoring the truth that human beings do not live in isolation. Indeed, the actions of one have a profound impact on all.

The Impact of Suicide on Survivors

The butterfly effect is a theory suggesting that the flap of a butterfly's wings in one part of the world generates enough motion to cause the formation of a hurricane in a far distant location and at a much later date. Though some may consider this a far out concept, it speaks directly to the impact we as humans have on one another. As the parent of a teenager who committed suicide, Sally Grablick, author of *The Reason—Help and Hope for Those Who Grieve,* shares about the ripple effect a suicide has on the living:

Death has a profound effect on our relationships. When the loss is unexpected and tragic, as it is with suicide, there is no time to prepare our foundations for the destructive impact. Stunned, we are slow to react, but when the shock subsides, our first inclination is to find someone to blame. This is where the shift begins; accusations, guilt, and shame spill out into the world that surrounds us. The ripple effect extends into the lives of our spouses, siblings, extended family, and friends. Some relationships are strong enough to sustain the weight and confusion that comes with suicide; but many are not.

Our reactions aren't always a response to the cause of death; it often has more to do with our relationship to the deceased. From this perspective, it is the death of a child that impacts us the most. Statistically, 30 percent of marriages that experience the loss of a child will end in divorce. This is due to the fact that as a parent, we believe our primary responsibility is to keep our children alive. The feelings of failure and guilt, combined with the intensity of grief, can be completely overwhelming. The desire to escape the trappings of this black hole can cause spouses to turn against one another, which not only affects their relationship, but the surviving children as well.

Having lost their mother and father to grief, the siblings are left to work through the pain and confusion on their own. They rarely discuss their loss, because they don't want to create more suffering for their parents. Feelings are at first concealed, and then buried deep inside. A number of siblings will turn to drugs and alcohol for some form of relief. Others may begin to approach things with a larger-than-life exuberance; the weight of their dead brother or sister fuels their need to experience everything, not only for themselves but for their lost loved one.

People rarely anticipate having to re-evaluate their relationships during the grief process, but the lack of support from extended family or friends may cause them to do so. I personally experienced several circumstances in which our connections with others were dramatically changed. Several couples began to avoid us, as if losing a child was contagious. Others stood back from us both physically and emotionally as if they were going to "catch" suicide. Then there were those who just wanted to pretend that nothing had happened, and completely avoided any conversation regarding our loss.

The examples throughout this chapter help to illustrate the fact that we all react to death differently … something Kyra noticed soon after Bradley's suicide. That is because, as individuals, our actions and reactions to loss will be as unique as we are. Support groups and talk therapy help us to realize these truths, and enable us to gain perspective. People need to understand that GRIEF is a process, and if we work at it, the balance to our lives and relationships can be restored.

Sally's dedication to raising awareness about teen suicide inspired me to do some research of my own. While the numbers themselves are shocking for any parent to read, I uncovered two important takeaways that I believe are essential for suicide prevention. The first is that the most common reason for teen suicide is depression. Over 90 percent of adolescents who die by suicide have a diagnosable mental illness at the time of their death, though it has often gone unrecognized or untreated for years. The other important finding is that a teen experiencing a suicidal impulse, who also has access to the means to carry it out, is a lethal combination. Studies show that many suicides could have been prevented by simply not having guns available (or having gun locks) or by installing barriers on bridges or other high places—anything to buy time for the impulse to pass.

The 1,300 people who have jumped to their death from the Golden Gate Bridge offer a powerful example of how our darkest impulses may in fact be fleeting. Of the 30 people who survived the fall from the bridge, 19 admitted that the instant they jumped, they knew they didn't want to die. Like waves, our impulses come and go. The challenge is to move through the impulse to harm ourselves without acting on it.

GOING RIGHT INTO THE EMOTIONAL FEELING

A suicide attempt by gun is fatal 85 percent of the time.
—National Public Radio

For those in despair … For teens or adults experiencing deep despair or suicidal impulses, use all your might to shift your focus out of the clouded mind. Know that in the midst of the negative emotions flooding your mind, you really don't have to believe everything you think. In fact, in this moment, believe nothing you think, because FEAR—the FRAGILE EXPERIENCE OF ANXIETY OR REGRET—is in charge, and this fear is a mirage distorting the truth. Practice the tools provided so far in this book, starting with the simple act of shifting your thoughts away from the idea of dying and into a greater awareness of your breath. Follow the inhale and exhale in detail. Use the power of this awareness to see your pain from a bird's eye corner of your mind, and use all your might to pull yourself free from the shadow of these dark thoughts and back to the light of noontime where the shadow disappears. Call a hotline. Reach out to someone you trust—choose this person carefully. **Kill time—not yourself.**

Managing Suicidal Thoughts

In my teens and 20s, it was common for restaurants to give away matches with their logos imprinted on them. I never was a smoker, but I used the matchbooks in another way—as a sort of diary of dining experiences. In that tiny "book," I logged the date, who I was with, and summarized our conversation in a phrase or two—or made a note about what I liked or didn't like about the restaurant … sort of my own personal version of Yelp or Twitter before the Internet. After taking a class on organizing and using feng shui principles to clear out clutter in my home, I found that matchbook collection in a jar I hadn't opened in decades. There in the midst of dozens of matchbooks was the double-edge razor blade I'd hidden back in the days of my hopelessness and despair.

In that dark period, when chronic depression stemming from the core belief that I was unlovable prevented me from seeing any way to turn my life around, I considered many different means to the end, including one I had forgotten about until I found this note in the box with my diary.

Janet, Age 19

A portion of a note I wrote in a moment of desperation.

I wish I would have died when I was in the hospital, I knew even then I wanted to. I remember crying every morning because I woke up. Of all the times I've been tempted to drive into a pole on Demers Ave., why don't I ever do it? I'm such a chicken. Just a worthless obstacle in everyone's way. I'm sick and tired of feeling alone, and knowing that I'm too much of an inconvenience to visit in the hospital. My attitude is so bad right now, AND I have no desire to make it better. I don't remember what it's like to have a happy day. When I wake up in the morning, I've already lost any chance at getting a grip on myself. I open my eyes and tears are already there. My only hope is to stay asleep.

Whenever I struggled to find the will to keep living, a wiser part of me would reliably step in, put down the blade and pick up the newspaper—opening to the obituaries. In one short column, a whole life was summarized. I wondered what my own obituary would say, and knew deep inside that the story of my passage to date was far from complete. I knew there was more to me—I was bigger than whatever words could be written and concluded by such an abrupt ending. The question was, what did I want my eventual obituary to say? Using that question as a focal point, I began therapy at the college counseling office where, for the first time, I learned there were other ways of viewing my situation. Looking back, I see how fortunate I was that I found the resources to resist the dangerous impulse to "end it all"—the impulse that leads to a tragic death for so many teenagers. To this day, I still read the obituaries; using them as signposts or mirrors to reflect and "course correct" as I strive to stay focused on my own goals and dreams for life on "this ole' planet," as Melissa's mom called it. Reminding me of this also is a story I once heard Eckhart Tolle share about a moment of awakening during a time when he was in the depths of despair to the point of feeling suicidal. He recalls having the thought, "I can't live with myself anymore," and then immediately asking, "Who is the "I" that cannot live with me, and who is the "I" that I cannot live with anymore?" In that instant, he realized that he is the observer; not the one stuck in the thought. He understood he was not the voice in his head, but the one who was aware of it. This realization, he explains, was the key to breaking free of the emotional imprisonment that had held him hostage.

I wish I could report that the suffering I endured is no longer an issue among teens in today's society; that all our technological advances and available resources over the decades have resulted in a happy ending to this problem, but I cannot. Why? Because the efforts to ease the desperation experienced by so many teens continue to circle around the real solution—to heal the soul, as individuals and as a society. We must acknowledge the epidemic of self-hatred that leads to suicide and begin to teach self-love and self-respect. These mind-boggling statistics regarding teen suicide deliver a powerful wake-up call: Suicide prevention is everyone's business.

Teen Suicide by the Numbers

- ✵ *Youth suicide is on the rise in the U.S. The rate of teenage suicide has **tripled** over the last six decades.*

- ✵ *4,600 youth between ages 10 and 24 commit suicide each year in the U.S. The most common cause of teen suicide is depression.*

- ✵ *Suicide is the third leading cause of death, behind accidents and homicide, of people ages 15 to 24. Suicide is the fourth leading cause of death for children between the ages of 10 and 14.*

- ✵ *Homes with guns, particularly loaded guns, pose up to a 30-fold increased risk for suicide. The risk skyrockets especially among individuals* without *a major mental disorder, because of the acting-on-impulse factor.*

DECISION TO
EXCLUDE AND
NEGLECT
INSIGHT
AWARENESS AND
LOVE

Children must be taught how to think, not what to think.
—Margaret Mead

Sadly, these statistics paint only a partial picture. To understand the full scope of the severity of the problem, we need to consider the number of suicide *attempts* as well. Among young adults, ages 15 to 24 years, there are approximately 100 to 200 attempts for every completed suicide. After conducting a nationwide survey of youth in public and private high schools, the CDC found that 16 percent of students admitted that they had seriously considered suicide; 13 percent reported going so far as to actually create a plan; and 8 percent revealed that they had indeed tried to take their own life in the 12 months preceding the survey. Whether from DENIAL, dysfunction or lack of support within the family or from a social climate of intolerance of those who are different from the majority, the pressures on our teens are mounting. One study involving 32,000 high school students reported in the journal *Pediatrics* found that suicide attempts by gay teens—*AND straight kids*—are more common in politically conservative areas where schools don't have programs supporting gay rights.

Only when teens learn how to relate to themselves and the world in a way that honors the SOUL will we begin to see a turnaround of these alarming statistics. As long as our interactions are dictated by the FEARSELF, we will continue to reenact the same vicious cycle as the one experienced by Linda, who found herself mindlessly following the same destructive path that had led her aunt Laura to take her own life.

Linda, Age 20

I am a person who has lost her soul and I am searching for it, chasing wildly after rainbows, trying to find myself, trying to know who I am. From the time I was 13, I have been taught to deny my feelings, my wants, my needs, my desires. I have been taught to feel guilt so well, that now when I try to discover who I am, I find I am confused and lost to even myself. Did Laura feel like I do now?

Aunt Laura, what did they tell you,
what did they make you believe?
Did they hurt you with all their moralizing,
did they tell you lies,
did they make you cry?
Did they tell you that you had to be just like them,
or else you weren't worthwhile at all?
You are gone Aunt Laura,
and we shall never meet on this earth again,
and go for walks
through the Philadelphia Zoo,
in Society Hill,
on Christian Street
again.

Laura was 32 when she thoroughly planned and carried out her own suicide. It was her sixth attempt. In life, she played the role of a secretary to earn money, but in her heart she was an artist. She was sad and lonely, lost and unloved. The only people at her funeral were her relatives, ten in all. Hers is a heartbreaking case in point that without community or a sense of connection to others, despair can turn into anger we inflict upon ourselves, as Laura did. Even worse, it can turn to rage that is channeled against others. Acts of random violence are a prime and tragic example of the latter.

When Suicide Turns to Homicide: Mass Violence and School Shootings

In an Atlanta-area elementary school in 2013, Antoinette Huff, the school's bookkeeper, provided one of the most powerful lessons of our time. On the heels of the tragedies in places like Newtown, Aurora, Columbine, Virginia Tech and others, Ms. Huff encountered what could have been an equally violent situation, yet her response produced a radically different outcome.

When a 20-year-old man barged into the school office armed with an assault rifle, Ms. Huff responded to the intruder not with anger, judgment or FEAR, but with love. Thrust into the center of a potential mass school shooting disaster, she tapped the source of soul-centered power that is far mightier than any weapon or the fear-based minds of those who wield them. In my observation, it was the soul-to-soul connection Huff established with the gunman that enabled her to talk him down and convince him to turn himself over to police. Coming from her heart with genuine compassion, she saw the would-be killer as a hurting soul calling out for help—and responded to his call. How did she accomplish this?

By becoming vulnerable and sharing her own struggles, she opened the door for him to do the same. In her presence he felt safe enough to confide in her the deep pain that had driven him to such extreme actions: No one loved him, he told her, and therefore he felt he had no reason to live. She told him she was proud of him for not hurting anyone, despite the fact that he himself was so deeply hurting. She even told him she loved him. By holding him in higher esteem than he was in that moment capable of holding himself, she conveyed the message that he—like every human being—is inherently valuable, and his life is too important to end. In so doing, she defused a potentially deadly situation.

Whether or not we ourselves would have the courage to follow in Ms. Huff's very big footsteps is not as important as absorbing the lessons she taught by her example. The infinite wisdom of this story is to understand the power of single-minded presence while being open to Guidance in a specific situation, no matter how large or small the task at hand may seem. By maintaining an ongoing practice of mindful AWARENESS, seeking safe and healthy ways to express painful emotions, and making use of other processes shared throughout this book, we gradually build a foundation of inner stability that enables us to RESPOND in the most nonviolent way possible, whatever that may be, to ensure the ultimate goal—in this case—of maintaining the safety of the children.

As for the young man behind the firearm, his story is strikingly similar to that of the majority of perpetrators of mass violence: He felt alone and unloved. He suffered from mental illness, just like Adam Lanza, the New-town killer, and so many others before him. A Federal study shows that most school shooters suffered bouts of depression or had even attempted suicide, and the diaries of mass killers confirm this finding. Entries in the diaries of Dylan Klebold and Eric Harris, the Columbine shooters, revealed that these boys felt unaccepted, unloved and not good enough. Compounding these feelings, both wrote of being intimidated and bullied. Dylan's diary exposed underlying untreated depression, while Eric expressed more hostility and tendencies toward gruesome violence.

Gun violence in PG-13 films has tripled since 1985, exceeding the amount found in R-rated films.
—Pediatrics

While the dramas played out from the FEARSELF within teenage boys is beyond the scope of this book, I would be remiss not to acknowledge that boys and young men suffer from—and act out in response to—early emotional wounding to the same degree that teen girls do. And yet because boys are so often taught to suppress or "suck up" their feelings and maintain control in the face of the uncontrollable, their unexpressed sadness and yearning for acceptance more commonly manifest as anger and rage that can erupt in externally destructive ways. The fact that random acts of violence like the one described above are occurring with greater frequency must serve as yet another wake-up call for all of us to meet every individual, male or female, with what I think of as a more elevated perspective on continuing education credits—or **CEUs**:

COMPASSION, EMPATHY AND UNDERSTANDING   ... CEU

In the field of human relationships, the qualities of COMPASSION, EMPATHY and UNDERSTANDING are the CEUs that foster an environment in which loving kindness replaces all forms of violence within our communities and ourselves. With this foundation, regardless of gender, the human spirit is nurtured at the level of the SOULSELF, where FEAR is a stranger and hatred is unknown. Behind every action originating in the FEARSELF is a wounded soul calling for help.

Dr. Frank Robertz, co-founder of the Institute for Violence Prevention and Applied Criminology, shared that the most surprising finding from his interviews with school shooters was how often these kids had cried out for help before going through with their violent plans. "All of the school shooters actually said—if someone would have approached me with how I'm feeling, what goes on in my mind, I would have told them." Robertz added that "if teachers actually approach kids, they have a very high chance that they will talk about what's going on in their minds, and will talk about their violent fantasies." When Eric and Dylan made a school video project that eerily depicted the acts of violence they ultimately carried out, what if a teacher had taken time to ask them what was on their minds? Of course this same power and sense of responsibility of paying attention to clues lie not only with teachers, but also with parents, family members, concerned onlookers, lawmakers and friends.

To have the ability to RESPOND without violence to a cry for help masked as an extreme threat is nothing short of a miracle. But this story out of Georgia delivers a more universal call to action. By frontloading values of compassion and understanding in the beginning of a child's life—by learning to LISTEN at the level in which we LET IN SILENCE, TRUTH, EMPATHY AND NON-JUDGMENT—we ease the desperation felt by those who harm themselves and others in the first place.

Building self-esteem and tending to the mental and emotional needs of each and every member of our society is not just a warm and fuzzy thing for touchy-feely people. Self-esteem is the birthright of all individuals, and it's critical to both the security of a nation and peace in the world. The website www.helpguide.org, founded by Robert and Jeanne Segal after they lost their daughter to suicide, identifies major risk factors—past or present conditions that increase the possibility of suicide—and offers helpful "do's and don'ts" when talking with someone who we may suspect is contemplating suicide.

Suicide Risk Factors

- ✪ *History of depression*
- ✪ *Childhood abuse*
- ✪ *Recent traumatic event*
- ✪ *Lack of a support network*
- ✪ *Availability of a gun*
- ✪ *Hostile social or school environment*
- ✪ *Exposure to other teen suicides*

Warning Signs That a Teen May Be Contemplating Suicide

The teenage years are a trying time, and sometimes normal behavior looks a lot like possibly destructive behavior. But it's important to know the following warning signs of teen suicide:

- *Shows signs of depression. (See Signs of Depression in Chapter 7)*
- *Withdraws from interacting with friends and family and regular activities.*
- *Talks about death and/or suicide (maybe even with a joking manner).*
- *Plans ways to kill him or herself.*
- *Expresses worries that nobody cares about him or her.*
- *Has attempted suicide in the past.*
- *Exhibits dramatic changes in personality and behavior.*
- *Shows signs of an alcohol or substance abuse problem.*
- *Begins to act recklessly and engage in risk-taking behaviors.*
- *Spends time online interacting with people who glamorize suicide and maybe even form suicide pacts.*
- *Stops making plans, and gives away belongings.*
- *Changes eating and sleeping habits.*
- *Has violent or rebellious behavior, running away.*
- *Shows an unusual neglect of personal appearance.*
- *Shows persistent boredom, has difficulty concentrating or experiences a decline in the quality of schoolwork.*
- *Frequently complains about physical symptoms, often related to emotions, such as stomach aches, headaches, fatigue, etc.*

SOURCE: Combined and adapted by www.teensuicidestatistics.com and the American Academy of Child & Adolescent Psychiatry

Ways to Start a Conversation About Suicide

Bringing up the subject of suicidal thoughts and feelings is a difficult conversation for anyone. But if you're unsure about whether someone you love is contemplating suicide, the best way to find out is to ask. You can't drive a person to this act by showing that you care. In fact, giving a suicidal person the opportunity to express his or her feelings can provide relief from loneliness and pent-up negative feelings and may actually prevent a suicide attempt. Here are a few non-confrontational ways to initiate the conversation:

Statements of concern:

- *I have been feeling concerned about you lately.*
- *Recently, I have noticed some differences in you and wondered how you are doing.*
- *I wanted to check in with you because you haven't seemed yourself lately.*

Questions you can ask:

- *When did you begin feeling like this?*
- *Did something happen that made you start feeling this way?*
- *How can I best support you right now?*
- *Have you thought about getting help?*

Supportive things you can say:

- *You are not alone in this. I'm here for you.*
- *You may not believe it now, but the way you're feeling will change.*
- *I may not be able to understand exactly how you feel, but I care about you and want to help.*
- *When you want to give up, tell yourself you will hold off for just one more day, hour, minute—whatever you can manage.*

When Talking to a Suicidal Person: Do's and Don'ts

Do:

- *Be yourself. Let the person know you care, that he/she is not alone. The right words are often unimportant. If you are concerned, your voice and mannerisms will show it.*

- *Listen. Let the suicidal person unload despair, ventilate anger. No matter how negative the conversation seems, the fact that you are having it is a positive sign.*

- *Be sympathetic, non-judgmental, patient, calm, accepting. Your friend or family member is doing the right thing by talking about his/her feelings.*

- *Offer hope. Reassure the person that help is available and that the suicidal feelings are temporary. Let the person know that his or her life is important to you.*

- *If the person says things like "I'm so depressed, I can't go on," ask the question: "Are you having thoughts of suicide?" You are not putting ideas in their head, you are showing that you are concerned, that you take them seriously, and that it's okay for them to share their pain with you.*

- *Finally, if you or someone you know is thinking about suicide, call 1-800-273-8255*

But do NOT:

- *Argue with the suicidal person. Avoid saying things like "You have so much to live for," "Your suicide will hurt your family," or "Look on the bright side."*

- *Act shocked, give a lecture on the value of life, or say that suicide is wrong.*

- *Promise confidentiality. Refuse to be sworn to secrecy. A life is at stake and you may need to speak to a mental health professional in order to keep the suicidal person safe. If you promise to keep your discussions secret, you may have to break your word.*

- *Offer ways to fix their problems, give advice, or make them feel like they have to justify their suicidal feelings. It is not about how bad the problem is, but how badly it's hurting your friend or loved one.*

- *Blame yourself. You can't "fix" someone's depression. Your loved one's happiness, or lack thereof, is not your responsibility.*

—Adapted from *www.helpguide.org* and *www.metanoia.org*

Our efforts to understand the pain and pressure that drives young people to suicide would not be complete without noting the disproportionate focus our society places on academics. It is a tragic irony that Hamilton High School—the school in Texas where the controversial "No Child Left Behind" Act was signed into law—has seen four students die by suicide in a matter of a few short months. There are seventeen indicators of success laid out in the No Child Left Behind Act; all seventeen are focused solely on academic performance. In the PBS documentary *Cry for Help* that tells the story, Principal Daniel Malone noted about the Act that "there is not one indicator that says, 'Did you take time for students who were having emotional problems?'" One thing is sure in the long term—academic success does not equal life success. Yet when education budgets are slashed, the first courses cut are usually those that nurture the right side of the brain, where abstract, empathic, and creative thinking takes place.

In her 2008 TED talk, neuroscientist Jill Bolte-Taylor, who suffered a stroke that impaired her left brain functioning, described how the increased access to her right brain opened her up to a more universal connection and sense of peace. It occurred to me, when I heard this, that the right brain—responsible for enriching the world through music and art—is a powerful gateway to the SOULSELF and universal mind and is an essential skill to nurture in developing teens.

What Really Matters

When I lived in Hawaii, I worked at the Kapiolani Medical Center for Women and Children in Honolulu, where thousands of babies are born each year. My office happened to be right down the hall from the room where parents met to grieve and support each other through the devastating loss of a child during birth or closely thereafter. On the days those grieving parents met and sobbed, I spent my lunchtimes outside the hospital, staring at the stained glass window of the chapel across the lawn, begging for these aching mothers and fathers to be carried through their pain. These parents who would give anything just for the chance to hold their precious babies; to look into their eyes ... to convey through every sense how deeply they are loved. Sometimes, when I see a mom in a shopping mall telling her daughter that her Ugg boots look silly with those short shorts, or when I realize that I've gotten so caught up in the logistics of running a household that I have neglected to carve out quality time with my own daughter, the memory of these parents' unspeakable GRIEF comes flooding back to me. It's so easy to lose sight of what's truly important. As we fill our roles as the invisible taxi driver, carting our kids to soccer or dance practice, we forget how fleeting our time with them truly is.

The near constant lament of hurting teenagers is that their parents don't care; and yet as parents, we know exactly how much we care. How then do we bridge this gap? By caring enough to show it. By pausing our busyness long enough to listen. By listening with the intention of understanding. By letting go, to the best of our ability, of our expectations of the person we aspire for our daughter to be, and placing more of our attention on helping her become who she naturally is. When we communicate in both words and actions that we care for her at the deepest level, and that our love for her transcends mother and daughter roles entirely, we are able to be with her in a way that allows us to connect soul to soul. Anytime we catch ourselves losing sight of what a precious gift our daughters are to us, we can ask ourselves the question posed by Nobel and Pulitzer Prize winning author Toni Morrison: "When your child walks into the room, do your eyes light up?" And if our honest answer is "no," we can take a moment to reconnect with how very much she means to us, and how essential she is to the world. There is no easy way to accept death, but we can use it to remind ourselves and teach our daughters about the preciousness of life and—again in Morrison's words—to "Let our faces speak what's in our hearts."

Living Life Unlocked

The following process, adapted from The Dougy Center for Grieving Children and Families, is one that supports all of us in stocking our emotional tool kit with practical, hands-on actions we can take anytime we are feeling anxious, depressed or overwhelmed. It's best to answer these prompts when things in your inner and outer world are relatively calm. Whether you complete it all at once or add to it over time, keep it handy so you can refer to it in times when you're feeling fragile, or would simply benefit from remembering just how emotionally resourceful and resilient you are.

- *Name three people you are comfortable talking to.*
- *Name a place you can go that is comfortable and safe.*
- *Name three things you can do, or three people you can be with, where you can let out anger without hurting yourself or others.*
- *Name three things you can do or three people you can be with to let out sad feelings.*
- *Name three non-harmful ways to release feelings of anger or sadness.*
- *Name three positive things you can do when life feels meaningless.*
- *Name three activities you can do that will help you express your feelings. Examples: writing, drawing, hitting pillows, singing, playing sports, dancing.*
- *Name three things that will help you get your mind off your loss.*

Chapter 9

What Is and What Could Be: Getting from Here to There

The privilege of a lifetime is being who you are.
—Joseph Campbell

Misty, Age 19
This serenity
this peace
this feeling I felt I lost
but yet remembered to keep.
I am free now
naturally.
I like to keep little things
so close to me
close to my heart
so it reminds my lungs to breathe.
Affirm that I am happy with a smile for once
so alive I can hear the birds sing
a forgotten prayer
to enjoy the Spirit inside of me.

Anne Frank, Age 14

Riches, prestige, everything can be lost. But the happiness in your heart can only be dimmed; it will always be there as long as you live, to make you happy again.

Whenever you're feeling lonely or sad, try going to the loft on a beautiful day and looking outside. Not at the houses and the rooftops, but at the sky. As long as you can look fearlessly at the sky, you'll know that you are pure within and will find happiness once more.

Throughout the pages of this book, we have been stirred by the personal stories of our daughters, our mothers, our friends and ourselves. The words penned by teenage girls navigating the complexities of high school cliques or struggling with an addiction, seeking guidance about how to deal with an unplanned pregnancy, or grieving the loss of a loved one show us that we are not alone on our journey through the twists and turns of life. In reading the words of each diarist as she describes the changing inner landscape of her thoughts, beliefs, perceptions and feelings, we become more deeply connected to our own.

These personal stories have awakened us to the universal themes that weave through each and every life script: our shared longing for love, acceptance and connection. The dramas of virtually all archetypes—transcending time, place and culture—are played out within these pages. In a very real sense, each diarist's tale has drawn us nearer to the heart of the human story as it has unfolded through the ages, illuminating the degrees of awakening that take place in the body, mind and spirit of individuals in search of themselves. Through their triumphs over fear and darkness, self-doubt and isolation, we watched girls evolve into women able to transcend their personal trials by engaging every aspect of their BEING in a soul-directed way, uncovering their own truth along the path. Thanks to these women and girls who have made it to the other side of many challenges to a more peaceful place in life, we too are now better equipped with AWARENESS, insight, and a treasure chest of transformational tools to accelerate our own journey of awakening.

While the dramas re-enacted on these pages reflect obstacles to peace that humanity has, for the most part, come up against throughout time, the diary entries herein have offered us a record of specific incidents that connect us all at the core of our deepest human fears and highest aspirations. One of the visions that inspired the writing of this book grew from a desire to offer women and teens a way to start conversations with one another about the real issues they face. Even before its publication, that goal had already been realized. Whether I was talking with people in the waiting room of a doctor's office, at the gym, or out at a coffee shop, just sharing the title of this book—*My Diary Unlocked*—sparked an opening. I have experienced firsthand the deep thirst among women for meaningful heart-to-heart conversations. After learning the mission of this book, many women—even some I just met—confided in me experiences previously entrusted only to their diaries. Providing teen girls and grown women with a forum that allows them to bring issues once locked away in their private thoughts into the full light of AWARENESS is, I believe, a key step toward helping them find acceptance, both within themselves and as a reflection back to them from their larger community.

If we look honestly at the stories shared from the most raw and intimate place of these private diaries, we can see that while each soul comes forth with its own unique expression, we are united in a way that, if fully grasped, would instantly end the madness of self-judgment and self-harm, of bullying, intolerance, divisiveness, hatred and even war.

In the midst of our own personal trials, it's easy to lose sight of the bigger picture; but in present-day reality, girls and women are living in a state of disempowerment that not only suppresses potential but also threatens basic safety. Over time, obedience to a misplaced source of external power has devolved into a degradation of our culture and of the human spirit in general. What begins as little rejections experienced by a young girl grows into a belief system that renders her powerless to create her own destiny. The painful distortions of reality reflected in the writing of today's girls demonstrate how the FEARSELF feeds on itself, spinning with an ominous momentum as it is passed down to each new generation. A look at the top five news stories on a local or national level any given day never fails to reflect the results of the collective FEARSELF at work.

If we could read the secret history of our enemies, we should find in each person's life sorrow and suffering enough to disarm all hostility.
—Henry Wadsworth Longfellow

We entangle our dramas with the FEARSELF of others.

The Tangled Web We Weave

The statistics are sobering. Yet it is in the AWARENESS and dissemination of these tangible facts that we are ultimately compelled to action, to become a force for good—for each other, for our daughters, and for ourselves. In the second decade of the 21st century in America, about two-thirds of women between the ages of 25 and 45 have disordered eating behaviors. Each year one in five girls becomes pregnant before the age of 20. Bullying is now an Internet phenomenon that plagues our girls 24/7 and in the most public and yet personal of ways. Alcohol and drug addiction and related abuse affect millions of families and are likely compounded by the co-occurrence of depression or other mental illness. According to author David Sheff, the total overall cost of drug abuse in the United States exceeds $400 billion a year, mostly in health care, crime-related costs and lost productivity. Anxiety disorders alone affect about 40 million American adults in a given year. Whether by natural or unnatural circumstances, one in seven individuals has lost a parent or sibling by age 20 and too often must live through the devastation of the death or suicide of a friend in a society where healthy grieving is still not part of the norm.

We mustn't just read these facts as numbers on a page, but open our hearts to how these experiences are affecting the self-esteem of the girls who are bravely weathering these teenage storms today. The compassion we feel must then be multiplied by the scores or millions just like them who share similar stories. Whatever our shared challenges, the solution always begins in each instant we become consciously AWARE (AWAKE WITH ALL REALITY EXPOSED) of the situation as it currently exists. Just as present-moment AWARENESS was pivotal in the transformation of every teenage girl who wrote a reflection long after she penned her original diary entries, the recognition of moment-to-moment CHOICE-making holds the key to breaking free from the repetition of age-old destructive habits, tendencies and thought patterns. This understanding is poignantly described in 17-year-old Beth's entry and reflection.

Awake
With
All
Reality
Exposed
Naturally
Expressing the
Soul-
Self

Beth, Age 17

I finally got up the courage to tell Mom what Dad is doing to me and I can't believe all she said was that he was a good provider for our family and that I must be making some mistake or dreaming or something. Dreaming?! She couldn't even call it a nightmare.

Beth's Reflection, 33 years later

For years I suffered in the wake of having been sexually abused and having my mom turn her back on me when I needed her most. I started using cocaine and I became promiscuous—especially with married men or others who were emotionally unavailable in some way or other. One day I woke up and realized that I would never be the one someone wanted to be with until I became a person who wanted to be with myself. Not the self I despised every day, but my true self. I started with baby steps. I lost some existing relationships as I slowly learned how dependent they were on my desperation. Since that day, I've been basking in life changing practices that can only create a shift when you take serious responsibility for your own direction in life. I began journaling. When I first began, I left many pages soaking wet as I fed my soul the tears it needed to be nurtured back to health. I've been through a lot of hypnotherapy that has opened the door for my trauma to surface and be replaced by guided visualizations in a context of love and self-acceptance. I listen to audio webinars that so many self-help experts offer.

As children, we don't have a conscious vote in the circumstances or beliefs handed down to us. Our identities are shaped not only by our parents' genes, but also by their worldviews, attitudes, and the ways they modeled (or didn't model) self-love and self-care. Although these factors shape us, they do not define us. In her song *I Am Light*, India.Arie echoes this truth in the following verse: "I am not the things my family did—I am not the voices in my head—I am not the pieces of the brokenness inside." Until, like Beth, we experience an "aha" moment of reckoning that sparks within us an insistence to overcome the limitations passed down from previous generations, we are bound to carry the scourge of a painful past into the future, where the saga of stress, heartaches and heartbreaks continues. Developing the AWARENESS, courage and discipline to remain AWAKE to each moment without allowing FEAR (FRAGILE EXPERIENCE OF ANXIETY OR REGRET) to be at the helm is critical to charting a life course that leads to the realization of our full potential.

The cave you fear to enter holds the treasure you seek.
—Joseph Campbell

Know that these "statistics"—these girls and women—have inherited the collective pain and suffering passed down from our ancestral sisters as a direct result of the suppression and degradation of the feminine spirit over centuries. What does this mean? In tribes and countries around the world and throughout time, girls and women have been shamed into sacrificing their true selves in the name of upholding beliefs and traditions that focus on the love of power, and not the power of love. That over 200 school girls were kidnapped from their Nigerian school by militants in 2014 is just one example proving this conquest lives on even in the 21st century. Girls all over the globe continue to be raised in cultures that demean the very nature of the feminine qualities that nurture the souls of all humans. Few people understand this as clearly as Elmira, who wrote in her diary as a teenage girl in Iran during the Iranian Revolution in the late 1970s, years before she became my dentist in San Diego.

When the power of love overcomes the love of power the world will know peace.
—Jimi Hendrix

Elmira, Age 16
The Iranian revolution has an ugly face of street massacres, nightly curfews and horrifying screams after sounds of shooting. It is now

against the law for all females regardless of religion to enter the streets without a complete veil covering all hair, arms, wrists, neck, entire legs, ankles and toes. No makeup, no nail polish and no perfumes are allowed. Listening to music, Western or Persian, is strictly forbidden. Absolutely no male-female interactions in public are allowed. Women cannot lick on their ice cream cones in public. No one is allowed to have a festive party; even in private. So much for the promised freedom!!!

Elmira's Reflection, 23 years later

To make a long story short, I left Iran in my last year of high school and made it to America. I kept thinking to myself that if I were able to endure the pressure of growing up in Iran, I can do anything. I became motivated and excited to start a new life in a world that promised freedom and opportunity. I knew once I left the oppressive regime, I would take every given opportunity and cherish it to the best of my abilities and never look back. I had survived the Revolution, the Bombardment, the missile attacks and the suppressive system and now I could feel and smell freedom. Real life began. I knew why I was here and did not want to waste any time. So I got my G.E.D and started UCSD right away, working full time all the way through to graduation. After graduation, I took the Dental Admission Test, and took one year off working as a Biology lab Technician doing research to save money to apply to dental schools. Got accepted in UCLA and the rest is history!!

Regardless of our past, whether individual or shared, the power of present-moment AWARENESS is central to the intersection of heart and soul, as every lesson learned ultimately circles back to a moment of consciousness when the recognition of CHOICE becomes available to each of us. Whether it's a CHOICE a girl faces about how she expresses her sexuality, the extent to which she is open with parents about her activities, or making the CHOICE to flee from any form of bondage to freedom, the power to choose based on one's own inner guidance is pivotal in moving once again toward the direction of the SOULSELF. Adolescence is a time when a lack of solid roots in the truth of our BEING can leave us susceptible to choosing a path that takes us deeper down the slippery slope of the FEARSELF, where each step brings higher winds in the storms of life. Every action taken from a false belief of oneself—eating less to look "good enough," drinking more to fill an emptiness, having sex in an attempt to secure love, or stressing out over

CONSTANTLY
HAVING
OPTIONS
IN
CREATING
EXPERIENCE

self-judgments that more must be done to prove ourselves worthy—leads to ever-increasing turbulence. These pressures, of course, are not limited to our teen years; they follow us until the moment we wake up to the AWARENESS that the FEARSELF can never lead us to a joyful life or a state of inner peace.

Butterfly Wings

Along my own lifelong journey of coming home to myself, I remember the words to a song written by Libby Roderick that poses a fundamental question: "How could anyone ever tell you you were anything less than beautiful?" Every time I LISTEN to it still I imagine being swaddled in the arms of a loving being with whom I can drop all my burdens and just be. I just finished listening to that song once again, and here I am just BEING. This book, which has been literally decades in the making, is fueled by my passion for each of us to join together to build a better world for our girls and to love our own inner adolescent. I sincerely believe that if you have read this far and are still with me, you are a kindred spirit who is ready to mend your broken wings so you can fly in a way that will turn this mad, mad world on its head and lead us back toward the SOULSELF residing within us all. Writer Aileen Fisher describes in poetic words what I have referred to as "Freeing Your BEING" throughout this book.

LET
IN
SILENCE
TOTAL
EMPATHY AND
NON-JUDGMENT

Butterfly Wings
How would it be
on a day in June
to open your eyes
in a dark cocoon,
And soften one end
and crawl outside,
and find you had wings
to open wide,
And find you could fly
to a bush or tree
or float on the air
like a boat at sea ...
How would it BE?
—Aileen Fisher

The era in which we are living is ripe to birth a transformation. But we must choose to channel the dynamism shared by so many women and girls on these pages who, through the exposure of their personal past, have laid the foundation for this altruistic vision. It is up to us to lift the veil of the false power that hides only pretentiousness and the empty eyes of *fear*, and to invest ourselves in *love* instead.

The Power of the Feminine

Something big is happening for us as women. We're on the brink of an evolutionary shift with the potential to alter the course of history. Millions of us around the world are feeling a calling to reclaim the feminine, and in so doing, to awaken our authentic power to co-create the future of our lives and shape the future of our world.
—Claire Zammit and Katherine Woodward Thomas

In 1933, Eleanor Roosevelt wrote a book called *It's Up to the Women* in which she declared, "The attitudes of women will shape who we become as a society." Over three quarters of a century later, in 2009, the Dalai Lama echoed these same sentiments in a lecture, saying, "The world will be saved by the Western woman." If the predictions of these two iconic leaders were on target, it's not because we Western women are the most balanced and centered—indeed we have much to learn from the East to mature in these areas—but because we have demonstrated the courage to become AWARE of what is happening around us; to embrace "what is," as Byron Katie told us, to move forward and to effect a change. For the only true way to create what is possible is to begin by accepting things as they are. Armed with this knowledge, we are now in a position to shake up the status quo, to wake up those kindred to our mission, and to take up an action plan to make a better world. For when we make a better world for our girls, we make a better world for everyone.

As women, we possess an innate capacity for the creative resourcefulness and intuition that our country and our world desperately need. And yet, at the time of this writing, American women are still being repressed politically—unbelievably earning the right to vote only within the last century! In 2013, women held fewer than one in five seats in Congress. This is the same year that the seated 113th Congress of United States was deemed the most unproductive Congress in our nation's history. I believe that had the scales been more balanced between masculine and feminine we would not have seen as much chaos or self-indulgence as egos trumped progress and sabotage outmaneuvered the duty to work for the good of the people. Our progress has been held captive and our nation's credibility jeopardized. In this sense—whether within the political arena or outside of it—"it is up to the women," as Mrs. Roosevelt primed us so many years ago, to harness our inner resources and stand united in a humanitarian approach that ensures the right of human dignity for every citizen—man, woman, and child. Heeding her own inner call to move a nation forward with its soul intact, Mrs. Roosevelt embraced the feminine spirit by travelling from coast to coast and listening to the personal struggles of Americans. The stories she heard around kitchen tables of average citizens were reported back to her husband, the President, whom she encouraged *and* convinced to create groundbreaking programs to aid those in need— many programs that are still in place today, including Social Security.

In Chapter 3, we learned that the majority of teen moms today are left alone at the table to feed their children while living in poverty, without support from the father of their children. A 2013 report by Wider Opportunity for Women revealed this problem doesn't go away once the teen reaches adulthood; and in fact, 70 percent of single mothers working full time do not earn economically secure wages. From 2007 to 2010, child homelessness rose by 33 percent in America. In 2012, women still earned only $0.81 for every dollar earned by men, even though they performed equal work. Do the math and you discover that over a 40-year period— the presumed length of a career—this means the average full-time female worker loses approximately $443,000 in wages (over $11,000 per year) because of the gender pay gap. The "glass ceiling" preventing advancement to leadership positions is still very much intact. In 2013, fewer than 5 percent of Fortune 500 CEOs were women. A worldwide view of females tells us there are some 66 million girls missing from classrooms— and this at a time when education is the primary vehicle out of poverty.

Extremists have shown what frightens them most: a girl with a book.
—Malala Yousafzai

In the face of these obstacles, why am I so confident that if every soul-directed person stepped up to the plate, now is the time we could overcome the challenges facing us in the 21st century? I believe this because we have the fire and passion within us to see what's wrong and use it as a force to make it right. The accessibility of information and knowledge has finally placed us on a level playing field; we have the means and technology to turn the tides of disconnection and join together, regardless of geographic limitations, and create a tipping point. We have proven our ability to rise above our circumstances. Just look at the great strides we have made in higher education and business ownership.

In the late 1970s, when I was studying for my Accounting degree, I was one of about 10 percent of females in most of my classes. Today females make up about half of business and management classes, receiving almost 60 percent of university degrees earned in America and in Europe. In 1960, only 22 percent of women even had a paying job; in 2012, women-owned businesses generated revenues of $1.3 trillion. The 2012 *State of Women-Owned Businesses Report* reveals that women-owned businesses are increasing at a faster rate than any other group; and according to the Center for Women's Business Research, Hispanic and African American women are the fastest growing entrepreneurial segments in the country. Progress, yes, but more is needed. Although 29 percent of businesses are women-owned, overall they only employ 6 percent of the country's workforce and account for less than 4 percent of business revenues.

In the majority of decades in the 20th century, female students spent class time mindlessly typing the message, "Now is the time for all good men to come to the aid of their country." Gratefully, the 21st century has seen the dawn of a new day. It is clear that the time has come for women—and everyone who values the CEU-based qualities of compassion, empathy and understanding—to come to the aid of our world.

John F. Kennedy, who rallied our nation in the 1960s to boldly change the trajectory of our future, said, "We choose to go to the moon in this decade and do the other things, not because they are easy, but because they are hard, because that goal will serve to organize and measure the best of our energies and skills, because that challenge is one that we are willing to accept, one we are unwilling to postpone, and one which we intend to win." This is the attitude we must embrace today. Changing the status quo is not an easy road. The current socioeconomic, political and environmental system—driven by a hunter-gatherer, fight-or–flight, fear-based instinct to survive and not to thrive—has failed contemporary humanity on so many levels that we must engage all our energies and all five aspects of BEING to build a soul-based society. Fear as a motivator is now obsolete in the continued evolution of human consciousness. In fact, FEAR is detrimental to progress in an age of wisdom—a barrier to sustaining the very survival of future generations. Love is our only answer.

As we awaken to the power of choice, we are always given the opportunity to start anew.
—Eleesha

BODY
EMOTIONS
IMAGINATION
NATURAL SELF
GENIUS MIND

Building a Soul Society

Charles Darwin, who first explained the concept of evolution in *On the Origin of Species,* elaborated in his sequel *The Descent of Man* on the role that love, morality, sympathy and mutual aid play in the continued evolution of humanity. Author David Loye, who has studied the works of Darwin for decades, noted that in *The Descent of Man*, "Darwin writes only twice of 'survival of the fittest,' but 95 times of love. He writes of selfishness 12 times, but 92 times of moral sensitivity. Of competition 9 times, but 24 times of mutuality and mutual aid." In my own content analysis of *The Descent of Man*, I found he discussed emotions 47 times, and sympathy (which he likened to empathy) 57 times. What does this tell us? The expert of all experts on evolution took the time to write over 800 pages to highlight the role that soul-based qualities like empathy and compassion play in humanity's steady march toward a better future—and yet, from Darwin's time and into the present day, the collective FEARSELF has been writing the script. We have become divisive to the degree we are more concerned about aligning with a particular political ideology than whether or not to feed the poor. We are living in an age that can no longer support the survival of the most aggressive. Marianne Williamson, who serves on the board for the RESULTS organization, a leading force in ending poverty in the United States and around the world, shares in her lectures a story about the nature of hyenas to rally inspired action for the benefit of the children of the future. The mother hyenas, she explained, instinctively encircle their offspring as they eat to make sure their young are fed before the males are allowed to partake in the feast. "Surely we can do better than the hyenas," Marianne pleads, by way of emphasizing the fact that on our planet, over 17,000 children die of starvation every day— one every six seconds. In America alone, the number of kids going to bed hungry every night is higher than it has ever been. Triggered by the onset of the economic crisis culminating in 2008, nearly 15 percent of households in the U.S. did not have adequate food to eat. A UNICEF study of 35 developed countries found the United States had the second-highest rate of child poverty after Romania.

Women make up 51 percent of the population. We are in a position to say enough is enough. Love and compassion are not "soft" concepts to be scoffed at in the boardroom. Policies that allow corporations or special interests to seize power at the expense of people, allow bankers to mislead hard working citizens into financial ruin for their own gain, and allow governments to build bombs instead of schools are unacceptable in the dawning of the age of wisdom.

This country cannot afford to be materially rich and spiritually poor.
—John F. Kennedy

American kids are more cynical than any other groups of kids I've worked with. I think this is the case because we, as a country, have gotten a little confused about the family's values of standing up for what's right.
—Rosalind Wiseman

No stranger to war or public policy, former President Dwight Eisenhower duly noted: "Every gun that is made, every warship launched, every rocket fired signifies, in the final sense, a theft from those who hunger and are not fed, those who are cold and not clothed ... this is not a way of life at all in any true sense." In the long run, war doesn't work—not just because military leaders like Eisenhower learned the hard way that it doesn't, but because the Universe is self-correcting. Nobody gets away with harming others; and deep within our souls, nobody really likes to harm others. A 2008 RAND study showed that nearly 20 percent of Iraq and Afghanistan veterans screened positive for Post-Traumatic Stress Disorder (PTSD) or depression, while an Army report issued in 2012 addressing all branches of the military revealed that self-inflicted deaths outstripped the number of troops killed in combat, with one active duty soldier committing suicide every 17 hours throughout the year. These staggering figures beg another level to the meaning of the adage, "We have met the enemy and he is us." The 20th century stood witness as some 100 million people on the planet were killed by the ravages of war. Every dying soldier is somebody's baby, a mother's son or daughter, a family's loved one. And many surviving soldiers are the parents of a child. It's estimated that as many as five million kids have had a parent or sibling serve in Iraq or Afghanistan since 9/11. The kids who are left to deal with the loss associated with a parent suffering from PTSD have been largely ignored, even though it is well established that mental illness impacts the affected individual's entire family. The fact is, the rate of suicide among kids from military families is much higher than non-military families. On behalf of the children of tomorrow, is it not time for those of us today who understand the urgency to thwart this descent into collective FEARSELF? Is it not time to recognize the power we have to design our reality without having to hurt ourselves or anyone else to bring it into BEING? Is it not time to begin to live our lives unlocked?

No one won the last war, and no one will win the next war.
—Eleanor Roosevelt

Freeing Our BEING

There must be a better way. Who among us hasn't said this—or at least thought it in the privacy of our own mind and heart? I know I have, and I believe there *is* a better way. The Freeing Your BEING Compass shown in the first chapter of this book is a roadmap that points the way to becoming

both AWARE and AWAKE. To make the progress we need to make, we must be AWARE—AWAKE WITH ALL REALITY EXPOSED, and AWAKE—ALIVE WITH ALL KNOWLEDGE EVIDENT. My hope is that the girls and women who have shared their stories inspire us all to recognize patterns, to delete programs that no longer serve our highest good, and to celebrate our newly forged path of healthy and healed experiences.

The following mantra founded upon the aspects of BEING reminds us it is our birthright to live lives that are truly unlocked, and to express ourselves in a way that is unblocked, unfettered, and completely free:

I AM MORE
(A Mantra/Affirmation for Freeing Your BEING)

BODY (physical): **I am more than my body**

EMOTIONS (emotional): **My feelings are sincere**

IMAGINATION (perceptual/visual): **I create my destiny**

NATURAL SELF (behavioral): **I express the best in me**

GENIUS MIND (mental/intellectual): **My mind is my frontier**

Dr. Gerald Jampolsky, whose lectures I have seized every opportunity to attend for three decades, is a true stand-out model of what it means to embrace the power of *being*. After I shared the Freeing Your BEING Compass with Jerry and his wife, Diane Cirincione, they in turn shared with me their "To Be" list, which is reprinted here, for it offers another powerful way to our consciousness with the essence of BEING:

The
TO BE
List

GERALD JAMPOLSKY, M.D. AND DIANE CIRINCIONE, PH.D.

WWW.AHINTERNATIONAL.ORG

WE HAVE DISCOVERED that starting our day with our "to be" list instead of our "to do" list brings us a sense of peace and happiness far beyond anything we have previously experienced.

IT IS A PROFOUND WAY of celebrating our "being," the essence of love that is our true identity and our true natural state of happiness. Doing this each morning has changed our state of mind far beyond anything we have ever experienced.

Our "to be" list serves to reminds us of our core self which is so often hidden from our daily awareness by the bus-i-ness of our daily doings and thoughts. It helps to remind us of our "spiritual self," rather than our "doing self" as we bring forth the essence of our being as the Love that we truly are. This daily reminder emphasizes that we are more than just our physical bodies and that the Love we give and receive is lasting and, literally, affects the world around us.

We say the list out loud and it has a deeper effect than just reading or thinking the words. We always begin with the commitment that "today is going to be the best and happiest day of my life." No matter what happens this day, the following thoughts on consciousness enable us to learn and grow from every situation without exception.

The "TO BE" List

TODAY, MY BEING IS:

THE LIGHT OF THE WORLD
THE ESSENCE OF LOVE
UNCONDITIONALLY LOVING
UNCONDITIONALLY FORGIVING
SPIRIT, NOT A BODY
A CO-CREATOR OF LOVE
ONE WITH ALL THAT IS
GUILTLESS
AGELESS
FEARLESS
PATIENT
FORMLESS
TIMELESS
PEACEFUL
COMPASSIONATE
KINDNESS
TENDERNESS
HAPPINESS
NON-JUDGMENTAL
GRATEFUL
GENEROUS
ETERNAL
HONEST
GRACE-FILLED
FAITHFUL
TRUSTING
OPEN-MINDED
OPEN-HEARTED
CARING
GIVING
INNOCENCE
UNMEASUREABLE

With all there is to *do* to change the state of our world, why is it so important to teach teens, parents and teachers the importance of simply *being*? Because when we learn how to *be*, who we *are* naturally unfolds in each moment. Accomplishing goals and building authentic relationships with others can only emerge from the SOUL when our actions are inspired from an organic "in the moment" expression of our BEING. No superficial acts, no influx of anxieties, and no amount of obligation or regret will ever hold a candle to the power of *being* in alignment with one's SOUL. That's the source of real power—what I call *SOULar* power.

SOULar Power Creates a Tipping Point

When I reflect on my own heroes who I feel have been powered by the soul, three people come instantly to mind. The first is the late Nelson Mandela, whose life demonstrated to the world the power of love and forgiveness as he transformed the hatred white people held toward blacks in South Africa into a united force of acceptance. "As I walked out the door toward the gate that would lead to my freedom, I knew if I didn't leave my bitterness and hatred behind, I'd still be in prison," Mandela replied when asked why he didn't seek vengeance against his prison captors. At the time of his passing—which coincided with the completion of this book—it was abundantly clear he is among the most revered leaders and role models of the virtues to which all of humanity aspires. His key message was to seek not revenge, but to release grievances and move forward to live in the now. I believe the collective potential we could unfold by embracing these values within ourselves is powerful enough to change the world.

The second example of a soul-powered individual is that of my friend Azim Khamisa. Azim did what Longfellow suggested and "read the secret histories" of his enemies. By looking into the eyes of his son's murderer—someone most would surely consider a lifelong enemy—he found within his heart the place all hearts join together. His compassion for the sorrow and suffering that drove a 14-year-old gang member to shoot and kill his 20-year-old son was powerful enough to disarm his hatred and rage. "When I walked into the prison to meet my son's killer, I was looking for a murderer," Azim explained. "What I found was a soul much like me. I was able to climb through his eyes and touch his humanity. At that level

The tipping point is that magic moment when an idea, trend, or social behavior crosses a threshold, tips, and spreads like wildfire.
—Malcolm Gladwell

we are one. He murdered my son—he made a mistake. We are not born with a spirit of violent intention to hurt others. It is learned."

Instead of seeking blame, he asked himself a much bigger question: What changes would we need to make in our society to eradicate bullying and violence? Accepting his share of responsibility for being a citizen in a culture which has allowed such hatred to flourish, he founded an educational program he now carries to schools around the country. He understands that hatred is learned, and what can be learned can be unlearned. Azim's program, The Violence Impact Forum, is dedicated to breaking the cycle of violence among our youth by empowering kids, saving lives and teaching peace. Together with an unlikely partner—the grandfather/guardian of his son's murderer—he teaches the futility of violence and revenge and the importance of making decisions from within the soul, not based on external circumstances. Knowing that the boy who killed his son was born to a 15-year-old girl, he does not underestimate the role that teen birth plays in jeopardizing a healthy society, and he mentors kids on preventing teen pregnancy. Over a lunch meeting to discuss this book, Azim asked that I share his passion for parents' involvement in their kids' lives in a real and tangible way: "What is teachable is for parents to open their *real eyes and realize* that as parents, their power lies in their ability to be transparent enough to share their stories with their kids. Not just the stories about how far they walked to school in the snow, or even what they did in school, but the ones that brought them joy and caused them pain and left them full of fear or courage. These are stories that speak to the *soul*. These are the ones that open our kids to the humanity within us all. The ones that dismiss the wall put up psychologically or by a computer or video game screen. Then the kids can see with their *real eyes* how everyone is connected, and learn that everyone is wired just like them, and they will be far less likely to impose acts of hatred or violence on anyone." In my eyes, Azim Khamisa is a leader in the arena of personal responsibility as much as he is an icon in forgiveness and a model of empathy.

The third model of someone who has mastered the balance between the analytical side of the left-brain with the qualities of compassion and empathy of her right-brain is Eleanor Roosevelt. Though born into an affluent family, she suffered many of the same trials endured by the diarists in the preceding pages: her father struggled with alcoholism and depres-

Any intelligent fool can make things bigger, more complex, and more violent. It takes a touch of genius—and a lot of courage—to move in the opposite direction.
—Albert Einstein

sion, while her mother focused on maintaining an external image—to the point of mocking her own daughter's physical appearance. Both her parents were dead before she was a teenager. Yet Mrs. Roosevelt persevered through life with her head held high as she fought for the rights of the underprivileged. Her statue in New York City bears an inscription of the words she delivered in her 1958 speech on the tenth anniversary of the Universal Declaration of Human Rights, a declaration she co-created. "Where, after all, do universal human rights begin? In small places, close to home. Such are the places where every man, woman and child seeks equal justice, equal opportunity, equal dignity." Like Azim, Mrs. Roosevelt saw those in need through eyes of love, and her story illuminates the full circle of life's circumstances—the ebb and flow of challenges serving as opportunities to make decisions from the core of our soul, where compassion and empathy are always available.

These heroes of mine have allowed me to see that the only path to my own freedom is to forgive those against whom I have held any grievance or whom I may have blamed as the source of my pain. They were never my captors; rather, they were offering me the key to my own personal liberty. From their messages, I have expanded my AWARENESS of the five aspects of my BEING to consider how I can both model empathy and unite in service with others. I call this expansion being ME ... and being US::

For to be free is not merely to cast off one's chains, but to live in a way that respects and enhances the freedom of others.
—Nelson Mandela

| MODELING EMPATHY | ... ME |
| UNITED IN SERVICE | ... US |

Empathy Is the Key

Over the past decade, my research on empathy—often described as the ability to put ourselves in another person's shoes—has suggested that it is key, if not the most essential key, to all human social interaction and integrity. I define EMPATHY as:

EMBRACING THIS MOMENT OF POWER AND AWARENESS TO TRULY HONOR YOURSELF AND OTHERS

... EMPATHY

Thanks to breakthrough discoveries in science, we now know that empathy is not just a concept; it is a measurable response in the human brain. When we observe someone else who is experiencing pain or any other uncomfortable emotion, mirror neurons fire in our own brains that enable us to empathize. While we now have scientific evidence that validates the wisdom of the ages, those of us who have experienced a connection with another person at the level of the soul don't need to be convinced of the fact that the power of EMPATHY is REAL—*real* in a way I define as the:

REAL ...

RAW ESSENCE OF AUTHENTIC LOVE

The symbol that appears on the cover of this book reflects its overarching vision and purpose—embracing EMPATHY. Within this icon is represented the love of parent and child; of inner mentor and inner adolescent. When met with the presence of BEING in relationship with self and others, this love is infinite—flowing into eternity. Eternity exists in the now—the only place of timelessness. By looking within (the keyhole), *being* in the present moment, this treasure is sure to be found.

EMBRACING THIS
MOMENT OF
POWER AND
AWARENESS TO
TRULY
HONOR
YOURSELF AND
OTHERS

EMPATHY crosses all boundaries of religion and mysticism throughout time and across the globe. It is manifested in the core principles we know as The Golden Rule—the universal law which advises us to do unto others as we would have done unto us. Yet a deeper understanding of this rule reveals that whether we are aware of it or not, what we do unto our brothers and sisters *we also do unto ourselves* —and which is reflected in the spirit of REAL-life heroes like Nelson Mandela, Azim Khamisa and Eleanor Roosevelt. As we read these statements from the world's religions, we realize that the power of EMPATHY is the common thread that connects humanity in ways both personal and universal.

The Golden Rule: A Broader Perspective

Buddhism:

"... a state that is not pleasing or delightful to me, how could I inflict that upon another?" *Samyutta Nikaya v. 353*

"Hurt not others in ways that you yourself would find hurtful." *Udana-Varga 5:18*

Christianity:

"Therefore all things whatsoever ye would that men should do to you, do ye even so to them: for this is the law and the prophets." *Matthew 7:12, King James Version*

"And as ye would that men should do to you, do ye also to them likewise." *Luke 6:31, King James Version*

Hinduism:

"This is the sum of duty: do not do to others what would cause pain if done to you." *Mahabharata 5:1517*

Islam:

"None of you [truly] believes until he wishes for his brother what he wishes for himself." *Number 13 of Imam "Al-Nawawi's Forty Hadiths."*

Judaism:

"... thou shalt love thy neighbor as thyself." *Leviticus 19:18*

"What is hateful to you, do not to your fellow man. This is the law: all the rest is commentary." *Talmud, Shabbat 31a*

"And what you hate, do not do to anyone." *Tobit 4:15 4*

Taoism:

"Regard your neighbor's gain as your gain, and your neighbor's loss as your own loss." *Tai Shang Kan Yin Pien*

At the level of the FEARSELF, we create borders and boundaries to keep each other separate. And yet we have seen—both from the single thread weaving together the world's seemingly disparate religions and from an inside view of the psyche of innocent teenage girls—just how indelible is the connection we share, and how deeply we yearn for that connection. At the level of the soul, truth is formless. It moves through each one of us, reconnecting us with the wisdom living in our hearts. There are no outsiders—no us versus them. It's all for one and one for all. E pluribus unum. Out of the many … one.

The degree to which teens learn to resonate with or separate from their soul's desires is largely dependent upon the environment in which they live. No one makes this point more beautifully than Dorothy Law Nolte and Rachel Harris in their poem, *Teenagers Learn What They Live.*

Teenagers Learn What They Live

If teenagers live with pressure, they learn to be stressed.
If teenagers live with failure, they learn to give up.
If teenagers live with rejection, they learn to feel lost.
If teenagers live with too many rules, they learn to get around them.
If teenagers live with too few rules, they learn to ignore the needs of others.
If teenagers live with broken promises, they learn to be disappointed.
If teenagers live with respect, they learn to honor others.
If teenagers live with trust, they learn to tell the truth.
If teenagers live with openness, they learn to discover themselves.
If teenagers live with natural consequences, they learn to be accountable.
If teenagers live with responsibility, they learn to be self-reliant.
If teenagers live with healthy habits, they learn to be kind to their bodies.
If teenagers live with support, they learn to feel good about themselves.
If teenagers live with creativity, they learn to share who they are.
If teenagers live with caring attention, they learn how to love.
If teenagers live with positive expectations, they learn to help build a better world.
—Dorothy Law Nolte and Rachel Harris

I have found that a powerful way to internalize messages of personal responsibility, like the one conveyed in this poem, is to write them in my DIARY, in first person: I write the first line of this poem "If I put pressure on myself, I learn to be stressed," etc. Then I take a moment to contemplate areas where I am placing undue pressure on myself and consider what I could do instead. Next, I move on to the second line, reflecting on where in my life I am failing to align with my truth … and continue through the poem. It's one way I've learned to put myself back in the driver's seat of my life and be a better role model for my daughter. In my workshops, I ask parents to close their eyes and think of something they wished their parents had said to them when they were a kid. Then I have them write it down and say it to themselves. Next, I ask them to go home and say it to their child. I believe this is a tangible way to bring the Golden Rule into our own hearts and homes.

The Tree of Life is another beautiful example that spans across world religions and mythologies to convey the deeper connection shared by all of humanity. To me, the painting on the next page captures the brilliance of the interconnectedness of life in the midst of all its unique expressions. At the picture's center is a key, symbolic of our inherent ability to tap into our essence, expressed by my friend Mary in her mysterious note: "I Am a conduit of Energy…I Am the flow of Spirit."

Humanity as a whole is in its latter stage of adolescence. The hour has come to make the leap into adulthood. It is time to wake up in full AWARENESS of our true identity as beings of love. We now have the means and the motivation to embody a kinder way of being. Together as a force of the feminine spirit united, we can refuse to drain our energy and resources by staying in an old déjà vu argument for argument's sake, and invest our energy instead to setting our sights on social justice for all. Breath-by-breath and CHOICE-by-CHOICE, we can change the world.

> *The arc of the moral universe is long,*
> *but it bends towards justice.*
>
> —*Martin Luther King Jr.*

Self-Exploration and Self-Expression

While the emerging of my own personal transformation began when I was a young adult, it is my hope that this book will shorten the number of years and experiences needed for girls to uncover the truth about themselves. My dream is that pitfalls and detours encountered by me and so many others are transformed into signposts that enable others to get on the road to self-discovery as early as possible. In a period of self-reflection inspired by unlocking my own diary after its 15-year hiatus in a sealed box, I wrote the following poem:

Who I Am

Is the Being I am who I see in the mirror?
And is who "I Am" becoming any clearer?
I hope I'm reflecting my sincerest desire
To achieve the dreams for which I do aspire.
I beg to know clearly the face that I see
That I may be true to the highest in me
That the peace I feel when my confidence is strong
Be maintained in my heart all the day-long.
Sometimes it's hard and I feel the pain
Of growing, becoming—of knowing again
That when feelings of loneliness take their toll
Just a spark of compassion rekindles my soul.
And on my path to the place I call home
The eyes in the mirror refrain from their roam
I'm learning to trust and I'm learning to feel
And my wish for us all is to know how to heal.
—Janet Larson, Age 33

For teens, my message is that you do not need to wait until you are an adult to know how powerful you really are. It can be scary to step into the realm of self-discovery, and change can be uncomfortable. However, in my own lifelong process of becoming—of building high self-esteem one CHOICE at a time—I have learned the seemingly upside-down secret that I need to become comfortable with the uncomfortable to make progress more effortlessly. Adolescent psychologist Roni Cohen-Sandler shares about the significance of beginning a path of self-discovery now:

> *I found that girls who have been given the chance to get to know themselves and to pursue their true interests are two steps ahead of*

the game. Teens who believe their parents and teachers have hopes for them that are realistic—and in line with their actual talents and passions—feel most equipped to succeed. Equally important, I discovered that while affluence and having exceptionally accomplished parents can increase teens' pressures and obligations, other factors protect them. What really matters is how resilient girls are to stress; this is determined by their self-confidence, social acceptance, validation, and coping skills. This is why intellect and fine schooling do not guarantee success. In fact, the research is clear: Most successful people are not necessarily brilliant, but they are self-directed and passionate about what they do. A 20-year longitudinal study of learning disabled individuals by the Frostig Center in Pasadena, California, corroborates the importance of resiliency. Researchers identified six attributes associated with long-term life success: self-awareness, proactivity, perseverance, goal-setting, effective support systems, and emotional coping strategies.

With a little patience and practice of the insights you've gleaned herein, I am confident the day will come when you wake up feeling more peace than pain, more discipline than sabotage, more love than fear, more self-respect than self-loathing. The next day, maybe you'll go in reverse a little bit, but you'll learn to shake it off, like Babe Ruth shook off two strikes before hitting his next home run.

For the inner adolescent in us all, we shake off the past and open ourselves to the future every time we look ourselves in the mirror and say (silently or out loud):

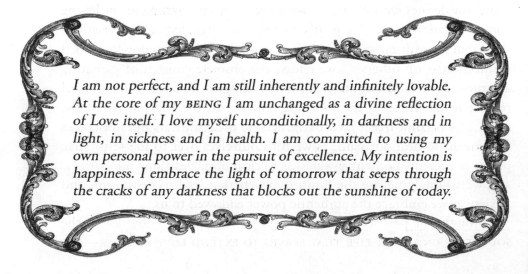

I am not perfect, and I am still inherently and infinitely lovable. At the core of my BEING *I am unchanged as a divine reflection of Love itself. I love myself unconditionally, in darkness and in light, in sickness and in health. I am committed to using my own personal power in the pursuit of excellence. My intention is happiness. I embrace the light of tomorrow that seeps through the cracks of any darkness that blocks out the sunshine of today.*

Self-love is the key to living life unlocked, and it is a call that applies as much to adults as it does to those on their way to adulthood. High self-esteem, achieved one CHOICE at a time is the portal to the SOULSELF. One powerful reminder of the importance of expressing every aspect of our BEING in the most authentic way we can was contributed by Bronnie Ware, a nurse in palliative and hospice care who captured the five most common regrets of those who are nearing the end of their lives and compiled them in her book, *The Top Five Regrets of the Dying*. It is my deepest hope that each one of us will meet our transition from this world knowing in our hearts that we have fulfilled most if not all of these wishes:

The Top Five Regrets of the Dying

1. *I wish I'd had the courage to live a life true to myself, not the life others expected of me.*

2. *I wish I hadn't worked so hard.*

3. *I wish I'd had the courage to express my feelings.*

4. *I wish I had stayed in touch with my friends.*

5. *I wish that I had let myself be happier.*

Do not regret growing older. It is a privilege denied to many.
—Unknown

Every worn-out paradigm leads to a sort of death, but only a death to the attachment of a smaller self that was never our source of strength to begin with. Together, we die to the attachment of the idea that the body somehow defines who we are, as we accept it as an instrument for loving communication ... we lay gently to rest the entanglements of relationships that cause distance and suffering, as we practice sustaining love-filled connections with others ... we release the obsolete concept of parenting as a means of controlling another human being, as we open to the mutual respect of parent/child relationships centered in the heart space of the soul ... we become free forever of the need to use chemicals and substances as a means to heal our pain, as we turn ourselves over to the restorative power of present-moment AWARENESS to clear obstacles along our path ... and we willingly release the limiting beliefs that lead to depression and anxiety as we embrace the authentic power endowed to us.

Through our practice of awakening to the truth, we now know the SOURCE OF UNIVERSAL LIFE THAT SERVES TO EXTEND LOVE FOREVER—our

SOULSELF. We harness its power to look at "what is" with our eyes wide open. It is from the bottomless well of compassion in our hearts that we draw the courage to stand up against forces fighting to keep us mired in the status quo, as we create the life we were meant to live and a world we are proud to bestow upon our daughters. We know that in this day and age, remaining complacent and assuming everything will take care of itself is a dangerous presumption.

As I pen the final words of this book, sitting by the fire with my zig-zag-patterned afghan made in those 1970s brown tones and crocheted for me by my Grandma Tillie, I reflect on my conversations with her decades ago. I thought I'd learned so much about her struggles and joys. I now realize I had only a snapshot; I barely skimmed the surface of her life. I have learned much more about her history, partially from piecing together new information from family members, but mostly from getting to know the inner workings of the Universal mind and soul of every girl as she grows and becomes a woman. What I know for sure is that behind each of the hardships my Grandma faced and every mistake she made—beneath the joy and tears, love and fears of everyone—is the innocence of a child.

Knowing that there was much more to the fabric of my Grandma's

Someday, beyond the clouds and all the world's wrongs, there will be love, compassion and justice, and we shall all understand.
—Flavia Weedn

Grandma Tillie at the age of 5 in 1900.

life that was buried with her, I am doing everything in my power to bring forth anything of significance from my own experiences that may make a difference in the lives of my own descendants, for this is the ultimate purpose of unlocking my own diary. I am daring to live my life unlocked, and I invite you to join me.

Invitation to **My Diary Unlocked** Circles

*How wonderful it is that nobody need wait a single
moment before starting to improve the world.*
—Anne Frank

You are invited to start improving the world ...

For too long, we have lived within a paradigm built on a hierarchy-based structure in which we yield our power to a chosen few at the peak of a pyramid. Regardless of the institution, whether it be financial, political, corporate, religious, educational or other, and no matter how well intentioned the creation of each entity or how noble its cause, in each one we have experienced the flaw in the basic structure of this paradigm—that providing too much power to too few people whose underlying motivations are driven by the FEARSELF ultimately results in an abuse of that power.

Remaining asleep to the power of the collective FEARSELF—acted out by those in control who take advantage of the rest of us—has led us to economic collapse, sabotage of the democratic process of government, personal suffering caused by unsafe products, abuse of our children, failure to secure a worthwhile education that ensures quality life skills and the overall well-being of our children, along with many more undesired repercussions. Yet the collective FEARSELF can only gain momentum when each of us makes individual choices that maintain an alliance with it. Throughout this book, we have learned to recognize that we have another choice. We recognize our responsibility to chart a new direction—a new paradigm.

In this new era, the age of wisdom, we commit to tearing down that wall—that hierarchy—and to rebuilding our communities, both globally and locally, within an all-encompassing circle of love and compassion in which every girl is empowered and every human is equal.

The good news is that we do not have to do this alone. Through the My Diary Unlocked movement, you can join a community circle to share your experiences, gain support, learn new tools, brainstorm ideas and become a powerful advocate for change. Join a virtual circle via the My Diary Unlocked community on Facebook at www.facebook.com/mydiaryunlocked, or meet in person with other members by starting your own local group or joining one already in place. New materials, guidelines and resources for the circles are always in development and available at www.mydiaryunlocked.com. I invite you to get involved, stay in touch and spread the word.

Through our commitment and action, the truth of the SOULSELF is becoming the guiding light for all of humanity, ensuring an environment in which high self-esteem is not only possible, but probable for every human BEING.

Glossary of Acronyms

ABC:

AWARE OF BEING CONSCIOUS

AFFIRM:

ACKNOWLEDGE FROM A FOUNDATION OF INTENTION REALIZED AND MANIFESTED

AWAKE:

ALIVE WITH ALL KNOWLEDGE EVIDENT

AWARE:

AWAKE WITH ALL REALITY EXPOSED

AWARENESS:

AWAKE WITH ALL REALITY EXPOSED NATURALLY EXPRESSING THE SOULSELF

BAR:

BOUNDARIES, AWARENESS, AND RESPONSIBILITY

BEING:

BODY, EMOTIONS, IMAGINATION, NATURAL SELF, GENIUS MIND

BREATH:

BRIDGE TO RECONNECT YOUR ENERGY AND TRUST YOUR HEART

BREATHE:

BRIDGE TO RECONNECT YOUR ENERGY AND TRUST YOUR HEART ESSENCE

CEU:

COMPASSION, EMPATHY, AND UNDERSTANDING

CHOICE:
Constantly Having Options In Creating Experience

DENIAL:
Decision to Exclude and Neglect Insight, Awareness and Love

DIARY:
Devoted Insights About the Real You

EMPATHY:
Embracing this Moment of Power and Awareness to Truly Honor Yourself and others

FEAR:
Fragile Experience of Anxiety or Regret

FEARSELF:
Fragile Experience of Anxiety or Regret Seeking Evidence of Limitations Forever

GOSSIPING:
Gestures Of Spreading Stories Igniting Personal Insecurities Native to the Gossipers

GRACE:
Genuine Recognition and Acceptance of our Connected Essence

GRIEF:
Going Right Into the Emotional Feeling

HELP:
Healing Essence of Love's Presence

LISTEN:
Let In Silence, Total Empathy, and Non-judgment

KEY:
KNOWING THE ESSENCE OF YOU

ME:
MODELING EMPATHY

NUMB:
NOBODY UNDERSTANDS MY BEING

REACT:
RACE TO EXERT ANY CONCLUSIONS TRIGGERED

REAL:
RAW ESSENCE OF AUTHENTIC LOVE

RESPOND:
REFRAIN AND ENTER A SILENT PAUSE IN ORDER TO NURTURE A DECISION

SOUL:
SOURCE OF UNIVERSAL LIFE

SOULSELF:
SOURCE OF UNIVERSAL LIFE SERVING TO EXTEND LOVE FOREVER

US:
UNITED IN SERVICE

I Am More—Mantra/Affirmation

BODY (PHYSICAL): I AM MORE THAN MY BODY

EMOTIONS (EMOTIONAL): MY FEELINGS ARE SINCERE

IMAGINATION (PERCEPTUAL/VISUAL): I CREATE MY DESTINY

NATURAL SELF (BEHAVIORAL): I EXPRESS THE BEST IN ME

GENIUS MIND (MENTAL/INTELLECTUAL): MY MIND IS MY FRONTIER

© MYDIARYUNLOCKED

Acknowledgements

I can't tell you how many people looked at me like I was crazy when I told them that my idea for this book idea included a collection or anthology of real-life diary entries shared by women and girls about the issues that are most personal to them. "Who in the world would ever share their private entries to be published in a book?" they asked. But then there were those who said, "I get it," and went digging for their own diaries hidden away in secret, and willingly exposed their deepest vulnerabilities for all the world to see. You are the ones I believe Steve Jobs was talking about when he said, "Here's to the crazy ones … the ones who see things differently … they push the human race forward … because the ones who are crazy enough to think that they can change the world, are the ones who do." Your willingness to share your most humbling moments underscores the power we generate when we unite to collectively face that which has kept us small. You are the soul sisters and kindred spirits doing your part to make life better and easier for yourselves and for others, shining a light on the message of compassion, empathy, and understanding that is central to the theme of this book. I am inspired by and grateful to all who stepped up to the plate and said, "I'm in." You are leading the way in making a better world for the future.

Contributing Diarists

These diarists (with names portrayed as requested), along with any credentials they chose to share include:

Celeste Krenz

Christy Dyer

Diana Fletcher, Author, Certified Life Coach, Speaker; www.thoughtsbydiana.com

Elisha

Elmira

Erin Mikelson

Erin T.

Jamie Miller, MA

Jenny Blake, Author and Career Strategies; www.lifeaftercollege.org

Karina Larson Greenway, M.Ed.

Kathryn (Katy) Butler
Kimberlee Dale Bishop-VanHeulen
Kristen Moeller, Bestselling author; www.kristenmoeller.com
Linda Smith
Lynette
Mary H. Shuler; www.maryshuler.com
Melissa Braverman; www.newyorkcitygal.com
Michelle
Mikaela
Misty Blankenship Valenta; www.mistyblankenship.com
Monique Muro; www.anovelquest.com (Blog)
Nathalie Hardy, Journalist/writer; www.nathaliesnotes.com
Sherry Duquet
Sherry Gavanditti
Toianna Wika

Anonymous Diarists

In my invitation to participate in this book, diarists were given the option of going public with their name or maintaining anonymity. I understand and respect that sharing these sensitive experiences is a very personal decision, and I appreciate the willingness of those who shared so that others may better understand that their situations and personal struggles are not occurring in isolation. As one diarist put it, "sometimes it's not friends or family who teach us to be brave. Sometimes it's complete strangers. As a contributor to this book, I am grateful to be one of those strangers." The message that we are not alone is key to the foundation of this book, and I appreciate all messengers, publicly identified or not.

Also, I am grateful to all the diarists who submitted entries for possible inclusion in this book. Even if your entries were not printed in the book, please know that your energy is present on every page.

Subject Matter Experts

Still others I met along the path of creating this book rose to the call to serve as subject matter experts, for part of my vision was to not only share the real-life dramas of "what is," but also to include a path to peace and happiness. These generous individuals—Alanis Morissette, Catherine Blyth, Joanna Poppink, Kristen Moeller, Andrea Kane, Alison Stewart Ng, Jane Nelsen, Kathryn Kvols, Brené Brown, Diana Loomans, Sara Tobin, Roni Cohen-Sandler, Byron Katie, Elizabeth Kübler-Ross, Barbara DeAngelis, Gerald Jampolsky, Diane Cirincione, Dorothy Law-Nolte, Rachel Harris, Azim Khamisa and Bronnie Ware—shared pearls of wisdom, insights, facts and figures on matters relating to their respective areas of expertise.

To Jack Canfield, my mentor in gaining both the skills and the courage to share the tools and insights that build high self-esteem, I am grateful for the support, and personal attention in helping to get this book off the ground so it can make a difference in the lives of so many others.

To Susie Walton, I am thankful for being a guiding light in teaching me (and teaching me to teach others) to be a better parent—the most important job in the world.

I am profoundly indebted to Anne Frank, who introduced me to the power of getting your story out of your mind and down on paper. From the time I first read her diary when I was in junior high school to this day as I continue to listen to it on audio over and over, I am humbled by the timeless messages that came from this precocious teenage girl. I am reminded of the genius spirit within each of us, regardless of our age.

For years I held the vision of this book in my mind as I circled around my own diary entries like a dog chases its tail. It wasn't until I met my editor, Danielle Dorman, that I was able to stop my dreams from spinning and chart a course to bring them into reality. Together with Danielle, I was able to create a meaningful direction and an organized process of bringing the concept of this book and the message of the My Diary Unlocked movement to fruition. To her, I am eternally grateful for her midwifery skills. Her breadth and depth of understanding of the human spirit, together with her professional acumen melded with my efforts to prove that when two or more are gathered, the prospect of miracles expands with exponential force. My passion and my life's work might still be locked away in the realm of the FEARSELF had she not been there to help me rediscover the light of my own SOUL and to let it shine for all the world to see. Danielle, thanks for being the kindred soul sister that you are, and for holding my hand through thick and thin with your kind and gentle spirit. To Arielle Ford, I express my gratitude for introducing me to Danielle.

My Supporters

There are many other individuals who believed in me and "got" the potential power of this book. Some offered moral support, others offered technical support, some guided me towards additional resources, and there were those bold enough to give me a "kick in the pants" at times to keep me moving forward. Their gentle prodding and encouragement helped me to stay the course, reminding me of my call to this mission when I might have otherwise rested by the roadside longer than necessary. A special thank you for all is this list, including Elise Abbott, Amy Ahlers, Lindsay Alt, Julie Anderson, Christine Arylo, Karen Billing, Mike Bosworth, David Coddon, Alyse Diamond, Sheri Fink, Jen Fry, Elise Gochberg, Carolina Gonzalez, Karina Larson Greenway, Arndís Halla Jóhannesdóttir, Ralph Hamm, Lisa Kaczmarczyk, Amanda Kane, Andrea Karp, Elmira Khodapanah,, Dee Kite, Julie Krenz, Tony Lasley, Eulalia Luckett, Jack Luckett, Ana Maltzman, Michelle A. Marzullo, PhD, Joy McCardle, Nermin Nergis, Heidi Niehart, Karla Olson, Helle Brisson Pearson, Susan Porjes, Valerie Rickel, Jim Riley, Cathie Roberts, Anna Savvas, Brad Schmidt, Karen Silsby, Lynette M. Smith, Connie Sorgdrager, Linda Tofte, Amy Torn, Mikaela Urman, Lynnsie Whitaker, Leslie Wicker, Emilie Winthrop and Pat Ybarra.

Thanks to artists Natalie Fry, Joanna Ding, and Paul Heussenstamm, whose art is featured, and to Paul Quarry, whose graphic design contributions have been immeasurable.

To the many more whose names I have not mentioned, please know that your services and your energy expended have not gone unappreciated. I will always be graced by the knowledge that those of you with seemingly nothing to gain reached out and invested your own time to help me help others. Some of you have no idea how much support you gave me to "keep on keeping on," just by showing me the goose bumps on your arms when I told you about the concept of this book. Trust me, I took it as a signpost I was moving in the right direction.

And last but certainly not least, I'd like to thank my husband, Clay, and our daughter, Angela, for their love, support, and patience through the process of writing this book. It is a true gift beyond measure to be supported in fulfilling your life's purpose, and one I receive with deep gratitude. I love you both.

References

Introduction

Anne Frank. *The Diary of a Young Girl: The Definitive Edition.* New York: Random House, 2011.

Mary Pipher. *Reviving Ophelia: Saving the Selves of Adolescent Girls.* New York: Penguin, 2005.

...Among young adults ages 15 to 24 years old, there are approximately 100-200 attempts for every completed suicide. http://www.cdc.gov/violenceprevention/pdf/suicide-datasheet-a.PDF (accessed June 14, 2014).

CDC. Suicide Facts at a Glance. Atlanta, GA: National Center for Injury Prevention and Control, Division of Violence Prevention, 2012.

...There were 74 school shootings out of the previous 270 school days prior to June 10, 2014. Assumes school year has 180 days. Sam Stein. 2014. "If It's A School Week In America, Odds Are There Will Be A School Shooting." Huffington Post, June 10. http://www.huffingtonpost.com/2014/06/10/school-shootings-since-newtown_n_5480209.html (accessed June 10, 2014).

Kathryn Kost, Stanley Henshaw and Liz Carlin. *U.S. Teenage Pregnancies, Births and Abortions: National and State Trends and Trends by Race and Ethnicity.* New York: Guttmacher Institute, 2010.

Andrea Cohn and Andrea Canter, PhD, NCSP. *Bullying: Facts for Schools and Parents.* Bethesda, MD: National Association of School Psychologists, 2003.

Childhelp: Prevention and Treatment of Child Abuse. "Cyberbullying, Teen Bullying and Abuse," http://www.childhelp.org/pages/988/

(accessed February 19, 2014).

Kate Kelland. *One in 12 Teenagers Self Harm, Study Finds*. Reuters, November 17, 2011.

National Collaborative on Childhood Obesity Research. "Childhood Obesity in the United States," http://www.nccor.org/downloads/Child-hoodObesity_020509.pdf (accessed February 19, 2014).

Chapter 1

My Freeing Your Being Compass is my own personal melding together of principles I've studied over the past several decades, including, but not limited to teachings by Plato, Gautama Buddha, Jesus Christ, A Course in Miracles, Jack Canfield's self-esteem model, the work of Ernest Holmes, John Gottman, Viktor Frankl, Carl Rogers, Alfred Adler, Norman Vincent Peale, Sonaya Roman, Rudolf Dreikurs and dozens of self-help authors who may have helped solidify the reality in my mind that we have the power to make choices and that we are worthy of make our own choices.

John Bartlett's book *"Familiar Quotations: Being an Attempt to Trace Their Source: Passages and Phrases in Common Use"* has been in print since 1868, first published in Boston by Little, Brown and Company.

Elizabeth Gilbert. *Eat, Pray, Love: One Woman's Search for Everything Across Italy, India and Indonesia*. New York: Penguin, 2007.

Leo F. Buscaglia. *Living, Loving and Learning*. New York: Ballantine Books, 1985.

Barbara Gordon. *I'm Dancing as Fast as I Can*. New York: Beaufort Books, 1979.

Shakti Gawain. *Creative Visualization: Use the Power of Your Imagination to Create What You Want in Your Life*. Novato, CA: Nataraj Publishing, 2002.

Stephen R. Covey. *The 7 Habits of Highly Effective People*. New York: Simon and Schuster, 1989.

Robert Frost. "The Secret Sits." In *The Poetry of Robert Frost: The Collected Poems, Complete and Unabridged*, edited by Edward Connery Lathem, 362. New York: Henry Holt and Company, Inc., 1969.

A Course in Miracles (ACIM) was written in 1976 to assist readers in achieving spiritual transformation. The person, Dr. Helen Schucman, who wrote the course down refuses to take credit for it and instead credits an "inner voice" with ACIM. https://acim.org/ (accessed February 20, 2014).

Chapter 2

Martin, J. B. (2010). The Development of Ideal Body Image Perceptions in the United States. *Nutrition Today, 45* (2010), 98-100. nursingcenter.com/pdf.asp?AID=1023485 (accessed February 20, 2014).

National Eating Disorder Association. "Get the Facts on Eating Disorders," http://www.nationaleatingdisorders.org/get-facts-eating-disorders (accessed February 20, 2014).

Center for Disease Control and Prevention report that the measured average height, weight, and waist circumference for American adults ages 20 years and over is: men height (inches) 69.3, weight (pounds) 195.5, waist circumference (inches) 39.7 / women height (inches) 63.8, weight (pounds) 166.2, waist circumference (inches) 37.5. Anthropometric Reference Data for Children and Adults: United States, 2007-2010. Vital and Health Statistics, Series 11, Number 252 (October 2012). http://www.cdc.gov/nchs/data/series/sr_11/sr11_252.pdf (accessed February 20, 2014).

The NIH calculates ideal body weight for adult (age 20 and over) females as 100 lbs. plus 5 lbs. for every 1 inch over 5 feet tall. A female who is 5 feet, 4 inches tall would have an ideal body weight of 120 lbs. A 5 foot, 10 inches tall woman has an ideal body weight of 150 lbs. National Institutes of Health, Department of Health and Human Services. "Aim for a Healthy Weight." http://www.nhlbi.nih.gov/health/public/heart/obesity/

lose_wt/ index.htm (accessed February 20, 2014).

Douglas Gentile and David Walsh found that 53% of girls are unhappy with their bodies by the age of 13 and this increases to 78% by the age of 17 (*A Normative Study Of Family Media Habits*. Minneapolis: National Institute on Media and the Family, 2002).

L. Cheung, A.M. Wolf, D. B. Herzog, S.L. Gortmaker and G.A. Colditz. "Exposure to the Mass Media and Weight Concerns among Girls." Pediatrics 103(1999): E36. http://www.ncbi.nlm.nih.gov/pubmed/10049992 (accessed February 20, 2014).

Mirasol Recovery Centers. "Eating Disorder Statistics: How Many People Have Eating Disorders?" http://www.mirasol.net/eating-disorders/information/eating-disorder-statistics.php (accessed February 20, 2014).

Food and Agriculture Organization of the United Nations. *The State of Food and Agriculture, 2013*. Rome, Italy. http://www.fao.org/docrep/018/i3300e/i3300e.pdf (accessed February 20, 2014).

Centers for Disease Control and Prevention. *Trends in the Prevalence of Extreme Obesity Among US Preschool-Aged Children Living in Low-Income Families, 1998-2010. Journal of the American Medical Association 308* (2012): 2563-2565. http://www.cdc.gov/obesity/data/childhood.html (accessed February 20, 2014).

Nanci Hellmich. Eating Too Much Added Sugar May Be Killing You. USA Today (February 4, 2012). http://www.usatoday.com/story/news/nation/2014/02/03/added-sugars-heart-disease-death/5183799/ (accessed February 20, 2014).

Jamie Oliver is a chef and media personality who has campaigned against processed foods in schools. See more at Jamie Oliver's Food Revolution: http://www.jamieoliver.com/us/foundation/jamies-food-revolution/home (accessed February 20, 2014).

National Association of Anorexia Nervosa and Associated Disorders (ANAD). "Eating Disorders Statistics." http://www.anad.org/get-information/about-eating-disorders/eating-disorders-statistics/ (accessed

February 20, 2014).

"At Issue with Ben Merens. The Lost Art of Conversation with writer and editor Catherine Blyth, author of 'The Art of Conversation: A Guided Tour of a Neglected Pleasure' (New York: Gotham Books, 2009)." First aired on Wisconsin Public Radio (an NPR affiliate), January 22, 2010: http://wpr.net/wcast/download-mp3-request.cfm?mp3 file=bme100122m.mp3&iNoteID=87762 (accessed February 20, 2014).

Portia de Rossi. *Unbearable lightness: A Story of Loss and Gain.* New York: Atria Paperback, 2010.

CNN reporter Moni Basi reported on Kevin Costner's eulogy for Witney Houston: ""You weren't just pretty. You were as beautiful as a woman could be…Whitney, if you could hear me now, I would tell you: 'You weren't just good enough. You were great.'" *Costner delivers poignant eulogy for co-star Houston.* CNN (February 19, 2012). http://www.cnn.com/2012/02/18/us/whitney-houston-costner/ (accessed February 20, 2014).

Chapter 3

Randy Pausch. 2007. "The Last Lecture." Lecture, Carnegie Mellon University, Pittsburgh, September 18. http://www.cmu.edu/randyslecture/ (accessed February 20, 2014).

Only 16 percent of protagonists in movies are female. They are usually "body props," sex objects. Only one out of five news stories are about women and girls. The academic term for this low profile played in culture is symbolic annihilation. Jennifer Siebel Newsom, producer. *Miss Representation.* 2011. "The Representation Project." DVD. http://www.missrepresentation.org/ (accessed February 20, 2014).

Alanis Morissette. 2002. "So Unsexy." by Alanis Morisette. On *Under Rug Swept.* Maverick. Digital recording, 2002. https://myspace.com/alanismorissette/music/song/so-unsexy-30865834-31257871 (accessed

February 20, 2014).

Gary D Chapman. *The 5 Love Languages: The Secret to Love That Lasts.* Chicago, IL: Northfield Publishing. 2010.

Sue Johnson. 2008. *Hold Me Tight: Seven Conversations for a Lifetime of Love.* New York: Little Brown and Company.

Sara B. Johnson, Robert W. Blum, and Jay N. Giedd. 2010. "Adolescent Maturity and the Brain: The Promise and Pitfalls of Neuroscience Research in Adolescent Health Policy." *Journal of Adolescent Health* 45: 216-221. DOI: 10.1016/j.jadohealth.2009.05.016 (accessed February 20, 2014).

The University of California at Los Angeles Rape Treatment Center reports about 50% of rape victims are under 18 years of age when they are victimized. http://www.911rape.org/for-teens/teens-rape (accessed February 20, 2014). Further, the 2012 Center for Disease Control's (CDC) National Center for Injury Prevention, Division of Violence Prevention, "Sexual Violence Facts-at-a-Glance" reports nearly 1 in 5 (18.3%) women and 1 in 71 men (1.4%) have reported experiencing rape at some time in their lives. http://www.cdc.gov/ViolencePrevention/pdf/SV-DataSheet-a.pdf (accessed February 20, 2014).

M.P. Koss, C.A. Gidycz, and N. Wisiewski. 1987. "The Scope of Rape: Incidence and Prevalence of Sexual Aggression and Victimization in a National Sample of Higher Education Students." *Journal of Consulting and Clinical Psychology* 55: 162–170. See also the National Institute of Justice, Office of Justice Programs, U.S. Department of Justice, "Rape and Sexual Violence," http://www.nij.gov/topics/crime/rape-sexual-violence/Pages/welcome.aspx (accessed February 20, 2014).

Holmes, M.M., Resnick, H.S., Kilpatrick, D.G., Best, C.L. 1996. "Rape-related Pregnancy: Estimates and Descriptive Characteristics from a National Sample of Women." American Journal of Obstetrics and Gynecology 175: 320-324.

Gavin de Becker. 1997. *The Gift of Fear: Survival Signals That Protect Us from Violence*. New York: Dell Publishing.

Tara Brach. 2003. *Radical Acceptance: Embracing Your Life with the Heart of a Buddha*. New York: Bantam Dell.

Janet Elise Rosenbaum's 2009 study published in the journal *Pediatrics* showed that teenagers who pledged virginity until marriage are just as likely to have sex before marriage as those who didn't pledge to remain virgins. And, the pledgers are much less likely to report using birth control or practice safe sex when they do resulting in a higher risk of pregnancy and sexually transmitted diseases. Janet Elise Rosenbaum. 2009. "Patient Teenagers? A Comparison of the Sexual Behavior of Virginity Pledgers and Matched Non-Pledgers." *Pediatrics* 123: e110 -e120. DOI: 10.1542/peds.2008-0407 (accessed February 20, 2014).

Ten thousand teens are infected with sexually transmitted diseases every day. CDC. *Sexually Transmitted Disease Surveillance 2009*. Atlanta: U.S. Department of Health and Human Services, 2010.

Kramer, A. 2012. *Girl Talk: What High School Senior Girls Have to Say About Sex, Love, and Relationships*. Washington, DC: The National Campaign to Prevent Teen and Unplanned Pregnancy. http://thenational-campaign.org/resource/girl-talk (accessed February 20, 2014).

... The United States still has the highest rates of teen pregnancy and birth among comparable countries. Despite declining by more than one-half since the early 1990s, the United States still has the highest teen birth rate among comparable countries. In 2011, the teen birth rate in the United States was 31.3 births per 1,000 girls age 15-19—nearly one and a half times greater than in the United Kingdom, which has the highest rate in Western Europe at 22 per 1,000, and nearly ten times greater than the teen birth rate in Switzerland, which has the lowest teen birth rate in Europe at 3.4 per 1,000. In addition, the U.S. teen birth rate was more than twice as high than the teen birth rate in Canada (14 per 1,000).

"Teen Birth Rates: How Does the United States Compare?" Washington, DC: The National Campaign to Prevent Teen and Unplanned Pregnancy. (2014).

E-gram from The National Campaign on August 22, 2013 citing study: "Encouraging teens to delay sex and providing teens with information about contraception are seen as complementary, not contradictory strategies by most adults regardless of age, race/ethnicity, or geography." Data in the new *Survey Says* were drawn from a national telephone survey conducted for The National Campaign by Social Science Research Solutions, an independent research company. Interviews were conducted in July 2013 among a nationally representative sample of 1,005 respondents age 18 and older.

United States: Martin, J.A., Hamilton, B.E., Ventura S.J., Osterman, M.J.K, & Matthews, T.J. (2013). Births: Final data for 2011. National Vital Statistics Reports, 62(1). Retrieved from http://www.cdc.gov/nchs/data/nvsr/nvsr62/nvsr62_01.pdf

Other Countries: United Nations, Department of Economic and Social Affairs. (2013). 2012 Demographic Yearbook. New York: Author. Retrieved from http://unstats.un.org/unsd/demographic/products/dyb/dybsets/2012.pdf

Guttmacher Institute. June 2013. "Facts on American Teens' Sexual and Reproductive Health." http://www.guttmacher.org/pubs/FB-ATSRH.html (accessed February 21, 2014).

Lorraine V. Klerman. 2004. *Another Chance: Preventing Additional Births to Teen Mothers*. Washington, DC: The National Campaign to Prevent Teen and Unplanned Pregnancy. http://thenationalcampaign.org/sites/default/files/resource-primary- download/anotherchance_final.pdf (accessed February 21, 2014).

Kost, K. & Henshaw S. (2014). U.S. Teenage Pregnancies, Births and Abortions, 2010: National and State Trends by Age, Race and Ethnicity. New York: Guttmacher Institute. Retrieved from http://www.

guttmacher.org/pubs/USTPtrends10.pdf.

Christopher Trenholm, Barbara Devaney, Ken Fortson, Lisa Quay, Justin Wheeler, and Melissa Clark. April, 2007. *Impacts of Four Title V, Section 510 Abstinence Education Programs*. Mathematica Policy Research, Inc. for U.S. Department of Health and Human Services, Office of the Assistant Secretary for Planning and Evaluation. Washington, D.C. http://aspe.hhs.gov/hsp/abstinence07/ (accessed February 21, 2014).

James Houston, director. 2009. *Let's Talk About Sex*. Documentary, DVD. http://www.letstalkaboutsexthefilm.com/ (accessed February 21, 2014).

Washington University School of Medicine in St. Louis. Winter 2013. "Access to Free Birth Control Reduces Abortion Rates." http://medschool.wustl.edu/news/patient_care/Contraceptive_Choice (accessed February 21, 2014).

The National Campaign to Prevent Teen and Unplanned Pregnancy. 2008. "Ten Tips for Parents To Help Their Children Avoid Teen Pregnancy." http://thenationalcampaign.org/sites/default/files/resource-primary-download/10tips_final.pdf (accessed February 21, 2014).

Mark L. Hatzenbuehler. 2011. "The Social Environment and Suicide Attempts in Lesbian, Gay, and Bisexual Youth." *Pediatrics 2010-3020*. Published ahead of print, April 18, 2011. DOI:10.1542/peds.2010-3020 (accessed February 21, 2014).

Gilbert Herdt. 1997. *Same Sex, Different Cultures: Exploring Gay and Lesbian Lives*. Boulder, CO: Westview Press.

Kramer, A. 2012. *Girl Talk: What High School Senior Girls Have to Say About Sex, Love, and Relationships*. Washington, DC: The National Campaign to Prevent Teen and Unplanned Pregnancy. http://thenationalcampaign.org/resource/girl-talk

Martha M. Lauzen. 2012. *It's a Man's (Celluloid) World: On-Screen Representations of Female Characters in the Top 100 Films of 2011*. San Diego, CA: Center for the Study of Women in Television and Film, San Diego

State University. http://womenintvfilm.sdsu.edu/files/2011_Its_a_Mans_World_Exec_Summ.pdf (accessed February 21, 2014).

Chapter 4

U.S. Department of Health and Human Services, Centers for Disease Control (CDC) and Prevention. 2006. "The Health Consequences of Involuntary Exposure to Tobacco Smoke: A Report of the Surgeon General." Accessed March 24, 2014. http://www.surgeongeneral.gov/library/reports/secondhandsmoke/secondhandsmoke.pdf

Students Against Destructive Decisions (SADD) and Liberty Mutual. 2005.

"Teens Today 2005 Report." Press Release, December 15. Accessed March 24, 2014. http://www.sadd.org/teenstoday/rites.htm

Peter Weir, dir. 1989. *Dead Poets Society*. DVD, Touchstone Pictures.

Stephen R. Covey. 1989. *The 7 Habits of Highly Effective People*. New York: Free Press.

Arianna Huffington. 2006. *On Becoming Fearless…in Love, Work, and Life*. New York: Little, Brown & Company.

Dan Siegel. 2010. Mindsight: *The New Science of Personal Transformation*. New York: Random House.

John Gottman. 1994. *Why Marriages Succeed or Fail*. New York: Simon & Schuster.

Child Welfare Information Gateway. 2013. 3.4 million referrals of 6.2 million children for abuse. "Child Maltreatment 2011: Summary of Key Findings." Washington, DC: U.S. Department of Health and Human Services, Children's Bureau. www.childwelfare.gov/pubs/factsheets/can-stats.pdf. (accessed March 23, 2014).

Tracie O. Afifi, Natalie P. Mota, Patricia Dasiewicz, Harriet L. Mac-Millan, and Jitender Sareen. 2012. "Physical Punishment and Mental Disorders: Results From a Nationally Representative U.S. Sample." *Pediatrics* 130, no. 2 (August): 184 -192. Doi: 10.1542/peds.2011-2947) Published online July 2, 2012. http://pediatrics.aappublications.org/content/130/2/184.full (accessed March 24, 2014).

Bonnie Rochman. 2012. "Hitting Your Kid Increases Their Risk of Mental Illness." *Time Magazine*, July 2. Accessed March 24, 2014. http://healthland.time.com/2012/07/02/physical-punishment-increases-your-kids-risk-of-mental-illness

Global Initiative to End All Corporal Punishment of Children. 2014. "States with Full Abolition." 37 countries and states with full abolition of corporal punishment for children. http://www.endcorporalpunishment.org/pages/progress/prohib_states.html (accessed June 16, 2014).

Kathryn Kvols. 2012. "Stop. Look. Listen!" *Family Living Magazine,* July 13. http://floridafamilyliving.com/listening-quiz (accessed March 24, 2014).

Dale Carnegie. 1981. *How to Win Friends and Influence People.* New York: Simon & Shuster.

Jane Nelsen, Lynn Lott, Cheryl Erwin, et al. 2006 (reprint). *Positive Discipline* (series). New York: Ballatine Books.

Brené Brown. 2012. *Daring Greatly.* New York: Penguin Group.

Diana Loomans. 1994. *100 Ways to Build Self-Esteem and Teach Value.* Tiburon, CA: H. J. Kramer.

Chapter 5

Simone Schnall, Kent D. Harber, Jeanine K. Stefanucci, Dennis R. Proffitt. 2008. "Social Support and the Perception of Geographical Slant."

Journal of Experimental Social Psychology 44, no 5 (Sept.): 1246–1255. http://www.ncbi.nlm.nih.gov/pmc/articles/PMC3291107/#R35 (accessed March 25, 2014).

Jill Feury Devoe and Monica R. Hill. 2011. "Student Victimization in U. S. Schools: Results from the 2009 School Crime Supplement to the National Crime Victimization Survey." U.S. Department of Education, National Center for Education Statistics. Washington, D.C.: U.S. Government Printing Office. http://nces.ed.gov/pubs2012/2012314.pdf (accessed March 24, 2014).

Tonja R. Nansel, Mary Overpeck, Ramani S. Pilla, W. June Ruan, Bruce Simons-Morton, Peter Scheidt. 2001. "Bullying Behaviors Among U.S. Youth." *Journal of the American Medical Association.* 285, no. 16: 2094-2100. doi:10.1001/jama.285.16.2094. http://jama.jamanetwork.com/article.aspx?articleid=193774 (accessed March 25, 2014).

Susan M. Swearer. 2011. "Risk Factors for and Outcomes of Bullying and Victimization." White paper prepared for the United States White House Conference on Bullying Prevention, March 20. http://digitalcommons.unl.edu/cgi/viewcontent.cgi?article=1131&context=edpsychpapers (accessed March 26, 2014).

Rachel Simmons. 2002. *Odd Girl Out.* Orlando, Florida: Harcourt Books.

Mark Traina. 2012. "Bullying and "Bullycide" national data and statistics." http://teachers.net/mentors/bullying/topic79/8.06.12.10.12.29.html. ...Each day, approximately 160,000 teenagers skip school because of bullying...

"Bullying Statistics." 2010. http://www.bullyingstatistics.org/content/bullying-statistics-2010.html (accessed March 26, 2014).

Frank Peretti. 2000. *No More Bullies.* Nashville, TN: W. Publishing Group.

Amy Pavuck. 2013. "Rebecca Sedwick's Suicide Highlights Dangers of Cyberbullying." *Orlando Sentinel,* Sept 15.

ABC News. 2013."Mom of Accused Teen Cyber Bully Arrested on Child Abuse Charges." Aired October 18. http://abcnews.go.com/US/mom-accused-teen-cyber-bully-arrested-child-abuse/story?id=20617247 (accessed March 26, 2014).

"Bullying of Brothers and Sisters Should Not Be Ignored."2013. American Academy of Pediatrics (June 17). http://www.aap.org/en-us/about-the-aap/aap-press-room/pages/Bullying-of-Brothers-and-Sisters-Should-Not-Be-Ignored.aspx (accessed March 26, 2014).

Tina Fey. 2011. *Bossypants.* New York: Little, Brown and Company.

Chapter 6

National Institute on Drug Abuse, National Institute of Health (NIH). 2012. "Illicit Drug Use."Accessed March 26, 2014. First time illicit drug users = 7,898 /day. 52% were under the age of 18. Excludes Marajuana use. http://www.drugabuse.gov/publications/drugfacts/nationwide-trends U.S. Department of Health and Human Services. 2012. "Results from the 2012 National Survey on Drug Use and Health." http://www.samhsa.gov/data/NSDUH/2012SummNatFindDetTables/NationalFindings/NSDUHresults2012.htm (accessed March 26, 2014).

National Institute on Alcohol Abuse and Alcoholism, NIH. 2009. "Underage Drinking." http://pubs.niaaa.nih.gov/publications/UnderageDrinking/Underage_Fact.pdf (accessed March 26, 2014).

National Institute on Drug Abuse, NIH. 2011. "Marijuana: Facts Parents Need to Know," March revision. http://www.drugabuse.gov/sites/default/files/parents_marijuana_brochure.pdf (accessed March 26, 2014).

Center for Disease Control and Prevention (CDC). 2013. "Policy Impact: Prescription Painkiller Overdoses," July 2. http://www.cdc.gov/

homeandrecreationalsafety/rxbrief/ (accessed March 26, 2014).

Brené Brown. 2012. *Daring Greatly.* New York: Penguin Group.

American Academy of Child and Adolescent Psychiatry. 2011. "Children of Alcoholics, Facts for Family Pages," No. 17, December. http://www.aacap.org/aacap/Families_and_Youth/Facts_for_Families/Facts_for_Families_Pages/children_of_Alcoholics_17.aspx) (accessed March 26, 2014).

E. Rosenbaum and D.B. Kandel. 1990. "Early Onset of Adolescent Sexual Behavior and Drug Involvement." *Journal of Marriage and the Family,* 52, no. 3: 783-798. F.L. Mott and R.J. Haurin. 1988.

"Linkages Between Sexual Activity and Alcohol and Drug Use among American Adolescents." *Family Planning Perspectives,* 20, no. 3:128-136.

The National Campaign to Prevent Teen Pregnancy. "Teen Pregnancy, Substance Use, and Other Risky Behavior." https://thenationalcampaign.org/sites/default/files/resource-primary-download/risky_behaviors.pdf (accessed March 29, 2014).

Claudia Black. 2002. *It Will Never Happen to Me.* New York: Random House.

"6 Parenting Practices." 2012. Treatment Research Institute and The Partnership at Drugfree.org. http://www.drugfree.org/wp-content/uploads/2011/07/partnership_components_tool_revised_031612.pdf (accessed March 31, 2014).

National Center for Injury Prevention and Control, CDC. 2012. "Vital Signs: Teen Drinking and Driving," Oct. 2. http://www.cdc.gov/Features/VitalSigns/TeenDrinkingAndDriving/ (accessed March 31, 2014).

Michael J. Bradley. 2009. *Yes, Your Teen is Crazy!* Gig Harbor, WA: Harbor Press.

...Score-It-Yourself... I combined resources to create this list, largely founded upon a pamphlet by Alcoholics Anonymous World Services, Inc. 2007. "Young People and AA." http://www.aa.org/pdf/

products/p-4_youngpeopleandaa.pdf (accessed March 31, 2014).

Barry Meier. 2007. "In Guilty Plea, Oxycontin Maker to Pay $600 Million." *New York Times,* May 10. http://www.nytimes.com/2007/05/10/business/11drug-web.html?pagewanted=all (accessed March 31, 2014).

Kelly Riddell. 2014. "Hoffman's Death Highlights U.S. Spike in Heroin Use." *The Washington Times,* Feb. 3. http://www.washingtontimes.com/news/2014/feb/3/hoffmanns-death-highlights-growing-trend-us-heroin/?page=al (accessed March 31, 2014).

Centers for Disease Control and Prevention. 2010. "New CDC Vital Signs: Prescription Painkiller Epidemic Among Women." http://www.cdc.gov/media/dpk/2013/dpk-Prescription%20drug%20overdose.html (accessed March 31, 2014).

L. Manchikanti, and A. Singh. 2008. "Therapeutic Opioids: A Ten-year Perspective on the Complexities and Complications of the Escalating Use, Abuse, and Nonmedical Use of Opioids." *Pain Physician*, March 11, no. 2 (Supplement): S63-88. Review. PMID: 18443641. http://www.ncbi.nlm.nih.gov/pubmed/18443641 (accessed March 31, 2014).

"Sex Slaves: Addiction." 2012. *MSNBC Documentaries,* May 30. http://www.msnbc.com/documentaries/watch/sex-slaves-addiction-44581955833 (accessed March 31, 2014).

Christina Huffington. 2013. "Addiction Recovery: Getting Clean At 22." *Huffington Post,* April 13. Accessed March 31, 2014. http://www.huffingtonpost.com/christina-huffington/addiction-recovery-getting-clean_b_3076391.html

Madhav Goyal. 2014. "Meditation Programs for Psychological Stress and Well-being."*Journal of the American Medical Association (JAMA), Internal Medicine* 174, no. 3: 357-368. doi:10.1001/jamainternmed.2013.13018. http://archinte.jamanetwork.com/article.aspx?articleid=1809754

(accessed March 31, 2014).

Eckhart Tolle. 2005. *A New Earth*. New York: Penguin Group.

Darrel A. Regier, Mary E. Farmer, Donald S. Rae, Ben Z. Locke, Samuel J. Keith, Lewis L. Judd, Frederick K. Goodwin. 1990. "Comorbidity of Mental Disorders With Alcohol and Other Drug Abuse." *JAMA* 264, no. 19: 2511-2518. Accessed on March 31, 2014. doi:10.1001/jama.1990.03450190043026. http://jama.jamanetwork.com/article.aspx?articleid=383975

Tommy Rosen. 2013. "Recovery 2.0: Yoga and Meditation for People in Recovery From Addiction." *Huffington Post, The Blog* July 2. http://www.huffingtonpost.com/tommy-roseTn/yoga-for-addiction_b_3523111.html (accessed March 31, 2014).

"Drug-Related Images Trigger Brain's Reward Center." 2008. *The Washington Post*, January 30. http://www.washingtonpost.com/wp-dyn/content/article/2008/01/30/AR2008013002728.html (accessed March 31, 2014).

Addiction. Unknown (pre-2007). "A Mother's Desperation." Susan Froemke and Albert Maysles, dirs. HBO. http://www.hbo.com/addiction/thefilm/centerpiece/613_segment_2.html (accessed March 31, 2014).

David Sheff. 2013. *Clean*. New York: Houghton Mifflin Harcourt Publishing.

Ernesto Londono. 2013. "As U.S. Withdraws from Afghanistan, Poppy Trade It Spent Billions Fighting Still Flourishes." *The Washington Post*, November 3. http://www.washingtonpost.com/world/national-security/as-us-withdraws-from-afghanistan-poppy-trade-it-spent-billions-fighting-still-flourishes/2013/11/03/55cc99d6-4313-11e3-a751-f032898f2dbc_story.html (accessed March 31, 2014).

Redonna K. Chandler, Bennett W. Fletcher, and Nora D. Volkow. 2009. "Treating Drug Abuse and Addiction in the Criminal Justice System." *JAMA* 301, no. 2 (January 14): 183-190. http://www.ncbi.nlm.nih.gov/

pmc/articles/PMC2681083/#__ffn_sectitle (accessed March 31, 2014).

Chapter 7

Associated Press. 2010. "Study: Students More Stressed Now Than During Depression." http://usatoday30.usatoday.com/news/education/2010-01-12-students-depression-anxiety_N.htm (accessed April 1, 2014).

National Alliance on Mental Illness (NAMI). 1996-2014. "Mental Illnesses." According to the NAMI web site, "The U.S. Surgeon General reports that 10 percent of children and adolescents in the United States suffer from serious emotional and mental disorders that cause significant functional impairment in their day-to-day lives at home, in school and with peers." http://www.nami.org/template.cfm?section=about_mental_illness (accessed April 1, 2014).

American College Health Association. 2013. "American College Health Association-National College Health Assessment II: Reference Group Executive Summary," Spring. Hanover, MD: American College Health Association. http://www.acha-ncha.org/docs/ACHA-NCHA II_ReferenceGroup_ExecutiveSummary_Spring2013.pdf (accessed April 1, 2014).

National Institue of Mental Health (NIMH). 2005. "Mental Illness Exacts Heavy Toll, Beginning in Youth." Press Release, June 6. http://www.nimh.nih.gov/news/science-news/2005/mental-illness-exacts-heavy-toll-beginning-in-youth.shtml (accessed April 2, 2014).

Brendan L. Smith. 2012. "Inappropriate Prescribing." *American Psychological Association* 43, no. 6 (June): 36. https://www.apa.org/monitor/2012/06/prescribing.aspx (accessed April 2, 2014).

Roni Cohen-Sandler. 2013. *Easing Their Stress.* Author and Company: Amazon Digital Services, Inc.

Tom Shadyac, dir. 2011. *I Am.* Shady Acres Film, Flying Eye Productions.

http://www.iamthedoc.com/thefilm/

NIMH. "Anxiety Disorders." National Institute of Mental Health. Accessed April 2, 2014. http://www.nimh.nih.gov/health/topics/anxiety-disorders/index.shtml

Mayo Clinic. "Post-traumatic stress disorder (PTSD)." http://www.mayoclinic.org/diseases-conditions/post-traumatic-stress-disorder/basics/definition/con-20022540 (accessed April 2, 2014).

Shakti Gawain. 1978. *Creative Visualization*. Novato, California: New World Library.

Deirdre Barrett. 2001. "The Power of Hypnosis." *Psychology Today Online,* January 1. http://www.psychologytoday.com/articles/200101/the-power-hypnosis

Arianna Huffington. 2006. *On Becoming Fearless…in Love, Work, and Life*. New York: Little, Brown & Company.

Teen Help. "Cutting Statistics and Self-Injury Treatment." http://www.teenhelp.com/teen-health/cutting-stats-treatment.html. (accessed April 2, 2014).

Lucie Hemmen. 2012. *Parenting a Teen Girl*. Oakland, California: New Harbinger Publications.

David Fitzpatrick. 2012. *Sharp*. New York: Harper Collins Publishers.

Mariel Hemingway, dir. *Running from Crazy*. 2013. Cabin Creek Films. Accessed April 2, 2014. https://www.facebook.com/RunningFromCrazy

Eckhart Tolle. 2008. *The Journey Into Yourself*. Audiobook. Vancouver, Canada: Eckhart Teachings Inc.

Byron Katie. 2007. *Your Inner Awakening: The Work of Byron Katie: Four Questions That Will Transform Your Life*. Audiobook. New York: Simon & Schuster Audio/ Nightengale-Conant.

Jeffrey Ressner. 2000. "New Age: Four Questions to Inner Peace." *Time Magazine,* December 1. http://content.time.com/time/magazine/article/0,9171,998759,00.html (accessed April 2, 2014).

Chapter 8

Mavis Staples. 2010. "You Are Not Alone." Written by Jeffrey Scot Tweedy. On *You Are Not Alone.* ANTI-Records. http://www.songlyrics.com/mavis-staples/you-are-not-alone-lyrics/ (accessed April 2, 2014).

Mothers Against Drunk Driving (MADD). 2013. "MADD Analysis Finds Majority of Underage Drinking Deaths Not Traffic Related." Press Release, April 17. http://www.madd.org/media-center/press-releases/2013/madd-analysis-finds-majority.html Each year, about 4,700 people die as a result of underage drinking (according to SAMHSA, the Substance Abuse and Mental Health Services Administration), but the majority of the deaths attributable to alcohol use among 15 to 20 year olds are not on our roadways. => 1 teen every 1.86 hours. (accessed April 2, 2014).

Center for Disease Control (CDC). 2010. "Suicide: Facts at a Glance." National Center for Injury Prevention and Control, Division of Violence Prevention. Based upon Center for Disease Control (CDC) Web-based Injury Status Query and Report System (WISQARS), "Leading Cause of Death Reports 1999-2010: Database query for 15-24 year olds in 1999-2010." http://webappa.cdc.gov/sasweb/ncipc/leadcaus10_us.html (accessed April 2, 2014).

Mitch Albom. 1997. *Tuesdays with Morrie.* New York: Random House.

Raymond A. Moody, Jr. 1975. *Life After Life.* San Francisco: HarperCollins Publishers.

Tim Townsend. 2013. "Is Grief Mental Illness?" *St. Louis Post Dispatch,* May 27. http://www.usatoday.com/story/news/nation/2013/05/27/grief-psychiatry-mental-illness/2359591/ (accessed April 2, 2014).

Elisabeth Kübler-Ross, David A. Kessler. 2005. *On Grief and Grieving*. New York: Scribner.

Jack Canfield, Janet Switzer. 2005. *The Success Principles*. New York: HarperCollins.

Barbara De Angelis. 1993. "Making Love Work." http://www.barbaradeangelis.com/

Sally Grablick. 2011. *The Reason*. Davison, Michigan: 4EVR Press.

National Alliance on Mental Illness. 2010 (July). "Facts on Children's Mental Health in America." "Suicide is the third leading cause of death in youth ages 15 to 24. More teenagers and young adults die from suicide than from cancer, heart disease, AIDS, birth defects, stroke, pneumonia, influenza and chronic lung disease combined. Over 90 percent of children and adolescents who commit suicide have a mental disorder." http://www.nami.org/Template.cfm?Section=federal_and_state_policy_legislation&template=/ContentManagement/ContentDisplay.cfm&ContentID=43804. (accessed April 2, 2014).

 Harvard Public Health. 2013. "Guns & Suicide: The Hidden Toll." "Though guns are not the most common method by which people attempt suicide, they are the most lethal. About 85 percent of suicide attempts with a firearm end in death. (Drug overdose, the most widely used method in suicide attempts, is fatal in less than 3 percent of cases.)" http://www.hsph.harvard.edu/news/magazine/guns-suicide-the-hidden-toll/ (accessed April 2, 2014).

New York Post. 2013. "He Jumped Off the Golden Gate Bridge…and Lived!" June 30. "Of the survivors, 19 of them have come forward and expressed words to this effect: 'The second my hands and feet left the rail I realized I had made a mistake, I realized how much I needed to live, or didn't want to die.'" http://nypost.com/2013/06/30/he-jumped-off-the-golden-gate-bridge-and-lived/ (accessed April 2, 2014).

CDC- National Center for Injury Prevention and Control Suicide. 2012. "Facts at a Glance-- Division of Violence Prevention. " "Among young adults ages 15 to 24 years old, there are approximately 100-200 attempts for every completed suicide." http://www.cdc.gov/violenceprevention/pdf/suicide_datasheet_2012-a.pdf (accessed April 2, 2014).

Linsey Tanner. 2011. "Gay Teen Suicides (And Straight) More Common In Politically Conservative Areas." Associated Press, *Huffington Post*, April 18. http://www.huffingtonpost.com/2011/04/18/gay-teen-suicides-and-str_n_850345.html (accessed April 2, 2014).

Lisa Belkin. 2013. "Antoinette Tuff's 911 Tape: What We All Can Learn About School Shootings." *Huffington Post*, August 22. *http://www.huffingtonpost.com/2011/04/18/gay-teen-suicides-and-str_n_850345.html).* (accessed April 2, 2014).

Wikepedia. 2012. "Sandy Hook Elementary School Shooting." Accessed April 2, 2014. *http://en.wikipedia.org/wiki/Sandy_Hook_Elementary_School_shooting*

United States Secret Service and United States Department of Education. 2002. "The Final Report and Findings of the Safe Schools Initiative." Accessed April 2, 2014. http://www.secretservice.gov/ntac/ssi_final_report.pdf

Public Broadcasting System (PBS). 2009. "Cry for Help: Teenage Mental Illness and Suicide, Resources: Wake-Up Call." PBS.org. Last modified April 20. http://www.pbs.org/wnet/cryforhelp/episodes/resources/wake-up-call/22/ (accessed April 2, 2014).

Teen Suicide Statistics. "Sources for Warning Signs that a Teen Might Commit Suicide." http://teensuicidestatistics.com/warning-signs.html (accessed April 2, 2014).

National Alliance of Mental Illness. https://www.nami.org/Content/ContentGroups/Illnesses/Suicide_Teens.htm (accessed April 2, 2014).

...Suicide help guide is adapted from multiple sources, primarily: http://www.metanoia.org/suicide/sphone.htm and http://helpguide.org/mental/suicide_prevention.htm (both accessed April 2, 2014)

Public Broadcasting System (PBS). 2009. "Cry for Help: Teenage Mental

Illness and Suicide,"April 23. PBS.org. http://www.pbs.org/wnet/cry-forhelp/episodes/the-film/watch-the-documentary/1/ (accessed April 2, 2014).

Jill Bolte Taylor. 2008. "My Stroke of Insight," February. *TED Talks*. http://www.ted.com/talks/jill_bolte_taylor_s_powerful_stroke_of_insight (accessed April 2, 2014).

Toni Morrison, interviewed by Oprah Winfrey. 2009. "Oprah's Life-class: Lesson 18: Do Your Eyes Light Up When Your Child Walks in the Room?" *Oprah Winfrey Talk Show*. http://www.oprah.com/oprahs-lifeclass/ Lesson-18-Do-Your-Eyes-Light-Up-When-Your-Child-Walks-in-Video (accessed April 2, 2014).

The Dougy Center: The National Center for Grieving Children and Families. Accessed April 2, 2014. http://www.dougy.org

Brad J. Bushman, Patrick E. Jamieson, Ilana Weitz, and Daniel Romer. "Gun Violence Trends in Movies." Pediatrics 2013; 132:6 1014-1018. http://pediatrics.aappublications.org/content/132/6/1014.full. (accessed June 16, 2014).

Chapter 9

Tula Karras. 2008. "The Disorder Next Door: Alarming Eating Habits." *Self Magazine*, April 26. http://www.today.com/id/24295957/ns/today-today_health/t/disorder-next-door-alarming-eating-habits/#.Uz3b-jlxcRnF) (accessed April 3, 2014).

David Sheff. 2013. Clean. New York: Houghton Mifflin Harcourt Publishing.

National Institute of Mental Health. 2009. "Anxiety Disorders". NIH Publication No. 09 3879. 2009. (accessed April 3, 2014).

http://www.nimh.nih.gov/health/publications/anxiety-disorders/index.shtml?wvsessionid=wv650bd43245ce405884dd789794894544

Stephanie Goldberg. 2010. "Kids Who Lose Parents Still Grieve as Adults." CNN, March 23. (accessed April 3, 2014).

http://www.cnn.com/2010/HEALTH/03/23/child.bereavement.study/

Aileen Fisher. Undated. "Butterfly Wings." *Angelfire*. Accessed April 3, 2014 http://www.angelfire.com/mi4/team_b/.

Eleanor Roosevelt. 1933. *It's Up To The Women*.

Dalai Lama. 2009. Vancouver Peace Summit. Quoted in Emily Bennington "The World Will Be Saved by the Western Woman," December 11, 2012. *Huffington Post*. http://www.huffingtonpost.com/emily-bennington/western-women_b_2277916.html (accessed April 3, 2014).

National Foundation for Women Legislators. 2014. "Facts About Women Legislators." Women Legislators. http://www.womenlegislators.org/women-legislator-facts.php (accessed April 3, 2014).

Shawn McMahon and Jessica Horning. 2013. *Living Below the Line: Economic Security and America's Families*. Washington, D.C.: Wider Opportunities for Women. http://www.wowonline.org/wp-content/uploads/2013/09/Living-Below-the-Line-Economic-Insecurity-and-Americas-Families-Fall-2013.pdf (accessed April 3, 2014).

Marisol Bello. 2011. "Report: Child Homelessness Up 33% in 3 Years." *USA Today*, December 13. http://usatoday30.usatoday.com/news/nation/story/2011-12-12/homeless-children-increase/51851146/1 (accessed April 3, 2014).

United States Department of Labor. 2013. "Pay Equalities," April 12. *http://www.dol.gov/dol/chat/chat-pay-equality-static-20130412.htm* (accessed April 4, 2014).

Catalyst. 2014. "Women CEOs of the Fortune 1000 List," January 15. Catalyst, Inc. http://www.catalyst.org/knowledge/women-ceos-fortune-1000 (accessed April 3, 2014).

Girl Rising: Global Campaign for Girls Education. Girl Rising, Inc. http://girlrising.com/grow-the-movement/ (accessed April 3, 2014).

Women Moving Millions. "Facts." Women Moving Millions, Inc. http://www.womenmovingmillions.org/how-we-do-it/facts/ (accessed April 3, 2014).

American Express. 2012. "New OPEN Study Reports Growth of Women-owned Businesses for 2012." American Express, Inc. https://www.americanexpress.com/us/small-business/openforum/articles/2012-american-express-open-state-of-women-owned-businesses-report/ (accessed April 3, 2014).

Natalie Madeira Cofield. 2013. "Minority Women Entrepreneurs: Go-Getters Without Resources," August 28. *Forbes.* http://www.forbes.com/sites/meghancasserly/2013/08/28/minority-women-entrepreneurs-go-getters-without-resources/ (accessed April 3, 2014).

American Express. 2012. "New OPEN Study Reports Growth of Women-owned Businesses for 2012." American Express, Inc. https://www.americanexpress.com/us/small-business/openforum/articles/2012-american-express-open-state-of-women-owned-businesses-report/ (accessed April 3, 2014).

Charles Darwin. 1859. *The Origin of Species.*

Charles Darwin. 1871. *The Descent of Man.*

David Loye. 2007. *Darwin's Lost Theory.* Carmel, California: Benjamin Franklin Press.

United Press International. 2012. "U.S.: Second-highest Child Poverty Level," May 29. http://www.upi.com/Top_News/World-News/2012/05/29/US-Second-highest-child-poverty-level/UPI-67641338349787/ (accessed April 3, 2014).

Rand Corporation. 2008. "Invisible Wounds of War: Psychological and Cognitive Injuries, Their Consequences, and Services to Assist Recovery," March 26. http://www.rand.org/pubs/monographs/

MG720.html (accessed April 3, 2014).

Nelson Mandela. 1990. Quoted in Faith Karimi, "Nelson Mandela, Anti-Apartheid Icon and Father of Modern South Africa, Dies," December 5, 2013. CNN News Online. http://www.cnn.com/2013/12/05/world/africa/nelson-mandela (accessed April 3, 2014).

Azim Khamisa. Founder, Thariq Khamisa Foundation (TKF): Stopping Youth Violence. *http://www.tkf.org*

Violence Impact Forum. *http://www.tkf.org/programs/educational-programs/*

United Nations. 1948. "Universal Declaration of Human Rights," December 10. http://www.un.org/en/documents/udhr/index.shtml For a history of this document, see http://www.un.org/en/documents/udhr/history.shtml (accessed April 3, 2014).

Dorothy Law Nolte and Rachel Harris. 2002. *Teenagers Learn What They Live*. New York: Workman Publishing Company.

Roni Cohen-Sandler. http://ronicohensandler.com

Bronnie Ware. 2011. *The Top Five Regrets of the Dying: A Life Transformed by the Dearly Departing*. La Jolla, CA: Hay House, Inc. / Balboa Press. http://bronnieware.com

Write It On Your Heart

Write it on your heart
that every day is the best day in the year.
[S]he is rich who owns the day, and no one owns the day
who allows it to be invaded with fret and anxiety.

Finish every day and be done with it.
You have done what you could.
Some blunders and absurdities, no doubt crept in.
Forget them as soon as you can, tomorrow is a new day;
begin it well and serenely, with too high a spirit
to be cumbered with your old nonsense.

This new day is too dear,
with its hopes and invitations,
to waste a moment on the yesterdays.
　　　　—Ralph Waldo Emerson, *Collected Poems and Translations*

Indeed, tomorrow is a new day, a blank page. Contemplate the empty space in the pages that follow. Consider the vast canvas of all the tomorrows of your own life. How will you fill your days? How will you create your future? Spend a moment or more remaining mindful of the possibilities, using the power of your IMAGINATION *to design what could be, what will be true for you—with your newfound level of* BEING.
　　　　—*Janet Larson*

Every block of stone has a statue inside it and it is the task of the sculptor to discover it.
—*Michelangelo*

Janet Larson, My Diary Unlocked® LLC
My Diary Unlocked Press
3525 Del Mar Heights Rd Ste. 1000 San Diego, CA 92130
www.mydiaryunlocked.com

Ordering Information:
Special sales may be available on quantity purchases by associations, organizations, schools and others.
For U.S. trade bookstores and wholesalers, please contact the publisher at: info@mydiaryunlocked.com

Companion *Diary—The Answers are Within* for *My Diary Unlocked* is available for purchase. Inspirational quotes that align with the 5 Aspects of BEING lead each page of blank lines. Available online and in select bookstores.

Keep on the lookout for workbooks, inspirational books, and more.
For more inspiration, sign up for eblasts at www.mydiaryunlocked.com
Remember to join a My Diary Unlocked Circle. See website for information.

Contact me to speak at your
organization, school, rally, bookclub or other gathering at:
info@mydiaryunlocked.com